TRAVELER'S
CUBA
COMPANION

by Kirsten Ellis and Joe Yogerst

Photographed by Mireille Vautier

Second Edition

The
Globe
Pequot
Press

GUILFORD
CONNECTICUT

Contents

The Traveler's Companions
ARGENTINA • AUSTRALIA • BALI • CALIFORNIA • CANADA • CHINA • COSTA RICA •
CUBA • EASTERN CANADA • ECUADOR • FLORIDA • HAWAII • HONG KONG • INDIA •
INDONESIA • JAPAN • KENYA • MALAYSIA & SINGAPORE • MEDITERRANEAN FRANCE •
MEXICO • NEPAL • NEW ENGLAND • NEW ZEALAND • PERU • PHILIPPINES • PORTUGAL •
RUSSIA • SOUTH AFRICA • SOUTHERN ENGLAND • SPAIN • THAILAND • TURKEY •
VENEZUELA • VIETNAM, LAOS AND CAMBODIA • WESTERN CANADA

Traveler's Cuba Companion

First published 1998
Second Edition 2002
The Globe Pequot Press
246 Goose Lane, PO Box 480
Guilford, CT 06437 USA
www.globe-pequot.com

© 2002 by The Globe Pequot Press, Guilford CT, USA

ISBN: 0-7627-2217-7

Created, edited and produced by
Allan Amsel Publishing, 53 rue Beaudouin
27700 Les Andelys, France.
E-mail: AAmsel@aol.com

Editor in Chief: Allan Amsel
Editor: Anne Trager
Picture editor and book designer: Roberto Rossi

Printed by Samwha Printing Co. Ltd., Seoul, South Korea

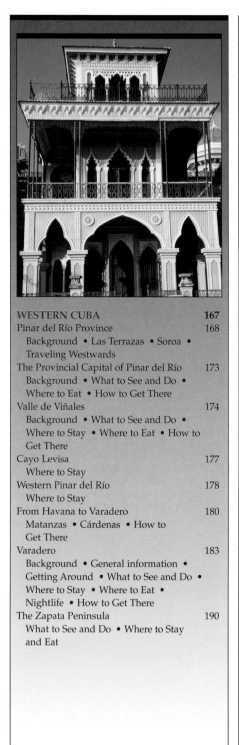

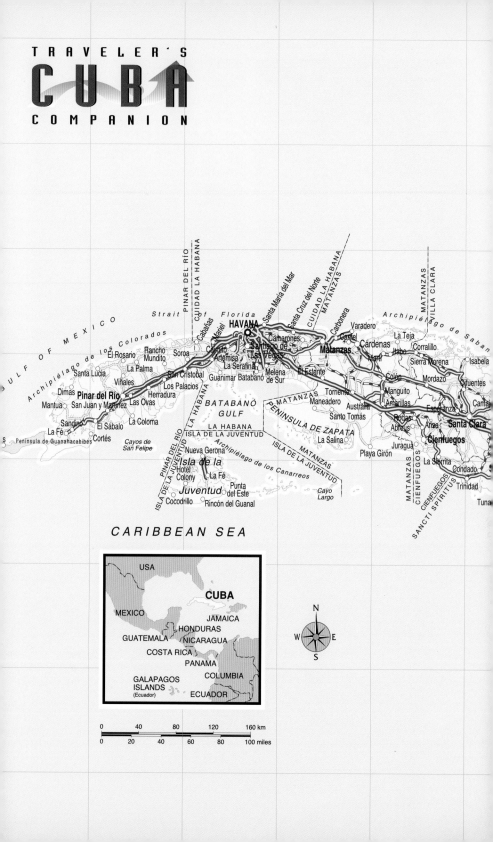

TOP SPOTS

Explore Old Havana

That aging beauty, La Habana Vieja, with its exotic mixture of historic buildings, has an enigmatic charm that invites the urge to simply wander. Whether you have several days or only a few hours, the time you spend exploring the evocative quarter of Old Havana — the colonial heart of the city near the waterfront — may well prove to be the highlight of your visit to Cuba.

Old Havana's stone fortresses and monuments, not to mention its labyrinth of magnificent houses, imposing columns, grand stone steps and tinted glass windows, offer an extraordinary, if somewhat worn-out, glimpse of the Spanish colonial era. At almost every step, the old city is literally four centuries deep. More than 900 of La Habana Vieja's

3,157 listed buildings have been deemed of historical importance, and only a fraction of these were built last century.

For many, Old Havana's streets exert a kind of siren call, and exploring them becomes a compulsion. For me, nothing quite compares to watching dawn break across the slate-colored stones of the ancient buildings on the Plaza de Armas, hours before the booksellers clatter across the cobbles to set up their stalls. Footsteps echo in the stillness of the vaulted archways of stone loggias on the restored Plaza de la Catedral. Over the years I have seen the old city's main boulevard of Obispo change dramatically: beleaguered historic façades and empty stores have been replaced by a flotilla of gaily painted, re-faced buildings bustling with commerce; in some cases, to my eyes, they look perplexingly brand-new. Yet, I remain captivated by the old city's many hidden corners and secrets; its quiet sun-filled courtyards and balcony hideaways. The narrow streets hum with people gossiping between balconies, lugging sacks of provisions or buckets of water and the "tring-tring" of bicycle bells. There is so much life here, so many layers of the past mingling with the quotidian, that every visit, each different street taken — and every change of the day's light — reveals something new.

Recent restoration has transformed Old Havana's most historic squares — Plaza de

Remnants of the past in Havana: the neo-baroque Gran Teatro OPPOSITE and a mosaic ABOVE.

Take a Trip to Trinidad

If Havana is Cuba's wild heart, then Trinidad is its calm soul. Where sugar once was king, the colonial city of Trinidad and its nearby Valle de los Ingenios offer a tranquil glimpse into the island's long-disappeared history. The perfectly preserved city radiates quiet colonial charm, lying in a beautiful spot between the sea and the nearby Escambray mountains close to the coast in Sancti Spíritus Province in central Cuba.

Intimate in scale, the city's winding cobbled streets and restored mansions make it easy to imagine how life might have been for Cuba's early sugar barons and their families in the seventeenth and eighteenth centuries, when this was the island's affluent sugar capital. Trinidad remains uncannily frozen in time: during the nineteenth century, it was all but abandoned, and nothing new has been added to the city's colonial core. Compared to Havana, Trinidad's pace is sleepy and traditional. Many of its stylish Creole *palacios*, have been turned into museums, some with preserved living quarters decorated throughout with murals, tiles of Italian marble and period furniture. Visit the Palacio de Brunet (now the Museo Romántico) and the Palacio Cantero (the Museo Histórico Municipal).

The nearby Valle de los Ingenios (Valley of the Sugar Mills) casts another light onto Trinidad's history as a bastion of provincial luxury. Here, thousands of African slaves toiled in the valley's many sugar mills, under harsh conditions and the unforgiving sun. Although this lush valley looks peaceful now, it once whirred and hummed with dozens of large sugar mills. A restored vintage steam train runs through the neck-high sugarcane fields making stops at El Guarisco, a stockpile center at Magua (where seasonal sugarcane harvesting still takes place today), the Guachinango estate (which has beautiful frescoes) and the charming Manacas-Iznaga plantation and tower, where you can have a delicious lunch on a

Armas, Plaza de la Catedral, Plaza Vieja and Plaza de San Francisco de Asís, which are a must on any visit.

Equally, you should see the interiors of the grandiose Palacio de los Capitanes Generales and the Casa de los Condes de Jaruco, among others, where you can admire the unique tropical Mudéjar style that flourished in Cuba during the seventeenth and eighteenth centuries, a decorative synthesis of Spanish and Moorish styles. From the same era, you cannot miss seeing Havana's formidable fortresses — the Castillo de la Real Fuerza, Castillo del Morro and the Fortaleza de San Carlos de la Cabaña.

The gentle lull of the early morning offers one face, allowing quiet contemplation of the old city's beauty; while the velvety Havana night shows another, where overt hustling by women in skimpy Lycra outfits and tugs at your sleeve to buy fake cigars or bootleg rum are hard to ignore. Those faint of heart and trusting of nature, take heed.

ABOVE: Many of Old Havana's grand buildings, such as this former presidential mansion, recall the wealth that flowed through the city under Spanish rule.
OPPOSITE: The beautiful Iglesia San Francisco de Asís dominates Trinidad's skyline.

balcony overlooking the entire valley before the return trip. Of course, you can also make your own way by road, if tagging along with large tour groups is not your idea of a good time.

Explore Tobacco Country

Famous for centuries for the quality of its tobacco, the western province of Pinar del Río is one of the island's most scenic areas to explore. Within easy driving distance of Havana, the province attracts cigar connoisseurs by producing the raw material for such renowned cigars as Cohibas, Coronas, H. Upmanns, Romeo y Julietas and now, Trinidad, Cuba's latest brand. The area's key tobacco-growing areas of Vuelta Abajo and the Partido look modest — plowed by oxen, dotted with traditional thatched *bohíos* (rustic huts) and archaic-looking drying sheds like a Hispanic version of a Monet haystack landscape. Yet it's quite something to see the entire process from the fields to the processing plant (where expert rollers make it look deceptively easy), and the humidored results are heaven for cigar aficionados.

You can combine a cigar safari with a foray into the province, whose landscapes range from the fertile plantation flats of the Vuelta Abajo to the forested heights of the Sierra de los Órganos and the Sierra del Rosario, and on to the gloriously green Valle de Viñales, where Jurassic-era limestone cliffs and unusual *mogotes* (flat-top hills) tower with eerie beauty like soldiers in the valley's vast open-air grotto. The mountains contain huge cave and underground river networks, only a few dozen of which have been officially mapped. These include the largest cave system in Cuba, part of which, Cueva del Indio, can be explored by boat on underground river.

The two hotels in the area, the Los Jazmines and La Ermita vie for perfect views across the entire valley. You can also stay at La Moka, Cuba's first so-called ecological resort, within the Sierra del Rosario's beautiful settlement of Las Terrazas. Here you can hike many

mountain trails, visit the ruins of former French coffee plantations along with natural waterfalls and pools, and drop in on Cuba's largest orchid collection at Soroa. From there, along the northern coastal road, stop at any of the seaside villages that catch your eye, most notably, Puerto Esperanza.

Revel in Cuba's Musical Heritage

The music created by Cuba's seasoned musicians — and by many of its young, up-and-coming performers — is, very often, pure magic. In Cuba, music seems to be everywhere, most of it happening right in front of you, with live bands, musicians and singers serenading almost literally at every street corner, in every restaurant and café, and even where you least expect it. Once when I was on one of the *playas* (beaches) near Santiago de Cuba, a quartet of formally dressed musicians (complete with a double bass) materialized across the sands and proceeded to stage an incredible an unforgettable performance.

Sleepy towns conjure up dynamic musical performances after the siesta hours just as Havana, Matanzas, Trinidad, Camagüey and Santiago de Cuba offer

OPPOSITE: A singer relaxes after rehearsal in Havana's Casa de la Obrapa. ABOVE: A stack of Cuba's famous cigars proudly displayed awaiting the connoisseur.

wonderful impromptu performances, often for the price of a cocktail or a coffee. Even remarkably talented musicians and singers can barely get by on what they earn, making their dedication to music even more impressive.

A local Casa de la Trova can be found in many Cuban cities or towns. These music venues are named for *trovas*, pre-Revolutionary poetic ballads — often about love — that originated during the island's colonial period, and more recently, *nuevas trovas*, contemporary ballads. At Casas de la Trova, *trovadores*, or exponents of the *trova*, often play for free, keeping the tradition alive. Of all these establishments, it has to be said that Santiago de Cuba's Casa de la Trova is a breed apart, its history intertwined with that of Cuban music itself. Generations of Cuba's music legends have played here, many from the eastern province of Oriente, the birthplace of improvisational *son* and *trova* music. Portraits of famous musicians who performed here line the walls, and include the Trio Matamoros, Beny Moré and Sindo Garay, the father of *trova* music.

Some of Cuba's most celebrated musicians are now in their 70s, 80s and 90s, yet have recently come back into the spotlight reviving this nostalgic, pr-Revolutionary music. One of these musicians, Ibrahím Ferrer, who once sang alongside Beny Moré, had been shining shoes for a living. Widely celebrated albums such as the Buena Vista Social Club and the Afro-Cuban All Stars have brought a new wave of appreciation for the nation's musical heritage.

Havana is widely regarded as Cuba's musical capital (although this title is hotly disputed by Santiago de Cuba and Matanzas) with many venues offering an array of musical styles. You should definitely visit the Casa de la Trova and the Casa de la Música — and if you enjoy bold, big-band salsa, the Palacio de la Salsa. Havana's Casa de la Música holds regular performances of popular music. Other venues to seek out include La Divina Pastora restaurant, and La Habana Vieja's Casa de la Amistad, Casa de las Infusiones and Bar Nostalgia.

Throughout the country, look out for touring performances by Conjunto Folklórico Nacional (the National Folklore Dance Group), Los Muñequitos de Matanzas (known as the "kings of rumba"), pianists Chucho Valdés and Gonzalo Rubalcava, the jazz fusion group Cuatro Espacio, famous salsa bands Los Van Van and Irakere, and the jazz singer Xiamara.

Relax on Cuba's Best Beaches

Few people come to Cuba just for its beaches, although the island does have its share of shores worth visiting. Cuba's premier beach resort is Varadero, which is

just over two hours' drive from Havana, with an 18-km-long (11-mile) strip that is increasingly built-up with modern hotels. It has all the watersports and nightlife anyone could want, but little in the way of real Cuban atmosphere. Varadero's beach is beautiful, but you may be disappointed if this is all you have come to see.

The tourist-only beaches of Cayo Coco and Cayo Guillermo in Ciego de Ávila, as well as Cayo Largo, which lies off the mainland's southeast coast, have been earmarked as Cuba's next hot sites for beach development. Both these isolated resort islands (Cayo Coco and the smaller, nearby Cayo Guillermo are reached by a causeway from the mainland, while Cayo Largo is reached by plane, increasingly by

direct international charter flights) already have a significant hotel infrastructure. Of these, Cayo Largo is closest to everybody's vision of an idyllic tropical island with its soft, snow-white sands at the aptly named Playa Sirena, Playa Blanca and Cayo Rico, all of which are bordered by blue-green sea. However, as with Varadero, the only Cubans you are likely to meet will be waiters and housemaids.

For beautiful beaches as well as a relaxed beach scene and some of the island's better resorts, head for Playa Esmeralda (also known as Playa Estero

María La Gorda beach, at the extreme western end of the island, is one of Cuba's finest and an excellent base for scuba diving.

Ciego) in the Bahía de Naranjo, near the beach resort of Guardalavaca in Holguín Province. Here you can find a series of calm, beautiful sandy bays amid lush vegetation and some very good hotels. Within this region, the lovely, sheltered beach of Cayo Saetía can be reached by helicopter and is a popular daytrip. Playa Santa Lucía in Camagüey Province is also recommended for both its beach (and nearby beaches) and resorts, with the exceptionally pretty, soft-sanded shores and clear seas of Cayo Sabinal within easy reach.

Elsewhere in Cuba, other notable beaches (most of which have adjacent tourist resorts and facilities) include Matanzas's Playa Girón and possibly

Cuba's most perfect snorkeling spot at Caleta Buena. Pinar del Río has the Cayo Levisa, and Sancti Spíritus Playa Ancón, a pleasant location from which to visit the nearby colonial town of Trinidad. At Santiago de Cuba's Playas Siboney, Bucanero and Sigua, great atmosphere and seaside restaurants attract local Cubans as well as tourists. Guantánamo's Playa Maguana offers a pleasant place to stay as well as swim.

Although near Havana, the beaches of Habana del Este are not especially recommended. Here there is an unrestful atmosphere, with soliciting *jineteras* (figuratively speaking, "female jockeys," or "women who go along for the ride"), littered sands and loud music.

See Havana's Museo de la Revolución

Icon of Fidel Castro's reign, Havana's Museo de la Revolución offers an essential showcase of just about all the memorabilia of the *Revolución* one might ever care to see. Overlooking Havana's Malecón stands the capital's former Presidential Palace (Palacio Presidencial), an imposing white Spanish Revival pile with glittering interiors designed by Tiffany's of New York. Cuba's former dictator Fulgencio Batista was once king of this castle — until students stormed the citadel in March 1957; Batista hid an an elevator shaft to escape being lynched.

Now this building is a virtual walk-through of the Revolution's history, with many exhibits offering detailed, even forensic, insights. Maps chart the day-by-day progress of Castro's ultimate victory, as he and his gang of revolutionary rebels withstood attack in the tangled undergrowth of the Sierra Maestra mountains. Photographs, yellowed communiqués, blood-stained clothing and personal items of fallen revolutionaries are displayed alongside hundreds of rifles and pistols. One room is dedicated to Che Guevara, where you can gaze at objects that once belonged to the larger-than-life hero.

In the Palacio Presidencial gardens, stands the *Granma*, the large cabin cruiser that bore Fidel and his followers from Mexico to Cuba in 1956. Enshrined in a glass case, the ship has become an object of patriotic veneration. You can also see the bullet-ridden "Fast Delivery" truck used in the student's assault on the palace, the Land Rover a victorious Fidel rode into Havana (it has *Commandancia General Sierra Maestra* painted on it), a remnant of a U-2 reconnaissance plane shot down by the Cuban military during the missile crisis in 1962, and the tank used by Fidel himself during the Bay of Pigs confrontation.

OPPOSITE: Museo de la Revolución.
RIGHT: Hemingway's former home, La Finca Vigía.

Walk in Hemingway's Footsteps

Gone but not forgotten, hailed as a demigod in Cuba, Hemingway's legend lives on at a number of places around the island. "Ernesto," as the Cubans called him, lived in Cuba between 1939 and 1960, the longest period of time the ever-restless writer was to spend anywhere. His ghost lingers at a number of haunts in Old Havana.

A perpetually crowded bar called La Bodeguita del Medio on Calle Empedrado was supposedly his favorite drinking spot and allegedly the place where the mojito (light dry rum, lemon, crushed mint, sugar, soda and ice) was born back in the 1940s. Somewhere among all that scrawl on the wall are Papa's own musings about life in Havana, but finding them brings to mind that saying about needles in the haystack.

A somber bust of Hemingway keeps watch on things at La Floridita, another old town bar where's it's said that he quaffed daiquiris each morning with other self-exiled gringos. A brass plaque marks his favorite place at the long, mahogany bar. Floridita, by the way, earns mention in *Islands in the Stream*.

Before he bought his own digs on the outskirts of the Cuban capital, Papa bedded down at the Ambos Mundos Hotel on Calle Obispo. According to legend, *For Whom the Bell Tolls*, his classic story about

the better part of 20 years. Hemingway used to dine with other fishermen at a local spot called La Terraza, which still serves some of the best seafood in Cuba. After lunch, take a stroll down to a waterfront bastion called El Terreon, where there's a memorial to the author inside a small Romanesque shrine overlooking the sea.

Elsewhere in Cuba are more places where Hemingway whiled away his latter years. During World War II, the author used the *Pilar* to patrol for German U-boats off the north coast. He was also a frequent visitor to Cayo Paraíso off the north coast of Pinar del Río province.

After winning the Noble Prize for Literature in 1952, Hemingway dedicated his success to the Virgin Mary and made a personal pilgrimage to the Basílica del Cobre near Santiago de Cuba, where he placed his medal inside the Virgin's shrine. There it rested peacefully for nearly four decades, until it was stolen by petty thieves in 1988. Later recovered, it is currently being safeguarded by the local Catholic diocese. Unfortunately, it's no longer on display.

Saunter Through Santiago

Cuba's second largest city has an appeal all its own, sometimes somnolent, sometimes saucy. Unlike Havana, which swirls in clouds of party politics and international intrigue, Santiago seems to take most everything with a very large grain of salt. Life here is boiled down to the only things that really count — good food, fine rum, excellent music and a luscious lover. The only time you break a sweat is on the dance floor. The only thing that prompts mass hysteria is the annual street carnival.

Santiago is patent-made for sauntering, simply roaming around, exploring little nooks and crannies, seeing what's around the next corner. The old town, especially between Parque Céspedes and Plaza Dolores, is rife with ancient buildings and venerable old institutions that hark back to an era when island life was somehow far less complicated and in a way far more

the Spanish Civil War, took root in the author's mind during his frequent stays at the hotel during the 1930s. For whatever reason, Ernesto always booked the same room — Number 511 — now preserved as a small Hemingway museum.

Author and aviator Martha Gellhorn (Ernesto's third wife) finally convinced him to purchase his own place in 1939. La Finca Vigía is about a 40-minute drive from central Havana, perched on a hillside atop the sleepy village of San Francisco de Paula. Over the next two decades, this is where he wrote some of his finest work (including *For Whom The Bell Tolls, Islands in the Stream* and *The Old Man and the Sea*), weathered two marriages and entertained a stream of famous visitors.

It is now a museum, preserved to a highly evocative degree, with many personal possessions, clothes, books and furnishings left just as they were when the Hemingways left Cuba. The writer's boat, the *Pilar*, is displayed in the garden, "like the *Granma*," commented Gellhorn, as she inspected the museum many years after having once lived there herself.

Nearby is the fishing village of Cojímar, the setting for *The Old Man and the Sea*, and the spot where Papa docked the *Pilar* for

engaging. Wander through the Museo Bacardí, the house that rum built, which is filled with the artifacts (and cultural artifice) of high-society colonial Cuba. Explore the dark recesses of the Casa de Don Diego de Velázquez, the oldest house in Cuba (1516) and the place from which the conquistadors staged their bloody conquest of the island.

Even more than Havana, where very little of real consequence has ever actually transpired, Santiago is a city of history and events that indelibly shaped the island's future. The Castillo del Morro at the entrance to Santiago Bay was the focus of repeated attacks by English, French and Dutch forces bent on snatching Cuba from the Spanish. The sea directly off Santiago

played host to the greatest naval battle ever fought in the Caribbean — an 1898 engagement in which United States ironclads destroyed the Spanish fleet.

The city is just as engaging after dark. Some of the most romantic restaurants occupy old colonial mansions and art deco houses in the leafy Vista Alegre district, while those arrayed around the Plaza Dolores sway to the beat of house bands and strolling musicians. After dinner mosey over to the Casa de la Trova, find yourself a dance partner and let that sultry Santiago vibe linger long into the night.

OPPOSITE: La Bodeguita del Medio, Hemingway's favorite Havana bar, still serves mojitos late into the evening. ABOVE: The fretted wooden windows of Casa de Don Diego de Velázquez in Santiago de Cuba.

YOUR CHOICE

The Great Outdoors

Lying like a crocodile caught between the fishing nets of its neighbors — the United States and Mexico — Cuba is the largest of the Greater Antilles, and by far the largest island in the Caribbean, stretching some 1,250 km (about 775 miles) in length and 191 km (about 120 miles) across at its widest point, although it is just 31 km across (about 19 miles) at its narrowest point.

This enchanting, beautiful island has three main mountain regions — the Cordillera Guaniguanico in Pinar del Río Province to the west, the Sierra del Escambray above Trinidad in Sancti Spíritus Province in the center, and the Sierra Maestra in the southeast Oriente Province — each with isolated pockets of tropical rainforest. The Pico Turquino in the Sierra Maestra is Cuba's highest point at 1,973 m (6,473 ft).

The island's scenery varies from snow-white sandy beaches, protected by coral reefs and shaded by sea grape and palm trees, to high mountains smothered with native forest and coffee plantations, not to mention the island's mangrove swamps, offshore islands, limestone caves, waterfalls and subterranean rivers. On vast plains, fertile ochre-colored soil grows abundant swathes of the sugarcane and tobacco that Cuba is so famous for. Cuba has more than 200 rivers, the longest of which is the 343-km (213-mile) Río Cauto in Oriente Province. Offshore, in addition to Cuba's second largest island, Isla de la Juventud, there are some 4,000 keys and islets, many of which are untouched.

Nearly half of the 6,000 plant types found in Cuba are endemic, as are many thousands of animal species. Although Cuban forests once teemed with teak, mahogany, ebony and cedar, Spanish colonials systematically deforested the nation, and it is rare to find these trees in any great number. Also, about 200 species of Cuba's plants and animals are on the United Nation's list of endangered species. Cuba does, however, have among the highest concentrations of palm trees in the world. Of the 60 species of palms, the royal

OPPOSITE: The Sierra del Escambray mountains overlook a patchwork of greens in the fertile Valle de los Ingenios, with its many sugarcane plantations. ABOVE: Exotic flora in the Valle de Viñales.

palm is the more impressive, with its towering height and smooth silvery trunk — it is the national tree. Other palms include the barrigona or big belly palm (rudely called *puta palma* because it looks pregnant) and the rare, stunted prehistoric cork palm, which dates from the dinosaur age and is seen in the hilltops of the Valle de Viñales, in Pinar del Río Province.

Other notable plants include the *jagüey*, a fig tree with aerial roots; the *ceiba*, the sacred silk cotton tree; and the fragrant white butterfly-like *mariposa*, the national flower. Many flowering trees burst into blossom during summer, such as the flame-red *flamboyán* and the African tulip tree. Throughout central Cuba are endless orchards of oranges, lemons and limes, mangos, soursops and guavas.

It is a curious fact that both the smallest bird in the world and the smallest frog in the world are found in Cuba. You are unlikely to see the frog, nicknamed *el sapito*, but you may possibly see the beautiful *zunzuncito* or bee hummingbird, which is just bigger than a grasshopper, weighs only two grams and flaps its wings at an astonishing speed, producing an unusual sound. The fingernail-sized frog lives under ferns within the dense forest of Cuba's eastern tip, in the Cuchillas de Toa region. Other unfamiliar species include the polymite, a land snail with a colorful swirled shell, found in abundance in the forested mountains near Baracoa, and two rat-like

mammals: the *almiqué*, with a long snout and large padded claws, and the *jutia*, which is the size of small beaver and a delicacy eaten in rural Cuba.

Cuba has over 300 bird species, of which 23 are endemic and found nowhere else in the world. South of Havana, the Zapata Peninsula is the Caribbean's most important stopover for migratory birds such as flamingos, and is a year-round home for many endemic species. Here, alongside Cuba's ubiquitous white egrets (and their constant companions, the cows), serious birders will see rare species, such as the *zunzuncito* and the national bird, the *trogon*, also known as the *tocororo*, which is a member of the quetzal family. It has red, white and blue plumage, the colors of the Cuban flag.

A strange and beautiful tailed and gilded moth, the Cuban *urania*, lives in the forests of the Sierra del Escambray and the Sierra Maestra. The profusion of exotic butterflies — among them the exquisite *Greta cubana* — along with the rare native orchids that line mountain trails, offers one of Cuba's more ephemeral and unexpected pleasures in the wild.

Cuba's rich reptilian life includes crocodiles, iguanas, lizards, salamanders, turtles and at least 15 species of non-poisonous snakes. Cuban crocodiles — potentially the island's most dangerous creatures — are found in only one part of the island, the swampy Zapata Peninsula, where they are protected under a breeding program after being an endangered species for many years. You may also see the alligator gar, an endemic fish and living fossil that lives in rivers.

Wild boar, deer and horses can be found in some parts of the island, including the Guanahacabibes Peninsula in Pinar del Río Province, and monkeys live in some isolated areas, including a key off Cayo Largo.

While Cuba is not exactly on the map as a destination for ecotourism, its large regions of bush have some potential for this sort of development. If you make time to appreciate it in this light, don't expect for a moment to be unimpressed by Cuba's natural beauty.

So far, Cuba's national parks — a relatively new concept whose definition remains somewhat loose — are not yet extensively developed to welcome visitors. Don't expect the sort of facilities you might associate with national parks and reserves elsewhere: Cuba is just catching up when it comes to promoting itself as a nature destination. Visitor centers, interpretative trails, park maps and camping facilities are few. Hiking is not really big in Cuba (at least, not since the days when Fidel Castro and his revolutionaries camped out in the hills), and Cubans tend to consider walking less macho than horseback riding — but the island's infrastructure for the lay-hiker is pretty good, especially if you are happy just to spend a few hours walking (in some cases climbing fairly steep trails) within the island's scenic forest reserves, although marked walking trails are rare.

Enterprising and experienced hikers may see this situation as an advantage: with perseverance and a yen for self-sufficiency, they will be able to explore much of the island's scenic wilderness almost entirely by themselves. However, it is impossible to get good, detailed maps for use as a navigational aid. Suffice to say that getting lost could be a problem.

Generally, hotels close to parks and reserves can assist with hiring a guide, although in some areas they are a rare commodity. Many so-called guides are nothing more than local residents, rather than trained naturalists who can explain something about the local flora and fauna.

To join a tour, contact **Cubamar** ((07) 338317, 662524, 305536 or 662523 FAX (07) 333111 WEB SITE www.cubamar@cubamar .mit.cma.net, Paseo 752 at the corner of Calle 15, Vedado, Havana, a Cuban entity set up to develop the camping and ecotourism infrastructure. **Alcona S.A**. ((07) 222526, 222529 or 845244 FAX (07) 241531, Calle 42 no. 514, at the corner of Avenida 7, Miramar, Havana, runs week-long "ecotour" package trips to nature reserves in Sierra del Rosario in Pinar del Río and Isla de la Juventud, as well as in the Parque Nacional Desembarco del Granma and the Parque Nacional Turquino. Many of the island's mainstream organizations also offer nature excursions or will be able to suggest tours (see TAKING A TOUR, page 70). Gaviota, which is backed by Cuba's

OPPOSITE: A resident of Las Salinas in the Ciénaga de Zapata. ABOVE: A typical coastline near Santiago de Cuba.

Ministry of Defense, has developed a good reputation for arranged excursions of all kinds — on foot, on horseback, by helicopter and by boat — into Cuba's protected natural regions, many of which are no-go areas taken over the military.

For lush scenery, mangrove swamps, rivers, clear lagoons and crocodile watching — but especially for eyeing birds — don't miss a visit to the **Parque Nacional de la Ciénaga de Zapata** on the Zapata Peninsula in the province of Matanzas, several hours' driving distance from Havana. You should aim to spend at least two or three days exploring the park and should visit, among other sites, the breeding grounds of birds and other wild fauna within the protected area of Las Salinas and the crocodile breeding grounds at La Boca. Ideally, make the trip in February, March or early April, and make your base in either Playa Larga (which has a bird-watching center) or Playa Girón. Like many parts of Cuba, mosquitoes are a part of the landscape: bring along some strong repellant.

The Zapata Peninsula is also wonderful for snorkeling: you are likely to see manatees as well as many species of tropical fish, and the submarine caves or *cenotes* provide dramatic opportunities for underwater spelunking.

For the latter, contact the **International Scuba Diving Center** at Villa Playa Girón ((059) 4118 or 4110 FAX (059) 4117, Peninsula de Zapata, Matanzas.

From Havana, it is an easy drive to Pinar del Río's spectacular **Parque Nacional Viñales**. There is something sublime about watching the sun rise and set here from the stillness of your own hotel balcony: the landscape — with its huge forested *mogotes*, or limestone humps that conceal hidden caves and subterranean rivers — resembles the shifting canvas of an ancient Chinese master. Just as beautiful, forested pathways harbor the Cuban *trogon* (also called the *tocororo*), nightingales, woodpeckers and many butterfly species, all of which lay their eggs in the crevices of the region's limestone cliffs.

If you plan to visit Trinidad, make an overnight side-trip to the **Parque Nacional**

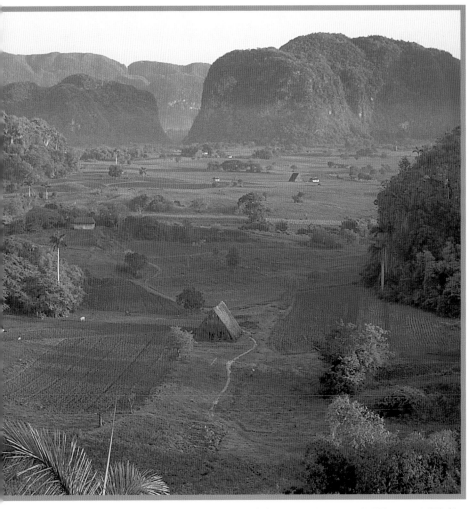

Topes de Collantes. You can hire a "nature guide" from either the Kurhotel or the Los Helechos hotels who can point out endemic species, including ferns, orchids, birds and butterflies. Trails vary from an hour's easy stroll to a very demanding six-hour round-trip hike to waterfalls along the Caburní and Vega Grande rivers, only recommended for people in good physical shape. You should make your preferences clear to the guide at the outset.

Further east, visit the island's largest natural reserve, Parque Nacional Sierra Maestra in Granma Province. It is an obvious attraction for serious hikers and trekkers and encompasses both the Parque Nacional Turquino, which has as its centerpiece the highest mountain in

Cuba, Pico Turquino (1,973 m or 6,470 ft), and the Parque Nacional Desembarco del Granma (Granma Landing National Park). Diehards can aim to complete the island's premier mountain hike: a strenuous three-day trek over the Sierra Maestra from Alto de Naranjo, south of Bartolomé Masó in Granma Province, to Las Cuevas on the southern coast, crossing Pico Turquino. The Desembarco del Granma reserve has two excellent trails, the Morlote-Fustete and El Guafe. The former requires some heavy-duty mountaineering. The latter is easier and

OPPOSITE: The coconut is one of the island's many palm varieties. ABOVE: Panoramic view of the Valle de Viñales with its *mogotes,* or flat-topped mountains.

winds through dense native forest to reach limestone caves, where you can see pre-Columbian cave paintings and stone idols. The Desembarco del Granma park is relatively easy to access by road from the provincial town of Bayamo. However, sections of the Pico Turquino reserve have been taken over by the Cuban military, making certain trails impossible unless you have authorized permission.

Parque Nacional Desembarco del Granma is also notable for its marine reserve, especially at Cabo Cruz, where scuba divers can explore a spectacular underwater terrace of coral, the "Stairway of Giants." Cabo Cruz can be reached by boat excursions from the Commonwealth resorts at Marea del Portillo.

Cuba has four UNESCO-designated biosphere zones, although they may not necessarily correspond to what you might expect. The recently reforested **Reserva Sierra del Rosario** and the **Reserva Península de Guanahacabibes** (more notable for its offshore diving sites than its onshore wilderness) are both in Pinar del Río Province. **Parque Baconao** in Santiago de Cuba Province contains the lovely reforested area surrounding the stone-outcrop of La Gran Piedra and several beautiful beaches. The **Reserva Cuchillas de Toa**, in Guantánamo Province, is home to the **Parque Nacional Alejandro de Humboldt,** which contains the island's largest expanse of rainforest and is one of the most isolated, pristine parts of the island. It is home to many endangered species, including the magnificent ivory-billed woodpecker. The Toa River, which flows through this region, is just about the only part of the island where it is possible to make short river-rafting trips. Walking and rafting trips can be organized from either the Hotel El Castillo or the Hotel Porto Santo in Baracoa. Although large parts of these reserves are off-limits to visitors, there are sufficient trails to allow at least several (guided) half-day walks through glorious landscapes.

A number of travel agencies in both Canada and the United States can tailor nature tours in Cuba. **MacQueen's Travel** TOLL-FREE IN US AND CANADA (800) 969-2822 WEB SITE www.macqueens.com, 430 Queen Street, Charlottetown, Prince Edward Island, Canada, offers cycling tours in rural Cuba including Pinar del Río, Granma and the Isla de la Juventud, as well as a two-week "Vuelta Cuba" cross-country ride from Santiago to Havana (see also SPORTING SPREE, below). In the United States, **Geographic Expeditions (** (415) 922-0448 TOLL-FREE (800) 777-8183 FAX (415) 346-5535 WEB SITE www.geoex.com, 2627 Lombard Street, San Francisco, California 94123, tenders quite a good selection of Cuba adventure trips including hiking and rock climbing. Geographic Expedition's premier trip is a 16-day "Exploration of Cuba's Conservation and Environmental Preserves" for US$4,190.

Another option is **Wings of the World** TOLL-FREE IN THE US (800) 465-8687, 1200 William Street, Suite 706, Buffalo, New York 14240, which offers tailored ecotours of Cuba, including the 11-day "From Mountain to Forest" trip. This all-inclusive US$2,695-tour visits the Zapata Peninsula in Matanzas, the Valle de Viñales and Las Terrazas in Pinar del Río, the Sierra de Nipe mountains and Pinares de Mayarí in Holguín and Parque Baconao in Santiago de Cuba (see also TAKING A TOUR, page 70). This company also offers all-inclusive eight-day bird-watching tours in January, February and March for US$2,295, visiting the Zapata Peninsula, the Long Point Observatory and La Güira reserve in Pinar del Río.

Sporting Spree

SCUBA DIVING

Although not exactly on the map as an international scuba-diving destination, Cuba's underwater attractions are comparable to the Bahamas, Cozumel and the Grand Cayman Islands — perhaps, in many ways, more impressive. Increasing numbers of enthusiasts are discovering how magnificent and unspoiled the archipelago's underwater world is. In addition, diving facilities offer, in some resorts, an international level of professionalism.

There is certainly no lack of potential diving locations to explore: offshore, more than 4,000 small (in some cases, tiny) islets and keys make up the Cuban archipelago. The southern Caribbean waters tend to be warmer than the Atlantic. Expect to see entire forests of multi-colored coral formations, dramatic drop-offs, gulf walls, caverns and wrecks alive with many species of fish and other marine life. The creatures that abound in Cuba's waters include rays, sharks, tarpon, turtles, barracuda, angelfish, grouper, bigeyes, butterflies, grunts, parrotfish, snapper, triggerfish, wrasses, as well as manatees, found offshore near mangrove swamps. Sunken galleons and even the odd U-boat can be seen off the island's southern coast.

Cuba's most important diving sites coincide with the four archipelagos which encircle the mainland: **Canarreos**, which lies to the southwest between Isla de la Juventud and Cayo Largo; **Jardines de la Reina**, located to the south, off Ciego de Ávila and Camagüey Provinces; **Sabana**, reached from Cayo Coco and Cayo Guillermo in Ciego de Ávila Province; and **Los Colorados**, off Cayo Levisa in Pinar del Río. Many sites are being explored off Cayo Largo, Cayo Coco, Cayo Guillermo, Playa Santa Lucía and off the tip of Cabo de Corrientes at the westernmost tip of Cuba.

Watchful crocodiles at La Boca Crocodile Farm in Ciénaga de Zapata.

As elsewhere in the Caribbean, water temperatures — which range from 27°C to 29°C (80°F to 85°F) — are perfectly suited to diving, and because so much of Cuba's marine environment has been left untouched and has not yet been affected by cruise liners, visibility is noticeably better. Outside of hurricane season (August to October), you can dive in Cuba all year round, but the period from November to March is the most agreeable, as the southern and western coasts are free of the *nortes*, or cold north winds that bring with them cold rains. The northern coast is generally calmer from May to September.

A number of international diving centers across the island offer organized dives, courses and equipment for rent. Cuba's premier diving destination is the Isla de la Juventud. The **Puertosol Hotel Colony International Diving Center** ((061) 26120 is among the best-equipped in Cuba (with one of the country's few decompression chambers). There are 56 marked dive sites offshore, which offer an incredible array of underwater landscape vistas. The Isla de Juventud has facilities for divers, from beginners to those seeking complete certification courses.

You can also contact the head office of **Puertosol** ((07) 245923 or 245782 FAX (07) 24-5928 E-MAIL comerc@psol.mit.cma.net, at the corner of Calles 1 and 30, Miramar, in Havana. This company specializes in organizing scuba diving, underwater photography, yachting, deep-sea fishing, freshwater fishing and boat rentals. However, beware: word has it their staff seeks clever schemes to have you pay more than is necessary.

In addition, Puertosol also operates the **Marina Tarara** ((07) 971462, outside Havana; the **Marina Dársena** ((05) 668060, in Varadero; the **María La Gorda International Diving Center** ((082) 78131, in Pinar del Río Province; the **Marina Cayo Guillermo Jardines del Rey Diving Center** ((033) 301738; the **Jucaro Nautical Base** ((033) 98104, in Ciego de Ávila Province (from which you can explore one of Cuba's most spectacular diving destinations, the Jardines de la Reina

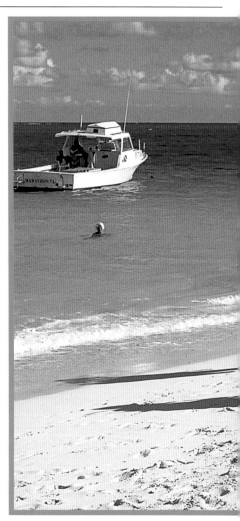

archipelago); and the **Marina Cayo Largo del Sur** ((05) 48213, on the tourist-only island of Cayo Largo.

Several other scuba companies are equally reputable. **Cubanacán Nautica** ((07) 246848 FAX (07) 245280 WEB SITE www.cubanacan.cu, Marina Hemingway, Avenida 5 and Calle 248, Santa Fe, Playa, Havana, operates another string of marinas and diving centers: **La Aguja Diving Center** at Marina Hemingway outside Havana; **Barracuda Diving Center** in Varadero; **Faro Luna Diving Center** in Cienfuegos; **Marina Cayo Coco** and **Coco Diving Center** at the Hotel Tryp Cayo Coco in Ciego de Ávila Province; **Santa Lucía Nautical Point** and **Diver Den and Shark Friends Diving Center** at Santa

Lucía in Camagüey; **Eagle Ray Diving Center** at Playa Guardalavaca in Holguín; **Albacora Diving Center**, Playa Marea del Portillo, Pilón, Granma; and finally, in Santiago de Cuba Province, **Marina Punta Gorda** and **Sigua Diving Center**, both in Parque Baconao, and **Marlin Diving Center** at Los Galeones, Chivirico.

Gaviota, the tourism wing of the Cuban Ministry of Defense, operates the **Marina Varadero**; **Bahía Naranjo Diving Center** and **Playa Esmeralda Diving Center**, near Playa Guardalavaca; as well as **Cayo Saetía Nautical Point** in Holguín Province. Contact them at ((07) 666777, 666773 or 666778 FAX (07) 332780 WEB SITE www.gaviota .cubaweb.cu, Third Floor, Edificio la Marina, Avenida del Puerto in Miramar.

In general, the diving centers cited above are professionally run, with modern, imported Mares and Cressisub equipment and CMAS- and PADI-trained instructors. By international standards, they are not expensive: expect to pay around US$40 per dive, with extra charges if you need to rent equipment. It's still a good idea to bring your own equipment, although you can rent tanks and weight belts on site. Diving lessons and packages of one or two weeks can be arranged on request, including study or photography tours specializing in underwater flora and fauna accompanied by researchers or university professors.

Vacationers scuba dive at Playa Esmeralda.

Less elaborate facilities for scuba diving can be found throughout the island at many beach resorts. You should contact **Villa Cayo Levisa** at Cayo Levisa in Pinar del Río; **Hotel Horizontes Costasur** at Playa Ancón near Trinidad in Sancti Spíritus; and **Villa Playa Girón** for scuba diving (and spelunking) in and around the Zapata Peninsula, notably near Playa Girón in Matanzas. Scuba diving in the Zapata Peninsula's submerged caves is only for experts.

In the future, Cuba will probably start drawing more attention to its considerable interest as a destination for underwater archaeology buffs. Official estimates put the number of ships sunk in the Cuba area over the centuries at over a thousand, only a few of which have ever been charted and explored. One of the best examples — and one that can be easily explored — is the *Nuestra Señora del Rosario*, a cargo galleon that was gunned down by an English pirate off the coast of Pinar del Río, laden with all its treasures. Expeditions to the sunken galleon can be made from the scuba diving center at Cayo Levisa.

Several travel companies can arrange dive-related trips to Cuba. From the United Kingdom, contact **Aquatours** ((020) 8398-0505 FAX (020) 8398-0570 WEB SITE www.aquatours.com, Milboa Lodge, Portsmouth Road, Thames Ditton, Surrey KTZ OES1; in South Africa contact the **Dive Travel Center** ((011) 326-3213 WEB SITE www.scubadiving.co.za/cuba, 376 Jan Smuts Avenue, Craighill, in Johannesburg, which organizes week-long diving expeditions to the wonderful Jardines de la Reina. In the United States, a good agency to try is **Wings of the World** TOLL-FREE IN THE US (800) 465-8687, 1200 William Street, Suite 706, Buffalo, New York 14240, which offers week-long all-inclusive diving packages to Isla de la Juventud.

If you are planning to do any serious diving, look for *The Diving and Snorkeling Guide to Cuba* by Diana Williams (Houston: Pisces Books, 1996), which is a detailed account of a great number of the island's diving spots.

SAILING

If you are interested in sailing around Cuba, or perhaps even sailing your own yacht into Cuba, your first points of reference should, without doubt, be the **Marina Hemingway**, in Santa Fé, about a 20-minute drive from central Havana, which is a one-stop facility for all nautical activities. It is the seat of Cuba's **International Yacht Club** and the **Club Náutico Internacional Hemingway de la Habana**, which between them organize a formidable annual program of yachting regattas and fishing tournaments, including the Havana Cup Regatta, which runs from Tampa, Florida, to Havana in May; the Key West–Varadero Regatta in November; the Christmas Regatta; and the Caribbean Conch Regatta (held in April), all of which attract many participants from the United States. (Cubans can participate in these regattas, but are barred from entering United States waters.) Cuba is keen to increase its profile internationally in this field and is forging good-will alliances with yacht organizations and clubs around the world. International yachties receive a warm welcome at the Marina Hemingway, and you'll usually see a large contingent of North American flags among the boats moored here.

Generally speaking, Cuba has good conditions for sailing throughout the year, although the months between December to April and June to November can bring unpredictable weather, affecting the island's northern and southern coasts at different times. The northern Atlantic coast tends to get the full brunt of storms and squalls, and is often rainier than the south coast. August to October are notable as months when hurricanes are likely to hit the region, although freak hurricanes can descend in other months too.

You can apply for temporary or so-called transient membership at the International Yacht Club if you are docked at the Marina Hemingway. Rates vary from US$25 to US$60 per boat per week, depending on the size of your boat.

Sailing on turquoise waters is a favorite activity of sea-loving visitors to Cuba.

To charter a yacht or to book a yacht cruise with others at the helm, contact Cubanacán Nautica. They supply a choice of fully equipped boats and crew.

The three marinas in Varadero — the **Marina Gaviota** ((05) 667755 FAX (05) 667756, Carretera Las Morlas, Punta Hicacos, Varadero; the **Marina Chapelín** ((05) 665750 FAX (05) 667093, Carretera Las Morlas, Varadero; and the **Marina Puertosol Dársena** ((05) 668060 FAX (05) 667456, Vía Blanca, Dársena, Varadero — also offer yachts which you can charter for crew-manned cruises. Prices range from US$20 for a two-hour cruise to US$150 for a day's charter.

Membership entitles you to discounts on berthing, accommodations throughout the country, car rental and any nautical activities, as well as free use of the gymnasium and the swimming pool of the Hotel Viejo y El Mar, also within the Marina Hemingway complex, which is run by **Cubanacán Nautica** ((07) 241150 or 246848 FAX (07) 245280 WEB SITE www .cubanacan.cu, Avenida 5 and Calle 248, Santa Fé, Playa, Havana.

The Marina Hemingway has four berthing channels — each a kilometer (half-mile) long and capable of holding a hundred vessels — and can cater to cruisers of all sizes. All the necessary amenities are provided: power outlets, water connections, telephone, guard service, supplies and land facilities. The complex includes several restaurants, supermarkets, shops, tennis courts, and bicycle and car rental.

If you are thinking of sailing to and around Cuba, look out for the excellent *A Cruising Guide to Cuba* by Simon Charles (Cruising Guide Publications, second edition, 1997). It has all the practical information you will need, as well as directives for entering Cuba by sea. In Cuba, get a copy of the detailed *Yachtsman's Guide Cuba*, published jointly by Marina Puertosol, Marina Gaviota and Marina Marlin. This useful guide is sold at the International Yacht Club and the Club Náutico Internacional Hemingway de la Habana.

FISHING

There are few better places than the Gulf Stream off Cuba's northern coast to catch blue marlin, dolphin fish, white marlin, sail fish, wahoo, barracuda, tuna, bonito, bonefish and tarpon.

From its headquarters at the Marina Hemingway, **Cubanacán Nautica** ((07) 241150 or 246848 FAX (07) 245280 WEB SITE www.cubanacan.cu, Avenida 5 and Calle 248, Santa Fe, Playa, Havana, offers daily boat rental for fishing in the Gulf Stream for around US$250 to US$350 per day, depending on the size of the boat and the number of passengers; rates include tackle and bait, snacks and lunch.

You can expect similar rates at Varadero's marinas. Several other principal resorts also have boats equipped for off-shore and deep-sea fishing, notably at Isla de la Juventud, Cayo Coco in Ciego de Ávila Province, Guardalavaca in Holguín Province, Marea del Portillo in Granma Province and the Sierra Mar Club Resort, Chivirico, Santiago de Cuba Province.

The Marina Hemingway stages a number of international events for visiting fishing enthusiasts (many of whom come from North America), notably the **Ernest Hemingway International Marlin Tournament**, founded by the writer himself and usually held each June, and the **Blue Marlin International Fishing**

Renting a boat ABOVE is the only way through the mangroves to Laguna del Tesoro OPPOSITE.

Tournament held in August or September, both of which are governed by the International Game Fishing Association. In an effort to conserve Cuba's marine environment, they have adopted the "tackle-release" procedure and urge visiting participants to do the same.

Fly-fishing is becoming increasingly popular in Cuba, and the current top destination for the sport is the Zapata Peninsula in Matanzas Province. Other ideal places for this type of fishing are Varadero, Santa Lucía in Camagüey Province, Marea del Portillo in Granma Province, Punta del Este in Isla de la Juventud, and Cayo Largo.

Inland, Cuba's most popular freshwater fish is the largemouth bass, which was introduced in 1928 from Texas and New Orleans. Good fishing spots include Lake Hanabanilla in the Sierra del Escambray, Villa Clara Province; Laguna del Tesoro (also known as Treasure Lagoon) at Guamá; Zapata Peninsula in Matanzas Province; Lago La Redonda lagoon in Ciego de Ávila Province; and Lake Zaza in Sancti Spíritus, which is the largest reservoir in Cuba. Specializing in excursions, the chain **Horizontes Hoteles** ((07) 334042 or 334090 FAX (07) 333722

WEB SITE www.horizontes.cu, Calle 23 no. 156 between Calles N and O, Vedado, Havana, specializes in excursions and has fishing lodges in these locations. **Cubamar** ((07) 338317, 662524, 305536 or 662523 FAX (07) 333111 WEB SITE www.cubamar @cubamar.mit.cma.net, Paseo 752 at the corner of Calle 15, Vedado, can help arrange fishing trips and accommodation at on-site lodges.

Contact the tourist organization **Viajes Cubanacán** ((07) 280607 or 286063 FAX (07) 280107 WEB SITE www.cubanacan.cu, Calle 160 and Avenida 11, Playa, Miramar, Havana, for information on their special fishing holiday program, as well as their lodge, the Viramas Hunting and Fishing Lodge, in Granma Province.

In the United States, **Wings of the World** TOLL-FREE IN THE US (800) 465-8687, 100 William Street, Suite 706, Buffalo, New York 14240, arranges deep-sea and bass fishing trips within Cuba. In addition to publishing a newsletter with regular information about fishing in Cuba, **Pan-Angling Outdoor Adventure** ((317) 240-3474 TOLL-FREE IN THE US (800) 533-4353, 5348 North Vermont, Suite 300A, Indianapolis, Indiana, arranges fishing trips to the Zapata Peninsula and elsewhere on the island.

Although not especially *de rigueur* in Cuba, surfing may well become more popular in years to come. Northeasterly trade winds bring good swells between December and April, but surfers will have to bring their own boards, as none are available locally for rent. This being said, you are not likely to see a single surfer during your stay.

For further information, contact the **Cuban Watersports Federation** ((07) 240945 or 621677 FAX (07) 241914.

SPELUNKING

Cuba has one of the most elaborate limestone cave systems in the Americas: its mountains conceal vast networks of subterranean caverns, galleries and rivers. Potentially, Cuba may develop into a popular destination for spelunkers. The most interesting and accessible caves are in Pinar del Río, where the galleries of the Cueva Santo Tomás stretch for more than 45 km (30 miles); the Cueva de Bellamar, outside of Matanzas, and the underwater caves along the Zapata Peninsula, both in Matanzas Province; the Cueva Jibara within the Parque Nacional de Sierra Maestra, which drops some 248 m (814 ft); and the Punta del Este caves on the Isla de la Juventud, which contain ancient cave paintings. For information on these caves, contact **Hotel Horizontes Los Jazmines** ((08) 936205, or **Hotel Horizontes La Ermita** ((08) 936071, in Viñales; or the **Villa Horizontes Playa Girón** ((059) 4118, near the Zapata Peninsula.

Cuba has great potential for spelunking activities, but experienced guides are few. Be careful about who you choose to accompany you.

OTHER WATERSPORTS

Generally speaking, most major beach resorts (especially those run as a joint venture with a foreign company) offer a full smorgasbord of Club Med-style watersports: para-sailing, water skiing, snorkeling, jet skis, banana boats, catamarans, water bicycles, kayaks. Charges for these activities can be quite pricey. By its own definition, Varadero is Cuba's capital of watersports, so this is probably the best place to come if a constant round of watersports is your idea of holiday heaven. Varadero holds various water-sports festivals and events, including the Water-bike Cuban Cup in March, the Caribbean Open Water-skiing Contest in June and the Rowing Regatta in July. Otherwise, other resorts that are exceptionally well equipped for watersports enthusiasts are the two Tryp hotels in Cayo Coco, Ciego de Ávila Province; the two Golden Tulip hotels in Playa Lucía in Camagüey Province; and the Sierra Mar Club Resort in Chivirico, Santiago de Cuba Province.

If you enjoy snorkeling and wish to head off on your own as much as possible, it's best to bring your own snorkeling equipment with you.

CYCLING

With its flat terrain, ever-changing scenery and relative lack of motor vehicles, Cuba presents almost ideal conditions for long-distance cyclers. Although often regarded as something of an oddity by ordinary Cubans, cycling enthusiasts find it fairly easy to arrange short itineraries or even to circumnavigate the island. It is certainly a unique way to see the country up close, and you are likely to encounter much curiosity

and warmth, and perhaps even hospitality from the people you meet along the way. It is a good way to get around if you savor the sensation of being off on your own, especially in a country where much interaction between foreigners and Cubans often feels somewhat monitored. You will certainly find the roads relatively free of traffic, due to the transportation crisis of Cuba's Special Period, and you won't see too many other tourists either, except those who are whisked by in air-conditioned buses, at the mercy of their tour schedule.

One of the most popular routes is a loop from Havana to Pinar del Río Province in western Cuba, a fairly easy ride that takes in the Gulf of Mexico coast, the incredibly scenic Viñales Valley, the local tobacco growing region and the sugarcane country east of Pinar del Río city. Another easy ride takes you east from the capital along the coastal Vía Blanca highway, with "surf and sun" stops at popular beach resorts like Playas del Este and Varadero.

A much more challenging cycle route is a loop from Cienfuegos to Trinidad on the south coast. On the outbound leg you can follow the narrow country road through the Valle de Yaguanabo at the foot of the Sierra del Escambray mountains, pedaling

your way up to the summit at Topes de Collantes. On the inbound leg you can follow the sinuous coast road past empty beaches and endless sugarcane fields.

Santiago de Cuba is good spot for bike trips. You can follow the coast road west toward Marea del Portillo, where it climbs inland over the Sierra Maestra, Cuba's highest mountains, or head east to Parque Baconao and up to the summit of Gran Piedra. Either way, the scenery is spectacular.

Cuba has a **Federación de Ciclismo** (National Cycling Federation) ((07) 663776 or 683661, but truth be told it's not equipped to help someone from overseas organize a long-distance bike trip. Your options are to bring everything with you on the plane (including your bike) or to join one of the many organized cycle tours that now ply the island. Otherwise you'll face renting Cuba's ubiquitous Chinese-made Flying Pigeon bicycles, or buying a modern mountain bike in one of Havana's dollar-shops. The supply of rental bikes can be quite unreliable, and is generally

OPPOSITE: A dolphin laughs at Bahía de Naranjo. ABOVE: Cuba's beaches are well-equipped for water sports.

limited to central Havana and the beach resort hotels.

Several companies in the United States, Canada and Britain offer Cuba bike trips. **MacQueen's Travel** TOLL-FREE IN US AND CANADA (800) 969-2822 WEB SITE WWW .macqueens.com, 430 Queen Street, Charlottetown, Prince Edward Island, Canada, offers all-inclusive cycling tours in rural parts of Cuba, such as Pinar del Río, Granma and the Isla de la Juventud, combining cycling with various cultural activities such as visiting tobacco and coffee plantations, a Cuban school, or even a Havana ball game. Packages cost under US$1,000. Hardcore cyclists might want to opt for MacQueen's "Vuelta Cuba" — a two-week pedal from Santiago to Havana.

HORSEBACK RIDING

Horseback riding is not a commonplace activity in Cuba. Generally speaking, horses are taken up with other activities, such as meeting the nation's agricultural quota. Don't expect great equipment for your horse-riding excursions: you will be lucky if you have a saddle, let alone a riding hat. Very often farmers lend out the meager equipment they possess along with the horse. However, some beach resorts and hotels can arrange horseback riding excursions. These include Varadero, Playa Santa Lucía, Guardalavaca, Marea del Portillo and — the most secluded of these beaches — Cayo Largo.

Of all these suggestions, Playa Santa Lucía, which is located within Camagüey

central Havana. Housed in the former Havana Biltmore Yacht and Country Club on Avenida 5, it is Havana's top-level sports center. Originally founded in 1943, it has nine holes and beautifully landscaped lawns. There are also tennis courts, a bowling alley, billiard tables, a swimming pool, two restaurants and the 19th Hole Bar. Contact your hotel concierge to help you arrange temporary membership, or contact the club directly.

The brand-new, 18-hole **Varadero Golf Club** ((05) 668482 OR 662113 FAX (05) 668180 or 668481 WEB SITE www.varadero golfclub.com, Avenida de las Américas, Autopista Sur km8.5, is between the Meliá and Tuxpan hotels and encloses the former Du Pont mansion, which is now the stunning Xanadú restaurant and bar. The course was designed by the Canadian firm Golf Design Services, headed by Les Furber, who worked with the great Robert Trent Jones.

BASEBALL

A reigning passion of this island nation, baseball has produced a handful of world-class Cuban players, a number of whom have famously defected, such as Livian Hernandez, probably the most famous Cuban pitcher since Fidel Castro himself, now with the Florida Marlins.

Beisbol, as it is called, has early origins in Cuba. The first recorded game of baseball was played in 1874, at what is now the world's oldest baseball stadium. The island's national team traditionally wins out over the United States team at the Olympic Games, and it is little surprise that United States professional leagues eye Cuba's star players with considerable interest. Although they earn only 400 pesos a month, Cuba's top players play more than a hundred games during the annual season, which lasts from December to June. It is well worth attending one of these games — even a local game — at one of the huge stadiums that have been built by the state throughout the island. Entrance to watch spectator sports in Cuba is generally free or nominal.

Province — renowned in Cuba for its ranches and *vaqueros*, or cattle-ranchers — has the best facilities. Your hotel can arrange rides at the nearby King Ranch, a working cattle farm. In addition, special horse ranches have been set up for tourists at the **Finca Guajira Rodeo** ((0226) 39526, at El Oasis (El Crucero) in Parque Baconao, and at the **Villa María Dolores** ((0419) 6481 or 6394, outside Trinidad.

GOLF

Havana and Varadero have the island's only golf courses. The private **Club de Golf Habana** (Havana Golf Club) ((07) 558746 FAX (07) 338820, Carretera Calzada de Vento, near Boyeros, is in the Diploclub complex in Boyeros, 20 km (12 miles) from

A traditional rodeo in Holguín Province.

The Open Road

You need at least a month to explore the island properly by car. Still, even if you plan to spend less than two weeks in Cuba, you can manage to see a great deal, especially if you opt to rent a car or jeep for at least part of your stay. Bear in mind that Cuba can be a surprisingly expensive destination in which to rent a car or jeep, with inflated rental and fuel costs. You may wish to investigate the **Horizontes Flexi Drive Program**, a car-rental and accommodation package that runs about US$95 per day. It should be booked before you arrive in Cuba (see GETTING AROUND, page 316, in TRAVELERS' TIPS).

If you're visiting the island for a week to ten days, you can design a road trip around specific themes such as beaches, nature areas and historic cities.

BEACHES

As a general rule, Cuba's best beaches are those along the country's northern shore, many of them easy to reach by side roads off the Autopista Nacional or the Carretera Central.

Start your beach tour from Old Havana by driving through the harbor tunnel and picking up a four-lane highway called the Vía Blanca on the outskirts of Cojímar. The first strands are about half an hour outside the city, a series of small beach towns (Santa María del Mar, Boca Ciega and Guanabo) lumped together under the title **Playas del Este**. On weekends these beaches are crowded with *habaneros* trying to escape the heat and humidity of the central city. These *playas* are great for people watching but not especially posh or peaceful.

For that you need to jump back into your car and drive about two hours farther east (along the Vía Blanca) to the island's biggest and, in many respects, best beach resort — the seaside city of **Varadero**. Once the haunt of American tycoons and gangsters, the peninsula has been often compared to Miami Beach. It's not quite *that* colorful — especially since the hustlers and hookers were banished by the Cuban government — but Varadero does have a certain savoir-faire that's lacking at the island's other big beach resorts. Some of the country's best hotels — such as the Meliá Varadero and Mansión Xanadú — make their home here. There's a wide

range of restaurants to choose from, good nightlife and lots of off-the-sand activities such as sailing, scuba and jungle safaris.

Reaching the next beach area takes about a day of driving on the Autopista Nacional via Santa Clara and Ciego de Ávila, where you turn north toward Morón and the offshore islands. A skinny causeway called the Pedraplen takes vehicles across the Bahía de Perros (Bay of Dogs) to the prawn-shaped **Cayo Coco** and tiny **Cayo Guillermo**, two of Cuba's most exclusive beach areas. Talcum-powder sand and turquoise water await along the five main beaches. You can simply lounge in the sun or partake of numerous outdoor activities including scuba, snorkeling, sailing, windsurfing, bird watching (flamingos on the bay) or horseback riding. Coco's horizontal terrain is also perfect for biking. But bring lots of bucks — resorts on both isles are among Cuba's most expensive.

Retracing your steps to Ciego de Ávila, drive the Carretera Central even farther east, to the industrial city of Camagüey, where you can pick up another country road that runs to **Playa Santa Lucía**. The beach is almost equally divided between a stretch of all-inclusive hotels aimed at foreigners and seaside vacation homes rented by Cubans. Santa Lucía is much quieter than the other north shore resorts, a place where you can find your own little patch of sand and chill out. It's also a perfect jumping off spot for diving trips, boat excursions and fishing expeditions to isolated islands like Cayo Sabinal and Cayo Guajaba.

Another half-day cruise along the Carretera Central brings you to the dreary inland city called Holguín, where you can turn off to the rapidly expanding **Playa Guardalavaca**. This is really two resorts separated by a small patch of undeveloped coast — the older Guardalavaca with its tree-shaded strand and slightly faded hotels, and the newer Playa Esmeralda on the Bahía de Naranjo (Orange Bay), dominated by the trio of dazzling Meliá resorts. If you find yourself bored by the endless beach, there are plenty of other options in the area including an aquarium, ancient Indian archeological site and the place where Christopher Columbus first set foot in Cuba.

OPPOSITE: Bicycles are one answer to fuel shortages. ABOVE: A young woman poses by a vintage car near Santiago de Cuba.

HISTORIC CITIES

Most of the island's old colonial cities lie on the south coast, where the Spanish galleons found fewer reefs and better harbors.

Ernest Hemingway waxed lyrical about the sunsets in **Cienfuegos**, which he called "a long trickle of gold." Three hours east of Havana via the Autopista Nacional, the old colonial town lies on the north shore of Bahía de Cienfuegos, one of Cuba's largest natural harbors. The spacious Paseo del Prado (Calle 37), with its throng of horse-carts and bicycles, takes you back to another age, while the stunning Palacio de Valle near the tip of Punta Gorda remains one of the most impressive structures in Cuba.

A narrow coastal road around the southern flank of the Sierra del Escambray

mountain range leads to **Trinidad**, crown jewel of Cuba's smaller colonial cities. Founded in 1514 by conquistador Diego de Velázquez, this town of cobblestone lanes, red-tile roofs and baroque churches is truly a place where time stands still. The entire central city has been declared a national historic monument and the area around the charming Plaza Mayor has been declared a pedestrian only zone. Many of the most important structures have already been restored and many more are currently under renovation.

An incredibly picturesque road through the **Valle de los Ingenios** (Valley of the Sugar Mills) winds past ancient plantations and over the Sierra de Banao hills to Sancti Spíritus and the Carretera Central. Once

44

you reach the highway, it's about a two-hour drive to **Camagüey**, a chaotic industrial city with a fine colonial core. The central city boasts three fine colonial squares including the Plaza de los Trabajadores, the Parque Agramonte and the cobblestone Plaza San Juan de Dios with its Creole restaurants. Three hours farther east (after turning at Las Tunas) is another overlooked colonial outpost called **Bayamo**, where historic structures cluster around two adjoining squares called the Parque Céspedes and the Plaza del Himno.

From Bayamo, it's an easy two-hour drive to **Santiago de Cuba**, the island's second largest city and a colonial gem in its own right. Santiago's old town seems hardly touched by the twenty-first century,

especially the ancient Casa de la Trova where the best of Cuban music pours forth from local bands each night. Protecting the harbor entrance are the stout walls of the Castillo del Morro and rising above its eastern suburbs is Loma de San Juan, where the Spanish-American War (and Cuba's liberation from colonial rule) reached a bloody climax.

NATURE AREAS

Cuba has some of the wildest and largest national parks and nature reserves in the Caribbean, although they remain largely undeveloped.

Two hours west of Havana via the Autopista Nacional are the celebrated *mogotes* (karst hills) and limestone caves of the **Valle de Viñales** in Pinar del Río Province. The valley's sheer cliffs are starting to draw the attention of international rock climbers, but they can just as easily be viewed from numerous vantage points along the highway and the park that spreads at the feet of the famed Mural de la Prehistoria.

Backtrack along the Autopista Nacional (take the ring road around Havana to avoid the heavy urban traffic) to the busy Jagüey Grande/Australia junction, where you can pick up a side road that leads due south to the **Zapata Peninsula**. Cuba's largest national park, the Parque Nacional de la Ciénaga de Zapata, sprawls along the coast here between the Bahía de Cochinos (Bay of Pigs) and the Ensenada de la Broa, a vast area that encompasses woodland, swamp, grassland, beach, coves and coral reef. Unless you've got your own boat, the park is almost impossible to explore. Best access is from the tourist complex at La Boca or the hotel at Playa Larga, where you can arrange boat trips and fishing expeditions.

The coast road beyond the Bay of Pigs is rough and not recommended. Better to backtrack to the *autopista* and drive east to Santa Clara, where you can veer onto a country road that runs straight south (via Manicaragua) to the wild and rugged **Sierra del Escambray**, the island's second

A horseman travels from Guantánamo to Baracoa in Cuba's most remote region.

45

The Cuban government is not exactly trying to encourage backpacking or budget travel as a trend, preferring tourists to stay in designated hotels and put as many dollars into the Cuban economy as possible. Although Cubans themselves seem to exist on next to nothing, you will soon realize that tourism is the bootstrap that the government hopes to use to lift the nation out of its economic crisis.

There are no youth hostels or student travel discounts in Cuba. The former standby for budget travelers used to be Cuban *peso* hotels and holiday camps (usually run through **Cubamar** or operated by the **Islazul** chain), but now these facilities are obliged to finance themselves in dollars. Many of their properties have been modernized for foreigners and remain modestly priced, just not as ridiculously cheap as before.

However, if you are resourceful, there are a number of ways to make travel in Cuba less expensive.

You may find it both more interesting and economical to stay — at least some of the time — in private homes, or *casas particulares*. Price is always a matter of negotiation. By law, Cubans are allowed to rent up to two rooms in their own home, and this practice is becoming widespread. The price for a room usually ranges from around US$10 to US$20 per day, and no two homestays will be the same. You will usually have to share the bathroom, and your hosts are usually happy to prepare meals for an additional cost. Homestays in *casas particulares* are more or less banned in major beach resort areas (even Varadero) because authorities want to channel as many dollars as possible into government-run accommodation.

It's not advisable to accept solicitations to stay in a private home from *jiniteros* (street hustlers) who may not have your best interest at heart and who will always demand a commission. Better to rely on the word of mouth of Cuban friends or other travelers.

highest range. Che Guevara and his guerillas took refuge in these mountains during the Revolution, but today Cubans and foreigners alike largely ignore them. There are two tourist centers: Topes de Collantes with its funky old mountain-top hotels, and the bass-filled Presa de Hanabanilla reservoir.

After visiting the Escambray you can return to Havana (about four hours) or continue oalong the *autopista* to Cuba's eastern provinces. The **Sierra Maestra** mountains, Fidel Castro's old stomping ground, spread along the south coast from Cabo Cruz to Guantánamo Bay, a paradise for hikers, birdwatchers, photographers and nature lovers. A large chunk of the high country (including Pico Turquino, the nation's highest peak) is protected within the confines of national parks west of Santiago. More scenic mountain real estate, including the towering Gran Piedra, falls within the Baconao Biosphere Reserve, east of Santiago.

Still farther east, Guantánamo Province offers a spectacular drive along its **La Farola** highway across high mountain passes to colonial **Baracoa**, Cuba's oldest Spanish settlement. The route is beautiful and varied enough to never become boring, within the space of an hour you pass from arid desert flatlands indented by pretty inlets to exuberant mountain vegetation, then, beyond Baracoa, to tropical groves of coconut palms. To many, this is the most beautiful road on the island.

Despite the number of years that Castro and Che spent sleeping under the stars during the Revolution, camping is virtually nonexistent in Cuba. The Cubans themselves seem to frown upon camping as a holiday option, and there are very few actual campgrounds, even in the national parks. You could bring along your own tent, stove, sleeping bag and other outdoor equipment. But theoretically you need permission from authorities (the National Police or the Ministry of the Interior) before you can sleep in the wild.

Attempting to get around the country by bus is cheap, but highly likely to try the patience of even the most budget-conscious traveler. Buses to just about anywhere in Cuba you could want to go depart from the **Terminal Nacional** ((07) 703397, near the Plaza de la Revolución in Havana, but only recently has the government cottoned on to the fact that many tourists will use buses if the service is provided.

At present there is only one major long-distance bus company that caters to tourists: **ViAzul** ((07) 811413, 815652 or 811108 WEB SITE www.viazul.cu, which offers coach service from Havana to Varadero, Santiago, Trinidad, Baracoa and Viñales, as well as Varadero to Trinidad.

OPPOSITE: Bus travel is cheap and readily available throughout Cuba. ABOVE: Relaxing at Playa Esmeralda, on the Bahía de Naranjo, one of Cuba's loveliest coastlines.

You may find that riding the island's railway network is not a bad option. Trains are a reasonably reliable and inexpensive way to travel long distances between major cities. Trains depart from the **Estación Central** ((07) 613509 in Habana Vieja (see GETTING AROUND, page 317 in TRAVELERS' TIPS).

The number of single woman sticking their thumbs out at any given intersection in the countryside is testament to the fact that Cuba is probably one of the world's safest places for hitchhiking. But given the number of Cubans who rely on hitching for basic transportation, thumbing between cities is not a reasonable option — unless you're willing to pay Yankee dollars for a lift.

Outside of Havana and Varadero, it's easy to find an inexpensive restaurant meal most anywhere in Cuba. If you're on a super-tight budget, the only options (short of cooking your own meals) are fast-food snack bars like **Rumbos** and **El Rápido** found throughout the country. Many local bars also serve sandwiches, pizza and other snacks at very low prices.

One of the best ways to ensure that you keep your travel costs low in Cuba is to arrive on an all-inclusive package tour booked through a travel agency overseas. If you are an ardent individualist, this can chafe. But if you shop around, you may be able to find a tour package that allows you a maximum amount of freedom for a minimum cost.

Living It Up

Despite the Revolution and all that egalitarian rhetoric, Cuba has some wonderfully decadent hotels and resorts. Although this is a socialist state, there is a *nouvelle* elite comprised of top Communist Party cadres and bureaucrat/businessmen who've earned fortunes off the dollar economy. Rather than flaunt their riches at home, they tend to party overseas in places like Madrid, Montego Bay and Nassau. When they live it up on the domestic front, privileged Cubans tend to flock to the same spots as the wealthy *turistas* — Havana's top hotels and the chic beach retreats of Varadero, Cayo Coco and Playa Guardalavaca.

STAYING IN STYLE

In Havana, the luxurious **Meliá Cohiba** and **Meliá Habana** both boast all of the facilities you might expect of five-star establishments. But the *louche* grandeur of such retro classics as the **Hotel Nacional** or the elegantly restored **Hotel Santa Isabel** offer far more character and style. You can also spoil yourself at the exquisitely renovated **Hotel Florida** and the charming **Hostal Conde de Villanueva** — both of them throwbacks to the bygone grace of Spanish colonial days.

Varadero boasts more extravagant hotels than any other Cuban destination (including the capital). Among the peninsula's best beach abodes are the superb **Meliá Varadero** and the **Meliá Las Américas**, while the **Hotel Internacional** has retro chic and the best stretch of beach. If money is absolutely no object, you can book the entire **Mansión Xanadú** (six guest rooms) and throw your own Roaring Twenties party, recreating the days when the sumptuous seaside villa was built by American tycoon Eleuthère Irénée du Pont. While you're in residence, get in a couple of rounds at the **Varadero Golf Club** (Du Pont's old private course), which surrounds the mansion.

ABOVE: Havana's neoclassical Hotel Inglaterra. OPPOSITE: The striking marble staircase of Havana's venerable Gran Teatro.

Yet Varadero doesn't own a monopoly on chic beach retreats. The twin paradise isles of Cayo Coco and Cayo Guillermo flaunt half a dozen resorts that could hold their own anywhere in the Caribbean, including the **Meliá Cayo Coco** with its romantic floating rooms, the intimate **Villa Vigía** and the veteran **Tryp Cayo Coco**. Among Cuba's other outstanding coastal abodes are the **Meliá Río de Oro** at Playa Esmeralda near Playa Guardalavaca; the **Gran Club Santa Lucía** at Playa Santa Lucía; and the **Brisas Trinidad del Mar** overlooking Playa Ancón near Trinidad.

In Pinar del Río, **Los Jazmines** in the Valle de Viñales is charming and has sublime views, and **La Moka** in Las Terrazas, Sierra del Rosario, is the island's first ecological resort, stylishly designed and rather luxurious to boot.

In Granma Province, the **Farallón del Caribe** in Marea del Portillo deserves praise for both its attractive landscaping and its relaxing atmosphere.

In Santiago de Cuba, the newly restored **Hotel Casa Granda**, which first opened in 1914, has elegant charm and outshines — in style if not in range of facilities — the city's longtime standby, the **Hotel Meliá Santiago de Cuba**. Meanwhile, towards the island's eastern tip, in Baracoa, the **Hotel El Castillo** has a commanding position and occupies what used to be a Spanish fortress.

WINING AND DINING

Cuba has many enjoyable and special restaurants, some of which are notable as much for their splendid settings as for their food.

Havana's best restaurant is **El Gato Tuerto** (The One-Eyed Cat), which nestles in an old colonial mansion in Vedado, just up from the waterfront. Everything about this place is stylish: impeccable service, elegant decor and an imaginative menu that combines Cuban ingredients and international flair. Havana's most romantic eatery is the rooftop **Terraza Florentina** at the Hotel Capri, where the resident violinist serenades with bygone boleros as you gaze down on the Malecón, Habana Vieja and El Morro castle. The cuisine is perhaps the city's best take on traditional Italian.

La Divina Pastora, one of Havana's most scenic restaurants, is set within the Morro-Cabaña fortress, overlooking the bay and the Malecón. Hemingway favorites such as **El Floridita** and **La Bodeguita del Medio** are classics from the pre-Revolution era, although neither should be visited with high culinary expectations. For the best of Cuban Creole cuisine amid stylish settings in Miramar mansions, **La Fermina** and **Tocororo** are both popular with Havana's cognoscenti.

Near Havana, in the fishing village of Cojímar (famous as the setting for Hemingway's *The Old Man and the Sea*), **La Terraza** serves the best seafood paella on the island.

In Varadero, aside from ubiquitous hotel buffets, the most sophisticated dining is undoubtedly at the Basque restaurant **Fuerteventura**, at the Hotel Meliá Varadero, and the **Mansión Xanadú**, set in the 1930s Du Pont mansion. In Pinar del Río, both the **Casa de Don Tomás** in the rustic town of Viñales, and the fresh prawns served at **La Casa del Marisco** in the Valle de Viñales should not be missed.

In Cienfuegos a meal at the **Palacio Valle**, for its grandiose setting alone, is a highlight of visiting the city, a description that also applies to Santiago de Cuba's **1900** restaurant, which occupies a former *palacio* and glitters with antique chandeliers and musty rococo elegance.

In Trinidad, try a *canchánchara* cocktail at **La Canchánchara**, while elegant dining is best at the **Trinidad Colonial**. In the nearby Valle de los Ingenios, lunches are served in historic **Manacas-Iznaga** plantation mansion. In Camagüey, for colonial ambience and excellent local food, **La Campana de Toledo** and **Parador de los Tres Reyes** both have beautiful settings in the historic Plaza San Juan de Dios.

In some cases, glorious surroundings appear to be everything, but the meals served also seem to rise to the occasion, assisted by the melting glow of the afternoon sun and the Mayabe beer.

Hotel Los Jazmines ranks among Cuba's most pleasant.

A special mention must be made of **La Taberna del Morro**, the restaurant at the harbor entrance to Santiago de Cuba, which has magnificent views across the sea and fortress of the same name; and the sea-facing restaurant **El Punte**, housed in the former fortress lookout in Baracoa.

Generally speaking, restaurants at hotels run by foreign chains, particularly the Spanish Sol Meliá group, offer fresh and varied food at reasonable prices, and the best food safety guarantees.

OUT ON THE TOWN

Cubans are a famously musical people and it is no exaggeration to say that music is an integral part of life here.

Almost every night in Havana, it is possible to find some of Cuba's best salsa and jazz bands playing live in various nightclubs. One of the best ways to start an evening out is with sunset cocktails at the Hotel Nacional's back garden bar and then wander down the waterfront to the Hotel Riviera's **Palacio de la Salsa**, or the **Casa de la Música**, depending on who is performing that night. The Meliá Cohiba's **Habana Café** is the capital's most exclusive nightclub, packed with trendy, young Cubans and featuring the

country's top musical acts. Almost all the capital's bars and nightclubs, notably **La Bodeguita del Medio** and **El Floridita**, have live musicians and singers who, even in more modest and less touristy surroundings, are shockingly professional. And of course, one must not forget Havana's legendary **Tropicana** cabaret. The two-hour show — a blizzard of samba, sequin and naked flesh — is worth every penny.

As you travel through Cuba, you can enter almost any of the island's many music halls, known as Casas de la Trova — from nondescript rooms in the countryside with peeling paint and a bar which has nothing to serve, to the more famous establishments in Trinidad and Santiago de Cuba — and hear the true soul of Cuban music. The Casa de la Trova in Santiago is the best of its kind, with memorable performances every night and regular appearances by its celebrated house band, Vieja Trova Santiguera.

GETTING AROUND IN STYLE

Until quite recently it was impossible to rent anything that even resembled a luxury automobile in Cuba. Enter a new rental car company called **Rex**, which

immediately took Cuban driving to a new level. Top-of-the-line at Rex is the Volvo S90 limousine, which comes fully equipped with refrigerator, video monitor, leather seats, air bags, anti-lock brakes and your own personal chauffeur. The price? A cool US$325 per day. If you don't mind driving yourself and you prefer something with a bit more zip, Rex also rents Audi TT 1.8 sports cars, with leather seats, Blaupunkt CD player, and electrically powered soft top.

If you long for legendary wheels, **Gran Car Autos Antiquos** in Havana rents out classic American cars from the 1940s and 1950s including DeSotos, Cadillacs, Mercurys, Buicks, Oldsmobiles and Chevys. They're all in mint condition, museum pieces on four wheels. But you can't drive them yourself — chauffeurs are obligatory.

Given the obvious security situation, it's not possible to rent your own aircraft in Cuba. But there is the possibility of getting whisked off by helicopter to an exclusive island retreat called **Cayo Saetía**, which lies off the north coast of Las Tunas Province. Contact Gaviota Tours at Playa Guardalavaca or Playa Esmeralda for details (page 246).

Just about any of the large marinas — **Marina Hemingway** near Havana, **Marina Chapelín** in Varadero, **Marina Vita** near Guardalavaca or **Marina Trinidad** at Playa Ancón — offer the opportunity of charting a yacht for private fishing, scuba or sailing expeditions. Large catamarans seem to be the most popular; they come fully staffed and stocked with all sorts of goodies (see SPORTING SPREE, page 35).

Family Fun

Cubans love children and treat them with genuine kindness and interest, a welcome attitude that you will encounter wherever you go. Many of the hotels — especially the beach resorts — offer special children's entertainment programs, and some hotels organize babysitting upon request.

Even children as young as two can check into Kids Kamp at the **Super Club Sierra Mar** near Santiago, which has a playground, Nintendo, a swimming program, a nightly movie and cartoon

Full comfort resort hotels ABOVE at the peaceful beach of Playa Esmeralda OPPOSITE near Guardalavaca.

brand new Cuban wing of **Museo Nacional de Bellas Artes** — the dazzling pop art, the modern sculptures and the mixed-media works are especially popular with children. When all else fails haul them off for some ice cream at Parque Coppelia in downtown Vedado.

Santiago has its own version of **El Morro**, which perches on a cliff above the harbor entrance and the sparkling sea. Inside the fort's coral-stone walls is a display on famous pirates who roamed the Caribbean. The **Museo Bacardí** in the old town displays old military uniforms and antique weapons, as well as Egyptian and Peruvian mummies. Another collection that will delight youngsters is the nearby **Museo del Carnaval** with its flamboyant costumes and giant papier-mâché heads. And don't think the **Casa de la Trova** is for adults only — children can also groove to the traditional tunes of Cuba, as evidenced by the number of local kids you see who accompany their parents and relatives to the nightly performances.

Just east of Santiago, **Parque Baconao** has a number of attractions that are tailor-made for children. You can see Cuban-style rodeo every weekend at the **Finca Guajira** or walk among some life-sized dinosaurs replicas in the bizarre **Valley of Prehistory**. Farther along the coast is a small **marine park** with aquariums and performing dolphin shows.

One of the best family daytrips from Havana is the **Zapata Peninsula** in Matanzas Province, where you can visit the Indian-style village at **Guamá**, the crocodile breeding farm at **La Boca**, and take a safari-style boat ride through the swamps of the sprawling **Parque Nacional de la Ciénaga de Zapata,** the country's largest wildlife reserve and nature area.

Another good family daytrip is the picturesque **Valle de Viñales**, about a two-hour drive west of Havana, in Pinar del Río Province. Take a motorboat trip through the **Cueva del Indio** (Indian Cave) with its dramatic rock formations and then admire the gargantuan **Mural de la Prehistoria** that Cuban artist Leovigildo Gonzáles painted on a limestone cliff in the Valle de Dos Hermanas.

program, watersports and activities for older children. On the other side of Santiago, the secluded **Carisol-Los Corales Resort** offers daily recreational programs for children and a range of sports activities for older kids including tennis, billiards, sailing, snorkeling and sea kayaking. The **LTI Tuxpan Resort** in Varadero has its own children's pool and a kiddy club with daily activities. **Club Amigo Guardalavaca** boasts a kid's club and other pre-teen activities. In addition to a wonderful beach and myriad watersports activities, the **Meliá Cayo Coco** also offers special programs for families with children.

Generally, children under the age of 12 traveling with their parents in Cuba are granted discounted accommodation. Check with your hotel beforehand. At some of the all-inclusives, children stay free. Depending on their age, children will probably enjoy the sights in and around the historic cities of Havana, Trinidad and Santiago de Cuba.

Havana is especially rich in sights that will intrigue young minds. **El Morro** castle with its lofty stone bastions and rusting Spanish cannon is a good starting point, although it's better to visit in the early morning and late afternoon when it's not so hot. Kids who like big machines will delight in the old tanks, planes and other military hardware on display at the **Museo de la Revolución**. Another good place to pass a couple of hours is the

Cultural Kicks

Some of Cuba's most remarkable museums are colonial mansions or *palacios* that have been turned into museums and are furnished in the traditional style — offering a most evocative look at Cuba's past. Some are steeped in history, such as the **Museo de la Ciudad de la Habana**, which is housed in the magnificent Palacio de los Capitanes Generales, seat of the colonial Spanish government, with private living quarters that saw many of the island's former masters come and go, or the city's first fortress, the **Castillo de la Real Fuerza**. You can also explore the museums housed inside the island's impressive colonial fortresses and wander their battlements afterwards, notably at the **Castillo de los Tres Santos Reyes Magos del Morro** and **San Carlos de la Cabaña** in Havana; and the **Castillo del Morro** fortress in Santiago.

Others are restored to an approximation of their original grandeur, like the **Museo Romántico** in the historic Palacio de Brunet overlooking the main square in Trinidad, which gives a very accurate sense of how the colonial sugar-rich aristocracy lived

during colonial times. The **Museo de Arte Colonial** and the **Museo de Artes Decoratives** in Havana, along with the **Museo de Ambiente Histórico Cubano** (also known as the Casa de Velázquez) in Santiago, house the country's most exceptional furniture and antiquity collections within historic former homes.

More contemporary museums on a slightly different theme are the **Casa-Museo de Hemingway** at La Finca Vigía, outside Havana, which displays the writer's home and possessions much the way they were left, and the **Museo Napoleónico**, in Havana, a quirky repository of one man's tribute to the great Corsican.

To become acquainted with Cuba's archaeological and natural history, the **Museo Anthropológico Montané** at the University of Havana and the **Museo Nacional de Historia Natural** on the Plaza de Armas, are worth a look, as are the **Museo Indocubano** in Banes, in Holguín Province, and the **Museo Matachín** in Baracoa, Guantánamo Province. The newly discovered site at **Punta Alegre**, in Ciego de Ávila, the country's largest extant Taíno

OPPOSITE: Children play in Old Havana. ABOVE: The modern-day Mural de la Prehistoria.

Indian settlement, may eventually become an important museum.

Cuba's single most important museum of art is the superb **Museo Nacional de Bellas Artes** in Havana, which opened its doors again in the summer of 2001 after a four-year, US$14.5-million renovation. The collection is now split between Cuban art (housed in the original post-modern gallery, built in 1954) and international art (housed in the Centro Asturiano, built in 1927). The latter boasts many works — including paintings by European masters — left behind by Cubans fleeing the Revolution or confiscated from wealthy families after Castro came to power. The two wings form the richest body of art in Latin America.

You should not miss the **Museo de las Parrandas Remedianas** if you visit the town of Remedios in Villa Clara Province. To learn about Cuba's Afro-Caribbean traditions, visit Havana's **Casa de Africa**, the **Museo del Regla** and the **Museo Histórico de Guanabacoa**.

You may become quite a connoisseur of Cuba's unique revolutionary museums, such as the capital's **Museo de la Revolución** (formerly the Presidential Palace of dictator Fulgencio Batista) with prize exhibits like the *Granma* boat that

brought Castro back from exile in Florida at the start of the conflict; the **Museo Girón** at Playa Girón, Matanzas Province, which concentrates on the infamous Bay of Pigs invasion of 1962; the **Tren Blindado** in Santa Clara, Villa Clara Province, where Che's brigade put the final nail into Batista's military coffin; and the **Moncada Barracks** in Santiago, where Castro kicked off his bloody campaign to destroy Batista's totalitarian rule.

Museum hours can be very erratic in Cuba. Generally, all the documentation about exhibits is in Spanish, but most museums allow language students training as guides to walk around with you. Although most museums are free for Cubans, the entrance fee for tourists is usually US$1 or US$2.

During your visit to Havana, you may wish to visit the venerable Gran Teatro to see a performance of the **Ballet Nacional de Cuba**. There is an almost surreal ambience to the moment when the lights dim, the orchestra begins to play and the faded red curtains part, created by the creaking majesty of the theatre itself, a glorious Miss Havisham out to trot. Here again, should you need any reminding, is another example of the outstanding talent shown by Cuban performers, especially musicians and dancers (not to mention baseball players). The Ballet Nacional follows a strong classical tradition, and its founding director, Alicia Alonso (Cuba's answer to Margot Fonteyn), runs a tight ship. It has produced an some internationally famous stars, most notably, Carlos Acosta, who has been heralded as the young Nureyev or Baryshnikov.

Shop till You Drop

When it comes to shopping, Cuba is best known for its preeminently popular export — its famous **cigars**.

You could always start your exploration with a visit to the **Hotel Meliá Cohiba's cigar bar** ((07) 333636, a veritable temple to cigar smoking, in which you can familiarize yourself with some of Cuba's many brands.

Cherished by tobacco lovers, the Cohiba is a symbol of the Revolution to many Cubans, because they were first made for Fidel Castro by a fellow soldier (a cigar-maker turned revolutionary), and it remained his favorite cigar until he gave up smoking. Equally famous is the Montecristo, which uses the specially graded Ligeuro leaf, followed by the Romeo y Julieta brand, famed for its consistency. H. Upmann and Ramon Allones are also fine examples, light-flavored and full-flavored respectively. Each brand — but most notably Cohiba, Montecristo and Romeo y Julieta — has a range which varies in size and quality. In 1998, Cuba launched a new brand, Trinidad, made at El Laguito — the same factory that makes Cohibas — and the Trinidad Fundador is currently the darling of the cigar-smoking world. Another new brand is named after Cuba's most famous tobacco-producer Alejandro Robaino.

The streets of Havana (and Santiago de Cuba) are full of hucksters trying to sell what they claim are boxes of fine cigars smuggled by employees from factories at a tenth of the usual price. Most of what they sell turns out to be a low-grade imitation, but some are not, as workers will

sometimes admit. It is not advisable to buy cigars on the street, especially if you expect them to be the real thing. There's a good chance that the Cuban customs authorities will take them away from you at the airport anyway, since they are trying to crack down on fake cigars, which they fear will ruin the reputation of the real ones.

If you shop for cigars at your hotel, you can expect to pay inflated prices, although the quality and selection will be good. One of the best government-run non-hotel shops in Havana for cigars is the **Casa del Tabaco** ((07) 241185, at Avenida 5 and Calle 16 in Miramar, where the staff is knowledgeable and helpful and the prices are about right. The shop at the **Fábrica Partagas**, behind the Capitolio, is also good, as is the **Casa del Tabaco** on Calle Mercaderes, near the Hotel Ambus Mundos.

Cuban Havana Club **rum** is something of a cult for some. A good place to buy rum, or Cuba's Cubita **coffee**, is the large **Supermercado de 70** ((07) 242890, at Avenida 3 and Calle 70 in Miramar, although you may find the **Casa del Ron**

OPPOSITE: Collectors prize vintage cigar box labels.
ABOVE: La Casa del Tabaco sells famed cigars.

((07) 331242, at the corner of Calles Obispo and Bernaza, next to El Floridita, is more conveniently located in La Habana Vieja.

It is ironic that you may find a better selection of superior quality recordings by Cuban musicians in New York, London and almost any other major city than in Cuba itself. However, many high-quality recordings of **Cuban music** produced in Canada and Mexico are available at competitive prices in Cuba. It is hard to go wrong if you buy any of the Cuban greats, ranging from classic recordings of Ernesto Lecuona, Beny Moré (the so-called El Bárbaro del Ritmo), Trio Matamoros, Machito, Issac Oviedo, Celia Cruz, Elena Burke and El Guayabero (master of the *guaracha*) to contemporary balladists Silvio Rodriquez and Pablo Milanes; salsa masters Los Van Van, Issac Delgado, NG La Banda, El Medico de la Salsa and Toto Gomez; or African jazz musicians such as Chucho Valdez and his band Irakere and newcomers such as Geraldo Alfonso.

The best place to buy music is the **Bazar La Habana Si** ((07) 553162, at the main outlet of ARTEX, the Cuban Art Export enterprise, which also has a better choice of CDs and cassettes than most of the government-run shops in Cuba. It is located at Calles L and 23 in Vedado. The **Casa de la Música**, at Calle 20 between Calles 33 and 35 in Miramar, has a good shop, but can run low on its stocks.

The **Palacio de la Artesanía** (Palace of the Artisans) ((07) 338072, on Calle Cuba between Calles Tacón and Cuarteles, in La Habana Vieja is worth a look. Its several floors of shops have a wide variety of Cuban-made arts and crafts, but is probably best as a place to buy Cuban music.

Cuba can be a good place to find old and **rare books and maps**, many of which turn up in street markets, but are most notably at the **Feria de Libros** set up every day in the Plaza de Armas. You can find all sorts of books here, including nineteenth-century architectural surveys of Havana, reproductions of works by Cuban artists, accounts by early travelers, works by the ethnologist Fernando Ortiz and by Natalie Bolivar, the Cuban expert on Santería, as well as political treatises written by Fidel

Castro and Che Guevara at the beginning of the Revolution. Some of the street markets sell what are certainly collector's items: comic books printed during the 1960s for schoolchildren to teach them about the Revolution. You can also find old movie posters and other pre-Revolution memorabilia at these street markets.

Havana's best bookshops include the **Libraría La Bella Habana** ((07) 628091, in the Palacio de Segundo Cabo in Plaza de Armas, and the **La Moderna Poesía** ((07) 616640, on Calle Obispo. The **Cuban Writers and Artists Union** (UNEAC), at the corner of Calles 17 and H in Vedado, sells the Union's small edition folios of poetry and other books.

If you are interested in purchasing **contemporary art**, start at the **Fondo de Bienes Culturales** ((07) 612859, the government-run artists agency, which runs several galleries around the country. The Fondo's main office is in the Galleria Diago on Plaza Vieja, in La Habana Vieja. The many art galleries along Calle Obispo and in Plaza Catedral may be able to help with introductions to local artists, so that you can visit their studios. It is important to know that if you leave Cuba having purchased original art, you need official authorization to export it. If you have purchased the art in a gallery or hotel, your receipt will include that authorization, but not if you have struck an independent deal with an individual artist. In that case, you'll have to take the art to the Ministry of Culture on the corner of Calles 17 and 12 in Vedado to get the necessary stamped piece of paper; the process usually takes several days.

The **Museo de Bellas Artes** ((07) 620141, and the **Centro Wilfredo Lam** ((07) 623305, sell art books, catalogues, posters and artistic T-shirts.

Cuban **postcards** and **revolutionary photographs** are good purchases. You'll find postcards in hotels and bookshops. Look out for photographic posters and books, particularly those by Alberto Korda, Raúl Corrales and Osvaldo Salas. You'll find a good selection at the La Terraza restaurant in Cojímar, as Raúl Corrales is a local (reclusive) resident. If all else fails, the airport shop is pretty good.

Dollar-shops and *supermercados* are appearing all over Havana, called *"shopees"* by locals, run by the Panamericanas and the Caracol chains, which accept only dollars and convertible pesos. They are useful for buying food supplies and bottled water.

Short Breaks

There are many places you can escape to for just a few days in Cuba. Some of the finest sand in the Caribbean is just a hop, skip and a jump down the coast from Havana. **Varadero** has attracted a trendy crowd for nearly a century, including such luminaries as gangster Al Capone and author Ernest Hemingway. Check into one of the posh all-inclusive resorts at the eastern end of the peninsula, or find a room at one of the modestly priced hotels in Varadero town. Either way, you've got smooth sand and turquoise water right outside your front door. Be it fancy hotel restaurants or grass shacks along the strand, Varadero boasts some of Cuba's finest dining. And there are plenty of things to do besides lying on the beach: golfing the country's best course, exploring the nearby mangrove swamps by jet ski, flitting off to various offshore cays on a luxury catamaran. By the end of your stay, you'll wish there was time for more.

Cloth dolls OPPOSITE and artwork ABOVE sold at the market in La Habana Vieja.

Nature lovers have several options for quick trips near Havana, including a jaunt down the **Zapata Peninsula**. Stay at one of the modest beach hotels on the Bay of Pigs or in a modern, air-conditioned thatched "shack" at the Villa Guamá hotel, in the middle of the swamp. Explore the national park by boat (bring binoculars for crocodile spotting and bird-watching) or organize your own bass-fishing expedition. You can explore the region's offshore waters via the International Diving Center at Playa Girón. Before you leave, duck into the nearby Museo Girón for a dose of Cuban history — fascinating displays on the failed Bay of Pigs invasion of 1962.

The easiest place to sink your teeth into Cuba's colonial heritage is the exquisite old town of **Trinidad** on the south coast. It's a good four-hour drive from Havana, half along the *autopista* and half along narrow country roads through sugarcane fields, so you'll need at least four days to do things right. Book yourself a roomy suite at the hilltop Hotel Las Cuevas and explore the town's cobblestone lanes by foot, starting at Plaza Mayor, the best-preserved colonial square in Cuba. If you've time, take the tourist train to nearby Valle de los Ingenios (Valley of the Sugar Mills) and visit one of the bygone plantations. Drive up to the Topes de Collantes and hike through the lush highland forest of the Sierra del Escambray. Or amble down to the beach, the little seaside village of La Boca or the fine white sands of Playa Ancón.

Festive Flings

Should you need any reminding that you are in Cuba, New Year's Day is celebrated as the **Anniversary of the Triumph of the Revolution**, which is often marked with a speech by Fidel Castro in the Plaza de la Revolución.

It is well worth coinciding your visit to Havana with the capital's annual week-long **International Jazz Festival**, held in mid-February. This is a heady time of year, with many of Cuba's great musicians such as Chucho Valdés and Irakere, Juan Formell and Los Van Van, and Silvio Rodríquez performing in venues across the city, notably the Hotel Riviera's Palacio de la Salsa, the Casa de la Cultura in the Plaza de la Revolución area, and the José Echeverria Stadium. You should check with your hotel about how to go about buying tickets at the Casa de la Cultura. If you want to be certain to have seats for performances, you may be interested in the pre-arranged tours offered by Australian-based **Our World Travel** ((03) 9614-1344 TOLL-FREE IN AUSTRALIA (800) 337-372 FAX (03) 9614-2992 WEB SITE WWW .ourworldtravel.com.au, Level 10, 34 Queen Street, Melbourne, Victoria 3000, Australia; or the United States-based **Global Exchange Reality Tours** ((415) 255-7296 TOLL-FREE IN THE US (800) 497-1994 FAX (415) 255-7498 WEB SITE www.gobal exchange.org/tours, 2017 Mission Street, Suite 303, San Francisco, California 94110, or **Wings of the World** TOLL-FREE IN US (800) 465-8687, 1200 William Street, Suite 706, Buffalo, New York 14240. All of these tours include reserved seating and visits to jazz workshops, and include round-trip airfare.

Also in mid-February, Havana gears up for its annual **Carnival**, which takes place in La Habana Vieja and along the Malecón, where a street party atmosphere takes over, along with skimpily-clad revelers, and outdoor performances of

ABOVE: Trinidad's El Museo Romántico dates from the early 1880s. OPPOSITE: A dancer pauses during a performance on Isla de la Juventud.

salsa, folkloric and jazz groups. The week-long festival culminates in a parade of floats, with conga-dancing being part of the scene. Although the Carnival is great fun, it can get a bit chaotic and crowded in La Habana Vieja, so take it at your own pace.

Later in February, the **Havana Book Fair** takes place, an interesting cultural event, which offers opportunities to meet Cuban writers. For more information, contact the **Cámara Cubano del Libro**, Feria Internacional del Libro Habana ((07) 329526 FAX (07) 338212 WEB SITE www.leedor .com, Calle 15 no. 604, Vedado, Havana. Or you can contact the **Center for Cuban Studies** ((212) 242-0559 FAX (212) 242-1937 WEB SITE www.cubaupdate.org, 124 West 23rd Street, New York, New York 10011.

In May, Havana stages its always-impressive **May Day Parade** on May 1 in the Plaza de la Revolución, where thousands of Cubans throng to wave flags and banners at the annual parade of the island's military might, along with school children in their Young Pioneer uniforms. Fidel Castro traditionally makes an appearance and a long speech, along with other Cuban leaders. If you happen to be in Havana, the event is not to be missed.

During May, the biannual **International Guitar Festival** held in Havana attracts many devotees.

In June, Trinidad's **Fiestas Sanjuaneras**, held at the end of the month, is a fun celebration of musical styles which centers on the Casa de la Trova, if you happen to visit during this hot month.

In July, the carnival in Santiago de Cuba, now relaunched as the **Fiesta del Caribe** runs from July 22 to 28. Despite the heat, this is probably the island's most exuberant and exciting music festival, held in the birthplace of son music and featuring musicians from Cuba and many other Caribbean island nations. It is impossible not to enjoy the street festivities, or not to be swept up in a rumba or conga line. The center of action is La Trocha, near the harbor at the southern end of Jesús Menéndez and the Avenida 24 de Febrero. Santiago's carnival is centuries-old, and was traditionally timed with the end of the

zafra harvest; however, it is no coincidence that today it is timed to culminate on the July 26 public holiday marking the day when Fidel Castro stormed the Moncada Barracks under the cover of carnival in 1953, honored throughout the nation as the **Remembrance of the National Rebellion**. It was cancelled for several years, but is now part of Cuba's festival scene once more, and includes dance, music and theater performances, as well a art exhibitions. Contact the Caribbean Music and Dance Programs and the Center for Cuban Studies (see above) for more details if you plan to attend.

August has two interesting music festivals: the **Boleros de Oro** in Santiago de Cuba and the **Beny Moré International Festival of Popular Music** in Cienfuegos,

YOUR CHOICE

notable if you happen to be in either of these cities.

Late August sees the biannual **Havana International Theater Festival**.

Held during the month of September every two years, the **Biennial de la Habana** (Visual Arts Biennial) celebrates work by artists from Cuba and abroad, providing a showcase for local artistic expression since it began in 1984. The most recent biennial included artists from some 50 countries, and also featured 30 North American artists. Exhibitions are staged throughout the capital, including the Centro Wilfredo Lam and the El Morro fortress. Contact the Centro de Wilfredo Lam ((07) 623305 or 613419 FAX (07) 338477, Calle Empedrado at the corner of San Ignacio, Habana Vieja.

October is a particularly active month: both the 10-day **Havana Festival of Contemporary Music** and the **International Ballet Festival** are held in Havana, and the **Festival de Bailador Rumbero** takes place in Matanzas.

In November, Trinidad stages its **Semana de la Cultura Trinitaria**, which takes place in the town's main cultural centers.

In mid-December, Havana is put on the map with the **International Festival of New Latin American Cinema**, when a flurry of international celebrities parachute in to glamorize the event. If you happen to have connections, this is a great time for parties, and if you can stand the lines,

Goats are sacrificed during a Santería ceremony.

the festival provides an excellent opportunity to see the latest Cuban and Latin American films.

Also in December, in Remedios in central Villa Clara Province, you might want to ask about a unique festival that used to take place here: **Las Parrandas de Remedios**. Apparently, this carnival-type event, which features colorful floats and festivities, was cooked up by the Catholic priests trying to stir up more enthusiasm for Christmas Mass during the town's early colonial era. It has been cancelled for several years during the Special Period, but may well be revived. Traditionally it was held on the Saturday before December 26.

Galloping Gourmet

It is best to preface any discussion on dining with a warning from *Mi Moto Fidel*, Christopher Baker's riveting account of a modern journey across the island: Cuban food is a "culinary catastrophe." If you crave truly exceptional Cuban food, try the Cuban restaurants in Miami, New York or Los Angeles, because you're probably not going to find it in Cuba. In sweeping capitalism into the Caribbean, one of the unexpected casualties of the Revolution was fine dining. Most of the country's best chefs fled to the United States, and those who remained behind are hampered by a lack of ingredients and the fact that all of the country's restaurants are somehow controlled by the state. Except at the very best hotels managed by European chains, menus are determined by bureaucrats in Havana who seem to think that tourists and locals alike will eat the same old thing day after day. Although the situation has improved over the last couple of years, as has the cuisine, we are still a far cry from the rich, inventive and savory cuisine of yesteryear.

Unless you are invited to a Cuban home, you are probably best off sticking to the dollar restaurants or *paladares* (private home-restaurants). It is something of an understatement to observe that Cubans frequently spend the better part of their days trying to obtain many of the

provisions that appear freely on hotel buffet tables.

Cuban restaurant food is frequently stodgy and bland, although if you are invited to private homes, you may be amazed at the way delicious meals can be magically prepared. Cubans often pride themselves on being excellent and ingenious cooks, and will go to huge lengths to make sure their guests are well-fed.

You should definitely visit a *paladar* during your stay. During the worst years of the Special Period, a popular Brazilian television series captured the heart of Cubans through the misadventures of a woman who triumphed over her daily difficulties (reflecting the quotidian trials of many Cubans) by opening a small restaurant called Le Paladar. Today, all of Cuba's small home-restaurants are called *paladares*, and although they began as more or less legal establishments, they are now officially allowed. There are many of these in Havana, as well as throughout the country. Like family *tavernas* in Greece, *paladares* are often full of character and authentic atmosphere.

The food in these *paladares* can be good or mediocre, the decor sumptuous or touchingly sordid, the service clumsy or already professional. They can range from very rustic establishments with simple Creole dishes to rather professionally run family mansions serving elaborate French cooking. Although you may not make any gastronomic discoveries, in any case, it's an experience that allows you to get that much closer to the Cuban reality. It's difficult to run a restaurant when it was not your original vocation, in a country where officially you have been condemned to the fires of hell for a shadow of a personal financial "profit" — a country where blackouts and water cuts are frequent, and where what is permitted today may be forbidden again tomorrow. It is generally best to seek out word-of-mouth recommendations for good local *paladares*, since their longevity can never be taken for granted. As a general rule, avoid eating fish and seafood dishes in such small establishments .

CREOLE CUISINE

Cubans like to start their meals with fresh fruits or a coleslaw salad to clear the palate, followed by a fairly heavy main course of grilled or Creole-style fried or fricasseed seafood, chicken or pork. But given the fact that the supply of fresh fruits and vegetables in Cuba can be sporadic, combined with the prevalence of meat dishes, vegetarians may find their choice very limited, however.

Suckling pig roasted on a spit, known as *lechón asado*, is Cuba's special national dish, and *chicharrones*, or pork cracklings, are a popular bar dish. Other staples include *congri* (rice with beans), *moros y cristianos* (rice with black beans), *yucca con mojo* (the potato-like cassava root covered in garlic-laced oil) and *maduros* (fried plantain bananas).

Given the fact that Cuba is an island surrounded by the rich waters of the Caribbean Sea, the Gulf of Mexico and the Florida Straits, you might expect a bounty of seafood. Such is not the case. The fishing industry has also declined since the Revolution, primarily because so many of the country's fishing boats have been used to transport refugees to Key West and Miami, never to return. However, the situation has improved in recent years, especially in the better hotels and

OPPOSITE: Santa Lucía's beachside fish restaurant.
ABOVE: A woman cooks traditional black bean and rice dish for a family celebration.

restaurants where you can now find a variety of underwater delights. Be on the lookout for special seafood dishes like *medallones de langosta a la criolla* (Creole-style lobster slices) and *camarones a la diabla* (shrimp in hot sauce).

Likewise, you might be lucky enough to come across some of Cuba's more interesting meat dishes — like *chilindrón de carnero* (lamb stew), *ropa vieja* ("old rope" a dish of spicy, fried, finely minced beef) or *costilla de lorno ahumada* (smoked loin chops). A wonderful variation of traditional fried chicken is *pollo maryland*, cooked with corn and pork.

The Cubans also have their own version of Jamaican jerk, a spicy beef plate called *tasajo a la Criolla*. Here and there you can even find offbeat dishes such as *fricase de conejo* (fried rabbit steak), *palomille grille* (grilled dove) or *codorniz* (quail eggs, usually served hard-boiled in some sort of vinaigrette).

You will probably find it hard to avoid indulging in a "*sandwich Cubano*" at some stage during your visit: these calorific door-stoppers are served as all-day snacks (as they are in Little Havana, Miami), with a combination of *jamón* and *queso* tucked into lard-smeared thick bread which is then grilled. Cubans regard *sandwich Cubanos* as a national dish, as Cuban as cigars, *cafecitos* and dominoes.

Dessert is often fresh fruit, Cuban-made ice-cream, cake or *dulce de leche*, very sweet caramelized milk.

After a meal, a bottle of *marasquino* — a sweet local liqueur — or rum is often passed around.

TRADITIONAL BEVERAGES

Coffee in Cuba is generally best when taken the Cuban way: as a tiny cup of *cafecito* — a concentrated expresso with lots of sugar. *Cafecitos* are for sale everywhere. Other variations include the short, strong *cortaditos* and *café con leche*, half milk, half coffee (and the nickname second- and third-generation Miami Cubans give themselves). If you order the mockingly named *Americano* coffee, you will get what usually tastes like mediocre dishwater. Good cappuccino and expresso made the European way are starting to make their appearance in several of the restored coffee shops and bars in La Habana Vieja.

As for alcoholic beverages, it doesn't take long to discover that rum is the national drink. A dozen distilleries across the island produce a variety of brands, the best known being the dry Havana Club and the sweeter Caribbean Club, preferred by locals.

You can choose from the transparent "Silver Dry" or the amber-hued, three-year-old Havana Club brands, as well as the smoother five- and seven-year-old varieties. The masterpiece of Cuban distilleries is the 15-year-old Havana Club Gran Reserve. Proudly exhibited at the Sevilla 1992 World's Fair, it has an international following. Both the Ron Matusalen and Pati Cruzada rums made in Santiago offer interesting variations. Bucanero, Caney and Varadero are other brands. You may hear about a rough, home-distilled version of rum, nicknamed *chispa del tren* ("train spark"), which you would be wise to avoid.

The best rum is generally consumed straight, however Cuba has many refreshing and delicious rum cocktails, notably the two Hemingway favorites, the *mojito* (light dry rum, lemon, crushed mint, sugar, soda and ice) and the daiquiri; others include the *cuba libre* (dry light rum, cola, lime and ice), the *cubanito* (a rum-based Bloody Mary), the *piña colada*, and the *isla de pinos* (light dry rum, grapefruit juice and red vermouth).

Cuban-produced wine is now a budding industry, the result of an Italian-Cuban joint-venture, and you may soon see red, white and sparkling brands in Cuban shops.

Cuba's more renowned national beers, such as Hatuey and Cristal, are very popular, but Polar and Bucanero, as well as many other regional brands, are worth trying too. If you don't want to drink alcohol, the malt-based drink, Mayabe, with its beer-like foam, provides a good alternative. Another one of Cuba's nonalcoholic specialties is *guarapo* — pure sugarcane juice made fresh by juicing a cane stalk through a grinder.

Special Interests

In addition to the special interest selections mentioned below, contact the recommended tour operators listed under TAKING A TOUR, below, about their wide range of special-interest tours.

MUSIC AND DANCE
With Cuba's world-renowned musical heritage, you could base an entire trip on visits to the island's many music and dance venues.

Havana's nightclubs are a good starting point. Many of Cuba's top bands appear each night at **Casa de la Música ((**07) 240447, in Miramar, which also stages *pena* folk music sessions every afternoon. Another great place for live tunes is the flashy **Habana Café ((**07) 333636, in the Hotel Meliá Cohiba, Vedado, where many of the country's top musical artists perform.

OPPOSITE: Café scene on Isla de la Juventud.
ABOVE: The Museo de la Musica offers a fine display of musical instruments.

Cuban-style modern jazz takes the spotlight at the moody **Café Concert Gato Tuerto** ((07) 662224 and the underground **La Zorra y el Cuervo** ((07) 662402, both in Vedado, and at the ever-mellow **Casa de las Infusiones**, opposite the Hotel Ambos Mundos in Habana Vieja.

The Teatro Nacional near the Plaza de la Revolución, harbors several popular music spots including the **Café Cantante Mi Habana** ((07) 766011, 793558 or 735713, which features jazz, salsa and a humorous variety show; and the intimate **Piano Bar Delirio Habanero**. The Latin big band sound predominates at the 1950s vintage **Salon Internacional Salsa** ((07) 334501, at the Hotel Riviera, Vedado.

Outside the capital, the best place to catch Cuban music is a local Casa de la Trova, a municipal music hall where traditional tunes are played on a regular basis by the best bands in the community. The name derives from Trova, a traditional Cuban ballad that blends passionate lyrics with African percussion and Spanish guitar rhythms.

Cuba's most renowned community music hall is the rowdy **Casa de la Trova** ((0226) 623943 or 651708, in Santiago's old town. Listening to veteran troubadours

perform here is one of the most memorable experiences of any Cuban visit, the tropical evening alive with intoxicating sound. An eclectic array of performers takes the stage, ranging from talented amateurs to national treasures.

Other lively Casas de la Trova can be found in Trinidad, Matanzas, Camagüey and Holguín.

You could coincide your visit with one of Cuba's annual musical events — the **International Jazz Festival** (Havana) in February, the **Sanjuaneras Fiesta** (Trinidad) in June, the raucous **Festival del Caribe** (Santiago) in July, the **Boleros de Oro** (Santiago) or the **Beny Moré Festival of Popular Music** (Cienfuegos) in August, or the **Festival of Contemporary Music** (Havana) in October.

The **Promotor Cultural at the Casa del Caribe** ((0226) 42285 FAX (0226) 42387, Calle 13 no. 154, Vista Alegre, Santiago de Cuba, organizes the Festival del Caribe and during the rest of the year runs courses and workshops on Cuban music and dance which last from two weeks to two months.

Several foreign travel agencies also organize special-interest tours based on musical themes including **Global Exchange Reality Tours** ((415) 255-7296 FAX (415) 255-7498 TOLL-FREE IN US (800) 497-1994 WEB SITE www.gobalexchange .org/tours, 2017 Mission Street, Suite 303, San Francisco, California 94110; **Wings of the World** TOLL-FREE IN US (800) 465-8687, 1200 William Street, Suite 706, Buffalo, New York 14240; **Womad-Karamba Arts & Dance Tours** ((01603) 872402 FAX (01603) 879053 WEB SITE www.karamba.co.uk, Ollands Lodge, Heydon, Norfolk NR11 6RB, Great Britain; and **Our World Travel** ((03) 9614-1344 TOLL-FREE IN AUSTRALIA (800) 337-372 FAX (03) 9614-2992 WEB SITE www.ourworldtravel.com.au, Level 10, 34 Queen Street, Melbourne, Victoria 3000, Australia.

CIGARS

It may not be politically correct in this era of health-conscious yuppies, but nothing says Cuba like a fine cigar. The country produces about 400 million cigar each year, about 40 percent for export. Although Fidel gave up smoking long ago, many Cubans still enjoy toking on a good stogie.

The vast majority of Cuba's tobacco crop is grown in the fertile Vuelta Abajo valley in western Pinar del Río Province, supposedly the world's best spot for growing the savory leaves. The harvest takes place in March and April. But whatever the season, you'll see some aspect of tobacco production when you visit the area: farmers tilling the orange soil or hanging leaves in drying sheds. Nearly every Havana travel agency offers fully guided daytrips to the region, with at least one stop at a tobacco farm where you can examine the crop and chat with farmers.

While you're in the area, be sure to sample the region's famed cigars at the Fábrica de Tabacos Francisco Dontien in Pinar del Río city. Housed in an old colonial-era prison, the factory produces six brands. You can watch the entire process, from leaf-selection and cigar rolling to label gluing and boxing. Afterwards browse through the factory shop and well-stocked humidor where local brands are on sale.

Havana has no less than five major cigar factories where many of Cuba's 500 different cigar types are manufactured with consummate skill. If you're not interested in joining an organized tour, several of the factories allows "walk up" visitors including the ancient **Fábrica Partagas** ((07) 624604 near the Capitola building, and **Fábrica La Corona** ((07) 338389 on Calle Agramonte in Habana Vieja. Others require prior permission before they will show visitors around: **Fábrica Romeo y Julieta** ((07) 781058, in Centro Habana, and **Fábrica El Laguito** ((07) 212213, on Calle 146 in the Cubanacán neighborhood of western Havana.

Several overseas agencies offer special tobacco and cigar tours of Cuba. **Special Places** ((0189) 266-1157 FAX (0189) 266-5670 E-MAIL specialplaces@cricketer.com, Brock Travel Ltd., 4 The White House, Beacon Road, Crowborough, East Sussex TN6 1AB, Britain, offers a one-week cigar tour among its other tour packages to Cuba.

Participants gain a detailed knowledge of how cigars are produced (from seed to factory) combined with a scenic sightseeing tour of Havana and Pinar del Río. Tours are run from January to March, which is the best period to see all of the main processes of local cigar production.

Other operators that stage cigar tours include **Wings of the World** TOLL-FREE IN US (800) 465-8687, 1200 William Street, Suite 706, Buffalo, New York 14240, and **Our World Travel** ((03) 9614-1344 TOLL-FREE IN AUSTRALIA (800) 337-372 FAX (03) 9614-2992 WEB SITE www.ourworld travel.com.au, Level 10, 34 Queen Street, Melbourne, Victoria 3000, Australia.

STUDY

Mercadu SA ((07) 333893 or 333087 FAX (07) 333028 OR 333090 WEB SITE www.uh .cu/infogral/cope, Calle 13 no. 951 at the corner of Avenida 8, Vedado, Havana, can arrange for study or work experience at Cuba's main universities and research institutes in the fields of agriculture, languages, science, education, technology and sports. Probably the most popular

Cigar rollers OPPOSITE are allowed to smoke on the premises ABOVE and to take home two cigars a day.

courses organized by Mercadu are the intensive Spanish courses at the University of Havana, which can last from two weeks to four months, with various levels of participation and costs.

ARCHITECTURE

The **Centro Nacional de Conservación, Restauración y Museología** ((07) 615043 or 335696, Calle Cuba 610, Havana, is a specialized government organization run under the auspices of Havana's city historian, Eusebio Leal, which offers courses in the architectural restoration, with the possibility of on-site work experience in La Habana Vieja.

Taking a Tour

Although not for everyone, joining a tour can be one of the best ways to get a first-hand look at as much of the country as possible in a limited time. Tours can offer extremely good value and may be the most effective use of your time in Cuba, with one other notable advantage being that you will not have to troubleshoot any potential travel hitches or problems that might crop up if you are traveling independently. Indeed, there may be minimal obligation to stay with the group once you arrive in Cuba.

Prices for all-inclusive tours, which include round-trip flights and accommodations, will vary depending on whether you will be arriving during peak season or not, the hotels you choose (or have chosen for you, as can be the case in some package tours) and the range of destinations you wish to visit. It is wise to compare prices and phone around until you are satisfied with what you are being offered, and also to query any hidden or add-on costs. Touring tourists generally enjoy a good level of comfort, and are ferried around in modern, air-conditioned minibuses and coaches.

AUSTRALIA AND NEW ZEALAND

Our World Travel ((03) 9614-1344 TOLL-FREE IN AUSTRALIA (800) 337-372 FAX (03) 9614-2992 WEB SITE www.ourworld travel.com.au, Level 10, 34 Queen Street, Melbourne, Victoria 3000, offers a number of unique Cuba excursions including photography, cigar country, music, women's perspective, history and dance tours. They also have a 17-day "Che's Footsteps" tour of Revolution battlegrounds and other sights and special "May Day Trip" for tourists with a more left bent.

Otherwise, contact **Cubatours** ((03) 9428-0385, 235 Swan Street, Richmond, Victoria 3121, and in New Zealand **STA Travel New Zealand** TOLL-FREE (0508) 782-872 WEB SITE www.statravel.co.nz. Various branches around New Zealand including: Auckland ((09) 309-0458 or 366-6673, 10 High Street; Wellington ((04) 385-0581 or 472-8510, 130 Cuba Street; Christchurch ((03) 379-9098, 90 Cashel Street; and Dunedin ((03) 474-0146, 32 Albany Street.

CANADA

Sunquest Tours ((416) 485-1700 TOLL-FREE IN US AND CANADA (877) 485-6060 WEB SITE www.sunquest.ca, 130 Merton Street, Toronto, Ontario M4S 1A4, runs various tours, ranging in price, destination and length of stay. For example, they offer seven-night beach holidays at five-star hotels in Varadero starting at CAN$899 per person.

MacQueen's Travel TOLL-FREE IN US AND CANADA (800) 969-2822 WEB SITE www.mac queens.com, 430 Queen Street, Charlottetown, Prince Edward Island, Canada, offers bike trips, fly & drive programs, camper rental and offbeat guided coach tours of the island.

Other Canadian operators include **Alba Tours** ((416) 746-2488 FAX (416) 746-0397 WEB SITE www.albatours.com, 130 Merton Street, Toronto, Ontario M4S 1A4; **Canadian Holidays** ((416) 620-8687 FAX (416) 620-9267, 191 The West Mall, Sixth Floor, Etobicoke, Ontario M9C 5K8; and **Hola Sun Holidays** ((905) 882-9444 or 882-0136 FAX (905) 882-5184 WEB SITE www.holasunholidays.com, 146 Beaver Creek Road, Unit 8, Richmond Hill, Ontario L4B 1C2.

Isla da la Juventud, Cuba's second-largest island.

SOUTH AFRICA
Dive Travel Center ((011) 326-3213
WEB SITE www.scubadiving.co.za/cuba,
376 Jan Smuts Avenue, Craighill,
Johannesburg, organizes both diving and
land-based Cuba tours.

UNITED KINGDOM
Special Places ((0189) 266-1157 FAX (0189)
266-5670 E-MAIL specialplaces@cricketer
.com, Brock Travel Ltd., 4 The White
House, Beacon Road, Crowborough,
East Sussex TN6 1AB, offers a one-week
cigar tour, among its other tour packages
to Cuba.

Progressive Tours ((020) 7262-1676
FAX (020) 7724-6941, 12 Porchester Place,
Marble Arch, London W2 2BS, organizes
intensive 14-day study tours designed to
meet Cuban people and learn about their
unique society with factory, hospital, farm,
university and school visits; they can also
arrange language courses in Santiago de
Cuba and Baracoa.

Havanatur has an office in the United
Kingdom ((01707) 665-570 FAX (01707)
663-139, 3 Wyllyotts Place, Potters Bar,
Hertfordshire EN6 2IN. Other operators
that handle Cuba include **Journey Latin
America** ((020) 8747-8315 FAX (020) 87472-
1313 WEB SITE www.journeylatinamerica
.co.uk, 12-13 Heathfield Terrace, Chiswick,
London W4 4JE; **Regent Holidays** ((0117)
987-2626 FAX (0117) 987-2627 WEB SITE WWW
.tripsworldwide.co.uk, 9 Byron Place,
Bristol; and **South American Experience**
((020) 7976-5511 FAX (020) 7976-6908
WEB SITE www.southamericanexperience.co
.uk, 47 Causton Street, Pimlico,
London SW1P 4AT.

UNITED STATES
The **Center for Cuban Studies** ((212)
242-0559 FAX (212) 242-1937 WEB SITE WWW
.cubaupdate.org, 124 West 23rd Street,
New York, New York 10011, organizes
custom-planned trips to Cuba for both
groups and individuals that fall within
legal exemptions to the United States ban
on travel to Cuba. These include, for
example, professional research, news-
gathering and educational study, as well
as cultural activities. They also offer fact-

finding tours each month for members of
their center, which, including airfares, cost
US$800. This is an excellent and well-
grounded organization to be in touch with,
and they have great contacts in Cuba.

Wings of the World TOLL-FREE IN US
(800) 465-8687, 1200 William Street, Suite
706, Buffalo, New York 14240, has 27 years
of experience organizing tours to Cuba
from the United States, all of which abide
by the United States State Department's
legal requirements because the company's
tours are "fully hosted and totally
prepaid" and technically speaking,
participants "neither exchange nor spend
money while in Cuba." Well-planned
tours include those with a bicycling,
hiking, bird watching, fishing theme.
Arrangements for attending festivals and
cultural events can also be made. Prices
and length of stay vary, with round-trip
flights frequently made from Toronto. This
company, which is a corporate member of
the New York Explorer's Club and the
Chicago Union League Club, often tailors
its trips to specific notable events, such as
the annual Hemingway International
Marlin Tournament. If you want to leave
on a Friday for a long weekend bass-
fishing in Cuba sure of arriving back in
your office first thing on Tuesday
morning, with all arrangements taken care
of, this is the company to call.

Global Exchange Reality Tours ((415)
255-7296 TOLL-FREE IN US (800) 497-1994
FAX (415) 255-7498 WEB SITE www.gobale
xchange.org/tours, 2017 Mission Street,
Suite 303, San Francisco, California 94110,
offers educational and study tours
focusing on Afro-Cuban culture, the arts,
as well as the Cuban healthcare system
and environmental issues. Among Global's
more offbeat Cuban tours are sustainable
agriculture, faith and spirituality, solar and
renewable energy, architectural trends and
African roots, rhythm and religion. It also
arranges individual trips on this basis.
Most trips are 10 days long and cost
around US$1,300, including round-trip
airfare from Mexico, Jamaica or the
Bahamas. This organization started the
so-called "Freedom to Travel" campaign,
which seeks to bring an end to the

restrictions on travel to Cuba by United States citizens.

Geographic Expeditions ((415) 922-0448 TOLL-FREE IN US (800) 777-8183 FAX (415) 346-5535 WEB SITE www.geoex.com, 2627 Lombard Street, San Francisco, California 94123, tenders a good selection of Cuba adventure trips including hiking and rock climbing. Geographic strives to expose travelers to Cuba's cultural, political and natural environment without political filters. It's also one of the few outfits that take you into the homes of ordinary Cubans and employs local guides from independent organizations rather than government agencies.

Marazul Tours ((201) 840-6711 TOLL FREE IN US (800) 223-5334 FAX (201) 861-9954 WEB SITE www.marazultours.com, Tower Plaza Mall, 4100 Park Avenue, Weehawken, New Jersey 07087; or ((305) 644-0255 FAX (305) 643-4474, 711 NW 37TH Street, Miami, Florida 33125, is a unique travel agency operating charter flights and tours to Cuba for United States citizens who satisfy all requirements under government regulations. This means you will need written permission from the United States Treasury Department. United States citizens who can book their travel to Cuba through this agency may include United Nations or United States government officials, reporters traveling on assignment, academics and teachers on research assignments and those visiting for humanitarian reasons, such as visiting a sick relative or attending a funeral. See ENTRY FOR AMERICANS, page 309 in TRAVELERS' TIPS, for more details.

MEXICO

The following operators work out of Mexico: **Divermex** ((998) 884-2325 FAX (998) 884-2325, Plaza de las Américas, Cancún; **Havanatur/Taíno Tours** ((55) 559-3907 FAX (55) 559-7754, Avenida Coyoacán 1035, Colonia del Valle CP, 03100 México DF, or ((664) 847001 FAX (664) 847077, Calle Ignacio Conmonfort no. 9330, Local 8 Zona Río CP 22320, Tijuana, Baja California; and **AS Tours** ((55) 575-9814 FAX (55) 559-5097, Insurgentes Sur 1188-602, 03200 México DF.

THE CARIBBEAN

Caribic Vacations ((809) 979-0322, 952-0116 or 979-9387 FAX (809) 952-0981, 69 Gloucester Avenue, White Sands Beach PO, Montego Bay, Jamaica, offers package tours to Havana or Varadero that include flights in Air Jamaica, hotel room, breakfast, city tour, airport transfers and visa fees. Tours range from two to seven days. Price depends on what hotel you choose, but the price of a three-night package at the Havana's Ambos Mundos Hotel is roughly US$600.

The Cuban Connection ((941) 793-5204 TOLL-FREE IN US AND CANADA (800) 645-1179 WEB SITE www.cuba.tc, in the Turks & Caicos Islands, offers a number of Cuba-related travel options including hotel and rental-car reservations, bookings for the Horizontes Flexi Drive program, and ground tours with Gaviota and Havanatur.

CUBA

Tourism agencies and operators in Cuba are government run, which does not mean they necessarily offer the same services

---

A 1959 issue of the weekly Bohemia, harvest "not tainted with blood."

and prices. We recommend you take the time to compare, ask many questions and try to get precise information. Remember that the people you will be dealing with have probably never traveled around Cuba, so you cannot always expect accurate advice concerning your destinations. Many operators offer discounts on hotel rates (up to 30 percent), at least for the more expensive venues.

Havanatur ((07) 242161, 242424 or 247541 FAX (07) 242877 or 240586, Calle 2 no. 17, between Avenidas 1 and 3, Miramar, Havana, pioneered Cuban tourism and has agencies throughout the world. They come recommended. Also among the older and more reputed operators are **Cubanacán S.A.** ((07) 280607 or 286063 FAX (07) 280107 WEB SITE www .cubanacan.cu, Calle 160 and Avenida 11, Playa, Miramar, Havana, and **Gaviota Tours** ((07) 666777, 666773 or 666778 FAX (07) 332780 WEB SITE www.gaviota.cuba web.cu, Third Floor, Edificio la Marina, Avenida del Puerto in Miramar.

Alcona S.A. ((07) 222526, 222529 or 845244 FAX (07) 241531, Calle 42 no. 514, at the corner of Avenida 7, Miramar, Havana, can help with outdoor options, as can **Cubamar** ((07) 338317, 662524, 305536 or 662523 FAX (07) 333111 WEB SITE www.cuba mar@cubamar.mit.cma.net, Paseo 752 at the corner of Calle 15, Vedado, Havana.

Other agencies include: **San Cristóbal** ((07) 339585 FAX (07) 339586, Calle Oficios 110, between Calles Lamparilla and Amargura, Havana; **Rumbos** ((07) 669538 or 633466, Calle Bernaza between Calles O'Reilly and Obispo, Havana; and **Easy Travel** ((07) 245263, 245265 or 244679 FAX (07) 244559, Bungalow 687, Hotel Comodoro, Havana. Also well known is **Cubatur** ((07) 334155 FAX (07) 333529, Calle F 157, between Calles 9 and Calzada, Vedado, Havana, although many travelers have complained about their services.

Thousands of birds migrate to the protected area of Las Salinas.

Welcome
to
Cuba

Evocative and lush, Cuba is a subtle country that nonetheless lives up to its larger-than-life reputation. It still has the white-sanded beaches and palm-trees of Caribbean postcards, the exotic hotels and bars where film-stars and Mafiosi swanned around in the 1950s, and the magnificent colonial fortresses and timeworn architecture left from the time when it was gateway to the Spanish Main. It remains the legendary place where a people's revolution was buoyed up by rum, cigars and salsa. Yet Cuba is also much more.

Lying off the coast of Florida, wedged between the Atlantic, the Gulf of Mexico and the Caribbean, the so-called "Pearl of the Antilles" has played host to many cultures: the indigenous Siboney and Taíno Indians, Spanish colonists and African slaves. Christopher Columbus described it as "the most beautiful land that human eyes have ever seen." Things have changed somewhat since then, of course, and aficionados of paradisiacal islands may not immediately think of Cuba. Although you may not visit Cuba for its exotic, tropical landscapes alone, expect some pleasant, if not spectacular, surprises. In fact, because it has been slow to develop tourism, Cuba is a rare find for delightful off-the-beaten-track places and experiences, even for the jaded or adventurous.

Don't expect many similarities to other Caribbean islands aside from the balmy climate and tropical flora: no Jimmy Buffet, legions of Spring Breakers, or packaged margaritas here. Cuba does not have a series of look-alike hotels, restaurants and shops dispensing practiced, efficient service. While it is often less polished, it is never dull, and has a quirky kind of charm.

Often, the rule is simple: get out of your hotel, rent a car and explore. If you can, meet Cubans and enter their world. You know you've arrived if you find yourself addressed as "*Chino*" or "Chinese," an affectionate term among friends.

Cubans themselves are your best guide to their own vibrant and passionate culture. Who else, for example, would you choose to teach you how to dance? For Cuba pulses to the music of salsa, son, rumba, mambo, cha-cha-cha — all of which originated here — and is, as Gabriel García Márquez, one of Cuba's most famous part-time expatriates puts it, "the most dance-oriented society on earth."

When the revolution of Fidel Castro and Che Guevara became superimposed on the sultry glamorous style of 1950s Havana, it proved to be a strange and compelling mixture. This was the canvas for the novels of Ernest Hemingway and Graham Greene. Then, after decades of the United States embargo, it became known to cinema-goers as the backdrop for such successful cinematic exports as *Fresa y Chocolate* (Strawberry and Chocolate) and *Guantánamera* by the late Cuban director Tomás Gutiérrez Alea, both bittersweet comedies which exactly convey love, tenderness and acid humor — Cuban style. Indeed, at times, you might feel you have to pinch yourself to make sure that you are not an extra in a giant open-air film set, with the last adjustments being made to the script after some four decades of directions by that well-known first-time author-director, Fidel Castro.

You are bound to encounter something of the strange mixture of ideologies and circumstances that have shaped the island. As one visitor joked, half-in-jest: "Cuba is like a 1950s Cadillac — held together by American design, Russian bits and pieces and Cuban imagination."

As you may be about to find during your travels, the term "magic realism" seems to have been coined just for this fascinating country, where as an outsider, trying to understand the real Cuba can feel like an excursion into the unexpected and improbable, a Spanish-speaking version of *Alice in Wonderland*.

Connoisseurs of the ironic, Cubans love bantering jokes, ripostes and a version of anecdotal word-play they call "double-morals." In the world of double-morals, nothing is quite as it seems, and every statement or remark can conceal at least one other meaning. Cubans have made flirting with contradictions and ambiguities part of their national character, along with a uniquely spirited humor that so often triumphs over adversity and a knowing attitude to sex, which many Cubans joke is the national pastime. After all, in a country where the national slogan is "*Socialismo o Muerte*" ("Socialism or Death"), it could be

argued that survival would be impossible without a sense of the absurd, or at the very least, a talent for living in the moment. Like the music and the dancing, these semi-secret jokes make the daily weight of life much easier to bear.

Arrive expecting appointments to be met, especially business meetings, but be prepared for the unexpected. After all, this is where "*ahorita*" means "any minute," which can be five minutes or five hours. Equally, as you may find, there is always something faintly unpredictable about even

the most carefully laid plans in Cuba. Sometimes what can follow is better than what you planned. Perhaps it's all about a certain outlook, expressed in the quintessential Cuban expression "*No hay mal que por bien no venga*," which roughly translates as "good can come from even the worst experiences." Cuban people are remarkable for their incredible exuberance for life, and their gusto for life is catching.

All in all, like trying to navigate Havana in one of its aged, but lovingly preserved chariots of chrome from Detroit, Cuba is unique, fun and worth any minor inconveniences.

PREVIOUS PAGES: Musicians play at El Morro, Santiago de Cuba LEFT and costumed women in Old Havana RIGHT. OPPOSITE: A colorful naïve painting. ABOVE: A musician from the Orquesta Siglo XX performs at La Casa de la Obrapía.

The Country and Its People

Since the early 1990s, Cubans have liked to joke that they live in the "Land of Miracles," a sarcastic popular term to describe the paradox of living in a Communist country at a time when the rest of world has all but decided that Marxism is outdated. For more than a decade, Cuba has existed in what is officially termed the "Special Period in the Time of Peace," a continuing regimen of economic hardship and cut-backs that followed the collapse of the Soviet Union. Still suffering from the United States embargo, the sudden deprivation of Moscow's sub-

sidies created desperate shortages of everything: medicine, food, water, housing, transportation and electricity. Endless jokes ensued about the "miracles" that ordinary Cubans have had to perform in order, say, to arrive at work on time during the transportation crisis ("the authorities are testing to see how many Cubans can fit on a bus," quip the people of Havana) or to put a decent meal on the table during the cut-back in rations.

When Pope John Paul II visited Cuba in January 1998, Cubans joked that the pontiff's motivation was, first, to visit hell; second, to see a people making a living out of miracles; and third, to meet with the very devil himself.

These days, Cubans remain a resolutely entrepreneurial people, although not in ways you might expect. *Resolver* (which roughly translates as "to fix a problem by any means available") is probably the most commonly used verb in Cuba, where for many, the difficulties of merely getting by involve all manner of daily struggles.

A girl's disco finery might be discarded for her usual costume of ragged shorts and T-shirt the next day; car engines revived with the help of a shoelace; cigarette lighters filled with fly spray; house paint concocted from quicklime mixed with kerosene; black-market beef bartered for rusty spare parts and cigarettes swapped for matches because of the frequent *apagones* or power cuts.

Throughout the island, shops and cafés with empty shelves are a common sight, especially in the provincial towns; yet the assistants keep working, explaining in answer to each request how they don't have this, and they don't have that, until finally the customer might ask, in exasperation, "Well, what do you have?"

"*Nada, ahora,*" ("Nothing, today") is often the answer.

When asked how they are, most Cubans, no matter what their profession, shrug and smile, and say, in what has become a catch-phrase: "Inventing and struggling, so what's new?"

Yet, no matter where you go, you are bound to encounter those qualities that are also so distinctly Cuban: an outgoing, welcoming attitude to foreigners and a sense of solidarity and community that has all but been lost in other societies, which some see as a touching by-product of the economic situation. In the words of Pico Iyer, author of the novel *Cuba and the Night*: "It's everyone against the system. It's: I'll give you a chicken and your brother can fix my TV. An ironist can have a field day in Cuba."

As a visitor, perhaps on your first trip, much of this might not be especially apparent. It is possible to see Cuba through a well-protected bubble if you are staying in one of the more luxurious hotels and are whisked

PREVIOUS PAGES: Passengers prepare for departure LEFT in Santiago Province. RIGHT: A rest in the shade in Trinidad. ABOVE: Magnificent but decaying houses dot Old Havana. OPPOSITE: Portraits of Che are everywhere, from T-shirts to mosaics.

by tour bus from one sightseeing jag to another. Increasingly, the Cuba that many visitors see is another emerging Cuba, one that is flush with new joint-venture businesses and foreign investments from Canada, Europe and Latin America. This new Cuba has a raft of gleaming hotels, expensive-looking restaurants and country clubs that cater to influential Cubans and the foreign business community alike. Is this a preparation for a political change that would put an end to the United States embargo, which so many in Cuba blame for

on sale, not by the United States, but by Cuba, which had received complaints from Guevara's widow, Aleida.

Along the familiar tourist routes, with Cuban bands playing irresistible salsa music, amid some of the most glorious and historic settings in the Caribbean, it is easy to sink into a blissful appreciation of the moment. And why shouldn't you?

Yet it is always interesting to probe beneath the façade a little, and to contemplate how this Cuba has come to be the way it is today.

all their problems? Perhaps. Or it may be possible to regard this new Cuba as experimental one that is trying to keep alive the most important values of the socialist system using the capitalist system.

Under the helm of Fidel Castro, Cuba is proving a canny self-marketer. After all, this is the country which exported radical chic to a generation of urban youth around the world. Its cigars are international symbols of costly fat-cat glamour, and it sells its tourists vast quantities of Che Guevara memorabilia. However, it did not approve when a United Kingdom company marketed its beer with Che's image and the slogan: "Banned In The USA. It Must Be Good." In a telling twist, the product *was* banned soon after it went

EARLY CUBA

The human story begins in Cuba almost two thousand years ago, when tribes from Central or South America began arriving on the island. The Siboney settled first, sheltering in caves and subsisting on fishing. They were followed by the Taíno (pronounced TIE-no), a tribe of Arawak Indians, who soon dominated the less aggressive Siboney, and whose agrarian lifestyle, which included making pots and figurines from clay, represented the peak of pre-Columbian culture in Cuba.

Christopher Columbus landed near what is now Baracoa at the eastern tip of Cuba on October 27, 1492, on his first voyage to the New World. Convinced he had reached a great Asian continent, he sent his men off into the mountains in search of great cities and a king, but instead they came back with reports of communities of near-naked Indians living in thatched huts. Spain did not immediately jump at the opportunity to colonize Cuba. However, Spanish occupation began in earnest in 1511, with the arrival near Guantánamo Bay in southeast Cuba of conquistador Diego de Velázquez and 300 men. Subjugation of the native Indian population was a fairly swift and brutal affair. Only one Taíno chief was able to

Cuban specialists discovered the first nearly complete piece of Taíno architecture — a community building of wood and thatch, as well as what may be as many as 25 preserved houses, which stood on Cuba's northern coast, in Punta Alegre, Ciego de Ávila Province, some 500 to 700 years ago. Archaeologists are now sifting through evidence that small communities of Taíno may have been able to survive along this isolated coast unnoticed long after the Spaniards arrived, perhaps even until the early seventeenth century.

briefly inspire any resistance among his people: Hatuey, who had come to Cuba after fleeing the Spanish in his homeland of Hispaniola (now Haiti and the Dominican Republic). When Hatuey (after whom the nation's premier brand of beer is named) was finally captured, he preferred to be burned at the stake than to be forced to convert to the Christianity of his captors. Within little more than a generation, the Taíno seem to have disappeared, leaving behind no written language or monumental structures. Today, only fleeting shadows of past ancestors live on in the features of some Cubans, mostly from the Baracoa region.

In July 1998, a Canadian archaeologist, Dr. David M. Prendergast, and a team of

SPANISH COLONIZATION

As patriarch of colonial Cuba, Velázquez set about founding seven *villas*, or fortified settlements in Baracoa, Santiago, Bayamo, Puerto Príncipe (now Camagüey), Trinidad, Sancti Spíritus and Villa de San Cristóbal de la Habana, later known simply as La Habana. Cuba's value to the Spanish was its position at the mouth of the Gulf of Mexico and its formidable network of fortresses which enabled crucial protection for Spanish ships from the constant threat of attack by pirates and foreign fleets as they ferried riches from

OPPOSITE: Returning from the fields in Santiago de Cuba Province. ABOVE: An unusual food stand in Santiago de Cuba's central market.

Central and South America back to Spain. Havana grew steadily in importance and soon became the jewel in the Cuban crown, becoming the capital in 1607.

Along with Mexico City and Lima, Havana became one of the most extravagantly imposing cities outside Europe, its militaristic fortresses beautified by elaborate stone pediments and cornices, with the wealthiest of the merchant and ruling class living in magnificent town palaces or *palacios* that still captivate the visitor today. Yet outside Havana, development elsewhere

in Cuba was sporadic. The early colonizers had adopted the *encomienda* system, in which each Spanish landowner was allotted between 40 and 200 indigenous Indians as forced laborers, who became *peones* or serfs. This unforgiving feudal regime ultimately destroyed the indigenous Indians through overwork, starvation, disease and suicide. The Spanish *conquistadores* were soon on the lookout for a new workforce for their tobacco and sugar plantations, and began importing thousands of African slaves. Slavery in Cuba was as brutal as anywhere, and most slaves were worked as many as 19 hours a day, every day of the week, with as many as 10 percent dying each year, literally like flies.

Those who managed to escape, known as *cimarrones*, formed surreptitious communities called *palenques* deep in the island's mountainous forests.

Yet Cuba's fortunes remained relatively modest until the mid-eighteenth century, when the British attacked and won Havana, marking a turning point in the island's history. The British occupation began in 1762 and lasted for almost a year, ending when they consented to return the city to Spain in exchange for Florida. By opening up restrictions that had banned the island from trading with any country other than Spain, the British had effectively launched Cuba's export trade, an achievement that was soon to prove enormously important for Cuba, albeit effected during such a relatively short stay. When the Spanish took Cuba back, they immediately set about making sure that their fortresses would be impregnable for any future attacks (which would remain the case until the Spanish-American conflict took the history of Cuba into an entirely new era). Another unexpected boost to the island's economy occurred with the slave revolution in the French-ruled half of Hispaniola (now Haiti), and Cuba soon took its place as the largest and most profitable sugar producer in the Caribbean, vying with British-occupied Jamaica for the profitable sugar market in the newly independent United States.

The sugar boom soon swallowed up almost all the island's hardwood forests, and Cuba prospered, exporting almost all of its sugar to the United States. Shackled slaves, on the other hand, were worked harder than ever. By the mid-nineteenth century, slaves made up almost half the population. Despite the abolition of slavery in most other Caribbean islands by 1848, slavery continued unabated in the Spanish colonies, largely due to an almost obsessive fear by the Spanish elite that history — in the form of the slave revolt in Haiti — would repeat itself in Cuba. Meanwhile, social unease was growing. Despite a shared fear of the oppressed and mutinous African slaves, the island's *criolles* (Creoles) — Cubans of Spanish descent — were increasingly resenting playing second fiddle to the so-called *peninsulares* — the island's designated aristocratic elite, who were born in Spain. Long after the independence of Spain's former South American republics and Mexico, anti-colonial unrest in Cuba finally crystallized into action. Calling for independence from Spain and the abolition of slavery, the *criolles* rebelled in 1868, led by Carlos Manuel de Céspedes, who launched the first war of independence by freeing his own slaves. The so-called Ten Year's War took the lives of more than 250,000 Cubans, including Céspedes, and saw the rise of two other early revolutionary heroes, Antonio

regarded as the George Washington of Cuba, and his statue can be seen in every town square and school. He passionately defended Cuba's right to self-rule, democracy, social justice and, importantly, for Cuba, racial equality. Enlisting Maceo and Gómez, Martí unified the island under the banner of his Partido Revolucionario Cubano (PRC), and by 1897, forced the Spanish authorities to concede autonomy.

With the Cubans on the brink of victory, the United States intervened. The island, although governed by an increasingly

Maceo, a rebellious mulatto known as the "Titan of Bronze," and Máximo Gómez, a defector from the Spanish army, whose forces were made up of disenchanted peasants and former slaves.

INDEPENDENCE AT A PRICE

Although brutally crushed by the Spanish, the resistance by the rebel army contributed to the abolition of slavery in Cuba in 1886. It took the unlikely figure of José Martí, a short, soulful man with a droopy moustache, to galvanize the next insurrection. Martí, a revolutionary and poet who lived an exile's existence in Spain and New York before dying a martyr's death in Cuba, is

weakened Spain, was by now tied economically to the United States, which was reluctant to forfeit such an advantageous relationship for the sake of an independent Cuba. Relations between the United States and Spain become increasingly strained, and the United States declared war after the USS *Maine* was blown up in Havana harbor in February 1898, although no evidence was ever found linking the Spanish to the downed battleship. Within months, the colonial army surrendered to the American occupying force, preceded by Theodore

OPPOSITE: Castro has delivered many speeches under the statue of Martí on the Plaza de la Revolución in Havana. ABOVE: An infant crocodile in the Ciénaga de Zapata reserve.

Roosevelt's famous charge against Spanish troops at San Juan Hill in Santiago that eventually propelled him into the White House. Washington contemplated annexation but finally decided to concede Cubans the right to elect their own government. On May 20, 1902, Cuba was declared a republic, and American troops withdrew. However it was freedom with a yoke: the United States had exacted acceptance of the Platt Amendment to the Cuban constitution, which gave Washington the right to intervene at any time "for the preservation of

Cuban independence." It also provided for the establishment of an American naval base at Guantánamo Bay.

Cubans found, to their dismay, that one colonial master now replaced the other. Cuban history books frequently refer to the five decades that followed the island's independence as the "pseudo-Republic." American monopolies swiftly took control over almost every economic activity on the island, turned Cuba into a giant sugar, tobacco and citrus-fruit factory, and forced islanders to import almost everything (apart from sugar and cigars) from the United States.

Amid public outrage at the widely known corruption within Cuban govern-ment, General Gerardo Machado won the elections in 1924 with the slogan "Honesty in Government." Soon, however, Machado was giving Cubans their first taste of a military dictatorship. In 1933, a rebellion by Havana University students and army sergeants led General Fulgencio Batista to take power. Meanwhile, the United States, although they distrusted the student rebellion, saw Batista as a military man on whom it could depend. He stepped down in 1944, but seized power again in 1952, holding onto it with a grip that was to prove both ruthless and brutal. He abolished the constitution, dissolved Congress and crushed his opponents, unleashing an orgy of police violence that killed estimated thousands.

During the 1950s, Havana was the belle of the Caribbean ball, presenting a beautiful face yet concealing dark secrets, attracting legions of America's rich and famous, Hollywood celebrities such as Marilyn Monroe and Frank Sinatra, not to mention its infamous Mafia. Between them, Batista and the mob (led by the Jewish mob chief, Meyer Lansky) controlled tourism. They built many of the city's high-rise hotels, including the Hilton (now the Habana Libre), the Riviera and the Capri, and the city thrilled to casinos, extravagant cabarets, salsa bands and glamorous showgirls.

In the meantime, many Cubans prospered: Havana's affluent suburbs of Vedado and Miramar glittered with grand mansions, where the elegant, cultured and largely contented bourgeoisie threw soirées, wore the latest European fashions and enjoyed the city's lively intellectual and cultural life, which attracted glamorous and worldly expatriates — many of them American — and refugees from Franco's Spain, a pattern echoed in many of the island's provincial towns. Yet underneath it all, rural poverty was widespread, unemployment was around 50 percent, many Cubans were illiterate and malnourished, and prostitution was rife.

This was the Havana that piqued the fancy of Graham Greene and Ernest Hemingway, and captivated the visiting Anais Nin; and for many now-aging exiled Cubans, this is the beloved island, splintered into fragments of memory, they strug-

gle to recall. For Cubans would soon become divided into two camps, and not only by the Florida straits: *los gusanos* (the "worms", as they would be called), who would leave the island, and *los comunistas*, who would stay behind.

REBELS IN THE MOUNTAINS

A clean-shaven, 26-year-old lawyer named Fidel Castro began the road to Revolution when, on July 26, 1953, he and 125 other militants attacked the Moncada Barracks in Santiago de Cuba. Although the assault was a disastrous failure, resulting in the death of most involved, its daring captured the imagination of the island, as did Castro's speech during trial proceedings against him. That speech, known as the "History Will Absolve Me" speech formed the basis for Cuba's new revolutionary movement, the *Movimiento 26 de Julio*, named for the series of coincidences involving the number 26 and devoted to the ousting of Batista. By another series of coincidences, Castro was released from prison after just 20 months (instead of the 15 years he had been sentenced). Castro left for Mexico City, where he gathered around him a group of idealistic revolutionaries, one of whom was the Argentinean doctor, Ernesto "Che" Guevara.

OPPOSITE: A crumbling rampart in Havana. ABOVE: Travel is slow on this remote dirt road between Baracoa and Moa.

In October 1956, Fidel, Che and 80 other rebels (including Fidel's brother Raúl) crossed from Mexico to Cuba in the leaking six-berth cabin cruiser, *Granma*, only just managing to avoid disaster. "It wasn't a disembarkation, it was a shipwreck," recounted Guevara of the landing, which took place in the eastern province now named Granma. Having lost all their equipment, the rebels soon lost many of their men: within a month they were ambushed by Batista's men, and only about 15 men (including Fidel, Raúl and Che) managed to hide out near Pico

Turquino in the Sierra Maestra mountains, west of Santiago. Here, the men adopted guerilla tactics, picking off soldiers at military outposts and broadcasting exhortations for a general strike from their makeshift radio station, *Radio Rebelde*. Within months, Castro's promises of agrarian reform had won over the landless farmers and laborers whose collaboration would be vital to his cause, and the insurgency began in earnest, supported by agitation in the cities by the underground M-26 movement. When Batista sent 10,000 soldiers into the Sierra Maestra to defeat the rebel army in 1958, many soldiers defected to the guerilla movement, and as Castro's army moved westwards, refused to fight. On January 1, 1959, as Castro's rebel army approached Havana, Batista fled to the Dominican Republic. Within a week, the 31-year-old leader, by now sporting his trademark beard and smoking Cohiba cigars, was greeted by thousands of jubilant Cubans as he traveled across the island from Santiago to a triumphant reception in the capital.

Around the world, but of course, especially in Cuba, the bearded, fatigue-wearing revolutionaries became folk icons overnight. However, despite the euphoria, many Cubans were apprehensive about the changes Fidel Castro had in store. The island's wealthy bourgeoisie had misgivings about the rather militant zealousness of this as-yet untested revolutionary movement. Large numbers left the island, especially those who had profited from the Batista regime, while revolutionary tribunals were set up to track down and punish (and frequently execute) those whose collaboration was alleged to have resulted in the persecution of Batista's victims.

Under Castro, the so-called Integrated Revolutionary Organization (re-named the Cuban Communist Party in 1965) assumed control of the country, and instituted widespread political, educational and agricultural reforms. A huge literacy campaign was organized, and eager revolutionary volunteers left the cities to live and work in the country. Within a year, the government had acquired more than 40 percent of Cuba's formerly foreign-owned farmland, dividing most of its up into state farms, and soon further nationalized foreign banks and other businesses.

INTERNATIONAL CONFLICT

For the United States, who had been increasingly alarmed at developments in Cuba, the wholesale nationalization of all American enterprises on the island — whose interests amounted to around US$1 billion — was an invitation to a showdown. In April 1961, anti-Castro Cuban exiles backed by the United States government attempted an invasion of Cuba at Playa Giró — forever after known as the Bay of Pigs — and were promptly routed by Castro's forces, led by *El Jefe Máximo* (the "Maximum Leader") himself. The United States, who had already imposed a partial embargo on trade with Cuba since 1960, retaliated by extending the embargo in March 1962 to include all goods. Thus began the United States trade embargo, which has remained in place ever since.

In what became another turning point in Cuba's history, Castro declared the socialist nature of the Revolution in mid-1961, just at the time of the Bay of Pigs invasion. He was later to proclaim, "I am a Marxist-Leninist, and I shall be to the day I die." Given that Cuba was by now facing complete isolation from the United States, the question of whether Castro was merely pragmatically paving the way for closer economic ties with Moscow has long been a matter of speculation.

In February of 1960, the Soviet Union agreed to an oil-for-sugar arrangement

which helped to bolster the Cuban economy through to the late 1980s. Trade with other socialist countries also became a priority. In October 1962, the Soviet Union had begun to move nuclear missiles to the island, shifting the balance of power between the two superpowers. President Kennedy sent a United States naval fleet out towards Cuba, and threatened war unless they were removed. In what was one of the most harrowing moments of the Cold War, six days of stalemate during the Cuban Missile Crisis brought the two nations to the brink of nuclear war. Without consulting Castro, Premier Krushchev and President Kennedy came to an agreement: the missiles would be withdrawn if the United

States pledged not to invade Cuba. Declaring, "We will build a wall around Cuba," President Kennedy tightened the trade embargo. This prompted another wave of emigration of some half a million Cubans, mostly urban, white and middle class, many of whom settled in Miami.

BUILDING THE REVOLUTION

The 1960s was a decade of major social and political restructuring in Cuba. Che Guevara took charge of centralizing the country's economy, becoming Minister of Industry. *Comités de Defensa de la Revolución* ("Committees for the Defense of the Revolution"), or CDR's, were deployed in every neighborhood, to monitor every aspect of Cuban life. Those not obviously enthusiastic about the Revolution often faced harassment or imprisonment, as did homosexuals, dissident intellectuals and Catholics. The regime mobilized hundreds of thousands of Cubans, so-called "volunteer workers," to increase its agricultural production, while "microbrigades" were set up to provide housing for the rapidly growing population.

In Cuba, the oft-heard phrase "Triumph of the Revolution" is generally used in reference to three things: education, medical care and relatively equal distribution of wealth. It is indeed one of Cuba's sources of pride that sufficient food, healthcare and education have been made available to all, particularly when compared to pre-Castro days or to the rest of Latin America. However, "moral incentives" for collective advancement were not enough to keep the Cuban economy from suffering a series of economic woes. Rationing was introduced in 1962, and Guevara resigned in 1965, going off to fight a series of guerilla wars before he was assassinated in Bolivia two years later.

By 1975, Castro's regime staged the country's First Communist Party Congress, launching a new centralized system of national and local government, called *Poder Popular*, or People's Power. The new constitution espoused Marxism-Leninism as the

OPPOSITE: Castro's famous slogan "Socialism or Death" neighbors an ad for a fast-food restaurant. ABOVE: Fidel Castro in the Sierra Maestra, 1959.

state's ideology, and recognized the Communist Party as the only legitimate political organization in Cuba. The early 1970s are remembered as tough and repressive years, with restrictions on personal freedoms such as choice of work and travel. Many so-called "social deviants" were jailed.

By the end of the decade, the economy had begun to improve and, with liberal peacemaker Jimmy Carter in the White House, it looked as if the United States-led boycott might melt away at any moment. However, 1980 marked the most signifi-

cant period of widespread dissatisfaction with Castro's government since 1959 and, in a massive exodus, 125,000 Cubans left for Florida with the Mariel boatlift. (Unbeknownst to United States immigration officials, with a timely opening of his country's prisons and asylums, Castro ensured that large numbers of these new immigrants were criminals.) The boatlift dramatically shifted public and political opinion in the United States, squelched any hope of an immediate end to the embargo and prompted several Cuban scholars to float a now widely held theory that Castro purposely scuttled rapprochement with Washington in order to maintain his own political raison d'être.

In an effort to rapidly improve living conditions and morale in Cuba, Castro initiated a series of changes, allowing private agricultural markets, so-called "farmer's markets," at which farmers could sell any surplus produce beyond the quota allotted to the state. These reforms were so successful, prompting many Cubans to abandon their state jobs to prospect in this new, albeit-limited free market, that Castro dissolved this reform, announcing a so-called Rectification of Errors program that reverted back to strict centralization under Party supervision.

During the 1980s, with President Reagan in the White House, American foreign policy within the region took a more hawkish stance against burgeoning socialist liberation movements in Grenada and Nicaragua, and stepped up its covert activities, many of them now notorious. Although Castro himself was the target of many assassination attempts, he wryly commented, "It's not my fault that I haven't died yet; it's not my fault that the CIA has failed to kill me!" Meanwhile, the island was sending its soldiers into the conflict in Angola — an involvement some refer to as "Cuba's Vietnam" — where Castro supported the Marxist government against rebels backed by the United States and South Africa. Some 370,000 soldiers went into action, and during the 15-year war, which ultimately ended with a negotiated accord in 1988, the number of those who died is debated as being anything from Cuba's official figure of 2,077 to at least five times that number. In the Soviet Union, President Gorbachev was spearheading widespread reform, a move that Castro pronounced himself as firmly against. *Perestroika*, he said, would never be allowed to bring down Cuban socialism.

However, the status quo in Cuba was shattered by the collapse of the Soviet Union. Over the years, Cuba had received over US$1 billion in aid, and it had largely survived, if not thrived, on its long-standing deal with Moscow in which sugar was bartered for oil. Confronted with its most serious economic crisis ever, the Castro government implemented the so-called "Special Period" in 1990, a severe austerity package that has drastically affected the lives of most Cubans. The already-depleted ration system was cut back, while queues multiplied; *apagones*, or power cuts, became ever-more frequent; the lack of fuel made public transportation virtually impossible, with many rural Cubans reverting to medieval methods of transportation and farming, replacing their machines with horses and oxen. Although education and medical care are free, even basic supplies are lacking.

In 1992, the United States tightened its embargo by introducing the Torricelli Bill,

CUBA TODAY

Since the 1990s, the Cuban leadership has begun to realize that restricted liberalization of its policies is inevitable. "To return to capitalism would be a step backward in history," Castro warned his people in 1991. Later, however, saying the move was "unavoidable to save the Revolution," he took a couple of tentative steps in that direction. In August 1993, in order to quash rampant black marketeering, he decriminalized the

which extended the embargo to foreign subsidiaries of American companies, including those shipping food and medicine to Cuba. In August 1994, widespread discontent and despair drove an estimated 30,000 Cubans to attempt to leave the island illegally, flinging themselves into the Gulf Stream off Cuba's northern coast on inner tubes and makeshift rafts, the largest exodus of refugees since the Mariel boatlift in 1980. Many of those who attempted this desperate measure did not make it to Florida's shores alive, and just as many were moved back to Cuba to be held in camps at the Guantánamo naval base while their request for asylum was processed.

possession of foreign currency and accepted the United States dollar as a de facto national currency circulated alongside the Cuban peso (referred to as "dollarization"). He legalized small private enterprises, such as *paladares* or private restaurants, and reinstated farmer's markets, thus allowing people to work independently of the state and, in effect, creating a small class of self-employed Cubans.

Another major reform was the promotion of tourism, which as an industry is barely a decade old in Cuba. Rather than wait decades for it to blossom of its own accord, the Castro

OPPOSITE: "Committee for The Defense of the Revolution." ABOVE: Approved reading in Old Havana.

regime decided to jump-start the industry by encouraging sex tourism, a move that immediately attracted thousands of male visitors from Europe, North America and Latin America, but that also generated profound and long-lasting social consequences.

Tourism sparked a parallel economy, where Cubans with access to dollars can buy supplies and consumer goods at hard-currency shops. Many trained professionals, including doctors and university professors, have opted to work in tourist hotels and restaurants, where they can earn considerably more with dollar tips than they would on their meager monthly peso wage, ranging from 200 to 700 pesos (US$9 and US$32). The average wage in Cuba has fallen to about US$13 a month. Most Cubans immediately convert their salary to American dollars because it is impossible to buy anything in pesos. The scanty food rations provided by the government usually run out about mid-month.

The depressing economic situation has also made young prostitutes more pervasive in Havana streets and bars, and bag snatching and other forms of petty crime more common. Meanwhile, the gap between the capital and rural provinces has grown ever wider, sparking a wave of migrants from the countryside (referred to in Cuban slang as "*palestinos*" or "Palestinians," alluding to their homelessness).

Another golden opportunity for rapprochement with Washington came in 1996 when President Bill Clinton announced that

he would seek an end to the Cuban embargo if he won a second term in the White House. But once again Castro proved his own worst enemy. In February 1996, just one month into Clinton's second term, Castro ordered the Cuban air force to shoot down two small planes operated by a Miami-based Cuban exile group called Brothers to the Rescue that flew into Cuban air space to drop anti-Castro leaflets. Four Cuban-Americans were killed, and once again any hope of mending fences with Washington was lost. Not only did the embargo remain in place, it was fortified. In 1997, despite wide opposition by United States trading partners in both Europe and the Western Hemisphere, the United States Congress passed the Helms-Burton Act, which discourages foreign investment in Cuba and allows Americans to sue foreign companies using property in Cuba confiscated from Americans after 1959. America's allies at the United Nations and the European Court strongly objected to the bill's extraterritorial nature. But once again, Cuban scholars viewed the whole affair as a carefully crafted plan by Castro to inflame sentiment in the United States and thereby maintain a boycott that hurts the Cuban people but gives his regime a reason for existence.

With Pope John Paul II's historic visit in January of 1998, Cuba — or rather the Castro regime — was seen by the world as taking a more conciliatory stance toward

The Cuban armed forces are numerous and well equipped under the leadership of Raúl Castro.

some change. In this instance, Castro lifted restrictions on the Catholic Church and allowed Christmas to be celebrated openly for the first time since 1969. While in Cuba, the Pope called upon the island to open up to the world and reiterated international opposition to the United States embargo.

In the wake of the Pope's visit, the Clinton administration once again moved to ease the embargo, announcing humanitarian initiatives to help Cuba become less dependent on the Communist government and to ease Havana's isolation. These measures included

authorities to repatriate the boy, but the boy's relatives in Florida refused to turn him over. During the ensuing standoff, Elián became an international media sensation and Castro found a ready-made excuse to rally the Cuban masses against their traditional enemy, Uncle Sam. The standoff finally ended in April 2000, when United States federal agents raided the home in which Elián was staying and reunited him with his father for a return trip to Cuba.

In June 2001, Castro showed his age and growing frailty by fainting during a public

a resumption of direct charter fights to the island, which had been cancelled in 1996; allowing Cuban-Americans to send US$1,200 a year to relatives in Cuba, which had been banned in 1994; and relaxing restrictions on the sale of medicine and medical supplies to the island. These measures had profound impact on the standard of living of many Cubans, although the demand for help was greater than the supply.

But yet again, Castro found a way to arouse American passion against his regime. His vehicle this time was a five-year-old Cuban boy named Elián González, the sole survivor of a refugee boat that sank off the Florida coast during a desperate bid to flee Cuba. Elián's father pleaded with American

speech in Havana. By August, he had recovered sufficiently to travel to Venezuela, where he celebrated his seventy-fifth birthday in the company of Hugo Chavez, that country's new left-leaning president. A spokesman for the United States State Department quipped that it was time for Castro to step down because the Cuban leader had "reached the mandatory retirement age for dictators." But there are no signs that Cuba's supreme leader plans to take a back seat anytime soon.

Meanwhile, the diplomatic struggle between Washington and Havana continues. When the Bush administration came to power in January 2001, the new president instructed the Treasury Department to step up enforcement of United States travel restrictions and other tenets of the boycott. The American Congress, however, seemed to head in the opposite direction. In June, the House of Representatives voted overwhelmingly to ease travel restrictions, a measure that was scheduled to go to vote in the Senate until the terrorist attacks of September 11 put the entire United States government on hold. Meanwhile, the 40-year embargo stays in place — much to Castro's delight — and ordinary Cubans continue to suffer.

Certainly, there is avid speculation about what the future holds for Cuba's estimated 11 million people. After four decades in power, Castro has formally selected his brother Raúl as his eventual successor. Raúl has been playing a more prominent role in the running of the Cuban government and the Communist Party. Another strong figure in Cuban politics is Ricardo Alarcón, President of the Cuban National Assembly of People's Power, whose articulate and moderating influence may offer Cuba its very own bridge to the twenty-first century.

These days, Castro is a gaunt and graying figure, yet he still commands respect and fascination on the world stage, despite his faults. Meanwhile, it appears that whatever Cuba's next big gamble with its future might be, it is waiting in the wings.

CUBA AND HUMAN RIGHTS

Most of the two million tourists who venture to Cuba each year never get beyond the beach resorts and the bars of Havana. They have virtually no contact with the government and very little understanding of domestic politics. Yet many of them go home with trinkets that reflect the enduring romance of the Cuban Revolution — postcards of young Fidel Castro chomping a cigar or T-shirts with images of Che Guevara — sold en masse at government souvenir outlets with much the same ardor as Disney employs in hawking Mickey Mouse hats or Tinkerbell wands. That's all fine and good. But there is another side of Cuba, indeed an entirely different take on the Revolution that is not so marketable or romantic.

The United Nations Commission on Human Rights, Amnesty International and the Paris-based Reporters Without Borders — independent bodies that are not beholding to the anti-Castro propaganda that pours forth from the United States government and exiled Cubans in Miami — continue to brand Cuba as one of the world's worst offenders of human rights. Cuba, in fact, is the only nation in the Western Hemisphere with no freedom of expression, freedom of the press or freedom of assembly, and the only nation in

the Americas that hasn't staged free and open elections in the last 40 years. The government continues to restrict the movement of ordinary citizens, determining where they can live, work and attend school. Many dissidents are arrested on trumped-up charges, and those whose cases reach the courts have no guarantee of fair trial or proper legal representation.

The human rights situation isn't nearly as heinous as during the 1960s, when thousands of people with connections to the Batista regime were executed and tens of thousands of dissidents jailed. But repression of one sort or another remains a way of life for most Cubans.

Within the framework of the Cuban constitution and penal code, suppression of dissent is completely legal. Among the official crimes for which you can be convicted and sent to prison are "disrespect" of the government or Communist Party and "dangerousness" to the state. According to

With dramatic shortages, stores are nearly empty OPPOSITE and the reality of rationing daily ABOVE.

the 2001 Amnesty International report on human rights, "The Cuban government has traditionally argued that it is justified in depriving dissidents of fundamental freedoms of expression, association and assembly in order to maintain the unity of the country against hostile forces abroad." In other words: anyone who doesn't agree with the government is deemed a threat to Cuban independence and sovereignty.

During the late 1990s, the release of several prominent political prisoners gave rise to hope that the Castro regime was softening its stance toward dissent. But new arrests and an escalation of repression have snuffed out any optimism. As the second edition of this book went to press, several hundred people — including journalists, human-rights advocates and political opponents — were being held in Cuban jails on purely political grounds. Among those who are more prominent are Dr. Oscar Elías Biscet González, president of a humanitarian organization called the Lawton Foundation for Human Rights, convicted of public disorder and "insulting symbols of the homeland," and Nestor Rodríguez Lobaina, head of the Cuban Youth Movement for Democracy, who is currently serving a six-year term for public disorder and disrespect.

Overseas watchdog organizations also bemoan the state of the Cuban prison system. Generally conditions are abysmal and some prisoners, according to Amnesty International, are subject to "cruel, inhuman and degrading treatment." Many prisoners are thought to be in poor health due to unsanitary conditions and inadequate medical treatment.

Dissidents who are not in prison are often subject to intense harassment or to house arrest. Many are denied jobs in their chosen profession and are forced into menial tasks.

Despite the repression, Cuba's dissidents continue to press for more freedom. One of the boldest groups is the Manuel Marquez Sterling Journalists' Association, which represents about 40 reporters who work for unauthorized, non-government media outlets including overseas news organizations. The group is currently seeking permission for five Cuban writers who have suffered lengthy persecution at the hands of the Castro regime to leave the country. So far their pleas have fallen on deaf ears and the writers remain under virtual house arrest.

The government continues to control and restrict access to all information including television, radio, newspapers, magazines and the Internet. Tourist hotels are allowed to download CNN and other foreign stations, but it's against the law for Cubans to have a satellite dish at home. Business centers in tourist hotels are allowed to offer Internet service to foreign guests, but it's against the law for Cubans to have their own private cyber connection. "The monopoly of the state over information is contrary to Cubans' right to be informed," Robert Menard, secretary general of Reporters Without Borders, declared during a recent interview on the state of human rights in Cuba.

And lest you assume that Cuba's lack of human rights doesn't impact your holiday, consider the fact that Cuban authorities monitor all outgoing communication from hotels and post offices. "They don't read every single e-mail," says the manager of an Internet center in Havana. "Only if you are suspicious."

PASSIONS OF A PASSIONATE ISLAND

Cuba has a culture like no other. The mixture of Spanish and African religious and artistic traditions — Roman Catholicism and Yoruba religious ritual — has created an exotic people — Spanish and Indian *mestizos*, Spanish and African *mulattos* and African *zambos,* among others — whose genes reflect history's conspiracy to blend together Spanish, African, French and even Chinese cultures, producing a culture that is passionate, mystical, literate, sensual and often self-ironic.

RELIGION

Although Cuba has many millions of baptized Catholics, the island's most popular religion originated in Africa. Known out-

A rumba dance is often a feature of the carnival festivities in Havana and Santiago de Cuba.

side Cuba as Santería, this religious tradition is a mixture of practices brought to Cuba by African slaves and the Catholicism they were forced to adopt under the Spanish. To a large extent, Santería evolved from the cult of Yoruba or Lucumi people of Nigeria. Many practitioners regard the term Santería as a misnomer, and call the so-called syncretistic religion by another name, "Ifaism." (In Haiti, a variant of the same belief is known across the world as "voodoo.") Experts estimate that 70 percent of Cubans practice Santería, whether through

energy behind creation." This supreme being presides over *orishas*, which could be described as anthropomorphic spirits, who watch over the human world. Because worshipping *orishas* was heresy to Catholics, the slaves managed to conceal worship of their own African deities behind the names and images of Catholic saints. Yet during this process, aspects of Catholicism became mingled with their own religion.

In the Yoruba celestial world, Olofí is regarded as the supreme *orisha*. He communicates through Orula, the *orisha* of wisdom,

daily ritual or merely an occasional offering. Even many of those who call themselves practicing Catholics also believe in Santería, which in Cuba, a deeply superstitious nation, could be regarded as keeping on the safe side, just in case. Tucked away in certain neighborhoods, you will always find a local *bótanica*, which sells special incense, herbs and amulets for Santería rituals, as well as the distinctive beaded necklaces and bracelets denoting a person's patron *orisha*.

Santería recognizes a single supreme being, of no known gender. As a practicing *babalao* or priest put it: "How can you describe the gender of electricity? For us, God is the energy that is created and it is the

whose corresponding saint is San Francisco. By means of divination, Orula allows believers to communicate with their patron *orisha*, although he is always consulted himself by Cubans before they make an important decision. For Cubans, the Virgen de la Caridad del Cobre (Virgin of Charity of Cobre) is identified with Ochún, the powerful goddess of rivers, lakes, beauty, love, money and maternity. Like Aphrodite, she is known for her dalliances with lovers, yet manages to somehow be ever-virtuous. Other central *orishas* include Yemayá, worshipped as the Virgen de Regla, Havana's patron saint, goddess of the sea and protector of loved ones; Elegguá, the warrior god, identified with San Antonio and the messenger of prayers between the human and the spirit world; Changó, god of thunder and lightning, music and virility, whose inseparable companion is Oyá, the *orisha* of winds, storms, night lightening and cemeteries; Obatalá, goddess of light, worshipped through the Virgen de las Mercedes; Babulu-Ayé, the *orisha* of healing, who is recognized in San Lázaro, a pilgrimage site in Cuba. Altogether, there are many hundreds of *orishas*, but these are the most dominant.

Santería *babalaos* (the priesthood is male-only) perform divination and other ceremonies in their own homes, and according to belief they should only take place during daylight hours.

Just as a doctor has a stethoscope, each *babalao* has an *okpele*, a chain with eight pieces of coconut shell which when swung onto the floor can produce one of a possible 256 combinations, each one with a specific interpretation that has been passed down and refined over the centuries, which the *babalao* relates to his client. Various devices are used in "cleansing" ceremonies, including certain herbs, smoke blown through a cigar, and spurts of *aguardiente* expelled from the mouth. No one who witnesses or is involved with a Santería ceremony will ever forget the experience.

In what is sometimes regarded as a controversial aspect of the religion, certain rituals and initiation ceremonies involve the sacrifice of animals, usually black chickens or roosters, but sometimes goats or larger animals. Its practitioners shrug their shoulders and say that all religions have been blood related at one time, while the animal that is killed is always eaten. Another contentious aspect is the fact that *babalaos* are known to demand quite hefty financial payments for their services. Santería apparently demands that those who practice it must be made to take

it seriously: free dispensing of the *orisha's* advice is not agreeable to the religion.

Initiates are known as *santeros* or *santeras*, and are recognizable by the immaculate white clothes and the colorful necklaces they must wear for an entire year; you will probably see one or two during your stay.

Cuba has two other important Afro-Cuban cults, Palo Monte and Abakuá, both of which have a limited and more secretive following. Palo Monte, also known as Regla Mayombé, is practiced mostly in eastern Cuba. It was brought to Cuba by Bantu slaves, and combines animal sacrifice with a fetish for skulls and spells, and in this respect, has much in common with Haitian voodoo. Abakuá, practiced only by white Cuban males, is a very secretive society, feared by many in Cuba. Initiates are known as *abakuás*.

MUSIC

Another aspect of the island's culture indisputably linked to its Afro-Cuban heritage is the rich mix of African rhythms and European instrumentation that form Cuban music. There is no question that Cuba has evolved one of the world's richest and most exuberant musical traditions. Music, song and dance are an inseparable part of the national identity. Equally, over the past century, the island's music has profoundly influenced the development of such international musical styles as jazz, blues, swing and the contemporary ballad structure.

Juan Formell, bassist and founder of Los Van Van, one of Cuba's leading music ensembles, has this to say about his country's music heritage: "Cuba is the historical source

OPPOSITE: Drummers play in a Santería ceremony in Havana.
ABOVE: One sees few sculptures in Cuba, this one is in Santiago de Cuba.

of Latin music, more so than any other Latin American or Caribbean country. The main elements of today's Latin music are directly descended from music of the 1920s and the 1930s, beginning with Miguel Matamoros, Ignacio Piñeiro, Orquestra Aragon and Beny Moré. Even today, popular salsa is still much more Cuban than anything else. In general, we utilize the same musical elements and forms our predecessors used. When you say the '*introducción*,' the '*montuno*,' the '*estribillo*' and the '*mambo*,' for example, much younger musicians from

the white *criolle* bourgeoisie and the newly enfranchised blacks. The power of African rhythm soon created a musical transformation of the more sedate European contradanse, incorporating the rhythms, chants and dances used ceremonially to summon *orishas*. Today, dance bands openly make Santería references.

Of all Cuban musical forms, rumba — which originated by the docks and poorest barrios of Matanzas and Havana as fiesta music, cathartic and intoxicating — expresses this fusion most openly. The most famous rumba dance is the columbia, a rapid, almost

other countries and from newer styles all recognize, respect and use these elements, and identify them as Cuban."

In the words of musician Ry Cooder (who produced the Grammy-winning album, *Buena Vista Social Club*, a compilation of son): "Music is alive in Cuba, not some remnant of a museum. In Cuba the music flows like a river. It takes care of you and rebuilds you from the inside out."

Fernando Ortíz, the late Cuban ethnologist famously wrote that the island's music stemmed from "the love affair of African drums and Spanish guitar."

The Cuban music we know today only took off after the abolition of slavery allowed cultural barriers to collapse somewhat between

gymnastic solo man's dance which conveys the contortions of devils, a feature of certain ceremonies of the Afro-Cuban cult Abakuá. Rumba has three main styles: the sensual and exciting guaguanacó, the columbia, and the yambú and conga. The latter styles are often a feature of the carnival festivities in Havana and Santiago de Cuba.

Over the past century, other musical styles evolved. Some are inseparable from the voices of singers: the romantic bolero and the more flirtatious guaracha, both of which began in nineteenth-century Havana as a form of serenading by suitors — the object of their affections was required by the social dictates of the day to remain coyly unseen behind colonial latticework screens. Others, such as the danza, the habenera and lastly, danzón, are known more as dance genres.

Son, which dates from the first decade of this century, has proved one of the most enduring and inspirational forms of Cuban music. It began in Oriente Province and involved an ensemble of a double bass, trumpets, bongos and other percussion instruments, as well as a three-stringed guitar called a *tres*. Cuba's most famous son artist was Beny Moré, the so-called "Barbarian of Rhythm." It was largely Moré's influence that inspired a generation of musicians to

Cuban bands, such as Los Van Van, N.G. La Banda, Issac Delgado, Grupo Sierra Maestra and El Medico de la Salsa have kept alive these rhythm phenomena while adding their own modern twists.

There are many other aspects and styles to modern Cuban music, as any musicologist will tell you. Even if you regard yourself as an absolute beginner when it comes to Cuban music, if you are acquainted with the mainstream sounds of Desi Arnaz (for the older generation) and Gloria Estefan, then you already recognize something of the

experiment with son during the 1950s, especially in New York where Machito, Chano Pozo, Xaiver Cugat, Mario Bauza, and Tito Puente and his Mambo Boys each had their moment of fame. Dizzy Gillespie and Charlie Parker listened, created their own fusion; and thus Cu-bop, Jazz Mambo or Cubano Jazz came into its own. Another offshoot of son was salsa — which, with its brass, syncopated percussion and choruses, became an international sensation.

While salsa, along with cha-cha-cha, swept the world, Cuba was busily concocting septets and charangas and other dance rhythms, and meanwhile, Joseito Fernandez's *Guantánamera* became internationally synonymous with Cuba. Contemporary

Cuban sensibility. Overall, it is accurate to say that Cuban music often fuses African sources and aspects of Santería rhythms with traditional folk dance music, along with jazz, rock and classical elements. Indeed, this description exactly sums up the sound of Irakere, one of Cuba's most popular jazz fusion bands, led by Chuco Valdéz, as well as the fusion group, Sintésis.

Since the Revolution, the most significant development in Cuban music has been the so-called *Nueva Trova*, typified by the ballads of Silvio Rodríquez and Pablo Milanés. More recently, singers such as Gerardo Alfonso, whose lyrics speak of the pain

OPPOSITE AND ABOVE: Cuba's famous cigars are made by hand, from the harvest to rolling.

of exile and the realities of modern-day Havana, represent the new wave, termed *Novísima Trova*. Outside Cuba, you may want to follow the career of the platinum-haired Albita, who was once one of the island's darlings, dubbed Cuba's Lili Marlene, but who defected to a new life in Miami in 1993.

If you want to familiarize yourself with the best of Cuban music, as well as those musicians mentioned above, you would do well to start with various compilation records, such as *Buena Vista Social Club*, *Afro*

ART

Prior to the Revolution, Cuba produced one major internationally renowned artist: Wilfredo Lam (1902–82), of Chinese descent, who was both a friend and student of Picasso. Despite the fact that Wilfredo Lam lived most of his life as an expatriate, his influence on Cuban art remains profound. Today, in Havana, the Centro Wilfredo Lam is one of the city's most vibrant cultural centers.

Cuban All Stars, and *I Am Cuba*. Some of the featured musicians in the *Buena Vista Social Club* album, such as Ibrahim Ferrer and Compay Segundo, were side men for the great Cuban innovators of the 1940s and 1950s. Ferrer worked as a shoe-shiner in Cuba for decades before making this album, yet recorded with Beny Moré; Rubén Gonsález, who had retired in 1991, played with Arsenio Rodríguez and Enrique Jorrin, Cuban greats both. Also, don't overlook the sweetly nostalgic compositions of Cuba's famous classical pianist, Ernesto Lecuona, who was born last century, or the voice of Celina Gonsález, born in 1920, Cuba's diva of guajira, Cuba's traditional country music.

René Portocarrero (1912–85) is one of Cuba's best-loved artists, known for his ethereal paintings and stained-glass windows of women and churches with their Marc Chagallesque quality. Two other artists, Amelia Peláez (1897–1968) and Mariano Rodríguez (1912–90) are known for their ceramics and murals, respectively. In the 1960s, Raúl Martínez created some of the Revolution's most memorable images, such as his poster paintings of Fidel Castro, Che Guevara and José Martí.

Today, Manual Mendive is Cuba's leading living artist, whose work features bold graphics and dashes of hot, earthy color, weaving themes from Afro-Cuban mythology and folklore. Another contemporary artist is Flora Fong, a Chinese Cuban, like Lam, who paints vivid, tropical landscapes.

A visit to the brand-new Cuban wing at Havana's Museo Nacional de Bellas Artes is a must for familiarizing yourself with the island's art.

The Biennial de la Habana (Visual Arts Biennial) celebrates work by artists from Cuba and abroad, providing a showcase for local artistic expression. Increasingly, young Cuban artists often address sensitive topics like emigration and economic hardship. An article in the *New York Times* noted: "Havana's still-young festival makes up in high spirits and unpredictable freshness what it sorely lacks in money or manpower." The biennial is held in several locations in the Cuban capital, including El Morro fortress and the Centro Wilfredo Lam.

As with all cultural institutions in Cuba, all art galleries are state-run.

FILM

Following the Revolution, Castro's government made the island's film industry a national priority. It created the Instituto Cubano del Arte y la Industria Cinematográficos (ICAIC), the Cuban Institute of Film Art and Industry, which has had a virtual monopoly on Cuban filmmaking ever since, producing everything from animated cartoons, features, documentaries and newsreels.

Cuba's best known film director is the late Tomás Gutiérrez Alea (1928–96), who worked with Juan Carlos Tabio on the critically acclaimed films *Fresa y Chocolate* and *Guantánamera*, both starring his wife, the luminous Mirtha Ibarra, and both reflecting ironically on the faults of the Cuban system, yet conveying the wit and passion of the Cuban soul. Earlier films by Alea include *La Muerte de un Burórata*, *Memorias del Subdesarrollo* and *Cartas del Parque*.

Another leading director is Humberto Solás (born 1941) whose 1968 film, *Lucía*, is one of the classics of Cuban cinema. More recently, two notable Cuban films, Daniel Diaz Torres's *Kleines Tropicana* and Arturo Sotto's *Amor Vertical* can be said to carry on the Alea's tradition of lovingly mocking the system.

ICAIC also runs the annual International Festival of New Latin American Cinema, founded in 1979 and usually held in the first two weeks of December. Bringing a whiff of business and glamour to the capital, the festival usually centers at the Hotel Nacional, with screenings at a dozen cinemas. The two-week run generally plays to packed audiences with at least half a million tickets sold.

Novelist Gabriel García Márquez (a part-time Cuba resident) is regarded as the founding godfather of the event. Many of the world's most talented filmmakers from other hemispheres come to take part too, including Robert Redford, who has visited several times, and who is instrumental through his Sundance Institute in bringing independent American films to Cuba and in screening the work of talented Cuban and Latin American filmmakers at his Sundance Festival. (In doing so, frequently they come up against the United States embargo on Cuba. Given the political situation between the two countries, Cubans have a peculiar interaction with American movies, which are often seen on borrowed satellite in a contraband kind of way.)

Previous years have featured a jumble of such visiting celebrities as Robert De Niro, Francis Ford Coppola, Peter Greenaway, Stephen Frears, Arnold Schwarzenegger, Gerard Depardieu, Sydney Poitier, Harry Belafonte, Helen Mirren, Taylor Hackford, Hanna Schygulla, Julian Schnabel, Matt Dillon and Treat Williams. And of course, there is always the nation's famous *deus ex machina*, Fidel Castro himself, who often chooses the festival to make one of his surprise entrances.

LITERATURE

Although Cuba prides itself on being a fiercely literary nation, many Cubans today have very restricted access to books beyond those deemed politically and ideologically correct. Indeed, as the Argentinean writer Jacob Timerman commented: "If it is true that every Cuban knows how to read and write, it is likewise true that every Cuban has nothing to read and must be very careful about what he writes."

Paintings by local artists are sold at street markets for dollars to access new food stores.

Although it has certainly proved to be an almost irrepressible topic one way or another, Cuba's Revolution has not always been kindest to the writers who have grown up in its shadow. Some went into exile, such as Guillermo Cabrera Infante, whose work was at the forefront of the 1960s renaissance in Latin American writing, and who was hailed by *The New York Review of Books* as Cuba's most important living writer. His books cannot be found in Cuba.

However, in Havana bookshops, along with the writings of Fidel Castro, Che Gue-

Valdés, about a tragic affair between a slave trader's son and a beautiful *mulatta*, who, it transpires, is his illegitimate half-sister.

José Lezama Lima (1910–76) caused ripples with his 1966 novel *Paradiso*, which explores homosexuality (a pet hate of Fidel Castro), and Miguel Barnet's *Biografía de un Cimarron* ("The Autobiography of a Runaway Slave") was published in 1967; both are regarded as seminal works.

In Cuba, younger writers such as Senel Paz and Reinaldo Gonsález have tackled subjects viewed as somewhat contentious, such as disillusionment, AIDS and poverty. This younger generation includes Zoé Valdés, an exile living in Paris, whose works have been banned in her native Cuba. Her book *La Nada Cotodiana* (which translates as "The Nothingness of Everyday Life"), published in English as *Yocandra in the Paradise of Nada*, paints a devastating portrait of Cuba during the Special Period.

In the United States, the novels of Havana-born Cristina García, *Dreaming in Cuban* and *The Agüero Sisters*, lift the troubled relationship between the two countries, as well as the emotional fallout created between those who left and those who stayed behind, into the realm of remarkable literature.

vara, Marx and Lenin (as well as agricultural handbooks and anti-CIA literature), you will find books by the revolutionary leader José Martí and by the two authors the island claims as its greatest: the avant-garde surrealist writer Alejo Carpentier (1904–80) and the mulatto poet Nicholas Guillén (1902–89), both of whom came of age well before the Revolution's triumph. Guillén is regarded as the father of Cuban letters: he helped found the Unión Nacional de Escritores y Artistas Cubanos (National Union of Writers and Artists). You can also look for works by Cuba's greatest nineteenth-century novelist, Cirilo Villaverde y la Paz, a revolutionary who foreshadowed José Martí. His best-loved work is *Cecilia*

ABOVE: Browsing on the Plaza de Armas.
OPPOSITE: A coconut plantation near Baracoa in Guantánamo Province.

Havana and Environs

HAVANA

0.2 miles
300m

VEDADO

Cristobal Colón
Necrópolis

Casa Garcia
● Calzada las Americas

Museo de Artes ●
Decorativas

Malecón

Teatro Nacional
Av. Carlos M. Céspedes

Plaza de la Revolución
● José Martí
Biblioteca Nacional
Aragüren
Feria de la Juventud
Castillo del Príncipe
Avenida Rancho Boyeros

Victimas del Maine ●
Malecón
Hotel Nacional ●

VEDADO

Linea
Paseo

23 (La Rampa)
23 (Rampa)
José Miguel Gómez
University of Havana

Hotel Cohiba ●

Estadio Juan Abrahantes ●
Zapata
Museo Napoleónico ●
Hospital

CENTRO

Parque Maceo

Calzada de Infanta
27 de Noviembre
Príncipe
Calzada de Infanta
Neptuno
San Francisco
San Miguel
San Rafael
Concordia
Hamel
Vapor
Aramburu

Quinta de los Molinos ●
Aguila
Mazón
Basarrate
Valle
Espada
San Martín (San José)
Zanja
Salud
Jesús Peregrino
Pocito
Soledad
Castillejo

Enrique Barnet (Estrella)
Sitios
Venus Oquendo
Marqués González
Lucena
Gervasio
Padre Varela (Belascoaín)

Animas
Trocadero
Concordia
Neptuno
San Miguel
San Rafael
San Martín (San José)
Zanja
Salud

CENTRO

Avenida Simón Bolívar (Reina)
Manrique

Palacio de Aldama ●
Aguila

Escobar
Lealtad
Perseverancia
Campanario
San Lázaro
Lagunas
Animas
Virtudes
Concordia
Neptuno

San Nicolás
Av de Italia
Blanco
Aguila
Crespo
Industria

Avenida Simón Bolívar (Reina)
Manrique

Maximo Gómez (Monte)
Revillagigedo
Aguila
Amistad
Industria

Plaza de la Fraternidad
Parque Central

Museo Nacional de Bellas Artes ●
Gran Teatro ●

Paseo de Martí (Prado)

HABANA VIEJA

Museo de la Revolución ●
Plaza de la Revolución

Corrales
Apodaca
Gloria
Misión
Factoria
Suárez
Diaria
Tallapiedra

Arsenal
Cienfuegos
Economia
Agramonte

Estación Central de Ferrocarriles

Monserrate (Bélgica)
Bernaza
Cristo
Villegas
Aguacate
Compostela

Iglesia y Convento de Belén ●

Paseo de Martí (Prado)
Museo Nacional de Bellas Artes

El Templete ✝
Castillo de los Tres Reyes del Morro

Casa Natal de José Martí ●
Maced
Factoria
Revillagigedo
Aguila

Sol
Muralla
Teniente Rey (Brasil)
Lamparilla
Amargura
Obrapia
Obispo
O'Reilly
Chacón

HABANA VIEJA

Picota
Acosta
Jesús María
Merced
Paula
Damas
Cuba

Habana
Compostela
Aguacate
Villegas

Catedral ✝
Palacio del Segundo Cabo
Plaza de Catedral
Palacio de los Capitanes Generales
Plaza de Armas
El Templete ✝
Castillo de la Real Fuerza ✝

Egido
Picota
Jesús María
Curazao
Leonor Perez

Conde de Jaruco
Luz
Santa Clara
Sol
Muralla

Iglesia de San Francisco de Asís ✝
Plaza Vieja
Plaza de San Francisco

San Isidro
Desamparado
San Pedro

San Ignacio
Cuba
Mercaderes
Oficios
Baratillo

Espíritu Santo
Jesús de
Inquisidor
San Ignacio
Chacón
Tacón
Cuarteles

Caleta de San Lázaro

Malecón

El Parque de los Martires
El Parque de la Punta
Castillo de San Salvador de la Punta

Maximo Gómez
Av de Bélgica
Parque Histórico Militar

Fortaleza de San Carlos de la Cabaña

Canal Entrada

N W E S

Strait of Florida

Marina Hemingway

Mariel
Guanajay
Cabañas
La Coloma

Playa Baracoa
Santa Fe
Bauta

José Martí International Airport
Jardín Botánico
Parque Lenin
Santiago de las Vegas

San Antonio de los Baños

HAVANA

Cojímar
Guanabacoa
Regla
Casablanca
Bahía de la Habana

Bejucal

San Antonio de las Vegas

Cotilla

Santa María del Rosario

San José de las Lajas

Campo Florido

Güines

Playas del Este
Guanabo

Cuatro Caminos
Cotorro

Central La Máquina del Mar
to Matanzas ➤

Esenada de Atarés

Havana ●

HAVANA

Something about the haunting beauty of Havana seems to affect the heart as deeply as a love affair, the memory of which brings a twinge of melancholy and has a compulsive pull on the emotions, triggered by an old song or the smell of a certain flower. It is impossible to forget the exotic decadence of Havana's crumbling mansions, the mesmerizing slap of waves against the Malecón, the summer air with its wistful traces of salt and frangipani. It is easy to romanticize Havana, but as visitors soon observe, perhaps harder to live like a *habanero* in matrimony with some of its imperfections.

For more than two decades, this most sensual of cities existed in a state of socialist purdah. Even now, a decade after Fidel Castro opened the doors to foreign tourists, those visiting the island nation can't help but feel a frisson of unreality as they contemplate the sight of one of the most remarkable cities in the world.

Havana has a beguiling flavor all of its own, a strangeness that is at first baffling. Its source is partly rooted in the paradox that Havana is a grandly extravagant city built with fortunes created by slavery and capitalism, but which has became more famous as the crucible of Fidel Castro's radical Revolution. Certainly, the city is better known for having the world's most famously obdurate Communist government than as the first to have a Spanish fortress in the Americas. (Indeed, it has both the oldest and the largest: the Castillo de la Real Fuerza and the Fortaleza de San Carlos de la Cabaña.)

BACKGROUND

Havana was one of the seven cities founded by the Spanish expeditionary Diego de Velázquez who, in 1514, established the colonial *villa* or settlement then called San Cristóbal de la Habana. The de facto capital of Cuba from 1553, Havana was officially declared the capital in 1607, and was always the island's most affluent and cosmopolitan city. By 1750, about one half of the island's entire population (some 170,000) lived in the city; today that figure is just over two million, making it the largest city in the Caribbean.

More recently, in the 1950s, Havana was considered by many to be the Las Vegas of the Caribbean, a playground for rich tourists run by the American mob, a palm-lined port city filled with casino wheels, rum cocktails and dancing under an open sky. It was sexy, decadent and corrupt to the core, underlaced with prostitution and smuggling. It was becoming one of Latin America's major financial centers when Castro took over in 1959.

As Cuba's principal city, Havana is the point of entry for most visitors, and unquestionably its main attraction for visitors. Over the centuries, Havana has developed into a beautiful but chaotic architectural jumble, with a constant juxtaposition of eras. In the capital's colonial core, La Habana Vieja, it is possible to walk along streets lined with grand baroque buildings that look little changed since the seventeenth and eighteenth centuries, with churches, plazas and imposing colonial mansions that were once places of elegant residence for the Creole aristocracy.

PREVIOUS PAGES — LEFT: Havana's Plaza de la Catedral. RIGHT: An elegant staircase in Vedado. ABOVE: Diego de Velázquez, founder of Havana.

As you wander the streets, many as-yet-unrestored mansions are propped up by scaffolding and tangled with electrical wires, with brightly colored washing suspended across peeling stucco, and the smell of sweet coffee wafting from portable heating coils. Very often, these narrow streets contain hidden marvels behind otherwise unremarkable walls notable only for their large iron-studded wooden doors. You may catch glimpses of carved stone and marble interiors, perhaps awaiting restoration. Distinctive features of Havana's colonial

deco houses, Spanish Colonial mansions and modernist architecture from the 1950s. Many of these buildings — some once occupied by sugar barons and industrialists who fled after the Revolution — are in a notoriously shocking state of disrepair; some have become *ciudadelas* — or "little cities" — home to more than a dozen families.

However, an ambitious drive for architectural restoration and renovation of Havana — most notably of La Habana Vieja — is underway, largely under the energetic direction of the city's historian, Eusebio Leal.

buildings include high, multi-colored stained-glass *mediopuntos* (fan-shaped windows divided with wooden struts) and *vitrales* (divided with metal instead of wood), elaborate carved window bars (*rejas*), louvered blinds (*persianas*) to keep out the sun, intricate latticework window screens (*celosias*), double-hinged half-doors (*mamparas*), upper balconies, inner *portales* or arcades, and intricately carved *alfarje* wooden ceilings.

In addition to the profusion of colonial buildings in the La Habana Vieja, other sections of the city, such as the formerly wealthy neighborhoods of Vedado, Miramar and El Cerro, have a varied mixture of twentieth-century architecture: art nouveau palaces, art

Although La Habana Vieja is protected as a UNESCO World Heritage Site, many visitors are surprised by the government's eagerness to transform the historic neighborhood into a quaint tourist attraction. While the city's aristocratic colonial buildings and monuments have received careful treatment and are nothing less than dazzling, many secondary buildings have lost their charming authenticity under solid coats of salmon pink and canary blue, creating a slightly surreal, too-quaint effect.

Certainly, the rash of newly constructed flashy hotels, shops, cafés and fast-food outlets in the old city give the impression that Cuba's new romance with capitalism is in full swing. Meanwhile, the architectural wonders in Vedado, Miramar and El Cerro, less likely to attract tourists, have been allowed to crumble into almost derelict state. On the outskirts of the capital, rundown military installations and crumbling Soviet-style apartment buildings (built by "micro-brigades," teams of volunteers who build their own homes with government-supplied cement and equipment) offer a harsher reality. It is true that the pervasive hardship experienced by most of the city's citizens during the on-going Special Period gives a stranger's enjoyment of Havana a certain sting. It is hard not to be moved by their optimism and warmth. In a profound way, Havana — the aging beauty — radiates real lusty life, and is not easily forgotten.

GENERAL INFORMATION

Most hotels, especially the four- or five-star ones, have information desks that are equipped to deal with most queries. They can also arrange prompt medical assistance should it be necessary.

Cuba's Ministry of Tourism operates several **Infotur** ((07) 333333, 247036 or 240624 tourist offices in Havana including branches at Calle Obispo (between Calles Bernaza and Villegas in La Habana Vieja), Calle 28 no. 303 in Miramar, Avenida 5 (at Calle 112) in Playa, and at all three terminals at Aeropuerto Internacional José Martí. In theory, Infotur has free brochures, maps and videos, and can make hotel or tour reservations. In reality, they are often out of printed information and what they do stock is generally for sale rather than gratis. Still, the staff can be extremely helpful when it comes to bookings and recommendations.

Asistur ((07) 338920, 338527 or 338339 FAX (07) 338087 WEB SITE www.asistur.cuba web.cu, Paseo de Martí (Prado) 212, La Habana Vieja, is a Cuban government company specializing in assistance to international visitors. The staff are friendly and speak English. A 24-hour service is available if you require any of the following: emergency medical aid or dental treatment, repatriation, legal aid, help with tracing lost baggage, various types of travel insurance, emergency foreign currency exchange and new travel documents.

Another handy place to make hotel reservations and garner general tourist information is the **Cubanacán** kiosk right outside the international arrivals area in Terminal 3 at José Martí airport.

Several publications cater to the tourist market. *Cartelera* a free weekly cultural and tourism newspaper has articles on local attractions and upcoming events. *La Isla Catálogo Cultural* is a free monthly magazine with stories about the Havana arts and culture scene. Both are (sometimes) available at leading hotels and travel agencies.

You will find plenty of travel agencies in Havana whose primary aim is to sell you tour packages and excursions. Among the oldest and most reputable are **Viajes Cubanacán** ((07) 280607 or 286063, **Havanatur** ((07) 242161 or 242248, **Gaviota Tours** ((07) 666773 or 339061, and **Tour & Travel** ((07) 247541 or 241549.

The Hotel Nacional and the Hotel Habana Libre have banking outlets where you can get cash advances on credit cards or cash traveler's checks even if you are not staying at the hotel; you will need to show your passport. Otherwise, try the privately run Banco

---

OPPOSITE: The tower of the Castillo de la Fuerza and El Palacio del Segundo Cabo at sunset. ABOVE: Stylish balconies in La Habana Vieja.

Financiero Internacional ((07) 333423 or 333424, Calle Línea 1, Vedado. It is open Monday to Friday from 8:30 AM to 3 PM, but lines tend to be lengthier than at the hotel outlets, which are also open on the weekend. You can exchange dollars for Cuban pesos at any of the capital's Casas de Cambio (Cadesa), although in theory there shouldn't be any need for you to do this because United States greenbacks are accepted everywhere. The most conveniently located one is near the Lonja del Comercio building in the Plaza de San Francisco de Asís in La Habana Vieja.

Unless you are staying at one of Havana's top hotels, the most convenient **post office** (which also offers international telephone service) is at the Hotel Habana Libre. Another convenient place to buy stamps or make long-distance calls is the **Telecorreo** on Calle Obispo in Habana Vieja, right across the street from the Infotur office.

Most tourist hotels throughout Cuba offer special low rates for overseas calls either directly from your room or the front desk. Per-minute charges are lower at two- and three-star hotels where rates run US$2.20 to North America, US$3.75 to South America, US$4.40 to Western Europe and US$4.86 to Australia, New Zealand and South Africa.

Unless you're staying at one of the five-star hotels, Internet service is rather Spartan in Havana. **Infotur** on Calle Obispo charges just US$1 for 15 minutes of web time, but you can only send one page to one address and you cannot check your mailbox. The business center on the first floor of the **Golden Tulip Hotel Parque Central** ((07) 606627 EXTENSION 1911 or 1833, overlooking the Parque Central in La Habana Vieja, offers Internet service to non-guests from 8 AM to 8 PM. Rates are US$4.50 for 15 minutes or US$12 for one hour. The **National Science Library** in the Capitolio Building in Havana Vieja also offers Internet service to foreign visitors.

Should you require medical attention, you can contact the **Hospital Nacional Hermanos Almeijeiras** ((07) 576077, Calle San Lázaro 701, off the Malecón in Centro Habana. Another option is **Servimed** ((07) 242377 or 247218, Avenida 41 no. 2206 in Playa. You can also contact the **Clínica International Cira García** ((07) 242673 or 240330, Calle 20

at the corner of Avenida 41 in Miramar. In the same complex is the **Farmacia Internacional** ((07) 242051. If it's urgent, call your hotel doctor and proceed from there.

In emergencies, the telephone contact for Havana's **Tourist Police** is ((07) 600106 or 820116; for an **Ambulance** call ((07) 551584 or 552785.

GETTING AROUND

Havana is a very spread-out city, divided into 15 municipalities; six of which — La Habana Vieja, Centro Habana, Miramar, Playa, Regla and La Habana del Este — border the sea.

Most museums, historical sites, restaurants, cabarets, nightclubs and bars are found in La Habana Vieja, Vedado, Centro Habana, Miramar and Playa, and are usually well-known to taxi drivers. You should, however, confirm they know the address before you set off. In some areas, such as La Habana Vieja — with its labyrinth of narrow cobbled streets filled with something interesting to see at every corner — it is much better to be on foot.

Havana has numerous car rental agencies including **Rex** ((07) 339160 or 337788, which rents new Volvos and Audis; **Transautos** ((07) 245532 or 245765; **Panautos** ((07) 553298; **Micar** ((07) 242444; **Veracuba** ((07) 330600 or 330601; and **Havanautos** ((07) 332369 or 332891. More details on car rental can be found in GETTING AROUND, page 316, in TRAVELERS' TIPS. If you rent a car, remember that driving around Havana can be hard on the nerves, involving a lot of dodging of pedestrians and cyclists.

If you don't have a rental car, the easiest option is to hail or book a taxi. Havana's main taxi services include **Panataxi** ((07) 555555, **Taxi Transtur** ((07) 335543, **Transgaviota** ((07) 272727, and **Fenix** (07) 635861, all of which operate modern, air-conditioned vehicles manufactured in Europe or Japan.

Official taxis operate by meter, which drivers are obliged to turn on as soon as you set off. Taxi services also offer special hourly and long-distance rates. You will also see peso-taxis cruising (or rather limping) along Havana's streets; these are generally service taxis operating along scheduled routes and accept only pesos; they generally do not take tourists.

A specialized taxi service called **Gran Car Autos Antiguos** ((07) 577338 or 417980 operates nothing but vintage American cars from the 1940s and 1950s including DeSotos, Cadillacs, Chevy Bel Airs, Oldsmobiles, Pontiacs, Fords and Buicks. Most don't have meters, so you'll have to negotiate a rate at the start of your ride.

You can opt to see some of Havana's sights by tour bus, which can be a useful way of quickly familiarizing yourself with the city, and perhaps returning to some places on your own later. One of the best tours is run by **Rumbos** ((07) 669538 or 633466, which has a fleet of Mitsubishi buses offering air-conditioned comfort as you zoom around the city. Another city tour on offer is operated by **Tour and Travel** ((07) 247541 or 241549, which has various minibus tours daily. **Agencia Viajes San Cristóbal** ((07) 617191, Calle Oficios 110, offers daily walking tours of La Habana Vieja. The price of most tours is around US$10 and most hotels can book should be able to book you a place.

Havana's public buses, referred to as *guaguas* ("wah-wahs"), are very often two buses hitched together. Nicknamed *camelos* or camels because of their odd shape, they are not recommended for tourists. Many depart from the Parque de la Fraternidad.

Increasingly, the bright yellow tricycle taxis (or "*ciclotaxis*") have become a feature on Havana's streets, and these can be an enjoyable way to be whisked around, especially around La Habana Vieja and the Malecón. However, the rate should always be negotiated beforehand, and prices tend to be about the same as regular four-wheel taxis.

If you are feeling adventurous, you could experiment with renting a bicycle, which in Cuba tend to be the Chinese, one-speed "Flying Pigeon" variety. Most hotels will, after some discussion, be able to direct you how to go about renting a bicycle. **Panaciclo** ((07) 453746 or 810153, at the intersection of Avenida Rancho Boyeros and Santa Ana, near the Plaza de la Revolución,

Colonnades on the Plaza de Armas in Old Havana.

is a subsidiary of Panataxi, and rents out bicycles. But you'll have to be extra-cautious about the risk of reckless drivers, potholes and possibly of having it stolen, so be prepared for almost anything.

In La Habana Vieja and Centro Habana, the *calles* or streets have names in the familiar mode of any other European city — Obispo, Prado, San Rafael, and so on. In Vedado and Miramar, streets and avenues are identified by numbers or letters. First is closest to the seafront, and Third, Fifth and Seventh located progressively further inland. In Vedado, streets are known by the letters A through P towards the east, and by even numbers 2 through 28 running west. In Miramar, streets are also labeled with even numbers, from 0 to 100, east to west. Although it is quite straightforward to locate any given address, it is essential that you are sure of the district, to avoid unnecessary confusion.

WHAT TO SEE AND DO

The first two tours suggested below can be made on foot, and together they cover the most important places to visit in La Habana Vieja, which is easily the most interesting area to explore for visitors. The remaining tours are best made with a rental car or taxi, and cover Havana's main neighborhoods and places of interest, including the historic fortresses built to protect the bay. Be sure to check EXCURSIONS FROM HAVANA, page 157, for several highly rewarding trips that can be made within an afternoon, including a trip to Hemingway's house-museum, La Finca Vigía, and the nearby fishing village of Cojímar.

La Habana Vieja — A Walking Tour of the Old City

If time is short, you can conceivably manage this walking tour, which covers the main sights in La Habana Vieja, in one day. Or, if time permits, follow parts of this suggested tour at your leisure, perhaps over repeated wanderings in the old city.

The place to begin is **Plaza de Armas**, in many ways the crucible of Havana's colonial history. Facing the mouth of Havana Bay, it is ringed with baroque stone buildings, walls and columns that are astounding to behold at any time of day, but especially at

dawn and sunset or beneath a full moon. To the right is the four-sided **Castillo de la Real Fuerza** (Castle of the Royal Forces) ((07) 615010, considered to be the oldest stone fort in the Americas, and Spain's first fort in Cuba. What you see now is an elaboration of the original fort, first begun by Governor Hernando de Soto in 1538. It proved to be vulnerable to attack, and in 1555 an infamous French pirate by the name of Jacques de Sores took Havana within half an hour. His men pillaged and torched the entire city, terrorizing and slaughtering its citizens, taking

to the seas again laden with treasures. This event, and the constant threat of roaming pirates, prompted the Spanish King Felipe II, in 1558, to commission military engineer Bartolomé Sánchez to construct the new Castillo de la Real Fuerza, which took until 1582 to be fully completed.

A deep, greenish-watered moat spanned by a drawbridge surrounds its formidable, six-meter-thick (20-ft) walls. The fort was both the seat of Cuba's colonial government and the residence of the Commander-in-Chief until 1762. These days, its vault-like interiors house a permanent collection of works by Cuba's top artists and ceramists, including Wilfredo Lam, Amelia Peláez and Mariano Rodríguez. Open daily 8 AM to 4 PM.

Passing through the entrance, embellished with a crest of the royal arms, you can wander up to the fort's battlements for a panoramic view across the harbor to the horizon beyond. A bronze weathervane, known as **La Giraldilla**, stands in a narrow tower, and is regarded as a symbol of Havana (also appropriated on the Havana Club rum label). It has a sad history. After Hernando de Soto ordered the fort's construction he sailed away from Havana in 1539 to attempt to conquer Florida, leaving his wife, Doña Isabel de Bobadilla, behind as

Calles O'Reilly and Obispo. During the sixteenth century, this square was known as Plaza de la Iglesia, after what was then Havana's main church (demolished two centuries later). It was later named after the Real Fuerza's troops who paraded here every day. To commemorate this, every day at 4 PM, a troop dressed in eighteenth-century garb parades ceremonially through nearby streets in La Habana Vieja and around the square. Although a quaint sight, this parade is not worth going out of your way to see.

governor in his place. She thus became the first, and only, woman governor in Cuba's history. By all reports, Doña Isabel was much-loved by the people, as much for her good judgment as for her lovely appearance. After four years of waiting, she learned her husband had died days after discovering a great river, the Mississippi. She herself soon died, heartbroken. Cast in 1632, La Giraldilla is said to portray the sad woman scanning the horizon for some sign of her husband's return. There is a pleasant terrace coffee shop here with tranquil views of the harbor.

The Plaza de Armas, the oldest and perhaps the most beautiful civic square in Havana, stands at the sea-facing end of

After 1750, the city's colonial masters built a series of grand military and administrative buildings around the square, planting its center with royal palms, laurel trees, fragrant plants, fountains and pathways. By the nineteenth century, it was considered Havana's most fashionable meeting place, around which elegant, elongated horse-drawn carriages with huge wheels known as *volantes* clattered, and the city's elite strutted jauntily on their dusk promenades. These days, book-sellers tirelessly unpack cardboard crates for another day of commerce at **La Feria de Libros** (Book Fair) in this leafy square, hoping to interest tourists in ethno-

A lighthouse looms over the entrance to Havana's old harbor.

logical studies by Fernando Ortíz, battered texts by Marx, Lenin, Castro or Guevara, as well as exposés of the CIA and the KGB. You are equally likely to find certain booksellers are nationally recognized poets, so do not be so hasty or dismissive of them as mere hustlers. The centerpiece of the square is a statue of rebel leader, Carlos Manual de Céspedes.

On the west side of the Plaza de Armas facing the square, stands the formidable **Palacio de los Capitanes Generales** (Palace of the Commanders-in-Chief), from which some 65 successive Spanish colonial governors enforced their rule over the entire island. Later it became the presidential palace and then the town hall. It is now the **Museo de la Ciudad de la Habana** (City Museum) ℂ (07) 612876, Calle Tacón 1, La Habana Vieja. This magnificent example of Cuban-baroque architecture was commissioned in 1776 by then-governor and captain-general Marqués de la Torre. It took 100,000 bricks from Malaga, quantities of marble from Genoa, wrought iron from Bilbao and 15 years to be completed. Outside, to the left, is the statue of Spanish King Fernando VII that originally stood in the center of Plaza de Armas.

As you pass through the exterior arcade and huge arched entrance with its mahogany doorway, you enter a stately inner courtyard encircled by cavernous chambers that once served as government departments. Side annexes led to sections that were formerly coach houses, stables, guardrooms and an underground dungeon. Above, luxurious upper quarters crammed with rich furnishings, treasures and works of art were reserved for the governor and his family. Apparently, the unusual wooden paving on the street outside was devised to muffle passing carriage wheels so as not to disturb the governor's sleep.

Open to the elements, the courtyard is filled with a fragrant tropical garden, draped with flowered creepers, and planted with varieties of the royal palm, the national tree. A statue of Christopher Columbus stands in the center, some discarded cannon balls at his feet. This beautiful setting is frequently as a background for photographic portraits of *quinceañeras*, girls of fifteen on their coming-of-age celebration day, who pose in full-

makeup, frilly white dresses, stockings, hats, ribbons and high heels as their first day as a young lady is captured for posterity.

As museums go, this is one of the best to visit in Cuba, as much for the building itself, as for its rich historical collection — with paintings, furniture, ornate ceramics, decorations, colonial military uniforms and all manner of weaponry (including an unusual cannon made completely from leather), important documents, utensils and relics — displayed in its original context. Upstairs, aside from the plum-red throne room (intended for the King of Spain and never used), don't miss seeing the two enormous marble baths shaped like nautilus shell chariots and the glittering shards of light cast onto gilded mirrors by enormous chandeliers.

On the ground floor, a nineteenth-century model train waits to be sent spinning around its tracks. A room is dedicated to the fight against colonial imperialism, displaying both a fragment of the stone "Eagle of Imperialism" from the USS *Maine* monument and various Batista-era relics). You can also see a small bronze replica of La Giraldilla. Some speculate that the palace ought to have ghosts: not only was it constructed over the ruins of a church graveyard, but many slaves died in its construction. A plaque commemorates the death of a young beauty, Doña María de Cepero, who was accidentally killed in the courtyard in 1557 during a ritual firing round of harquebuses at a feast held in her honor. In addition, an open-air shaft reveals an mysterious metal casket adorned with a sword. Open daily 9:30 AM to 6:30 PM. Entrance costs US$3 (and US$2 extra for cameras). A guided tour costs US$1, and a small tip is often expected. You may want to buy the US$9 museum pass which can be used for admittance for all museums in Havana.

As you leave, to your left is the darker-hued Moorish-style baroque masterpiece **Palacio de Segundo Cabo** (Palace of the Second Lieutenant). Completed in 1772, it was originally used as the city's *casa de correos* (post office), then later used successively as the office of the royal estate and

TOP: The Mudéjar-style Palacio de las Ursulinas. BOTTOM: The Museo de la Ciudad de la Habana.

the court of justice, then finally as the residence of the second lieutenant, who was, in effect, the vice-governor. It now houses the offices of a government publishing institute, the Instituto Cubano del Libro, as well as the **Bella Habana** bookshop at street level. This beautiful building, with its row of neoclassical columns and two-story Andalusian-style courtyard is worth a look, and visitors can enter and go up to the first floor to wander around its gallery and look down into the courtyard; there's a US$1 charge if you want to take photographs.

From here, cross the square (passing the Castillo de la Real Fuerza on your right) to **El Templete**, a small neoclassical temple built in 1828 on what is regarded as the site where Havana, then San Cristóbal de la Habana, was founded. Next to it a *ceiba* (silk-cotton) tree, marks the spot where the city's first mass and town council meetings were held in 1519. It is said that the *ceiba* tree (one of a long line planted here, this one in 1959) has sacred powers, and that the spirit of the tree will grant your wish if you walk three times around the tree in silence. The Templete contains three large paintings by the French artist Jean-Baptiste Vermay, worth seeing for their portrayal of contemporary personalities and events in Havana. Vermay, who was a student of Jacques-Louis David, had studied in Florence and Rome and founded Havana's first art school. Both the artist and his wife died in Havana's 1833 cholera epidemic; their ashes are interred in an urn in front of the paintings.

Completing this side of the square is the **Palacio del Conde de Santovenia**, now transformed into the elegant Hotel Santa Isabel. It was the residence of the Count of Santovenia, whose nineteenth-century parties were the talk of Havana. At one, a hot-air balloon carrying revelers set off from the roof. In 1867, it was converted into the city's most exclusive hotel, and in many ways, this can also be said of its current incarnation, which has been beautifully restored and preserves a period ambience throughout and indeed is perhaps the loveliest hotel in Havana. Aside from the stone structure, which has been gleamingly scrubbed down, you can see the original grand interior

columns and stone staircases, as well as the restored crescents of tinted-glass known as *mediopuntos*.

On the plaza's southern flank is the fascinating but little-visited **Museo Nacional de Historia Natural** ((07) 620353, Calle Obispo 61, where amazingly life-like renditions of Cuban flora and fauna are on display. The collection is open Tuesday to Friday 10:30 AM to 5:30 PM, Saturday and Sunday 9 AM to 3 PM.

From here, follow the cobblestones down **Calle Obispo**, La Habana Vieja's main street, lined with grand old *palacios* and shops, painted up in candy-spiced stucco and festooned with delicate iron balconies as part of the old city's restoration project. Obispo has changed almost beyond recognition several times. It went from being the city's most fashionable shopping district to showcasing nothing but empty shelves, with only the most pathetic array of consumer items at its worst moment, while today, there is a proliferation of dollar-shops as well as new galleries and shops selling Cuban art. You will pass the restaurant **La Mina**, housed in a former girl's convent and the **Amistad** café, where, side-by-side, bands of musicians seem to be in full swing at almost any time of day.

Further along is **La Tinaja**, which during colonial times dispensed stone-filtered water from its underground source (originally discovered in 1544) and now sells glasses of mineral water. Next door is the nineteenth-century **Dulceria Doña Teresa** bakery, where you can buy fresh cakes and breadsticks. It is flanked by the **Oficina del Historidades de la Ciudad** (Office of the City Historian) at Calle Obispo 117, marked by a miniature copper galleon hanging above its doorway, with a bookshop at street level. This is notable as Havana's first residence, dating to 1570; you can peer inside a grilled gateway to see various artifacts in the courtyard, including a two-wheeled *volante*, the common means of transport in early colonial days. Next door, is the **Boutica Francesa de Santa Catalina**, an historic pharmacy with a beautiful wooden interior with rows of antique bottles.

At the corner of Calle Mercaderes, you will come to the **Hotel Ambus Mundos**. Ernest Hemingway spent long sabbaticals here before moving into La Finca Vigía. While staying in Room 511, he wrote *For Whom The Bell Tolls*, and the room is now a Hemingway shrine, displaying his typewriter, his shoes, books, fish-hooks and other memorabilia. You can ask to visit for a US$1 fee, and have the windows thrown open to see his majestic harbor view.

Opposite, you can see the stunning new **Hotel Florida**, renovated from the historic former Palacio de Joaquín Gómez.

If you are in need of a rest, try **La Casa de las Infusiones**, just around the corner on

At the corner of Calle Obrapía are three cultural institutes. **Casa de Benito Juárez** ((07) 618166 is a museum of Mexican art and culture funded by the Mexican government; it stages shifting exhibitions and musical performances. **Casa de la Obrapía** ((07) 613097, at no. 158, is a beautifully restored two-story seventeenth-century mansion, built on a grand scale by a wealthy philanthropist who gave the street its name (*obra pía* means "pious act"). It is now preserved as one of Havana's finest house museums, with fine painted frescoes, period

Calle Mercaderes, which serves excellent cappuccinos, and all types of teas. Down the street is the **Casa de Puerto Rico**, which also houses the small but interesting **Museo del Tabaco** with its exhibition of Cuban cigar wrappers and humidors; it is open Tuesday to Saturday 10:30 AM to 1 PM and Sunday 10:30 AM to 5 PM. At street level is the **Casa de Tabacos**, which is as good a place to buy cigars as any in La Habana Vieja. Both are located at Calle Mercaderes 120. One block south is the **Casa Simón Bolívar**, which houses the Venezuelan Embassy and the **Museo de Simón Bolívar**, which has a collection of paintings and artifacts from Venezuela, but is most impressive for its nineteenth-century interiors.

furniture and wall-hangings. It is open Tuesday to Saturday 10:30 AM to 5:30 PM, Sunday 9:30 AM to 12:30 PM.

Last but not least is the **Casa de Africa** ((07) 615798, at Calle Obrapía 157, also housed in a former colonial *palacio*, is a museum, gallery and study-center dedicated to Afro-Cuban history as well as the works of ethnologist Fernando Ortíz. Music and dance performances take place here on important Santería festival days. You can call ahead to check whether your visit coincides with any interesting events. There is a fantastic collection of paraphernalia used in various Santería and other African religions.

Straw hats for sale at the market in Old Havana.

Statues of the leading *orisha* divinities — Elegguá, Changó, Yemayá and Ochún — are surrounded by objects associated with them. Fidel himself made a triumphant tour through Africa in 1977, and many of the zebra skins, chief's chairs and other ceremonial gifts he brought back with him are displayed here, as are many contributions from the some 17 African embassies represented in Havana. It is open Monday to Saturday from 10:30 AM to 5 PM and Sunday from 9:30 AM to 1 PM.

From here, continue back along Calle Obrapía, and you will find **Casa Guayasamin** ((07) 613843, between Calle Mercaderes and Calle Oficios. This beautiful colonial mansion with its open interior courtyard is both an art gallery and home to Ecuadorian artist Oswaldo Guayasamin. If he is out of town, you can be guided through his living quarters upstairs, seeing original eighteenth-century wall frescoes as well as Guayasamin's portrait of Castro, given to *El Jefe* for his seventieth birthday. Havana's historian, Eusebio Leal, initiated a project wherein local children take painting lessons from the city's well-known artists here.

Turn left into Calle Oficios, one of the oldest streets in Havana, named for the *oficios de escribanos* or scribe's offices where early settlers could commission documents to be drawn up. On the left is the exotic Casa de los Arabes ((07) 615868, which in the late seventeenth century was purchased by the then-bishop Diego de Compostela to open as Havana's first school. It has a lovely interior courtyard and exhibits on Cuba's Arab immigrants. To your right is the Museo de Autos Antiguos (Vintage Car Museum), which displays a small, but diverse array of cars, with past owners ranging from Beny Moré to Che Guevara. However, you are likely to see equally remarkable old cars parked on Havana's streets.

Turn into Calle Justiz, which has several places of interest: the **Casa de la Comedia**, one of the city's oldest buildings; the **Salon Ensayo**, founded in 1990, which showcases Cuban dramatic talent; and the characterful **Caserón de Tango**, where gray-haired aficionados celebrate the dance with agile

Milling crowds and craft wares at the street market on the Plaza de la Catedral.

enthusiasm. From here, a left-hand turn along Calle Baratillo brings you back to Plaza de Armas and Calle Obispo.

From Calle Obispo, continue west one block, turn right on Calle San Ignacio and walk two blocks, crossing Calle O'Reilly (named after the Irish General who gave the key to Havana back to the Spanish in 1763) until you reach the other great square in Havana, the Plaza de la Catedral. It is adorned with some of the prettiest and most sophisticated examples of colonial baroque palacios to be seen, with sternly solid stone

miles) away — was situated. The people of Havana once collected their drinking water here, commemorated by a late sixteenth-century plaque. Today, the small side street is lined with artist's galleries, including a government collective.

To your left as you approach the cathedral is the site of Havana's first public baths, it now houses the **Galería Victor Manuel** ((07) 612955, a well-stocked arts and crafts gallery. Next door is the sixteenth-century **Palacio de los Marquesas de Aguas Claras**, lived in by a series of well-born, well-con-

exteriors belied by enormous loggias, coquettish stained-glass windows, brightly painted shutters and tiny romantic balconies. Despite the crowds of stalls, hawkers and tourists, it is still easy to imagine that these mansions were once places of splendid retreat for the Creole aristocracy.

During Havana's early colonial period, this spot was so flood-prone that it was referred to as the Plazuela de la Ciénaga, or "the Little Square of the Swamp." But all that changed when this became the site of the first Spanish aqueduct in the New World. When you enter the square, look to your left to see where the Zanja Real (Royal Aqueduct) — an irrigation channel which carried water from the Almendares River, 11 km (about seven

nected Spanish colonists. Now it is the restaurant El Patio, which has the best vistas across the square.

Havana's cathedral, **La Catedral de la Virgen María de la Concepción Inmaculada**, to give its full name, dominates the northern end of the square. Its eccentric, almost whimsical asymmetry somehow only enhances its majesty. "Music turned to stone," breathed Cuban novelist Alejo Carpentier, adding that the baroque façade was "huge, but not fine, old yet not ancient, dilapidated and, as it were, worm-eaten." It was almost entirely built by the Jesuits, whose work on this site began in 1748, but after the order was expelled in 1767, the Spanish crown took over the cathedral's completion.

Its weathered, six-column façade is flanked by two unmatched bell towers, and seems to change its mood with the light. For over a century a casket containing what were believed to be the mortal remains of Christopher Columbus was kept in the cathedral, after being transferred from Santo Domingo — after Hispaniola (now Haiti and the Dominican Republic) passed to France in 1795 — and before being taken to Seville in 1898. The cathedral is open Monday to Friday, 9 AM to 11 AM, then 2:30 PM to 6 PM, and for Mass on Sunday, 9 AM to 11 AM.

As you stand at the cathedral door looking back onto the square, the first building to your left is the grand, arcaded **Casa de Lombillo**, lived in by various colonial aristocrats, including a somewhat notorious slave-trader after whom the building is named. Notable for its exterior decorative paintings, it now houses the **Museo de la Educación** (Museum of Literacy) ((07) 615468, Calle Empedrado 151, which proudly documents Castro's 1960s *campagna de alfabetizacion* (literacy campaign).

The palace facing the cathedral is the **Casa de Chacón**, an eighteenth-century building that was built for the island's then-governor, Don Luis Chacón. Its unembellished simplicity makes it look more ancient than other buildings in the square. It has been used variously as offices, first for notaries, and later a newspaper and a rum manufacturer. Now it houses the **Museo de Arte Colonial** (Museum of Colonial Art) ((07) 626440, Calle San Ignacio 61. It is crammed with a fascinating profusion of architectural details and household ware: stained-glass *vitrales* and *mediopuntos*, carved furniture, elaborate door-knockers, wrought-iron lamps, silver, porcelain, marble baths, varieties of the quirky carriages known as *volantes*, and an entire set of *caoba*-wood bedroom furniture. It is open daily from 10:15 AM to 7 PM.

A block away from the square, on Calle Empedrado, you will see the sign for the **Bodeguita del Medio**. Although everything else has changed since Hemingway's time, his favorite drink here, the famous *mojito* (a mix of rum, lemon juice, crushed mint leaves, soda water and sugar) remains excellent, although for some reason, the bar upstairs seems to produce a superior version. Errol

Flynn's remark that this was "the best place to get drunk" seems to remain an apt one. Despite an abortive bomb attempt in 1997, which caused non-fatal injuries and considerable damage to the interiors, which have since been revamped, La Bodeguita is perennially popular, with visitors eager to add their signature scrawl to walls already crammed with graffiti. Although it is a tourist trap, it is nonetheless fun, especially when the crowds thin out later in the evening.

Leaving La Bodeguita, retrace your steps towards the cathedral, and turn left into

Calle San Ignacio. Continue to walk along the side of the cathedral, and beside it, you will see the **Semanario de San Carlos y San Ambrosio**, with its huge façade facing the bay. It, like the cathedral, was built by the Jesuits. It has an exceptionally beautiful and peaceful inner garden, lined with columns and full of trees and vines — frangipani, ginger-lilies, and many varieties of palms — bounded by ancient stairwells.

Continue along, and near the intersection of Calle Cuba and Calle Tacón, opposite the ruins of Havana's colonial armory, is the

OPPOSITE: Ernest Hemingway drank his *mojitos* at the Bodeguita del Medio. ABOVE: Detail of Havana's cathedral, built by the Jesuits in the eighteenth century, prior to their expulsion from Cuba in 1767.

Palacio de la Artesanía (Palace of the Artisans) ((07) 338072. This charming colonial mansion has been converted into a shopping complex, with several floors in which you can browse for recordings of Cuban musicians, coral jewelry, beaded necklaces, Che Guevara T-shirts, rum and embroidered tablecloths under less pressure to buy than in the Plaza de la Catedral.

A Second Walking Tour of Old Havana

From Plaza de Armas, a two-minute stroll along Calle Oficios brings you to **Plaza de San Francisco de Asís**, a graceful, wide-open square facing the city's main port and dock warehouses, with a central stone fountain adorned with lion statues. Gleaming from a spate of recent restoration, the square is enclosed by various historic buildings. To the left is the Italian Renaissance-inspired **Lonja de Comercio**, built in the early twentieth century and now renovated into a swanky office complex, with Café Mercurio on the ground floor. Opposite are several symbols of creeping consumerism: a Benetton franchise and the "Novio Wedding Shop" specializing in wedding finery that looks straight out of a Fellini film. You may want to stop for a cappuccino at the nineteenth-century style Café del Oriente.

Although the order of San Francisco de Asís was founded in 1563, the majestic **Iglesia de San Francisco de Asís** was constructed much later during the 1730s, above an earlier, modest hermitage. Its 40-m-high (130-ft), three-tiered bell tower was added as an afterthought. During the English occupation of Havana this church was commandeered by the Earl of Ablemarle as a place of Protestant worship. Afterwards it was largely shunned by the devout Catholics of Havana, who even let it be used it as a military warehouse. Today however, classical concerts are frequently held within its immense barrel-vaulted interior, and you can often hear singers practicing. A passage leads to the portico cloisters of the adjacent convent, which in 1915 was converted into a telephone exchange. Part of the cloisters displays gilt-accented statues, bejeweled crosses and delicate ceramics. It is a lovely place to linger in the quiet of the afternoon. If a choral performance in the church coincides with your

stay, try to attend: a notice of upcoming performances (usually held at 6 PM on Saturdays) is posted at the church's main entrance. Entrance costs US$2.

Across the way, looking towards the port, you'll see the **Terminal Sierra Maestra**, the city's main cruise terminal.

At the corner of Calles Oficios and Brasil (Teniente Rey), you will reach the **Convento de Santa Clara**, a renovated seventeenth-century convent, encircled by an imposing wall, between Calles Sol and Luz. It was founded as a haven for young dowry-less women who had no other prospects, and built to house hundreds of nuns and slaves. It is now the headquarters of Cuba's **Centro Nacional de Conservación, Restauración, y Museología** (CENCREM), the institute responsible for the

country's conservation research, training and architectural preservation. The center was founded in 1982, the same year UNESCO recognized the international historical and archaeological value of La Habana Vieja by declaring it a World Heritage Site. The center is open Monday to Friday from 9 AM to 4 PM. Next door, a small seventeenth-century house that is part of the convent, **Casa del Marino**, has been renovated for visiting scholars.

From here, follow Calle Brasil (Teniente Rey) until you reach **Plaza Vieja** (Old Square), which after Plaza de Armas and Plaza de Catedral, is one of the city's three great squares. Unlike the other squares, it is not dominated by churches or government buildings, but is purely residential. Begun in the late sixteenth century, it became home to many wealthy families, although many of the existing Creole *palacios*, with their arched *portales*, curved stained-glass windows and filigree balconies, were built a century later. Markets used to be held in its grand square, peasants and freed slaves selling meats, vegetables and fruits. In recent years Plaza Vieja has undergone dramatic renovation, involving the removal of a subterranean parking lot (added in 1952), renovation of former *palacios* into cultural centers and apartments, and the addition of a hotel, as well as a cinema and shops.

One of restored mansions that now has the appearance of emerging unblemished from the eighteenth century is the **Casa de**

The recently restored sixteenth-century Plaza Vieja.

los Condes de Jaruco at Calle Muralla 107-111 between Calles Inquisidor and San Ignacio. It was built in the late seventeenth century by the Count of San Juan de Jaruco, whose taste in interior and exterior decoration was clearly exuberant and whimsical. Lyres, fruit, flowers and scrolls embellish the mansion's walls, offset by a giant entrance hall; carved *rejas* or fretted windows bar the upper gallery, but allow a gentle breeze. Look out for the macabre lock fashioned in the form of a female slave. The building now houses the **Cuban Foundation for the Fine Arts**, and the ground-floor gallery is a good place to start looking if you are interested in buying works by Cuban artists. On the other side of the square, is the **Casa de Esteban José Portier**, which is now a photographic gallery. Art nouveau admirers should look out for **Hotel Palacio Vienna** at the corner of Calles Muralla and Inquisidor, recently unveiled from scaffolding and divided up into apartments.

From here Calle Muralla, heading west, will lead you to Calle Cuba. By continuing south several blocks, passing the Convento de Santa Clara, you will come to the Gothic **Iglesia Parroquial del Espíritu Santo**, Havana's oldest church and one of the most moving to visit, full of architectural quirks and surprises. It was originally a hermitage built in 1638, and was dedicated to "the devotions of free Negroes." Inside is a statue of Saint Barbara, the Catholic saint associated with Changó, the god of fire, thunder, passion and dance in the Santería religion. On each side of the church nave is a small catacomb; the more recent one dates from 1783 and is decorated by macabre fresco paintings featuring skulls adorned with tiaras and miters. The church was popular among sailors and travelers, who used to pray for a safe voyage here.

If you turn right on Calle Acosta you will pass the monumental **Convento de Nuestra Señora de Belén**, which occupies the entire block. Look for the **Arco de Belén** (Belén Archway), and head for Calle Leonor Pérez (Paula), where you will find the tiny, yellow-painted **Casa Natal de José Martí** ((07) 613778, where the nation's great independence hero was born in 1853. It is now a house museum which details his life and times. It is open Tuesday to Saturday from 9 AM to 5 PM, Sunday from 9 AM to 1 PM, and is closed Monday.

Opposite the neo-Moorish **Estación Centrale de Ferrocarriles** (Central Railway Station) exhibits *La Junta*, a European-style 1843-model steam engine, Cuba's first.

From here, you can take a look at Havana's **Mercado Central** (Central Market), located opposite the Railway Station. This is the city's largest and most patronized market, but the image of plenty is somewhat misleading. What people can't afford to purchase, either with their ration books, pesos or dollars, they come to look at.

It's a chaotic scene, with live roosters and chickens, goats and tortoises; piles of vegetables; tins of sweetened condensed milk, flowers and medicinal herbs. Outside, rows of *habaneros* sit on hemp sacks, some trying to sell just a single item, such as an old rusty lock, or to barter possessions for food. Young boys sell re-filled plastic lighters that most often contain fly-spray or solvents.

From here, you can either take Calle Leonor Pérez as a shortcut or meander along the seafront Désamparados. Look for the former **Iglesia Antigua de San Francisco de Paula**, now used as a small exhibition space. Further along, near the seafront Avenida Paula, at the corner of Calles Acosta and Oficios, is the **Centro Wilfredo Lam** ((07) 623305, an important cultural and arts center and the sponsor of the Havana Biennial. It is open Monday to Friday, and every other Sunday from 8:30 AM to 4:30 PM.

From here, take Calle Oficios back into the heart of La Habana Vieja, or perhaps make a detour along Avenida San Pedro (Avenida del Puerto) to stop for a drink at the **Bar Dos Hermanos**, an atmospheric place where locals like to unwind. It is named for the two American brothers who were former proprietors during the Batista years.

Parque Central and the Prado

This walking tour begins at Parque Central, where the edges of the old city blur with the new. Suddenly the architecture is from a different era, streets widen into boulevards, hulking makeshift buses lumber to a halt for yet more passengers, people stand in line outside government department stores. Formerly called the Parque de Isabela, the leafy, dilapidated Parque Central has a statue of José Martí as its centerpiece. Although lovely, it's hard to ignore the park's somewhat desperate ambience. This being said, unlike many of Havana's other main squares, it is also a gathering place for Cubans rather than tourists, and consequently you'll often see groups of men of all ages playing chess or discussing baseball results, and office workers having a break. Hawkers sell twists of salted peanuts along the dank, tree-lined boulevard.

Looming over the park is the ornate whitewashed façade of the 1927 **Centro Asturiano**, which now houses the international collection of the **Museo Nacional de Bellas Artes** ℂ (07) 620141 WEB SITE www .museonacional.cult.cu. Opened in the summer of 2001, the museum boasts works by a number of the European masters including Murillo, Zurbaran, Gainsborough, Reynolds and Turner, as well as displays of Egyptian antiquities, Greek sculpture and Roman decorative arts. There are also rooms dedicated to South and North American art. Many of the paintings and sculptures were left behind by wealthy Cubans who fled the Revolution, and this marks the first time they have been on public display. "They donated us their properties," Fidel Castro declared during the museum's ribbon-cutting ceremony. "Thank you very much!" The museum is open Tuesday to Saturday 10 AM to 6 PM, Sunday from 9 AM to 1 PM. Admission is US$5, but you can purchase a combined ticket to both branches of the Bellas Artes for US$8.

A few steps away, at the beginning of Calle Obispo is **El Floridita**. El Floridita is one of Havana's fixtures. More than 70 years ago, the frozen *daiquirí* was created here by barman Constante Ribailagua. But it was Hemingway who made daiquiris famous, and this is where he drank them; you can see the Napoleonic-style barstool where he sat. In Havana's giddy pre-Revolution days, El Floridita was all the rage, and its enthusiasts also included Gary Cooper, Ingrid Bergman, Tennessee Williams, Jean Paul Sartre, Marlene Dietrich, Spencer Tracy and Ava Gardner. Like the Bodeguita del Medio, it is a tourist trap, but worth at least one visit, and sampling its truly delicious daiquiri is a must. Above El Floridita, you can sample

and buy most brands of Cuban rum at the **Casa de Ron**.

Across the street is the **Manzana de Gómez**, a turn-of-the-century department store occupying the entire block, once filled with the latest Paris fashions but now rather desolate and empty. From here, a few steps take you into the lobby of the charming nineteenth-century **Hotel Plaza**, where you can take a lift up to its top floor terrace and perhaps have a cold drink while admiring the view, which looks back into parts of La Habana Vieja and across Centro Habana. As

you walk around the terrace, you'll have an excellent view of the **Edificio Bacardí**, built in 1929 for the rum and sugar tycoon, Emilio Bacardí, and the most impressive art deco building in Cuba, decorated with beautiful ceramic tiles and stylized nymphs. It has been restored as an office building and is leased out to foreign companies.

Back on the street, at the corner of Calle Animas, look out for the mosaic in the pavement and for **Sloppy Joe's**. As legendary in its own time as El Floridita, fictionalized by Hemingway as Freddy's Bar in his *To Have and To Have Not*, it now awaits restoration before reopening to quench the thirst of new admirers.

Grandmother and grandchild in the Callejón de Hamel, Central Havana.

Heading back to the Parque Central, you'll see the extravagant, neo-baroque façade of the **Hotel Inglaterra**, opposite. This is Havana's oldest hotel, first opened in 1884. It has been restored, and its dining room and patio are cool havens of patterned tiles, potted palms and stained glass. At its side, across a small alley, is the **Gran Teatro de la Habana** ((07) 613078, formerly known as the Centro Gallego, built as a private club for descendents of Galician immigrants. This extraordinary architectural confection is a wonderful, slightly surreal sight, full of neo-baroque ornamentation, with statues depicting illustrious muses and winged angels atop each of its four towers. The Gran Teatro was an ambitious renovation of Havana's former nineteenth-century Tacón Theatre, which was absorbed into the new design by its Austrian architect, Paul Belau. Inside, grand staircases and elaborate marble detailing were once the backdrop for the club's libraries and its smoking, billiard and dining rooms. A performance of Aida marked the inauguration of the club in 1915. Today, this is where the Ballet Nacional de Cuba performs.

It is impossible to miss the nearby **Capitolio**. Built in 1928, it is the spitting image of the United States Capitol, although it was styled by Cuban architects. The Capitolio was intended to be the sparkling centerpiece of that democracy-averse dictator, Geraldo Machado, and he spent a quarter of his US$50 million annual budget on it. Like the original, it is magisterially lined with marble, and has two long lateral galleries leading from a central vestibule. A compass set into an inlaid rose on the floor beneath the 91-m-high (300-ft) dome marks the point from which distances from Havana are measured. Looming beneath the vaulted ceiling is a massive bronze statue representing the Cuban Republic. Guided tours (for US$3) run through its grandiose interior, now a technical library, into the former presidential offices and halls of the pre-Revolution Cuban congress. The Capitolio is open Monday to Saturday from 9 AM to 5 PM.

To the left of the Capitolio is the **Parque de la Fraternidad**, which is chiefly known these days as a gathering place for freelance *taxis particulars* or private taxis. These are no ordinary taxis, as their proud owners will attest. On an average day there is an extraordinary line-up of antique American cars, with Chevrolets, Buicks, Plymouths, Packards and Studebakers in various states of polish and still-operable decay. For car buffs, this is a good place to meet your fellow Cuban enthusiasts. Opposite the square is the **Palacio de Aldama**, possibly Havana's most splendidly decorative example of an aristocratic nineteenth-century residence, with ornate neoclassical frescoes, intricate carvings and a beautiful cloistered patio. It is now the **Instituto de Historia del Movimiento Obrero de Cuba** (Cuba's Worker's Movement) which, unfortunately, is not generally open to the public.

Tucked behind the Capitolio and the Parque de la Fraternidad, on Calle Industria, is the **Fábrica Partagas**, one of the oldest and largest cigar factories in Cuba. You can take a guided tour through the building's several floors, where cigars are handmade from the sorting of leaves to the packaging, or simply browse from the extensive and well-stocked array of cigars, and sample their delicious expresso coffee in the shop. It is open for tours Monday to Friday, from 9 AM to 3 PM. Guided tours are at 10:30 AM and 1:30 PM, for US$5. The shop is also open on Saturday.

From here, retrace your steps past the Hotel Inglaterra, and you will find yourself facing the **Paseo del Martí** (also known as Paseo del Prado), a raised boulevard lined with laurel trees, statues, wrought-iron lamp posts and coral-rock benches laid out in the late seventeenth century. For two centuries, this promenade was frequently a crush of horses and carriages. It was the favored meeting place for an hour or two of decorous dalliance by Havana's high society, while military musicians in bright uniforms marched up and down playing overtures, polkas and marches. Often referred to as the Prado, this boulevard remains a popular place to stroll, and there's always something interesting to see. About half-way down, there is a sort-of open-air housing bureau which specializes in "*Se Permuta*" ("For Swap"), where people animatedly discuss swapping their house or apartment for another property, either in Havana or in another part of Cuba — the only legal way Cubans are allowed to move, with no cash

changing hands. You might see a wedding party file out of the **Palacio de Matrimonio**, the grand mansion that conducts civil weddings at the corner of Calle Animas, where shining Chevrolets festooned with bouquets and streamers are the day's chariot of choice. Teachers gossip while their charges play; urchins compete with their homemade skateboards. On either side, the Prado is also architecturally interesting, full of once-aristocratic mansions and quirky residential façades, many of them *ciudadelas*, or home to a dozen or so families.

As you walk towards the Malecón, to the right you will see the back of the **Hotel Sevilla**, the former Sevilla-Biltmore, another of the city's classic and beautifully restored nineteenth-century hotels, which is where Graham Greene had his character Wormold stay in Room 507 while on his beleaguered undercover mission, in *Our Man in Havana*.

Just beyond the Sevilla lurks a huge modern building that houses the domestic collection of the **Museo Nacional de Bellas Artes** (National Art Museum) ((07) 613858 or 620140 WEB SITE www.museonacional .cult.cu. Originally built in 1954, the building

OPPOSITE: Paseo del Martí was once an elegant place to see and be seen. ABOVE: Edificio Bacardí is Havana's finest example of art deco.

was in sorry repair by the mid-1990s when the Cuban government decided to sink US$14.5 million into a total renovation. The result — in terms of both the architecture and the art inside — is nothing short of stunning, perhaps the finest art museum in all of Latin America and certainly one of the most pleasant to visit. All of Cuba's top artists are represented including Victor Manuel, Guillermo Collazo, Wilfredo Lam, René Portocarrero and Amelia Pelaez, Antonia Eiriz. Don't miss the Revolution-era pop art paintings of Raúl Martínez, who surely must have

used by Fidel Castro in Playa Girón during the Bay of Pigs invasion. The museum has an exhaustive display that covers Cuba's history from Spanish colonization to the wars of independence and the subsequent Republican era. Then, having set the scene for the Cuban Revolution, it proceeds to detail almost everything you ever wanted to know about Fidel, his modus operandi in the Moncada Barracks and the Sierra Maestra and his triumph as *El Jefe* over the Bay of Pigs debacle. The profusion of charts, maps and 3-D models of battle sites is fascinating, and the

taken his inspiration from Andy Warhol. The museum is open Tuesday to Saturday 10 AM to 6 PM, Sunday from 9 AM to 1 PM. Admission is US$5, but you can purchase a combined ticket to both branches of the Bellas Artes for US$8.

Farther along the Prado, at Calle Refugio 1, is the former **Palacio Presidencial**, notable as the place where Batista only just escaped being lynched when it was attacked by 40 students in March 1957 — he hid in an elevator shaft. Built in 1920, this Spanish Revival former presidential palace is now the **Museo de la Revolución** ((07) 624091, with three floors devoted to what it describes on its pamphlet as "the natural rebellion of the Cuban people." At the entrance is a tank

photographs are evocative: an American marine drunkenly urinating on a statue of José Martí, Celia Sánchez gravely loving look towards her comrade-lover Fidel in the depths of the jungle, the many faces of Che Guevara. Touching remnants are preserved: the blood-stained uniforms of unlucky revolutionaries, Che's black beret and his asthma inhaler, Fidel's trousers, Celia's shirt. A bizarre touch is added by the mock *mise en scène* capturing the moment when Che and Camilo Cienfuegos emerged from the mountains, leading their horses — their *actual* horses, which were stuffed for posterity.

Outside, in an open-air glass-walled pavilion, sits the *Granma*, the famous leaky cabin cruiser in which Fidel, and 81 other revolutionaries, including his brother Raúl and Che, returned to Cuba from their exile in Mexico. Trying to visualize how all these men actually managed to fit themselves aboard this modestly sized boat is something of a mental challenge. Other icons of the Revolution include the delivery van used by the students in their raid against Batista, pieces of an American B-26 shot down over the Bay of Pigs, and a U-2 reconnaissance plane downed by Russian missiles during the Cuban Missile Crisis. The museum is open daily from 10 AM to 6 PM.

From here you can stroll out towards the Malecón. As you leave the museum, to your left you'll see the white **Iglesia de Santo Ángel Custodia** (Church of the Holy Angel Savior), largely destroyed by a hurricane in 1844. Gothic spires were added as part of its nineteenth-century restoration; the extravagant art nouveau architectural confection is now used as the Spanish Embassy. At the northern end of Avenida de las Misiones at Calle Capdevila 1 is the **Museo Nacional de la Música** (Music Museum) ((07) 619846, which has an extensive collection of Cuban instruments as well as a shop selling CD and cassette recordings. It's open Monday to Saturday 10 AM to 5:45 PM, Sunday 8 AM to noon.

The avenue continues down to the seafront, and beyond the mounted statue of the Cuban independence hero, General Máximo Gómez, is the small fortress of **Castillo de San Salvador de la Punta**, known by all as "La Punta."

Centro Habana
Central Havana, often referred to by *habaneros* as "Centro," stretches between its boundary with the Malecón, the Paseo del Prado, which connects it to La Habana Vieja, and the Calzada de Infanta, which marks its border with the district of Vedado. While there are few obvious attractions for tourists, sections of Centro Habana are interesting, for this was Havana's former commercial district. Today, plenty of street life spills out from its run-down, turn-of-the-century apartments and depressed-looking shops. Most of it is safe to walk around in, although it is disreputable in parts, which you should be alert to. Avoid this area at night, when it is almost completely blacked-out, with no streetlights. If you are driving, the main streets — Calles San Rafael, Zanja, Neptuno and San Lázaro — provide a fast route through the district.

Centro's main shopping district is along **Calle San Rafael**, which begins behind the Hotel Inglaterra, and is a somewhat miserable medley of 1950s-era department stores. The furtive spirit of free enterprise is more in evidence on the streets, with people offering things for sale, such as newspaper twists of peanuts, shots of *guarapo* (sugarcane juice), or Santería amulets.

At the intersection of Calles San Rafael and Galiano, continue until you reach Calle Dragones, then turn on Calle Zanja. This will bring you to Havana's own Barrio Chino or **Chinatown**, centered on **Calle Cuchillo**, a block-long street that runs between Calles Zanja and San Nicolás, a few blocks west of the Capitolio. This unexpected part of Havana is all that is left of a once-thriving district that was traditionally home to many thousands of Chinese immigrants during the nineteenth century. Many of these immigrants came from Guangdong Province and were imported — albeit voluntarily — as workers on Cuba's sugar plantations. They

School children cluster on Paseo del Martí.

faced tremendous hardships once they arrived and discovered they had become virtual slaves. Many moved either to Havana or Santiago de Cuba to establish themselves as traders. Many Chinese *habaneros* chose to leave Cuba after the Revolution, and now only around 700 remain.

Although this is not one of Havana's obvious attractions, it is interesting to explore this tiny section — which used to be a thriving tourist attraction in the 1950s — and see its remaining shops, restaurants and pharmacies. Look out for the ornate, dragon-festooned **Restaurant Pacifico** (on Calles San Nicolás and Cuchillo); the **Casino Chino**, the headquarters of the **Mi Chang Society** (a brotherhood founded 400 years ago, which has 300 active members); and the office of the **Partido Democrata Chino**.

It's too far to walk from here, but you must include a visit to **Callejón Hamel**, which lies between Calles Hospital and Aramburo, best reached from the nearby Malecón. It is known for one of its residents, the painter **Salvador**, an easily recognizable figure with his white beard, light skin and head of gray curls. He has a small gallery here, but it's his work outside that's better known: Salvador is Havana's best-known muralist and has used the city's dilapidated walls as his canvases for many years. His bright, bold murals have a folkloric quality, charged with painted words and phrases and the best place to admire them is this narrow road, also called by some, Callejón de Filin ("Street of Feeling"). Come on Sunday to see the neighborhood transformed by Santería dances accompanied by musicians playing rumba.

The Malecón

The sweeping Malecón is Havana's much-loved and most recognizable feature, a constant symbol of its enduring attachment to the sea. Tightly packed around a splendid bay, its famously decayed mansions and apartments resemble a curving stage set on the sea rim, open to the immense emptiness of the horizon. It stretches seven kilometers (just over four miles) between the La Punta fortress and the mouth of the Almendares River, and is the fastest route from La Habana Vieja to Vedado as well as to Mira-

mar. You might want to walk part of the way, and explore the rest by taxi.

Laid out in 1901, the Malecón's sea wall is fronted by an arcaded row of sea-pocked mini-mansions, each house different from the next: Moorish-domed windows, mosaics, calligraphic iron balconies, crumbling stone caryatids, and heavy carved doors. Seen from a distance, the paint on the stone buildings fades into a nostalgic patchwork of soft pastels. Up close, their former brilliance (pink trimmed with purple, green with cobalt, blue with yellow) has been worn away by salt, heat and high humidity, not to mention periodic hurricanes.

At times, the Malecón has a festive air, an almost giddy mood of camaraderie. On hot days, children (and adults) flirt with the salty

sea spray, shrieking with glee when they are drenched, and dare-devils launch themselves off the rocks and then clamber back to shore. A popular salsa song on a crackly sound system gets its listeners on their feet for an impromptu dance. Lycra-clad young women drape themselves on the sun-warmed wall, chatting among themselves, keeping an eye out for admirers. At other times, it can seem almost desolately sad, when, as your late-night taxi speeds back to the hotel, you see a small army of disturbingly young *jiniteras* in micro-skirts and spandex.

The promenade has many guises, changing with the light and the color of the sea and sky. When the tropical storms rage, the waves can knock pedestrians off their feet, and sometimes sweep cars across the pave-ment. On still, clear days, you can see sun-scorched men casting themselves into the sea in inflated tires (the same used by the *balseros* or rafters) in their attempts to catch a meal for their families. The Malecón itself is changing quickly, for as part of Havana's restoration program, 14 square blocks of the Malecón are scheduled to be rehabilitated and work has already begun, as evidenced by the transformation of the Catyrid's House, close to La Punta, now the Spanish government's office for cultural affairs. The project is estimated to eventually cost US$50 million, of which more than a half has been pledged by the Spanish government.

As you continue along the seafront promenade, you'll see the **USS *Maine* Monument**,

The former Palacio Presidencial was completed in 1920.

just west of the Hotel Nacional, constructed in memory of the 267 sailors who died when the American warship exploded in Havana Bay in 1898. Shortly after the Revolution, jubilant anti-American crowds knocked off the stone eagle that used to adorn this monument. Its broken wings can now be seen in the Museo de la Ciudad de la Habana. The *Maine* has a different meaning in Cuba than in the United States. "To the victims of the *Maine* who were sacrificed to imperialist greed in its fervor to seize control of the island of Cuba," reads the inscription at the

base of the monument. The head of the stone eagle is now mounted on the wall of the snack bar at the American Interests Section, Washington's quasi-embassy in Havana.

As the Malecón curves still further on, it is impossible to miss the seven-story mirror-plated, hermetically sealed **United States Special Interests Section**. In the sort of quirk to be expected given the political stand-off between Cuba and the United States, the building is in fact, sub-leased to the American government by the Swiss Embassy, and a similar arrangement characterizes Cuba's Special Interest's Section in Washington.

Continuing along the Malecón, various places of interest loom into view: the **Calixto García monument**; the art deco **Casa de las**

Américas ((07) 323587, at the corner of Calle 3 and Avenida G, founded in 1959 as a forum to showcase cultural exchanges between Cuba and Latin America; and the open-air **Mercado Feria Malecón**, where you can browse among old political comic books, 1950s movie posters, curios and many second-hand goods. It has a very Cuban atmosphere and is open daily except Monday.

You can turn off the Malecón momentarily to see the **Museo de Artes Decoratives** (Museum of Decorative Arts) ((07) 308037, Calles 17 and E, housed in the former man-

sion of the Countess Revilla de Camargo, a famous lady about town. It has a charming and in many ways exceptional display of important European and Oriental decorative arts from the eighteenth century through to the twentieth century. You can admire the rococo gilt neoclassical hall that was once the Countess's bedroom. The museum is open Tuesday to Saturday from 11 AM to 6:30 PM.

Two hotels come next, both symbols in their own way of their own era, representing the Cuban tourism industry, past and present. First is the **Meliá Cohiba**, considered one of the most up-to-date and luxurious hotels in Cuba. Further along is the 20-story **Habana Riviera**, which had major backing from the Mafia when it opened as a hotel-casino in

1957, just before the Revolution took over and dashed their expectations that Havana was about to become the next Las Vegas. Mob boss Meyer Lansky lived in the top-floor suite, which is now the hotel's business center with staggering views across the sea.

Farther west, beyond the spot where the Malecón dips down into the underground tunnel, lays the district of Miramar. Just before you enter the tunnel, to your right you can see the small **Torreón de Santa Dorotea de Luna de la Chorrera**, a seventeenth-century fort that was part of the city's protec-

century that the forests were razed, to make way for larger and more modernized homes for Havana's elite who had began to desert La Habana Vieja, a phenomenon which accelerated during the 1930s. Many elaborate stone mansions — some small palaces — date from the art deco and art nouveau period, mostly one or two stories high, with decorative patios and eclectic stucco façades often bearing French, Italian and even Mayan designs. During the 1950s, when reinforced concrete was all the rage, the Hilton, Riviera and Capri hotels as well as the hulk-

tive phalanx. Near the fort's parapet is **Restaurante 1830**, housed in an elegant white colonial mansion, and you can stop at its open-air terrace to enjoy a much-deserved drink and the view.

Vedado and La Rampa

Along the Malecón, mid-way between La Habana Vieja and the tunnel to Miramar, lies the district known as **Vedado**, which is now Havana's business district with many commercial offices, including agencies for airlines and tour companies. During the early colonial era, this area was deliberately left densely forested as an additional deterrent to pirates, to protect the city from attack by land as well as by sea. It was not until early this

ing FOCSA building, rose on Vedado's skyline, along with New York-inspired high-rise apartment blocks and prefabricated-looking government offices.

Laid out like a chessboard in grid-like squares with streets identified by numbers or letters, this immense neighborhood is easy to wander around in and offers compelling glimpses of its former glory amid its ugly tower blocks. Off its main avenues, tranquil streets reveal many lived-in scenes of Havana life: falling-down mansions where frangipani trees blossom in the hot shadows, and

OPPOSITE LEFT: The Hotel Nacional, a Havana icon, was inaugurated in 1930. OPPOSITE RIGHT AND ABOVE: Nineteenth-century Hotel Sevilla played a role in Graham Green's *Our Man in Havana*.

bedraggled, tail-down dogs find respite from insults while old ladies in frayed dresses keep vigil on their verandahs, their world-weary eyes softening at the sight of their grandchildren. For many exiled Cubans who fled after the fall of Batista, Vedado *is* Cuba, or at least the Cuba they remember as children. Fluttering laundry suggests that these once-stylish private houses are now multiple dwellings. During the early days of the Revolution, the Castro government ordered enforced squatting in Vedado's abandoned houses, in order to ensure that their former owners would find it all but impossible to reclaim their possessions.

If you are exploring Vedado on foot, begin at the **Hotel Nacional**, perhaps Cuba's only truly legendary hotel, modeled on the Breakers Hotel in Palm Beach, Florida. Since it opened in 1930, this has been the hotel of the rich and famous, including Winston Churchill, the Prince of Wales Edward VIII, Charles de Gaulle, Buster Keaton, Frank Sinatra, Ava Gardner, Nat King Cole and Marlon Brando, among others. It also featured as the site of a lengthy (and bloody) siege during a coup-attempt against dictator President Machado during the 1920s. In 1955, part of the hotel was converted into a Mafia-owned casino, managed by the mobster Meyer Lansky. Like a stately old ship ebbing with the tide of visitors, the Nacional is an essential part of experiencing Havana, so a drink on its verandah and a stroll through its gardens is called for.

After walking through the entrance gates of the Nacional, the **Hotel Capri** is a glance away; shabby these days, it is a far cry from its incarnation as the libidinous playground of the Mafia, built by the notorious American Mafioso, Santo Traficante Jr. Just northwest of the Hotel Capri looms the massive concrete **Edificio FOCSA**, Cuba's largest building, a 1950s apartment block that used to house visiting Russian delegates, officials and technicians during the Cold War period. Today, it is chiefly known for its rooftop **La Torre** restaurant and its dollar *supermercado*.

Walk downhill, turn right, and you will find yourself at the corner of Avenida 23, the main thoroughfare of the city center, which, on its uphill rise, is known by all as **La Rampa**, lined with offices, shops, cinemas

and fast-food parlors. You can browse for publications and pick up an English-language copy of *Granma* at the **Centro de la Prensa** (Press Center) directly on your right.

Up the hill, on Calle L, is the ugly, albeit recently modernized and much-patronized **Hotel Habana Libre**, the former Havana Hilton, which in the heady early days of the Revolution served as Fidel's headquarters. A few days after Fidel claimed Havana, a memorable interview was filmed here, with the seasoned American broadcaster Edward R. Murrow laconically questioning Cuba's new leader, who, with his small son, Fidelito on his lap, spoke halting English and was clearly a little overwhelmed at his sudden transformation of history. Later, Fidel, Che and other revolutionary leaders were prone to sweep in unannounced for ice-cream milkshakes at the poolside bar here, leading to an famously bungled CIA assassination attempt by an operative posing as a bartender. Then, as now, the top floors offer fantastic aerial views across the entire city.

Opposite the Habana Libre is the spaceship-like **Heladería Coppelia**, one of the fixtures of the Revolution, a cafeteria that used to specialize in many varieties of Cuban-made ice-cream, including guava, mango and papaya. Unfortunately, choices are now limited due to the shortages of the Special Period. Tomás Gutiérrez Alea's film *Fresa y Chocolate* (Strawberry and Chocolate) sets its memorable opening scene here. Most *habaneros* have to wait in long lines to be served, but tourists or those with dollars can bypass the lines and head straight for the first floor to be served promptly.

Several blocks away from the Habana Libre, continuing up Calle L, is the **University of Havana**, an acropolis-like complex begun early this century intended by its planners to be the epitome of classical monumentality. Its impressive Corinthian columns and 88-step entrance were the scene of many political demonstrations during the Republican era of Machado and Batista. Aside from wandering through its leafy campus, one of the main reasons to visit the university is to drop in on two museums here, housed in the Felipe Poey building, which is named for the Cuba's eminent nineteenth-century naturalist. The **Felipe Poey Museo** de Historia Natural is crammed with stuffed and pickled exhibits of Cuban wildlife, including some rare endemic species. The **Museo Anthropológico Montané** ((07) 793488 displays the island's most important archaeological artifacts, and there is no better place to discover the history of Cuba's earliest inhabitants, although the sketchy labeling of the exhibits can be frustrating. There are many fascinating artifacts, including carved turtle shells and shark-teeth necklaces, reconstructions of pre-Columbian burial rituals, and two stylized carved idols, one thought to be a god of tobacco, dating from AD 1500.

Across the road from the university entrance, at the corner of Calles San Miguel and Ronda, is the **Museo Napoleónico** (Napoleonic Museum) ((07) 791412, at Calle San Miguel 1159. Set in a beautiful Italianate mansion that is perhaps Havana's most unexpected museum, the legacy of the building's former owner, Orestes Ferrara, who had a magnificent obsession for all things Napoleonic. Imperial-era furniture adorns every room, and there are some fine paintings and weapons in the Hall of the First Empire. Among the personal effects on display that belonged to Napoleon are a lock of his hair, a toothbrush and the hat he is said to have worn on St. Helena, as well as the pistols he used at the battle of Borodino, his spy-glass and a unique piece, his death mask, brought to Cuba by Dr. Francesco Antommarchi, the doctor who attended him until the end. The museum is open from Monday to Saturday, 10 AM to 6 PM, and Sunday 9 AM to 12:30 PM.

In the vicinity, you may wish to explore a little-visited gem. Tucked away the extensive and tranquil gardens of Havana's **Jardín Botánico**, with its entrance on Avenida Salvador Allende, south of the university, is the graceful house-museum, **Quinta de los Molinos**. It was built for as a summer residence for Governor Tacón in 1837, and named after the royal snuff mills, which used to be located on the site. Just beyond the Quinta is the eighteenth-century **Castillo del Principe**, an inland fortress that has been converted into Havana's main prison.

The much-adorned roof of the Gran Teatro.

Plaza de la Revolución and Necrópolis Cristóbal Colón

Due the distances that have to be covered to explore this area, you will need a rental car or taxi. South of Vedado lies the Plaza de la Revolución, the political nerve-center of the Cuban nation, around which is the district known as "Plaza." The square's wide paved expanse dominated by the towering **José Martí monument** — a huge white marble statue of the nation's hero that stands in front of a giant four-sided obelisk. The observation platform (reached by a 567-step climb;

there is an elevator) is not always open. The stand in front of the monument has often been used by Fidel for his marathon speeches, and by other leaders to address the mass rallies that take place here. It was here that Pope John Paul II addressed the Cuban people during his landmark visit in January 1998, and here that the body of Che Guevara — for a long time, the equivalent of Cuba's patron saint — lay in state in 1997, after its return from being unearthed in a mass grave in Bolivia in 1997.

Surrounding the square are the most important government buildings in Cuba: the former Justice Ministry, now the **Central Committee of the Communist Party** (where Fidel's office is rumored to be); the Ministry of Communications; the Ministry of Defense; and the Ministry of Industry, which has an enormous metal sculptural portrait of Che. All of these monolithic edifices have a rather foreboding, slightly Orwellian look about them, and show the influence of Le Corbusier. None are open to the public — except for the **Biblioteca Nacional** and the **Teatro**

Nacional ℂ (07) 707655 or 785590, which presents mainly symphonic music and operas. All of these civic buildings, as well as the José Martí monument, were completed before the Revolution. An eccentric postal museum, the **José Luis Guerra Aguiar Museo Postal Cubano** ℂ (07) 705193 or 705043, is in the Ministry of Communications.

Head back to Vedado, taking the roundabout route looping back via Avenida 23. At its intersection with Calle 12 and Avenida Zapata is the grand Romanesque entrance to the nineteenth-century **Necrópolis Cristóbal Colón**. Unusual as it may seem, this historic cemetery is one of Havana's hidden marvels, with its many mausoleum equivalents of architectural follies, decorated with cherubs, angels, griffins and life-size statuary, set along tree-lined avenues where you can wander at whim, or rest on strategically placed benches. Since 1871, this has been Havana's city for the dead. At 56 hectares (138 acres), it is the largest cemetery in Latin America, with mausoleums, tombs and vaults laid out in gridlike blocks. A yellow-hued Greek Orthodox church stands at its core, the **Capilla Central**. Traditionally, plots were segregated by social status; professional and mutual societies also built tombs for their members. Just across Avenida 26, at the cemetery's southwest corner, lies the cemetery for Havana's Chinese community. Many of Cuba's greats are buried here, including Máximo Gómez, Alejo Carpentier, Celia Sánchez and Haydee Santamaría. Just left of the main entrance gate is the **Buro de Turismo**, which sells entrance tickets for US$1 and offers free guided tours of the main tombs; tips are welcome. The cemetery is open from 6 AM to 6 PM daily.

Follow Avenida 23 back to central Vedado. At the intersection with Calle 12, look for a bronze plaque on the corner which commemorates the spot where, on April 16, 1961, Fidel first proclaimed the "Socialist Nature of the Revolution" to listening masses, exhorting them to offer armed resistance to the Bay of Pigs invasion.

Miramar and West Havana

From Vedado, the Malecón continues west, through an underground tunnel, to reach the residential suburb of Miramar, which in many ways is a respite from the rest of Havana with its leafy parks and spacious boulevards lined with flame and jacaranda trees. This is where many of the wealthiest *habaneros* lived before the Revolution. Perhaps it is no mistake that its main boulevard is called **Quinta Avenida** (Fifth Avenue), a continuation of the Malecón. Miramar is a constantly fascinating place if you are interested in seeing the evolution of Havana's residential architecture, which ranges from formal turn-of-the-century decorative buildings set in elaborate gardens to more whimsical eclectic designs with stucco embellishments in stucco and concrete built

end of the exhibition, you will be comprehensively briefed about the activities of the Ministry of the Interior up to the present day.

Further west, at the corner of Avenida 5 and Calle 16, the **Casa del Tabaco** is one of the best cigar shops in Cuba, with knowledgeable staff and a wonderfully aromatic environment. A block south, at the corner of Avenida 7 and Calle 16, is **La Maison**, a colonial mansion with the soul of Imelda Marcos that has become the playing ground for Cuba's nouveaux riches. At night there are fashion shows; by day, you can come here to

during the 1940s and 1950s. Miramar still has an air of privilege, and is largely occupied by embassies, diplomatic residences, private schools, exclusive dollar boutiques, *supermercados* and ritzy restaurants.

The **Museo del Ministerio del Interior** (Museum of the Interior Ministry), at the corner of Avenida 5 and Calle 14, is strangely overlooked by visitors, but it is a not-to-be-missed glimpse into the paranoiac mechanics of the Cold War spying game between Cuba and the United States. All sorts of tools of the trade are displayed, ranging from exploding soap dishes to plastic rocks hiding radios. There is a comprehensive description of the many attempts on Castro's life made by his opponents over the decades. By the

browse in its dollar-boutiques, cosmetic and jewelry shops or indulge in the beauty parlor or shiatsu clinic. Fidel's daughter Alina once worked as a model here, before she defected in 1993. During the day, La Maison's café-restaurant is also open.

Further along Avenida 5, at the intersection of Calle 60, you will see to your left the imposing **Iglesia de San Antonio de Padua**, perhaps Cuba's only air-conditioned church, built after World War II. As you continue on, next in view is **Cubanacán**, also known as the "Country Club," a more secluded, greener neighborhood where gated walls offer glimpses of palatial mansions and

OPPOSITE: In Havana, you can see the making of Partagas cigars. ABOVE: The Marina Hemingway.

estates, some of which are now home to Havana's foreign ambassadors and senior Cuban government officials, while others have remained locked and empty, their original occupants long since fled. The **Palacio de las Convenciones** is located here, where international conferences are held in its numerous meeting rooms and halls.

Marina Hemingway

On the western outskirts of the city, just off Avenida 5 in the suburb of Santa Fé is the Marina Hemingway ((07) 241150, the home of the Havana Yacht Club. An increasing number of yachting enthusiasts — roughly half of whom are Americans — have been sailing to Cuba and this is where they berth their yachts. The marina compound includes various dollar supermarkets, bars and restaurants, like **Papa's**. You can stay here at the **Hotel El Viejo y el Mar**, or in pleasant condominium-style apartments run by the marina. Every year, the marina hosts several international fishing events and regattas including the **Ernest Hemingway International Marlin Tournament** in June, and the **Blue Marlin International Fishing Tournament** in August or September.

If you continue beyond Santa Fé, the road passes the Granma Naval Academy and an industrial zone, then Playa Salado, you would arrive in **Mariel**, the industrial port that was the embarkation point for the 1980 boatlift, which resulted in the emigration of 125,000 Cubans. If you plan to take the coastal route to Pinar del Río, on an excursion out of Havana, this is where the route begins.

Havana's Fortresses

To explore the fortresses in the route suggested here, you need a rented car, or to hire a taxi for a few hours, or perhaps to join a tour group. You may want to combine your excursion with a drink or meal at **La Divina Pastora** or **Los Doce Apóstoles**, perfect for watching the sunset glow across the Malecón.

Devised to keep warring armies and aggressive pirates at bay, it is no mistake that the fortress megaliths that now stand as Havana's architectural emblems look downright formidable. Like scimitars of stone, these impressive military forts straddle the strategic harbor entrance, one on each side of

the narrow channel, towering over passing freighters and tankers. When finally completed, this became the best-defended harbor in the Americas, unchallenged for nearly two centuries.

Construction began in 1590, under the command of Giovanni Baptista Antonelli, an Italian military engineer selected to construct Havana's defensive fortresses by the Spanish crown. Taking the city's traumatic earlier experience of pirates into account, he cast his eye on the ridge buttressing the entrance to the city's harbor and pronounced: "Whoever is master of this hill will be master of Havana."

Antonelli designed two forts — the **Castillo de los Tres Santos Reyes Magos del Morro** ("El Morro") and the **Castillo de San Salvador de la Punta** ("La Punta") — which

together were intended to form a staunch defensive triangle with the already-built Castillo de la Real Fuerza. Although both were begun at the same time, El Morro took some 40 years to reach final completion, with requests for more money and new consignments of slaves a constant refrain from the then-governor. The two bastions make up the **Parque Histórico Militar Morro-Cabaña (** (07) 620607, and are managed by Gaviota, the travel wing of Cuba's Ministry of Defense.

Begin at **La Punta**, located at the seafront tip where the Malecón begins. Facing El Morro across the harbor mouth, La Punta seems rather undramatic as a defense installment, with its low walls shaped in a rough quadrilateral and small bastions or watchtowers. Bear in mind that much of it has already been eroded by battering waves over the centuries. It was devised to work in tandem with El Morro, and if any danger was sighted on the horizon, a vast chain of metal and wooden logs could be launched into the channel between the two forts, creating an effective seal to the harbor entrance. These days, La Punta is where scores of *habaneros* congregate, hoping to hitch a ride home through the tunnel to La Habana del Este (East Havana). Past the tunnel, road signs lead you to **El Morro**.

From any angle, El Morro is impressive indeed, and as you look down from its battlements to see the huge green waves thrashing against its base far below, the difficulty

The Castillo de San Salvador de la Punta, completed in 1600, marks the start of the Malecón.

faced by potential aggressors becomes apparent. El Morro looms over the harbor entrance, has a tall nineteenth-century lighthouse tower in its northwest corner and is connected to the shore 150 m (490 ft) below by a series of ramps. A very deep dry-moat protects its inner citadel, which comprises officer quarters, a chapel, cisterns, a wine cellar, stables, dungeons and vaults.

For decades, El Morro held out against attacks by French, Dutch and English pirates. But in 1762, an English fleet consisting of over 11,000 troops and a formidable lineup of ships and frigates took the fort after a 44-day siege. It was hardly a bloodless battle: the English burst through the breach into the fort with mines, and both sides hacked at each other in hand-to-hand fighting. Some 400 Spanish soldiers died, more were taken prisoner, and many drowned trying to escape. For nearly a year, the English occupied Havana, and it was only due to the Treaty of Versailles that Spain was able to recover Cuba in return for Florida and Louisiana.

An extraordinary museum-piece in itself, El Morro will soon open a new maritime museum detailing the history of navigation in and around Cuba, with some actual historic ships on display, as well as replicas, and salvaged relics from galleon wrecks. You can climb to the top of the lighthouse, perhaps meet its keeper, who continues to operate its strong beam across the harbor entrance. El Morro is open daily from 8 AM to 8 PM.

As soon as Spain regained possession of Havana, Carlos III set out to ensure that they never again would they face such a humiliating defeat. He immediately ordered the construction of a new fortress, **Fortaleza de San Carlos de la Cabaña**, on the ridge close to El Morro. This was by far the largest and most ambitious fortress to ever be completed by the Spanish in the Americas.

You can wander through the restored San Carlos de la Cabaña fortress, seeing where, at one time, some 3,000 soldiers were housed in barracks, the cannon-dotted battlements, magazines and moats. You may want to hire a horse-drawn *calesa* to explore this large military settlement, which is almost a small city in itself. From 1926, the fortress was used as a military prison; after the Revolution, Che

Guevara himself was commander here and married his wife Aleida in the fortress chapel in 1959. It is worth looking at the museum's collection, which details the history of fortress design, and displays many medieval weapons, from catapults made with animal skins to fearsome antique muskets and daggers.

Come here for the **Ceremonia del Cañonazo**. Each evening at 9 PM, soldiers dressed as eighteenth-century guards march through the fortress accompanied by the beat of drums, and light a cannon flare, a ritual that announced the closing of the city's gates and the raising of the chain to seal the harbor mouth during Spanish colonial times. The atmosphere of the fortress at night, its cobbled streets lit by burning staffs, creates the almost eerie impression that you really have stepped back two centuries in time. You should arrive at the fortress by 8:45 PM at the latest to be in time for the ceremony. You may wish to repair to the nearby **El Bodegón de los Vinos** tavern, located in the old fortress, which serves a good selection of wine and Spanish snacks. San Carlos is open daily from 10 AM to midnight.

WHERE TO STAY

Deciding where to stay hinges on which part of Havana you prefer to wake up in and the nature of your trip, whether you want to be surrounded by the historic colonial center of La Habana Vieja or the newer Vedado district, with its concentration of government and business offices, as well as hotels, restaurants, bars and nightclubs. Some luxurious hotels, such as the unquestionably magnificent Hotel Nacional and the exceptionally elegant Hotel Santa Isabel, as well as the inexpensive but stylish Hostal Valencia, are destinations within themselves. In La Habana Vieja, a string of classic hotels dating from the turn of the twentieth century — the Sevilla, the Inglaterra, the Plaza and the Ambus Mundos — have been restored to their former colonial-era glory, offering modern comfort as well as quirky charm, although rooms themselves don't quite match up to the wonderful exteriors.

Over the past few years, the number and quality of Havana's hotels has improved dramatically, and a slew of new hotels are in the process of being constructed, and in some cases restored, most notably in La Habana Vieja. Most hotels — especially the (Cuban-designated) four- and five-star hotels — have security safes, satellite television and mini-bars in their rooms. The Miramar district also offers a choice of excellent hotels — the Meliá Habana, the Novotel Miramar and the Copacabana — with beaches and natural swimming pools on the coast, but unless you prefer to be at a distance from central Havana, you may find that you are spending a lot of time and money taking taxis.

For information about Havana's *casas particulares*, or privately rented accommodation, see the end of this section. For details on price categories, see ACCOMMODATION, page 321, in TRAVELERS' TIPS.

Expensive
The beautifully restored **Hotel Santa Isabel** ((07) 609619 OR 608201 FAX (07) 608391 E-MAIL reserva@habaguanexhsisabel.co.cu, Calle Baratillo 9, between Calles O'Reilly and Narcisco López, Plaza de Armas, La Habana Vieja, is decidedly the most charming and benignly staffed place to stay. Originally, this was a palace built for the Count de Santovenia in the nineteenth century, and its historic exterior is notable for half-moon

shaped stained-glass windows, while the inner courtyard is open to the sky. Each of its 27 rooms has a period feel, with attractive colonial-style wooden furniture, iron beds and swish bathrooms. Third-floor rooms have a semi-private terrace from which to survey the Plaza de Armas below, while the so-called Junior Suites contain a living room area and have a Jacuzzi. Even if you are not staying here, breakfasts here are the best in town. There is a restaurant specializing in Cuban and international dishes, a lobby bar and coffee shop, and a small shop. You can climb to the rooftop for stunning views across the old city. Future plans for this hotel include an adjacent swimming pool and hotel-style apartments.

A similar bygone ambience pervades the nearby **Hotel Florida** ((07) 624127 or 615621 FAX (07) 624117 E-MAIL reserva@habaguanex hflorida.co.cu, Calle Obispo 252 at the corner of Calle Cuba, an eighteenth-century colonial administrative building that was renovated into a gorgeous boutique hotel in 2000. From the rich tropical woods of the lobby area to the leafy central courtyard to the antique-filled rooms, everything about the Florida seems to transport you back to another time. Be sure to reserve early, especially during the high season when the hotel is often booked up weeks in advance.

Don't be fooled by the colonial façade of the **Golden Tulip Parque Central** ((07) 606627 or 606629 FAX (07) 606630 WEB SITE www.gtparquecentral.com. This is a completely new luxury hotel designed to fit in with the glorious architecture that surrounds its location in Habana Vieja. Already a favorite with visiting businessmen and up-market tour groups, the Parque Central has everything you expect from a five-star establishment — gourmet restaurants, comfy bars, 24-hour room service, dry cleaning and laundry service, a great business center, a rooftop swimming pool, a sports and fitness center with massage, and around-the-clock medical personnel. Rooms are spacious, well appointed and have that very unusual Havana treat — separate shower and tub in the bathroom. Add super-efficient Dutch management to the mix and it's hard to go wrong with this place.

The Cuban flag flies above the Hotel Plaza.

Hotel Meliá Cohiba ((07) 333636 FAX (07) 334555, Paseo between Avenidas 1 and 3, Vedado, among the slickest of Havana's five-star hotels, designed to be comfortable and efficient, is much like any other international hotel, except of course, it has a specialist bar devoted to the appreciation of fine cigars. Each of the 342 rooms and 120 suites is equipped with mini-bar, satellite television and a direct-dial telephone. If you bring a laptop, they can also hook up an Internet connection in your room. The hotel facilities include Havana's nicest swimming pool,

gymnasium and sauna, squash courts, beauty salon, conference room and banquet rooms that can accommodate up to 900 people. It also has an Executive Floor for business travelers, a choice of restaurants, shops, nightclub and 24-hour room service. The Italian restaurant serves a decent rendition of pasta and pizza.

There's nothing quite like raiding the mini-bar and watching the sea wash across the Malecón at dusk from one of the upper stories of the **Hotel Nacional (** (07) 333564 to 333567 FAX (07) 333899, Calle 0 and Avenida 21, Vedado. Set on a promontory that has unrivalled views across the sea and the Malecón, El Morro and the Vedado district, it is Havana's most majestic and ele-

gant hotel and gives a powerful impression of the decadent splendor of the city during the 1940s and 1950s. It was recently renovated, but with its colonnades, old Cuban tiles and wrought-iron lifts, the period ambience remains. The sixth floor caters to business travelers, and is smart and comfortable, with special work and meeting rooms, and separate check-in. Its many restaurants and bars are good, and its swimming pool, steam room, beauticians and barber add a pampering touch. The wide verandah bar is perfect for sociable lolling, at any time of day or night.

Hotel Habana Libre Tryp ((07) 334011 FAX (07) 333141, Calle L and Avenida 23, Vedado, is located on La Rampa, Havana's main thoroughfare. With its 534 rooms, the Habana Libre is the city's largest hotel and is managed capably by the Spain's Tryp group. It attracts a steady clientele of business and package travelers, as well as journalists. Despite its convenient location and the fact that its arcades contain many useful tourist offices, agencies and shops, is has the feeling of a large impersonal mall, reflected most dismally in its breakfast room. However, rooms have fantastic views, and the Turquino Bar on the top floor is a must for cocktails at dusk.

The best of Miramar's many seafront hotels is the new **Meliá Habana (** (07) 248500 FAX (07) 248505, Avenida 3 between Calle 76 and 80, which caters to both business travelers and ordinary tourists. The sprawling pool area out back is reason enough to stay here, but the Meliá also boasts four superb restaurants, an excellent business center, one of the city's best health clubs and outstanding service.

A block away is another debutant on the Havana hotel scene, the French-managed **Novotel Miramar (** (07) 243584 FAX (07) 243583, Avenida 5 between Calle 72 and 76, which also caters to the international business crowd. It's got all the bells and whistles — 376 well-equipped rooms, an efficient business center, several restaurants and a range of sports facilities including tennis, squash, gymnasium and large garden pool.

Moderate

One of the most romantic places to stay in all of Havana is the **Hostal Conde de Villanueva**

((07) 629293 or 629294 FAX (07) 629682 E-MAIL hconde@ip.etecsa.cu, Calle Mercaderes 202 at the corner of Lamparilla, Habana Vieja. The structure alone is reason enough to stay in this former home of the Claudio Martinez Pinillo, the Count of Villanueva, who made a fortune off cigars and railroads before his death in 1853. The hostel has only nine rooms, each of them named after a famous Cuban tobacco-growing area, and all of them set around a colonial-style central courtyard with potted palms and other tropical plants. Keeping with the tobacco theme, the lobby

friendly and courteous. All rooms have television, private bathrooms and mini-bars. The restaurant, La Paella, serves good renditions of the Valencian dish, and the Bar Nostalgia showcases local musical talent and is quite a soulful place. It also has a good Casa del Tabaco. Reserve your room well in advance.

The beautifully restored **Hotel Sevilla** ((07) 338560 FAX (07) 338582, Calle Trocadero 55 at Prado, Habana Vieja, has plenty of colonial-era charm, with its splendid, Moorish tiled marble lobby and fountains. It remains one of the loveliest of Havana's traditional late-

features a cigar shop, cigar bar and its own humidor room.

Another charming place to sleep in the old town is the colonial-era **Hostal Valencia** ((07) 671037 or 616423 FAX (07) 605628 E-MAIL reserva@habaguanexhvalencia.co.cu, Calle Oficios 53 between Calles Obrapía and Lamparilla, Habana Vieja, located just off the Plaza de Armas. It has a total of 12 rooms — including three suites — around its upper story (each named after a province of Spain) all lofty, with ceiling fans and decorated in a simple, authentic old-style with tiled floors and shutters. The upper verandah overlooks the cobbled, bougainvillea-festooned courtyard, where breakfast and drinks are served. The staff — as well as the house band — are

nineteenth-century hotels, and has a swimming pool, sauna and gymnasium. Readers of Graham Greene's *Our Man In Havana* may recall the scene that takes place here in Room 501, with the fictional protagonist, Wormold. Opera legend Enrico Caruso stayed here, and so did Josephine Baker, mobster Al Capone, world heavyweight champ Joe Louis, baseball legend Ted Williams and actress Gloria Swanson. Even if you are not staying here, the Roof Garden Restaurant is worth bearing in mind for dinner, with its city views and excellent trio of classical musicians. It is within easy walking distance of the old city.

OPPOSITE: Los Portales attracts many tourists, while Hotel Inglaterra ABOVE boasts nineteenth-century charm.

Havana's oldest hotel, **Hotel Inglaterra** ((07) 608595 FAX (07) 608254, Prado 416 next to Calle San Rafael, Habana Vieja, first opened in 1875, still retains a nineteenth-century feel, with its high ceilings, overhead fans, mosaic tiles, stained-glass windows and idiosyncratic lifts. Past guests include Sarah Bernhardt and Cuba's independence movement hero, Antonio Maceo. Although not the best buy for your money, some of the 83 rooms have balconies that overlook Parque Central and across to La Habana Vieja. The Sevillan-style patio bar on the ground floor is a popular meeting point. Talk of modernization is in the air, not a moment too soon.

The **Hotel Plaza** ((07) 608583 or 608589 FAX (07) 608591, Calles Ignacio Agramonte 267, Habana Vieja, is another Havana classic with a recently modernized colonial ambience and an ideal location for exploring the old city, just a few steps from Hemingway's famous haunt, El Floridita. One of its best features is the roof terrace, where a daily breakfast buffet is served, from which there are panoramic views across all of the old city as well the harbor. There is no swimming pool. Anna Pavlova and Isadora Duncan stayed here in the hotel's heyday.

The salmon-pink **Hotel Ambus Mundos** (Both Worlds) ((07) 609530 or 609529 FAX (07) 609532 E-MAIL diana@mundo.cu, Calle Obispo 153, at the corner of Calle Mercaderes, Habana Vieja, is chiefly known as the place where Ernest Hemingway sporadically based himself while writing *For Whom The Bell Tolls*. You can ask to see Room 511, which has been turned into a museum of Hemingway memorabilia. The hotel has a faux-1930s atmosphere, with the antique elevator and original marble staircase restored, and an art gallery exhibiting work by Cuban ceramists. Ask for a room overlooking the old city — the views are best on the top floors. The rooftop bar is one of the best places to while away a cocktail or two, with wraparound views across the city. There is no swimming pool — but really, who cares?

One of the city's best business abodes is the **Hotel Victoria** ((07) 333510 FAX (07) 333109 E-MAIL reserva@gcvicto.gca.cma.net, Calles 19 and M, Vedado, with its fast and friendly service and a choice location in the heart of the Vedado central business district. You can hire just about anything you need for commerce in the Cuban capital including computers, cell phones, meeting rooms, interpreters and secretarial support. The Victoria also garners high marks for cuisine.

When it opened in 1957, the **Hotel Habana Riviera** ((07) 334051 or 334055 FAX (07) 333739, Paseo and Malecón, Vedado, was one of Havana's most popular hotels, with Hollywood stars making a regular appearance. Although it's been modernized, the Riviera still feels steeped in the 1950s, and it's almost possible to imagine the time when notorious mob lawyer, Meyer Lansky, ran his operation from the twentieth floor. Its superb location on the Malecón affords outstanding views from its sea-facing rooms. In addition to its regular rooms, there are two executive floors at the top of the hotel and a presidential suite. Its seawater swimming pool is often used as a venue for afternoon salsa concerts. But the real draw is the hotel's Palacio de la Salsa, which showcases the best of Cuba's salsa bands.

The best thing about **Hotel Comodoro** ((07) 245551 FAX (07) 242028, Calle 84 and Avenida 3, Miramar, is its conscientious service — it is attached to Havana's tourism and hotel school. It has a swimming pool and overlooks a nice little man-made beach. Bungalows are available for little more than regular rooms.

With its dramatic location right on the seafront, the **Hotel Copacabana** ((07) 241037 FAX (07) 242846, Calle 1, between Calles 44 and 46, Miramar, is both a city hotel and a beach resort. During the 1950s, this was a hugely popular playground, and it has recently undergone extensive renovations, with a Brazilian theme throughout. Rooms are average, but the sea views and the wonderful natural swimming pool at the rim of the Caribbean are the compelling features here. Amenities include a discotheque, tennis and squash courts, shopping center and a marina from which you can go on fishing or diving excursions.

Inexpensive

Notorious as the place where the Mafia bosses went to unwind before the Revolution, **Hotel Capri** ℂ (07) 333747 FAX (07) 333750, Calles 21 and N, Vedado, is even mentioned in Mario Puzo's *The Godfather*. The Salon Rojo cabaret is no longer quite so outrageous, but still attracts swarms of young *habaneros* for its nightly musical performances. (This is not the place to stay if you like early nights.) Badly in need of renovation, the best thing about the Capri is its central location, being very close to the Hotel Nacional, the Hotel Habana Libre and La Rampa.

Located just off La Rampa in the heart of Vedado, the small **Hotel St. John's** ℂ (07) 333740 or 329531 FAX (07) 333561, Calle O between Avenidas 23 and 25, is a popular budget choice. The rooms are nothing lavish, but they are clean and comfortable, with air conditioning, satellite television and safe-deposit boxes. Breakfast is barely enough to feed a bird, but there is a handy parking lot next door (US$2 per day) where you can stash your rental car for the duration of your stay in Havana.

A sort of ramshackle charm permeates the waterfront **Hotel Deauville** ℂ (07) 338812 or 338813 FAX (07) 338148, Calle Galiano and Malecón, Centro Habana, is right on the Malecón and has seen better days. In fact it is worth staying in only to experience its historic terribleness: it could be viewed as a symbol of Cuba's Special Period. It used to be a favorite with foreign journalists, and is vividly described with affection by the writer Martha Gellhorn, who was Hemingway's third wife. Its main attraction is its location and its views across to the fortress of Los Tres Reyes del Morro.

Established in 1926, the **Hotel Lincoln** ℂ (07) 628061 or 338209, Calle Virtudes 164 at Calle Galiano, Centro Habana, is one of the better inexpensive hotels — it does have television and air conditioning — as long as you can put up with the uninspiring decor. The hotel's terrace bar has live music daily from 4 PM to 8 PM.

One of the few cheap sleeps in the old town is somewhat seedy and definitely down-market **Hotel Horizontes Caribbean** ℂ (07) 608233 or 608210 FAX (07) 669479, Prado 164 (between Colón and Refugio). The friendliness of the staff hardly makes up for small, gloomy rooms with threadbare sheets,

dilapidated bathrooms and cockroaches. Still, there are bright spots: a location in the heart of historic Havana and rates that no other hotel in the area could possibly match.

Casas Particulares

Casas particulares, or "private houses," are a definite option for visitors who would prefer to have more interaction with Cubans, as well as cheaper accommodation, during their stay. Prices per night are usually in the US$20 to US$25 range.

Vedado and Miramar have the largest number and variety of *casas particulares*. Many families rent out rooms in their houses, or in some cases will rent you their entire house. Prices can usually be negotiated, as can requests for meals. Facilities and comfort can vary, and in general, your experience will be colored by your rapport with your hosts, so don't commit yourself until you have met them and seen the premises. Unfortunately, there is no tourist agency specializing in recommendations and the business of finding a good *casa particular* is very much by way of word of mouth. Once you start asking around, offers will start multiplying, but bear in mind that touts receive a commission.

WHERE TO EAT

Havana has some excellent restaurants and *paladares* at which to enjoy Cuban cooking; and generally visitors bask in that wonderful trademark knack possessed by Cubans to make you feel both indulged and relaxed at the same time, whatever the surroundings.

Despite the fact that the Cuban capital has become increasingly cosmopolitan, don't expect *haute cuisine* in Havana. You can, however, expect to pay quite high prices, especially if you order imported wine, which can be up to five times its usual price despite being of indifferent quality, so it can be a good idea to check the wine list carefully. Most restaurants offer a mixture of Caribbean seafood, meat and Creole dishes, as well as memorable Cuban cocktails which are usually variations on the theme of rum.

Most hotels in Havana offer at least one daily buffet meal, if not three, which is an option if you want to dine quickly on what is generally dreary food in a cafeteria-style atmosphere.

Expensive

Havana's hottest restaurant at the moment is **El Gato Tuerto** ((07) 662224, which occupies the second floor of an old colonial mansion on Calle O (between Calle 17 and 19) in Vedado. From the impeccable service to the breezy dining room to the live classical music, everything about this place is classy. And we haven't even gotten to the food: an imaginative menu that combines Cuban ingredients and international flair — Caribbean-style fish filets, *camarones rellenos*

they wish to pay per head — which can be anything from US$15 to $35 — and the chef will whip up a meal of several courses accordingly, taking guest preferences into account. You can always just order an array of the house *tapas*, especially *pechitos de camarones*. Excellent live music features Cuba's famous white-haired jazz pianist, Bola de Nieve ("Snow Ball").

Despite the tour buses that pull up outside and the constant photo flashes and video cameras at **El Floridita** ((07) 631060, Calle Monserrate 557 at Calle Obispo, Habana Vieja, the daiquiris themselves are consistently good, as are the seafood specialties served in the adjacent salon. Aside

(shrimp cooked with ham, cheese and tomatoes in a seafood broth), *pollo maryland* (chicken roasted with corn and bacon) or the amazing *olla de diablo* (a filling and delicious seafood soup with shrimp, lobster, corn, peas and pepper). After dinner you can duck downstairs for some live tunes at the popular Café Concert.

El Tocororo ((07) 242209 or 224530, Calle 18 between Avenida 3 and 5, Miramar Playa, is named after Cuba's national bird, is another sophisticated restaurant, popular with executives working for joint-venture companies. Here, diners decide how much

from entering the computer era, El Floridita still seems steeped in the 1930s, its low-lit rococo interior dominated by a mahogany saloon-style bar nearly chest high to its bartenders, backed by an antique mural depicting eighteenth-century Havana. A bust of Hemingway looms over his favorite seat, while the resident band, Trio Brindis, entertains.

Thursday to Tuesday is formal dining at its most elegant in Havana at **Roof Garden** ((07) 338560, Hotel Sevilla, Calle Trocadero 55, Habana Vieja, with international dishes served by almost painfully correct waiters and classical music played by gifted musicians. Views across the city are stunning.

Despite its reputation as the city's most luxurious place to dine, the most impressive thing about **Comedor de Aguiar** ((07) 333564, Hotel Nacional, Calles O and 21, Vedado, is its surroundings, although service is good. Overall, the dishes are both expensive and mediocre, as is the wine list.

Pleasantly located within the marina, **Papa's** ((07) 297920 or 241156, Calle 248 and Avenida 5, Santa Fé, Marina Hemingway, is an enjoyable place for lunch or dinner, especially if you feel like escaping the city for a few hours. Seafood dishes are excellent, and can be pricey. You can order a whole roast fish in advance for US$50, or lobster can be prepared in many different ways. Naturally, they serve good daiquiris and *mojitos* here, and there's plenty of Hemingway memorabilia.

Located in the leafy diplomatic district, the very popular **El Ranchón** ((07) 339346 or 235838, Avenida 19 and Calle 140, Cubanacán, Playa, has generous servings of Creole and international dishes on the menu, and a jovial atmosphere.

Moderate

La Divina Pastora ((07) 608341, Parque El Morro-La Cabaña, Habana del Este, is easily the most romantic place to dine in Havana — perhaps in all Cuba — set among palm trees within the battlements of the city's great fortress, and with sweeping views across the bay. In addition, the musical trio that performs here is exceptional. Watching the sun smolder across the Malecón as it sets while drinking a *mojito* and enjoying them perform is an unforgettable experience. Seafood and Creole dishes are the specialty; stick with the simplest dishes on the menu, such as grilled fish. You can always just have a drink at the bar and enjoy the same ambience.

Anyone with a carnivorous appetite should duck into **El Conejito** ((07) 324671, Calle M at the corner of Calle 17, Vedado, where the menu runs a meaty gamut from pork and chicken to a dozen different types of rabbit (including roasted, fried and garlic). If you're really famished, try one of the four-course rabbit combo meals (US$15). The unusual (for Cuba) "English tavern"

decor adds to the gamy ambience. Service is fast and friendly.

Havana's most romantic perch is the rooftop **Terraza Florentina** ((07) 333747 EXTENSION 230, on the nineteenth floor of the Hotel Capri in Vedado. The view up the Malecón to Habana Vieja and El Morro castle is nothing short of spectacular. Fernando, the resident violinist, can play anything from Vivaldi to traditional Cuban boleros at your table. And the Italian cuisine is perhaps the city's best, especially the offbeat dishes like penne a la vodka, Sardinian-style calamari, seafood pizza with lobster and shrimp, risotto alla marinera and lobster ceviche.

Another good Italian eatery is **La Dominica** ((07) 602917 or 602918, at the corner of O'Reilly and Mercaderes in Habana Vieja. Located just off the Plaza de Armas, this pleasant sidewalk café has all the standbys including Caesar salad, cannelloni, pizza and Cuba's most delicious version of spaghetti carbonera. It's one of the few places in town with two house bands.

La Ferminia ((07) 336555 or 336786, Avenida 5 no. 18207, between Calles 182 and 184, Miramar Playa, is set in a lovely colonial house with extensive paved gardens and tables both inside and out. This is the most relaxed place for formal dining in Havana, and is a must. The extensive menu is traditional and refined, and well-served, with great efforts made to create the impression of European-style elegance.

The traditional Creole food served at **La Bodeguita del Medio** ((07) 618442, 671374 or 624498, Calle Empedrado 207 between Calles Cuba and San Ignacio, La Habana Vieja — roast pork or beef, usually accompanied by rice or beans — is good, from the diet-busting *chicharrones* (pork cracklings) to the the *arroz congri* (rice with spiced meat sauce) and the *picadillo* (shredded meat sautéed with garlic, onions, tomatoes and olives).

Located right on the seafront, an eye-catching, elegant colonial *palacio* has been converted into the partly open-air restaurant **1830** ((07) 334521 or 553090, Malecón and Calle 20, Vedado, which becomes a popular discotheque at night. The atmosphere is more compelling than the food.

President Gomez's former mansion is now a hotel.

La Cecilia ((07) 241562, Avenida 5 and Calle 110, Miramar, specializes in Creole cooking with mixed grills of seafood and meats. Well-spaced tables in the pretty garden allow unobtrusive enjoyment of the music performed at night. This is a popular dinner-dance spot after 10 PM.

El Barracón ((07) 334011, Hotel Habana Libre, Vedado, is considered one of Havana's best restaurants for Creole food. Its specialty is roasted pork, or pork in the form of *masas fritas* (fried pork skin), the *yucca con mojo* (cassava root covered in garlic-laced oil), and the *frioles dormidos.*

The main attraction of **La Torre** ((07) 553088, Calle 17 between M and N, Vedado, is the panoramic view from its location on the thirty-third floor of the FOCSA building. In its heyday this was the most swank joint in town; now it is worth coming for a drink at the bar.

Al Medina ((07) 671041, Calle Oficios 112, Habana Vieja, is an Arabic restaurant that does have an atmospheric courtyard setting in a traditional, two-story colonial house, but the food isn't all that good. Kitsch amusement value is provided by the psychedelic artwork of ample-breasted maidens and the waitresses, clad in harem pants, who perform belly dances in between serving the delicious kebabs.

Inexpensive

The house specialty at **Al Aljibe** ((07) 241583, Calle 24 at Avenida 7, Miramar, of roast chicken *con mollo* (with garlic sauce), is reliably good, and the *el aljibe* itself, a combination platter of chicken, beans, rice, salad, meat and dessert, is very good value.

Dos Gardenias ((07) 242353, Calle 26 at Avenida 7, Miramar, is a complex of restaurants and bars that serves Cuban, Chinese and Italian food, all inexpensive and of unremarkable quality. However, it is chiefly known for its **Salon Bolero,** which every night stages a tribute to Cuba's much-loved musical form, the bolero. There is also a shop that sells Cuban CDs and cigars.

You should at least have a coffee or a drink at **El Patio** ((07) 671034, Plaza de la Catedral, Habana Vieja, for its lively and relaxed setting in a beautiful three-story *palacio* overlooking the cathedral. Inside, light

filters through colored stained-glass windows, caged parrots entertain, and children watch turtles clamber inside the trickling marble fountain. Outside, there's always a fabulous musical ensemble performing, at almost any hour of day or night.

La Mina ((07) 620216, Plaza de Armas, Habana Vieja, is set in the courtyard of a delightful, colorfully painted *palacio* with crescent-shaped stained-glass windows, rambling plants, pet roosters and vibrant musical performances. This is an enjoyable place you should visit at least once, perhaps even to sample their *guarapo frío* (cold sugarcane juice), along with typical Cuban Creole food and coffee.

Located right next to Plaza de la Catedral, the Italian restaurant **D'Giovanni** ((07) 605979 or 671036, Calle Tacón next to Calle Empedrado, Habana Vieja, is not especially authentic; the best thing about it is the pleasant setting in a three-story colonial house, which also has pretty tables overlooking the harbor.

Los Doce Apóstoles ((07) 638295, Parque Morro-Cabaña, Habana del Este, located in the Castillo de los Tres Reyes del Morro (very close to the restaurant La Divina Pastora), is a little Creole restaurant that offers stunning views, along with modest, but satisfying Cuban dishes, such as rice, beans, pork and *yucca* (cassava root).

Café El Mercurio ((07) 666188, Lonja del Comercio, San Francisco de Asís, La Habana Vieja, is an excellent place for good coffee, sandwiches and salads, with great fresh fruit shakes.

As you might expect, paella is the specialty at **La Paella** ((07) 671037, Hostal Valencia, Calle Oficios 53, Habana Vieja, and their classic rendition of the dish actually won the prize for Best International Paella at the annual contest held in Sueca in Valencia, Spain in 1996.

Backpackers and Cuban students flock to the **Café del Prado** ((07) 608233 or 608210, Prado 164 (between Colón and Refugio) on the ground floor of the Hotel Caribbean, for cheap Italian eats like gnocchi, lasagna, ravioli, pizza and panini sandwiches. They've also got gelati ice cream.

A slightly rough-and-ready atmosphere pervades **Café Paris** on Calle Obispo, Habana

Vieja, a popular meeting spot where *habaneros* and foreigners intermingle. It's known for its slabs of pizza and cheap drinks.

Café O'Reilly, Calle O'Reilly 203, between Calles San Ignacio and Cuba, is a renovated version of one of Havana's oldest cafés and is good place for snacks and coffee.

Hanoi ((07) 671029, Calle Teniente Rey at Calle Bernaza, Habana Vieja, is an unpretentious little eatery serving Vietnamese dishes as well as the usual Cuban ones. It's a good place to stop if you're tired out from walking around the old city.

fried chicken, pizza, sandwiches, salads and milk shakes. The service can be glacial; sit at the counter if you're in a rush.

Paladares

Havana has a large and ever-changing number of *paladares*, or private restaurants, which offer an alternative to the usual government-run tourist restaurants, as well as a chance to meet with hospitable and enterprising Cubans. Licensed *paladares* are preferable because they have to observe strict hygiene requirements (they also have to pay high

Open until very late, the seafront restaurant **Cabañas** ((07) 605670, Calle Cuba 12, next to Peña a Pobre, Habana Vieja, has a very casual, friendly atmosphere popular with *habaneros*, who swear that the best dish is the house *Cabañas pollo*, which is chicken cooked with cheese and jam.

La Torre de Marfil ((07) 671038, Calle Mercaderes, between Calles Obispo and Obrapía, Habana Vieja, serves so-so Chinese food, in a restaurant run by Chinese-*habaneros*.

If you've got a hankering for something besides Cuban food, **La Rampa Café** ((07) 334011, at the corner of La Rampa (Calle 23) and Calle L in Vedado, does a passable job of imitating a 1950s American diner and its food. Among the offerings are burgers, fries,

taxes). Although meals are generally cheaper, always remember that wine can be surprisingly expensive (especially as its quality is generally not very good), so ask the price first. Reservations are always appreciated.

With flowers and candles on its verandah tables, the owners of **La Casa** ((07) 817000, Calle 30 no. 865 between Calles 26 and 41, Nuevo Vedado, which is set in a spacious and modern Vedado home, have managed to create a restaurant atmosphere in their family home. The specialty is Cordon Bleu chicken (stuffed with ham and cheese).

El Elegante ((07) 238215, Avenida 33 no. 3140 between Calles 34 and 36, Playa, is

Lounging in a Havana horse carriage.

set in an airy private home that lives up to its name. You can expect excellent home-cooking and solicitous service by Rafael and Joaquín. It is open for lunch and dinner.

Hurón Azul ((07) 784189, Calle Humboldt 153, next to Calle P, Vedado, is a very pleasant *paladar* specializing in Creole dishes. **Long Sai Li**, Sociedad de Instrucción y Recreo, Calle Dragones 313, between Calles Rayo and San Nicolás, Barrio Chino, Habana Centro, is run by the descendants of Chinese immigrants and has an unusual mixture of Chinese and Creole in its cuisine and ambience. On the menu, you'll find the typical Creole *pollo fritto* and the traditional Chinese fried rice served with Hatuey beer, the whole set against a backdrop of a large Chinese painting and salsa music.

NIGHTLIFE

When the light fades and the streets take on their half-lit hue (both dodgy electrics and power shedding mean blackouts are a regular occurrence), Havana's exuberant nocturnal spirit asserts itself. *Habaneros* take their partying very seriously, even if it just involves assembling around a fragile sound system blurting out high-velocity salsa.

The city's fabled nightlife is what you make of it, whether you chose to have a quiet moonlit drink next to the vine-covered old fort listening to Cuban ballads, or whether you decide to take your partner by the hand and start executing crazy salsa steps with the best of them. There are cabarets with elaborate dance acts, and many musicians playing salsa, conga and rumba rhythms, as well as live jazz and other types of music. Most hotels and restaurants feature soloists, trios or musical groups. Whatever you do, you may develop a newfound interest in rum and cigars, and almost where ever you go, the level of live music will range from the merely infectious to the sublime. Expect to a pay US$5 to $15 cover charge, especially at nightspots located within hotels.

Live Music

Tucked away on a quiet street in suburban Miramar is a coral-stone building with blue trim that houses the popular **Casa de la Música** ((07) 240447, Calle 20 between Calles 33 and 35, the Havana equivalent of Santiago's Casa de la Trova, where almost every night, you can expect to hear top-quality Cuban musicians amid an appreciative audience. There is also a shop with a good selection of Cuban CDs and cassettes. Bands take the stage Tuesday to Sunday nights from 10 PM to 3 AM. In addition, there are daily afternoon *pena* sessions from 4 to 7 PM. The music store is open daily from 10 AM until just after midnight.

Another great place to catch live music is the popular **Café Concert Gato Tuerto** ((07) 662224, Calle 0 (between Calles 17 and 19), Vedado, where modern Cuban jazz takes the spotlight each evening. The tunes flow from around midnight until 6 AM in a dark, smoky post-modern atmosphere replete with marble and stainless steel. The cover charged is normally US$5, or free if you eat dinner in the upstairs restaurant.

Cuba meets Hollywood at the flashy **Habana Café** ((07) 333636, in the Hotel Meliá Cohiba, Vedado, which fancies itself as a Latino version of the Hard Rock Café. Despite the pretense, some of the country's top groups perform here on a regular basis. Shows kick off at 9:30 PM nightly. **Café Cantante Mi Habana** ((07) 766011, 793558 or 735713, inside the Teatro Nacional, Paseo and Calle 39, Plaza de la Revolución, features nightly live music showcasing jazz and salsa, and a humorous variety show, although some travelers report having encountered a rather unsavory crowd. The national theater also hosts the intimate **Piano Bar Delirio Habanero** where this is live music nightly from around 10:30 PM.

The cozy **Bar Nostalgia** ((07) 671037 or 616423, Hostal Valencia, Habana Vieja, is a good place to catch budding local musicians. Evening performances vary, so check for their latest schedule.

La Zorra y el Cuervo ((07) 662402, on Calle 23, between Calles M and N, Vedado, features nightly live "Caribbean jazz," starting at 10 PM. The cover charge is US$5. Every Friday and Saturday night, contemporary groups perform rumba and jazz at **Casa de las Infusiones**, Calle Mercaderes 109, right opposite the Hotel Ambos Mundos in Habana Vieja.

The Afro-Cuban group Oni Ire performs every Friday from 10 PM to 3 AM at **Ribera Azul** ((07) 338812, Hotel Deauville, Centro Havana. The rest of the week, there's other types of live music, usually salsa or rumba. Cover is only US$1.

Salon Rosando, at the Jardín Tropical, Playa, offers an intensely Cuban night-out — you won't see many foreigners. On weekend nights, this open-air stadium is packed for popular salsa performances, at this peso-only venue near the Havana stadium.

Salon Internacional Salsa ((07) 334501, Hotel Riviera, Vedado, with its 1950s setting, showcases nightly performances by Cuba's top salsa bands, making it a venue not to be missed.

Bars

You could quite easily while away an entire evening cruising the many bars along Calle Obispo in Habana Vieja, places where Cubans mix freely with tourists in an atmosphere that Hemingway would have adored. There's very little difference among most of them. All boast US$1 beer, Cuban hustlers (both male and female), and live music of some sort.

One of the most spirited is **La Lluvia de Oro** (The Golden Ring) ((07) 629870, at the corner of Obispo and Habana, a raucous joint that rocks both afternoon and evening to the sound of the house salsa band. Don't be

A local musical institution, La Casa de la Música.

socked by the hordes of "working women" — they're usually here to drink rather than to trawl for tricks.

Down the block, at the corner of Obispo and Compostela, is a tiny place called **La Dichosa** that also serves up music and *mojitos* in the afternoon and throughout the evening.

Another local hangout is **Café Paris**, at the corner of Obispo and San Ignacio, often so crowded that patrons spill out the front door and down the street.

If you need a break from the crowds and the noise, duck into the **Piano Bar Maragato** ((07) 624127, on the ground floor of the Hotel Florida, at the corner of Obispo and Cuba, where the ambience is about as mellow as it gets down around the old town. Another quite spot is the **Bar Ambos Mundos** ((07) 669529, in the hotel of the same name at the corner of Obispo and Mercaderes, where the *mojitos* are tasty and the piano rifts sweet.

In pre-Revolutionary days, two American brothers ran **Dos Hermanos**, Avenida del Puerto at the corner of Calle Santa Clara, La Habana Vieja, near the Havana docks, and it was a rough-and-ready watering hole for sailors and dock workers. Today, it's a fun, out-of-the-way place to linger and meet Cubans.

Cabarets

The legendary **Tropicana** ((07) 270110, 279147 or 271548, Calle 72 between Calles 41 and 45, despite being an obvious monument to 1950s decadence, was one of the symbols of pre-Revolutionary Cuba that was not allowed to die. Night after night, this socialist show, whose slogan is "Paradise under the Stars," goes on, celebrating more than six decades of existence with so much kitsch flamboyance that it is hard to resist, and many of its performers are clearly very talented. Since the Tropicana first opened in 1939, it has been renowned for its scantily clad and outrageously costumed dancers. Its central stage is surrounded by tropical gardens and is open to the sky, which means that a rainstorm cancels the evening's performance. The cabaret is undeniably spectacular, with a huge cast of *café-con-leche* dancers who manage to be theatrically

dressed and semi-naked at the same time, sometimes teetering beneath chandelier headdresses that light up on cue. They gyrate to the music of a massed choir and a swing band playing Afro-Caribbean rhythms. In addition, acrobats perform dare-defeating acts, and the entire performance is delivered at a slick pace. Although the show is meant to begin at 9 PM, it usually does not get going until a half an hour or an hour afterwards. Cover charge is Havana's most expensive (US$40 to $60) and includes a cocktail. If it rains, you can opt for another performance

or (apparently) are refunded for your ticket. Closed Monday.

From 10:30 PM until midnight, the **Club Turquino** ((07) 334011, Hotel Habana Libre, Vedado, on the twenty-fifth floor of the Habana Libre, presents a rather lack-luster musical revue, after which it becomes a discotheque. But the views — especially at sunset — are wonderful.

La Maison ((07) 240126 or 241543, Calle 16 no. 701 near Avenida 7, Miramar, set in a white colonial mansion with a large garden terrace, is a magnet for well-connected and moneyed Cubans, who come here to enjoy the nightly fashion shows and cabaret performances, and to drink on into the night. The show begins at 9:30 PM. It is closed on Monday.

The restaurant **La Cecilia** ((07) 241562, Avenida 5 and Calle 110, Miramar, has a very popular performance show at night, with excellent salsa groups. It is open Thursday to Sunday, from 10 PM.

For a traditional hotel floor show with more than a little touch of Las Vegas try **Cabaret Parisien** ((07) 333564, held at the Hotel Nacional, Vedado. The nightly show starts at 9 PM and lasts until midnight; after that there is disco music.

Less expensive, the cabaret show at **Salon Rojo** ((07) 333747 EXTENSION 120, Hotel Capri, Vedado, also has something of a following. Shows are held from Tuesday to Sunday, starting at 10:30 PM.

EXCURSIONS FROM HAVANA

THE HEMINGWAY TRAIL

When he wasn't drinking daiquiris at El Floridita or drinking *mojitos* at the Bodeguita del Medio, Ernest Hemingway could most often be found either writing at his home outside Havana or fishing for marlin from his custom-made boat, the *Pilar*, off the Cuban coast.

To follow his trail, you should ideally combine a mid-morning visit to his former home, now a museum, with lunch at La Terraza restaurant at Cojímar; and you will need a taxi or rental car.

Overlooking Havana in the tiny San Francisco de Paula, 15 km (nine miles) southeast of the capital, is **La Finca Vigía** ((07) 910809 or 335335, the handsome white mansion Hemingway bought with the advance from *For Whom The Bell Tolls* in 1940. Here, surrounded by *flamboyán* trees and *areca* palms, Ernesto, as the Cubans called him, spent the last two decades of his life and worked on some of his finest works: *To Have and Have Not*, *For Whom the Bell Tolls*, and dozens of short stories and novellas, including *The Old Man and the Sea*.

Hemingway moved to La Finca with the journalist Martha Gellhorn, his third wife, and was later to live here with his fourth, Mary Welsh, telling her that this was the only place he ever felt at home. Feeling that Cuba was too unstable to live in during the early days of the Castro takeover, the Heming-

ways left for Idaho, where on July 2, 1961, Ernesto committed suicide.

A month after Hemingway's suicide, Welsh received Fidel Castro on La Finca's front porch, and in a brief ceremony, she handed the house over to the Cuban government. The next year, Castro turned La Finca into the **Casa-Museo de Hemingway**. Unlike Hemingway's house in Key West, Florida, La Finca remains much as it was left, preserving all his books, papers, personal effects and furniture. His aura is strongly, almost eerily present.

Inside the mansion is the writer's idiosyncratic collection of African fetishes, Picasso sculptures and Goya reproductions, and everywhere are books — more than 5,000 of them, including the intriguingly titled *Nine Lives Before Thirty*, and another used as a doorstop. Stuffed victims of hunting expeditions stare glassily down from almost every room, impalas and antelopes, buffaloes and brown stags, pronghorns and Grant's gazelles. In the living room, next to his favorite armchair, are empty bottles of Gordon's gin; next to his bed was the last book he read here, on which his wire-frame glasses perch, as though absent-mindedly left behind. On the bookshelf in the bedroom is the Royal portable at which he wrote standing up for the last 17 years of his life. In the bathroom are the hieroglyphic-like scrawls of the daily register he kept of his weight, which fluctuated between 190 and 242 pounds. There are also pickled frogs and lizards in a jar on top of the toilet. In the closet, some military-style jackets, and many pairs of worn but dashing "war correspondent" leather boots, shoes and sandals, all Hemingway's size 48, as well as smaller pairs that belonged to Mary.

In Hemingway's office, unused rounds of ammunition, including a dozen 20-gauge Winchester cartridges, stand upright on his desk. In the last few years of his life, Hemingway frequently tormented his wife and friends by rehearsing his suicide: he would brace the barrel of his Mannlicher Schoenauer .256 against the roof of his mouth and play with the trigger with his big toe.

Although you are only allowed peer inside the mansion from the verandah and

A Cuban icon: Hemingway's favorite Bodeguita del Medio.

through open doors, you can wander through the lush frangipani-fragrant gardens to see the outdoor tower where Hemingway often worked, the now-empty swimming pool, the guest-house (guests included Gary Cooper and Ava Gardner) and the cemetery he created for his beloved dogs, Black, Negrita, Linda and Nero. His boat, the *Pilar*, is on display here as well.

If you are driving by rental car, take the Primer Anillo de La Habana (Havana's First Ring Road) then follow the Carretera Central to Güines and onwards to San Francisco de Paula, in San Miguel de Padrón. La Finca Vigía is open Monday to Saturday, 9 AM to 4 PM, Sunday, 9 AM to 12:30 PM, and is closed on Tuesday and rainy days.

As you leave La Finca for Cojímar, get back onto the Primer Anillo de la Habana which joins with the Vía Monumental to lead directly to **Cojímar**, the tiny fishing village where Hemingway used to keep the *Pilar*. The crescent-shaped bay of Cojímar (pronounced Co-HEE-mar) was the setting for *The Old Man and the Sea*. A pergola shades a bronze bust of the author, smiling, in a fishermen's sweater. A little further on is **La Chorrera**, a seventeenth-century tower-like colonial fort, and the port, where a few boats are moored to a rickety wooden pier, around which barefoot children cast their reels to the sea.

More recently, Cojímar has been notoriously popular as a launching ground for thousands of attempts by *balseros* (rafters) to cast themselves across the Florida Straits — locals still talk about the scandal when two *balseros* were shot as they tried to escape in 1993, and the frenzied scenes in 1994, when a riot in Havana sparked the biggest exodus since Mariel.

Cojímar's most famous resident, Gregorio Fuentes, recently passed away at the age of 101. He was Hemingway's longtime fishing-boat captain, and remained a passionately loyal defender of his friend's memory until his death in 2002. Fuentes was rarely seen without a half-smoked *puro* between his lips, and for years posed good-naturedly for the steady parade of tourists who asked to take his photograph. There is plenty of

Santería celebration of the Yoruba god of fire and war.

Fuentes's spirit in the fictional character of Santiago, the old man in *The Old Man and the Sea*, which was to win the 1954 Nobel Prize for Literature. "Everything about him was old except his eyes," he wrote of Santiago, "and they were the same color as the sea and were cheerful and undefeated."

For the past 30 years, Fuentes was a guest of honor at Cojímar's seaside restaurant **La Terraza de Cojímar** ((07) 559486 or 559232, Calle Real 161 next to Calle Candelaria, where he would sometimes have a meal and a double whisky. With the terrace's windows open to the sea breeze, this is one of the most delightful and relaxed places to while away an hour or two: whether it's just for a *cafecito* and rum, or for their delicious fish soup or seafood paella with Spanish wine. The walls are lined with photographs of Hemingway (with some of Fuentes too) in their glory days.

THE PLAYAS DEL ESTE

Once you have reached Cojímar, you are halfway to the Playas del Este (Eastern Beaches) the long string of beaches to which *habaneros* traditionally flock during the stiflingly hot months of July and August to escape the humidity of the city.

From Cojímar, the Vía Monumental runs eastwards, turning into the Vía Blanca, the four-lane highway that runs all the way to Matanzas and then to Varadero. Leaving Cojímar, you'll pass the Revolution-era prefabricated apartment buildings made with unpainted cement — known as microbrigade housing — of **Alamar**, a glum seaside dormitory suburb of Havana, and further east, **Celimar**, another fishing village with similar micro-brigade housing built by untrained volunteers.

Here begins the undulating expanse of blue water and wide, white-sanded beaches dotted with coconut palms that makes up the Playas del Este. **Bacuranao** is the closest, no more than 20 minutes from Havana. Then comes the seaside towns of **El Mégano**, **Santa María del Mar**, **Boca Ciega**, **Guanabo**, **Jibacoa** and **El Trópico**. Especially during the peak summer months, these beaches have an intensely Cuban atmosphere, with entire families decamped here: old men

sticking to their game of dominoes in the shadows, toddlers having their first dip in the sea, and the inevitable rum, cigars and salsa music permeating the beach. Off-season, it's the closest place to Havana for a swim, although drifting pollution has been reported and beaches are often left littered with trash.

Although the hotel and restaurant facilities are pretty rough, this is a much more gratifying place to spend a few days by the sea than the more celebrated Varadero if you want to meet and mingle with ordinary

Cubans. On the downside, prostitution is becoming a much more visible problem here. The beach communities mentioned above are lined with inexpensive tourist resorts catering to both Cubans and tourists, private holiday homes dating from the 1920s and 1930s, cafés, shops and discotheques. However, the gloom of the Special Period can be felt here: the Playas del Este suffer from the lack of transportation and food supplies.

Where to Stay

If you want to spend a day — or a few days — at the beach at the Playas del Este, the beach at Santa María del Mar is probably your best base and its also has the nicest beach. It has to be said that none of the hotels are especially attractive.

Although it's not a traditional hotel, the best accommodation is **Villa los Piños** ((07) 971361 or 971269 FAX (07) 971524, Avenida las Terrazas 21, between Calles 4 and 5, Santa María del Mar (expensive). This Gran Caribe operation manages two dozen vacation houses in the beach area that can sleep two to four people. Most have their own small swimming pools and all are within four blocks of the strand. There is also a motel-like room block with slightly lower rates. Leisure

971637 FAX (07) 971494, across the street from Club Atlántico and about a block off the sand. Rooms are fairly Spartan, but there's a nifty pool area and a range of watersports options. All units come with air conditioning, private bath, safe-deposit box, kitchenette, refrigerator and satellite television.

Where to Eat

There are plenty of casual eateries and pizza bars along the strip at Playa Santa María del Mar. In adjacent Playa Boca Ciega, try the seafood restaurant, **La Casa de Pescador** at

activities include tennis and various watersports. The resort also has its own restaurant and pizza parlor, as well as a bar, workout room, sauna and massage.

Hotel Club Atlántico ((07) 971085, Avenida de las Terrazas, Santa María del Mar, offers moderately priced, all-inclusive accommodation. This rather Retro-style hotel could be a good base to hang your beach hat, although a few days may be enough if the constant stream of *jiniteras* is not for you. It is located right on the sand beach and within walking distance of most of the local nightspots.

Santa María del Mar is another hotbed of the Horizontes chain, with six budget hotels in the immediate beach area. Best of these is the **Aparthotel Atlántico** ((07) 971636 or

the corner of Avenida 5 and Calle 440, for its simple Creole dishes and beach atmosphere. The sign is sometimes hard to spot, but look for the house with the red-tile roof.

Boca Ciega has a number of other modest eateries including **La Rotunda** on Avenida 5 near the Calle 462 traffic circle (opposite the gas station), and **Restaurante d'Prisa**, a *parrillada* and seafood place adjacent to the municipal park at Avenida 5 and Calle 474. At press time, Cubanacán was constructing a brand new air-conditioned restaurant called **El Criollo** overlooking the vacant lot at the corner of Avenida 5 and Calle 456.

The windows of the Palacio del Segundo Cabo decorated with *mediopuntos*.

REGLA AND GUANABACOA

Across the harbor from Havana, two historic neighborhoods offer an alternative view of the city.

The easiest and most atmospheric way to reach the maritime hamlet of Regla is to take the stalwart ferry which regularly commutes to and from the Muelle de la Luz dock on Avenida San Pedro (Avenida de la Puerte) across from the Plaza de San Francisco de Asís. Buy a ticket for 10 centavos each way and see Havana from this unique perspective. (If you drive or take a taxi, you will be able to roam further afield and visit Guanabacoa, which is too far to walk from Regla.) From the boat, you have a wonderful view of Havana Bay, passing under the gaze of the large sculptured Christ figure near the city's observatory in the suburb of **Casablanca** immediately south of La Cabaña. From the station here, the electrified Hershey train runs to and from Matanzas.

When you disembark at the Regla docks, you can't miss seeing (along with the eyesore of a large thermo-electric plant) the harbor-front **Iglesia de Nuestra Señora de Regla**, one of Havana's most important places of pilgrimage. Here, the Virgin of Regla, patroness and protector of all travelers, can be called upon to give her blessings, also in her incarnation as Yemayá, the Santería goddess of the sea. Presiding over a blue and white tiled, flower-bedecked altar, the blue-robed Virgin of Regla is black, although the infant she cradles is white. Every September 8, the Virgin's feast day is celebrated here with both a Catholic Mass and Santería rituals. Many have come here to say an emotional farewell to Cuba, or to pray for their loved ones in other countries. A small adjacent museum displays objects and figurines used in Santería practices. The entrance fee of US$2 also covers the Museo del Regla.

From the church, you can happily wander through Regla's warren of old streets. Here, the traditional tempo of life remains unchanged: there are few cars but many bicycles, children play in the streets and modest wooden houses have a ramshackle quality, many emblazoned with socialist slogans faded along with the paint. The **Museo del**

Regla ((07) 976989, at Calle Martí 158, between Calles Facciolo and La Piedra, has a good collection of antique religious art, as well displays relating to the neighborhood's history during the Spanish colonial period. A special place has been reserved for the accoutrements of the **Tabla de Ifa**, divining instruments of Santería. It is open from Tuesday to Friday, 9 AM to 6 PM; Saturday, 9 AM to 7 PM and Sunday from 9 AM to 1 PM.

If you are feeling energetic, you can walk up winding streets and hillside steps to the neighborhood's highest point on **Lenin Hill**. It is graced by a rather surreal sculpture of androgynous post-modernist mannequins hailing the giant death mask-like face of the Russian revolutionary. Puzzlement over the sculpture is forgotten in the panoramic views of Havana, which also take in the creeping industrialization of the foreground.

The seemingly sleepy, unpretty town of Guanabacoa is a few kilometers away, renowned in Cuba for its deep connections with Santería, as well as the other Afro-Cuban belief systems, Palo Monte and the secretive Abakuá. If a *habanero* has a string of misadventures, he's likely to say, with a laugh, "I'm heading for Guanabacoa!" for a purifying ritual from the *babalao*.

From the earliest times of Spanish colonial rule in Cuba, Guanabacoa was associated with the trafficking of African slaves. This painful history is reflected in the name of **Calle Amargura** (Bitterness Street), where slaves who had been sentenced to death were dragged away to be executed. There are several historic churches and a monastery: the **Parroquial Mayor**, founded in 1644, overlooks the main square; the early baroque **Iglesia de Santo Domingo**; and the monastery complex of the **Iglesia de San Francisco**, founded illegally by Spanish missionaries, both of which date from the early eighteenth-century.

One very good reason to visit for anyone interested in Santería is the **Museo Histórico de Guanabacoa** ((07) 979510, Calle Martí 108, housed in an attractive colonial house, which has Cuba's most comprehensive display of lore relating to the Afro-Cuban religion, Santería, and the other related cults. You can see ritual tools that belonged to some of Cuba's most respected *babalaos*, or priests. Santería dance performances and rituals are frequently enacted in the museum and in the nearby **Casa de la Cultura**. The museum is open Monday to Saturday, 9:30 AM to 4:30 PM and is closed Sunday.

Whether you walk or drive through the streets of Guanabacoa, you can feel how steeped it is in Santería. White-clad *santeros*, or initiates, are a common sight, and through open doors, in gloomy interiors, you catch glimpses of shrines to the *orishas*, the gods or goddesses, with dolls dressed as Santa Barbara, bead necklaces, bottles of rum and plas-

tic flowers. You can also browse at the **Bazaar de los Orishas**, near the town's main square.

If you have time, make a detour further south along the Autopista Nacional, to reach **Santa María del Rosario**, a charming town of crumbling mansions and well-established trees founded by the sugar-baron Counts of Bayona. Its barely visited **Iglesia de Santa María de Rosario** is a beautiful baroque church built in 1776, which, with its richly carved pulpit and altar, is the most sophisticated rural church interior in Cuba. The paintings are by an artisan from the Canary Islands, José Nicholas de la Escalera. Across the cobblestone plaza is the restored mansion that belonged to the aristocratic Bayona clan. Unfortunately, the church is only open

on Sunday between 5:30 PM and 7:30 PM. Cuba's greatest contemporary artist, Manuel Mendive lives here, and you can see his mural on the town's **Casa de la Cultura** opposite the church. Santa María de Rosario lies 19 km (12 miles) southeast of Havana.

SOUTH OF HAVANA

If you have a day or two to spare and want to see something of the "real" Cuba — as well as to visit untouristed regions, you might consider combining several of the following places, all easily reached by car and within an hour's drive south of Havana. If you try to use any form of public transportation, you soon experience how great the daily obstacles faced by many Cubans are.

PARQUE LENIN

Due to transportation problems, not many *habaneros* have been going to **Parque Lenin** ((07) 443026, a huge recreation park area, which lies just off the Calzada de Bejucal in Arroyo Naranjo, 20 km (just over 12 miles) southeast of Havana. If you are driving a rental car, you can reach it by the Vía Monumental, then by the Primer Anillo de la Habana, which traverses La Habana del Este. The park lies southeast of Guanabacoa and just south of Arroyo Naranjo. The park has a giant white marble bust of Lenin and encompasses an amusement park, Havana's only *autokine* (drive-in cinema), a small aquarium, various equestrian centers, a theatre and the Paso Sequito lake, where you can rent boats. Most of these amusements are either closed or in a state of neglect. Hopefully, this park and its many activities will once again be restored and operational.

Where to Eat
Las Ruinas ((07) 443336, Calle 100 and Cortina de la Presa, Parque Lenin, is a 1970s-style restaurant that serves good Creole food at moderate prices and can cater to large parties. Its interesting setting incorporates fragments of an eighteenth-century sugar mill. Located in the park's southeast corner, it is open Wednesday to Sunday.

A lovely building converted into a broadcasting station.

JARDÍN BOTÁNICO

Further south of the park is the Jardín Botánico Nacional (National Botanical Gardens) ((07) 547278, where you can see an extraordinary array of exotic trees and plants imported from all over the world, as well as those endemic to Cuba itself. The gardens cover some 12 hectares (30 acres) and over 32 km (20 miles) of roads. The many varieties of Cuba's palm trees are a specialty, but there is also a charming Japanese garden and extensive varieties of bougainvillea and orchids. Tours take up to three hours and vary in price — you should be able to book ahead from your hotel. Try to visit during the months of April and May, when the gardens are at their most beautiful. The opening hours are Wednesday to Sunday from 9 AM to 5 PM.

Further south, beyond the Aeropuerto Internacional José Martí, is the small traditional town of **Santiago de las Vegas**, which is primarily of interest for a nearby church, **San Lázaro**. On the night of December 16 every year, an extraordinary religious procession celebrates San Lázaro's Day, dedicated to one of Cuba's most venerated saints, the patron of the old and sick. Each year, thousands of pilgrims, many of them barely able to walk, gather here in the hope that San Lázaro will answer their prayers. Most make the journey on foot from Santiago de las Vegas. Everywhere, there are cries of "Viva Lázaro," and the church itself is crammed with flowers and candles, with much emotional singing and praying. It is significant that Pope John Paul II chose to visit El Rincón on his landmark visit to Cuba in 1998.

SAN ANTONIO DE LOS BAÑOS

An hour's drive — some 37 km (23 miles) along the Autopista del Mediodía — southwest of Havana, San Antonio de los Baños is close enough to the capital that many residents commute to their jobs in the city. It is the closest that Havana has to a small country town. Rich in mineral waters, it was a fashionable spa town during the nineteenth century. The advantage of coming here is to see how ordinary, educated Cubans live out-

side the urban perimeter. It is known for its biennial international humor festival, held in April, when cartoonists and humorists converge to discuss the serious business of satire. At the entrance to the town, a sign announces that you have entered "San Antonio del Humor." The **Museo del Humor** ((0650) 2817, housed in a rose-colored colonial mansion on Calle 60 at Avenida 45, declares itself devoted to the "conservation, study and dissemination" of humor, and has a visual tour of Cuban graphic humor from the first extant Cuban caricature (1848) to the present. Open Tuesday to Saturday from 2 PM to 7 PM; closed Sunday and Monday.

On the town's outskirts, is Havana's **International School of Film and Television**, located amid leafy, tranquil surroundings. It is often referred to as Gabriel García Márquez's school, since the novelist (and former television scriptwriter) was actively involved in its creation in 1986. Since then many greats from the film world have offered themselves as visiting professors for the school's workshops, including Márquez himself, Constantin Costa-Gavras, Francis Ford Coppola (who also cooked pasta for the students), George Lucas, the late Tomás Gutiérrez Alea, Istavan Svebo, Robert Redford (whose Sundance Institute frequently participates in the annual International Festival of New Latin American Film) and actors Hanna Schygulla and Matt Dillon. The school, which is open to international students — mostly from Latin America, Asia and Africa — and only accepts a limited quota of Cuban students, has a two-year film-making program as well as shorter and experimental workshops.

TOP: Watching street life from a balcony. BOTTOM: The Malecón also serves as a playground for children.

Western
Cuba

Within easy driving distance from Havana, it is possible to explore a highly varied array of places and landscapes in the island's western region, even if you have just a week or a few days to spare.

Travel west, through the lush, tobacco plantation-filled province of Pinar del Río — Cuba's tobacco heartland — to relax amid some of the island's most spectacular scenery, laced with sleepy villages and cigar factories.

Also within western Cuba, yet to the east of Havana, the resort of Varadero may appeal if beach hedonism is what you have in mind.

More adventurous forays may lead you south to the wildlife-rich Zapata Peninsula and Playa Girón (site of the abortive Bay of Pigs invasion), where secluded, translucent waters offer some of the island's best spots for swimming and scuba driving.

PINAR DEL RÍO PROVINCE

The spectacular, beautiful and tranquil mountain province of Pinar del Río boasts some of the island's most dramatic and varied landscapes. Within this region's scenic Valle de Viñales, vegetation-covered Jurassic-period mountains of limestone schist tower over hidden caves, tobacco farms and unexpectedly charming colonial towns. The distinctive *mogotes* or high flat-topped mountains seen here are rarely found in such profusion elsewhere.

This is also the region of the classic *guajiro*, or Cuban peasant farmer, who you are likely to see wearing a weather-beaten straw hat astride his horse, chomping a cigar between his teeth.

Pinar del Río's fertile plantations — especially those in its Vuelta Abajo region — have been renowned for centuries for the exceptional quality of the cigars produced here, adding an additional lure for cigar connoisseurs. Whatever the season, you will see some aspect of the tobacco production process: from freshly-tilled red ochre soil, to bright green plantations, to the stacking of leaves in palm thatched *vegas*, or tobacco drying sheds.

Although some tourists manage to whisk through Pinar del Río in a one-day dash, if you can spare a few days, you will be rewarded by letting the region's relaxing hill-station ambience seep gradually into a sense of well-being — a rare mood in the heightened rush and blast on the senses that characterizes much about being in Havana. At least that's the idea: the lack of obvious distractions at night is an incentive to have distracting company, a yen to practice your Cuban-Spanish in small village taverns, or at the very least a good book. In addition, come equipped with some strong insect repellent — the Cuban forest teems with little mosquitoes.

BACKGROUND

For centuries, even for much of the colonial era in Cuba, the province of Pinar del Río, which occupies the westernmost end of the island, was a forested backwater. It was the last refuge of the Siboney, Cuba's early tribe of hunter-gatherers who were forced here from other parts of the island by the fiercer Taíno. Later the same mountains — which are riddled with caves and underground rivers — helped conceal communities known as *palenques*, where escaped slaves or *cimarrones* hoped to evade detection by so-called *ranchedores*, the ruthless bounty hunters who were paid to find or kill escaped slaves.

Today, the main attraction of Pinar del Río is simply to admire and explore the shifting moods of its changing landscape. There are plenty of possibilities to walk through forests, to swim in natural rivers and to enjoy the gentle tempo of life in this predominantly agricultural region. It has to be said that the quality of the food served in Pinar del Río's hotels is generally of a higher standard than elsewhere in Cuba.

LAS TERRAZAS

You may wish to make the delightful Hotel Moka within the forest reserve of Las Terrazas your base for all or part of your stay in Pinar del Río. Located within Sierra del Rosario, the so-called tourist complex of Las Terrazas is also home to a community of some 890 local people, most of whom are farmers and agricultural workers, who live amid what is Cuba's first exercise in sustainable development. The largely self-sustaining community of Las Terrazas was founded in 1968. Its low-lying bungalows, apartments, school, clinic and other buildings — including the region's traditional rodeo — lie in a narrow valley around Lake San Juan. Initially, the community undertook large-scale reforestation and the terrace building that gives the region its name. In 1993, the Ministry of Tourism stepped in and created Cuba's first ecoresort, La Moka.

What to See and Do

The **Sierra del Rosario**, with its upper reaches of thick tropical forest and highland rocky outcrops, is one of the most rain-prone regions in Cuba. It is one of the island's most concentrated habitats for migratory and endemic bird species, including the *zunzuncito* and the *trogon*. The cave-filled hills are home to other endemic species, such as the pygmy boa and an unusual-looking water lizard, as well as sheltering many varieties of trees, plants and flowers. Most of this large reserve is closed to visitors, however there is still plenty to see.

At Las Terrazas, the **Ecological Research Center** can provide maps of the walking trails in the area, which can lead to the splashing cascades of waterfalls and pools perfect for swimming or to the ruins of former nineteenth-century coffee plantations. Walks around the hills reveal an abundance of plant species, including native orchids.

PREVIOUS PAGES — LEFT: María La Gorda in the far west. RIGHT: Tending young tobacco plants. ABOVE: Aquatic plants cover the Ciénaga de Zapata marshes.

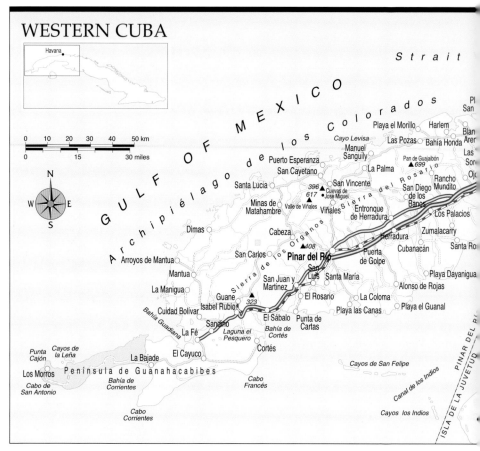

WESTERN CUBA

You can explore some of these trail by horse-back, or ask for a guide to accompany you for longer walks. Both activities can be organized by contacting the Hotel Moka in advance.

The most beautiful lookout point in the area is the **Buena Vista**, a narrow ridge from which, on a clear day, you can see both the Florida Straits and the Caribbean Sea. This was a former nineteenth-century coffee plantation, run by a French planter who kept close guard on his 120 slaves: to the right of the plantation you can see the ruins of the stone barracks they were bolted into at night. The planter's house has been turned into a restaurant that specializes in French-Creole food, notably the dish they call "witch chicken." It also has outdoor tables so you can appreciate the charming view, which sprawls across vine-canopied forests and blossoming flame-red *flamboyán* trees. The air has an invigoratingly alpine scent and coolness.

Hotel Moka can arrange visits to the studio of Lester Campa, a talented artist who was raised in Las Terrazas, and whose detailed landscapes reflect his fascination for nature.

Where to Stay and Eat
Set amid forested hills, **Hotel Moka (** (07) 335516, Las Terrazas, Autopista Nacional km51, Candelaria, is a comfortable hotel built using natural woods and incorporating much of the natural surroundings. A large tree grows up through an open-air atrium in the reception hall and a stream runs through the garden and under the hotel. All the air-conditioned bedrooms have bathrooms faced entirely with glass so you can lie in your bath and look out through the trees. All rooms have safe-deposit boxes, satellite television and refrigerators. Facilities also include a charming swimming pool and tennis court. Horseback riding, fishing, bird watching and guided tours can be arranged.

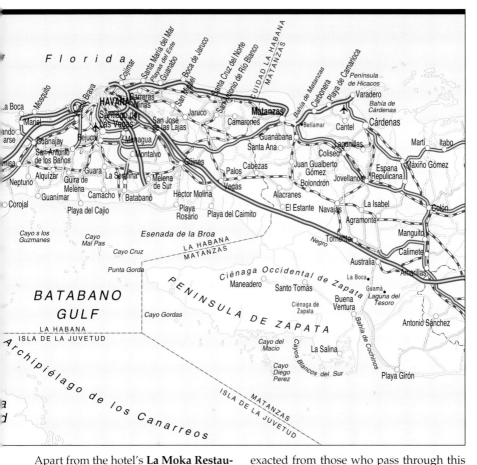

Apart from the hotel's **La Moka Restaurant**, you should have lunch at the **Cafetal Buena Vista** (it is open only between noon and 4 PM). In the Las Terrazas village, you can try the local *paladar*, **Terraza de la Fondita** in Unit 9, which is a great place to socialize with locals, and the Cuban fare is very good.

How to Get There

Las Terrazas is a 75-km (nearly 47-mile) drive west of Havana, off the Autopista Nacional at km51. Look carefully for this marker on the highway, since only one small sign announces the four-kilometer (two-and-a-half-mile) turnoff to Las Terrazas. You pass through steep green hills to reach a guard booth at the edge of the ecological reserve. It is best to advise La Moka of your arrival in advance, so that the guard can expect you and wave you through. Also, drivers be aware that a road toll of US$3 is

exacted from those who pass through this essentially private road for a scenic short-cut through to the town of Soroa.

SOROA

Only 18 km (11 miles) from Las Terrazas is the tiny settlement of Soroa, best known for its extensive *Orquideario* or **Orchidarium**, which contains some 750 species of plants, including over 200 endemic to Cuba, all thriving in this lush, humid hillside environment. It was founded in 1943 by a native of the Canary Islands, a botanist named Tomás Felipe Camacho, in honor of his daughter Pilar who had a great passion for orchids before she died during childbirth. Today it is maintained by the University of Pinar del Río. Look out for the tiny yellow orchids from Thailand, and the "Queen's Clogs" from the Philippines. The gardens are also landscaped with many other plants, including endemic palms and wildflowers. The best months to visit are between November and March when the orchids flower, although the gardens are pretty all year round. Entry costs US$2.

Close by, on the right side of the road near a small cafeteria, a sign marks the way to the **El Salto Falls**, which is a 10-minute walk away through leafy forest. Should you feel so inclined, you can bathe in the surrounding pools.

Soroa's other main attraction, at the very least a good rest stop or coffee break, is its

post-modern, Gothic-style restaurant **El Castillo de las Nubes** (The Castle of the Clouds), which is located at the area's lookout point, from which you can see lovely views of the surrounding countryside, peppered with *flamboyáns*. Within the area, the Manantiales River is renowned for the mineral and medicinal properties of its water.

Where to Stay and Eat

For inexpensive accommodations, try **Horizontes Hotel & Villas Soroa** ((085) 2122 or 2041, Carretera de Soroa km8, Candelaria. Located at the crossroads of the valley, this hotel is probably the least appealing of the options listed for Pinar del Río due to its bland *cabaña* rooms. But it is comfortable enough, has a pleasant restaurant and swimming pool, and is well located as a starting point for hikes walks in surrounding tropical forest.

The restaurant **Castillo de las Nubes**, Alto de Villa Soroa, Sierra del Rosario, features spectacular views across the valley, and is a good place for lunch.

TRAVELING WESTWARDS

From here, the Carretera Central continues westwards through the picturesque rural town of **San Cristóbal**, where tumbling-down red-tiled wooden *bohíos*, or cottages, are set against the green expanse of tobacco fields and thatched *vegas* (tobacco-drying sheds). Here, as throughout Pinar del Río, humped Indian Brahman cows plow the soil in a centuries-old method.

Continuing on, look out for the turnoff for the hamlet of **San Diego de los Baños**, once-popular for its spa waters. It lies on the fringes of another of Pinar del Río's nature reserves, the **Parque Nacional La Güira**, which sprawls across the sloping mountains of the Sierra de los Órganos. The 22,000-hectare (54,000-acre) wilderness of the national park remains undeveloped, although perhaps not for long. It is already on the itinerary of visiting bird-watching groups, and although its trails are limited, they offer satisfyingly predictable glimpses of the resident bird life, as well as the occasional deer. This reserve is located within the former private estate of Manuel Cortina, whose property was nationalized after the Revolution. You can visit Cortina's elegant house and garden, now a museum with his possessions on display. The town's only hotel, **El Mirador**, is a good place to stop for cold drinks or lunch.

On the western edges of the reserve, on the Río Caiguanabo, is **Cuevas de las Portales**, a giant free-standing *mogote*, riddled with cavernous chambers, and an amazing spectacle of stalagmites and stalactites. Just as remarkable is the fact that Che Guevara made these caves his headquarters during the Cuban Missile Crisis in 1962, when he was commander of Cuba's western army.

On the way back onto the Autopista Nacional en route to Pinar del Río, a turnoff to the south leads to the sparsely populated coastal settlement of **Maspotón**, notable as Cuba's largest hunting and fishing preserve, where the Horizontes hotel group operates a *casa de caza*, or hunting lodge, however this is not recommended as a place to stay. Don't make the disheartening mistake of coming here to bird-watch.

THE PROVINCIAL CAPITAL OF PINAR DEL RÍO

The provincial capital of Pinar del Río, 176 km (109 miles) from Havana, is not recommended as a place to stay, but using La Moka or Viñales as your base, you should certainly come here to spend an hour or two touring its cigar factories and museums. Include a walk along Calle Martí between Calles Medina and Colón, which is full of Cuban atmosphere, with bars, cafés and shops.

Since its rapid post-war expansion, Pinar del Río has lost whatever previous claims to charm it may have had, although tucked amid its colonial center you may find the occasional architectural gem.

BACKGROUND

The city's expansion has been largely due to the development of the tobacco industry, signaled by the many tin-roofed *casas del tabaco*, which contain the leaves harvested from the surrounding plantations of Vuelta Abajo and Viñales. The region's tobacco-growing soil and climate is universally recognized as being unsurpassed anywhere. Tobacco production reached its peak in the mid-1970s at 50,000 metric tons (55,115 short tons) per year and then was crippled by a blight of blue mold. Although it nearly recovered in 1990, 1991 saw the first of many poor harvests. Since 1995, production has increased steadily as has foreign investment in the industry.

You can sample the region's famed cigars, in the very factories where they are hand-rolled.

WHAT TO SEE AND DO

Head for the **Fábrica de Tabacos Francisco Dontien** on Calle Antonio Maceo near the Plaza de Independencia, the oldest and most established in the city, and housed in a former nineteenth-century jail. Here you can watch the cigar-making process, which includes leaf-selection, cigar rolling and label gluing. Over six brands are made here by skilful Cuban workers of both sexes and all ages.

As always, a man at the front of the room reads to the rollers over a loudspeaker — usually the day's news from the official state newspaper, *Granma*.

They also have an excellent shop and well-stocked humidor where you can browse or buy both the local brands, some of which can be very good, as well as the smoother export cigars. A guided tour costs US$2. It is open Monday to Friday from 6:30 AM to 4:30 PM and Saturday from 7:30 AM to 11:30 AM.

Another visit you should not miss is to the **Casa Garay** on Calle Isabel Rubio. Here a production team of garrulous women in white kerchiefs make Guayabita del Pinar, the alcoholic liquor made from the local *guayaba* or wild guava plant that grows everywhere in this region. You can tour the plant and sample the sweet and dry forms of this slightly spicy concoction; bottles are on sale. It is closed during the weekend.

Aside from these two factories, little else holds much attraction for visitors, except perhaps the 1909 **Palacio Güasch**, on Calle José Martí. The home was designed for a wealthy doctor who traveled extensively and wanted to live in a building inspired by architecture around the world, including Moorish arches and French Gothic spires. It now houses the **Museo de Ciencias Naturales** (Museum of Natural History), which is crammed with collections of shells and stuffed birds, fish and animals, and has an outdoor display of two concrete dinosaurs and a stone *megalon*, a large extinct rodent that was once endemic to Cuba. This is a good place to see examples of the archaic corkscrew palm tree (a contemporary of the dinosaur) and a stuffed pygmy boa constrictor in a case. Further up Calle José Martí is the smaller **Museo Provincial**, housed in a less dramatic colonial mansion, which has a display of local memorabilia. Across Calle Colón is the decaying Greek Revival-style **Teatro Milanés** which does have a pretty, if crumbling, nineteenth-century interior.

As you leave the city, it's difficult not to notice the shabby Soviet-era Hotel Pinar del Río, notable only as a place not to stay.

Cuban cigar boxes often retain designs from a century or more ago.

WHERE TO EAT

Located on the outskirts of the city of Pinar del Río, **Rumayor** ((08) 63051, Carretera de Viñales, is an Afro-Cuban restaurant whose specialty is smoked chicken. The *cherna frita* (sea bream sautéed in butter, garlic and onions) is also very good. At night, this establishment transforms into an open-air cabaret.

It's worth knowing that the only decent place to stop on the way to Pinar del Río for a break and refreshments (or even a meal, given the lack of appetizing restaurants in the township of Pinar del Río) is the roadside truck stop **Las Barrigonos**, on the north side of the Autopista Nacional, 27 km (17 miles) east of Pinar del Río.

HOW TO GET THERE

The Autopista Nacional from Havana will get you to the provincial city of Pinar del Río, 176 km (109 miles) away, within three hours. This is a relatively bland route aside from the great slogans-to-socialism billboards, agricultural scenes and the increasing numbers of Cuba's prized palm trees, banana trees, corn fields and rice paddies along the way.

Aside from joining an organized tour, another way to reach Pinar del Río is by train; there is a daily scheduled service from Havana. The trip is meant to take five hours, but can be much longer. See GETTING AROUND, page 316 in TRAVELERS' TIPS to make reservations through the state railway agency.

If you have time to spare, you might consider taking the Circuito Norte, the longer, more scenic coastal road which runs parallel to the Autopista to the north. It begins near Havana at the outlying town of Mariel and follows the coast all the way up to Puerto Esperanza, passing through rustic farming scenes and villages with plenty of opportunities to stop and talk to local people.

VALLE DE VIÑALES

From the city of Pinar del Río, a small two-lane highway (full of bicycles, horse-drawn carts and exhaust-spewing buses) leads north to the Valle de Viñales, which is 26 km (16 miles) away, formed by the convergence of two mountain ranges, the Sierra del Rosario and the Sierra de los Órganos.

BACKGROUND

It is generally acknowledged that the Viñales valley contains the most breathtaking scenery in the region. This is largely due to the strange, almost primeval spectacle of the landscape's row of free-standing sugarloaf hills called *mogotes* that tower over everything else in sight. They rise sharply from the valley floor to a flat top, with cliff-like flanks covered in green vegetation.

These fossil-filled geological formations are the oldest on the island, dating back to the Jurassic era, 150 million years ago, and are found only in Cuba and in parts of China, Vietnam and the Philippines. They are mainly limestone karst formations, shaped when underground rivers cut through the soft rock, forming caves and cliffs. These formations came about by the differential erosion of two types of rocks: slate and limestone, with the latter eroding more easily, so that with time, the action of the water formed the valleys that you see today.

These mountains also conceal spectacular cave corridors, apparently the largest in Latin America, with countless underground streams and gorges. Only 30 cave systems have been charted, and many more wait to be explored, making the area of considerable interest for speleologists. The largest of the caves is the Cueva Santo Tomás, which has more than 45 km (28 miles) of galleries. Particular caves of interest that you can visit include the Cueva del Indio, through which runs the Río San Vicente.

WHAT TO SEE AND DO

The main settlement in the valley is the charming town of **Viñales**, whose preserved nineteenth-century buildings appear almost frozen in time. The main street is lined with red-tiled wooden houses with verandahs and pine trees. The town's oldest house, **Casa de Don Tomás**, was built in 1822 and has now been turned into a delightful restaurant and bar. Within the town, a small, white nineteenth-century church and the

Casa de la Cultura are ringed around the main square's inevitable bust of José Martí.

Aside from La Moka, the two best hotels in Pinar del Río — **Los Jazmines** and **La Ermita** — are located in the mountains surrounding Viñales, both perfectly sited for their panoramic views across the entire valley. The experience of watching dusk fall over the landscape — seeing the light fade the shapes of the mountains to stencils against the sky, farmers leading their horses home, and the quiet punctuated only by chattering birds — makes the trip here worthwhile in itself. Needless to say, there are no such views from the town of Viñales itself, given that it lies in the valley bowl.

From Viñales, follow the road west of town for several kilometers to reach the

Valle de Dos Hermanas (The Valley of the Two Sisters) and the **Mural de la Prehistoria** (Prehistoric Mural), a huge mural depicting the process of evolution, from snail to dinosaur and chimpanzees to *Homo sapiens*. Set amid a landscape of such dramatic delicacy that it is somehow reminiscent of a Chinese brush painting, this gauche mural certainly adds an incongruous element to the scene. It was designed by Leovigilda Gonzáles, a former student of the famous Mexican mural-artist Diego Riviera, and work was completed in 1966. Despite the imposing scale, the mural remains somewhat of an artistic eyesore. A restaurant in the shadow of the cliff provides good Creole

The odd Mural de la Prehistoria was painted in 1966.

dishes for the large tour bus groups that tend to come here for lunch.

North of Viñales, follow the main road between the hills toward Puerto Esperanza, a road that ultimately leads to the coast. The atmosphere is very rural, with small farming communities clustered in the shadows of the *mogotes*. After crossing Ancón Pass, to your left you will see a sign for the **Cueva de José Miguel** where a bar and discotheque has been built in a dripping cave. On the other side of the cave is one of the largest cave *palenques* in Cuba, where up to 200 escaped slaves managed to survive and you can see a recreation of how they lived here, and perhaps have lunch at the restaurant **El Palenque de los Cimarrones**.

The **Cueva del Indio**, a few kilometers ahead on the right, was discovered by local farmers in 1920 and takes its name from the burial bones of the Siboney — also known as the Guanahatebeys — the Indian tribe that once lived here. You can explore part of this enormous cave system by foot, and along part of the underground river, a small motorboat tours through a gallery of dramatic stalagmites and stalactites before emerging from the hillside. The cave is some 1,700 m (nearly 5,600 ft) long, but less than a third of that is open to the public. It is open daily from 11 AM to 5 PM and the entrance fee is US$3. The riverside restaurant here is good. Watch out for the swarms of tiny mosquitoes.

From here, after continuing north for two kilometers (slightly over one mile), you will come to **Rancho San Vicente**, a spa-hotel catering mainly to Cubans, who come here for its complex of thermal waters and sulfur baths in search of a cure for various ailments.

WHERE TO STAY

Moderate

The **Hotel Horizontes Los Jazmines** ((08) 936205 FAX (07) 936215, Carretera de Viñales, 25 km (about 15 miles) from Pinar del Río, is the nicest of the hotels in the Viñales. This attractive pink colonial building with traditional stained-glass windows has fantastic views across the valley. Apparently, Castro himself suggested the site as an ideal honeymoon retreat. All of the simply furnished rooms are air conditioned, and they have balconies from which to enjoy the sunset. There is a large swimming pool. Horseback riding can be arranged, or you can explore tracks leading down into the valley by foot. It is prudent to reserve in advance.

The **Hotel Horizontes La Ermita** ((08) 936071 or 936100 FAX (08) 936091, Carretera de la Ermita, is two kilometers (slightly over a mile) from Viñales. The best thing about this hotel is its restaurant which has a large open-air balcony from which you can enjoy another view of the valley. Rooms are comfortable and air conditioned, and there is a pleasant swimming pool. Reserve well in advance.

Inexpensive

The **Horizontes Rancho San Vicente** ((08) 936201 or 936271 fax (007) 936265, Valle de San Vicente, off the road to Puerto Esperanza, is a no-frills, 33-room hotel with simple, comfortable rooms and a restaurant and bar. They offer guided tours by horseback or on foot through the nearby mountains and caves. In addition to the thermal waters and sulfur baths, the hotel also specializes in mud packs, using local mud which is rich in "algae, marine organisms and biologically active substances." Don't expect a luxury spa.

WHERE TO EAT

Moderate

Casa Don Tomás ((08) 93114, Calle Salvador Cisnero 140, Viñales, is set in a charming, two-story wooden colonial house on the main street of Viñales. This is the best place for lunch or dinner in town. You can dine outside or on the verandah. The Creole food and the service are very good. Among its specialties is a rice dish with ham, pork, lobster and sausage. The *tasajo de campesino* (*guajiro*-style dried beef) is another dish of the region.

Aside from this site's dramatic history as a *palenque*, **El Palenque de los Cimarrones**, Valle San Vicente, Viñales, has been modeled on a Santería theme, with each section inspired by a different *orisha*. The Creole dishes are good, especially the *pollo asado*, *arroz morro* and *yucca* (cassava root); and be sure to also try their house drink, *chinguirito*, which is a mixture of rum, honey, lemon, mineral water and ice.

Mural de la Prehistoria, Valle de Viñales, a ranch-style restaurant next to the Mural de la Prehistoria, caters mainly to large groups, but manages to keep a good standard of service and food, serving regional Creole dishes.

Inexpensive

Paladar Valle Bar, Calle Salvador Cisneros 100, Viñales, is a fun place at night, when the town's local personalities gather to banter with visitors and play the battered, much-loved piano. They appreciate reservations so they can prepare in advance.

La Casa de Marisco, Cueva del Indio, Valle de Viñales, is a modest establishment, across from the entrance to the Cueva del Indio. It serves Creole food, and its specialty is the freshwater prawns caught in the nearby underground rivers. Located next to the entrance of the Cueva del Indio, the restaurant **Cueva del Indio**, Valle de Viñales, features charcoal-grilled chicken, *cassava* cakes and *ajiaco*, a meat and vegetable stew.

How to Get There

Viñales lies 26 km (16 miles) north of Pinar del Río by way of a sinuous mountain road. The direct journey from Havana via the Autopista Nacional is 212 km (130 miles).

All the big Havana hotels and travel agencies can arrange guided excursions to the area. You can also negotiate a taxi ride, but the journey will cost at least US$100. The only cheap and efficient way to reach Viñales by public transportation is the daily **ViAzul (** (07) 811413 or 815652 bus service from Havana.

CAYO LEVISA

Most visitors generally head back from here to their hotels in Viñales. However, it would be a shame to miss one of Pinar del Río's prettiest, secluded beach resorts. Beyond San Vicente, turn left at the crossroads toward San Cayetano and soon you will reach Puerto Esperanza, a small fishing village which is the nearest point from which to reach the small offshore island resort of Cayo Levisa, a 45-minute boat ride away.

Until recently, Cayo Levisa was a destination for day-long excursions, which could include lobster fishing, snorkeling over the rim of coral reefs and lunch on the beach. Recently, a tourist resort has been developed on the three-kilometer-long (nearly two-mile) island, the Villa Cayo Levisa, which specializes in diving and watersports. It is becoming an increasingly popular destination for Spanish and Italian divers, who rave about offshore black coral formations, abundant tropical fish and lobsters. Lounging on its soft, creamy sands is equally pleasant.

From Cayo Levisa, it is easy to arrange (through Villa Cayo Levisa) boat excursions to **Cayo Paraíso**, beloved by Ernest Hemingway, who frequently anchored his yacht here during the 1940s. Plans are afoot to build a marina for yacht enthusiasts and scuba divers, who swear that diving here — the loveliest *cayo* in the Archipiélago de los Colorados — is nothing less than spectacular.

WHERE TO STAY

To ensure that this small key remains pristine, the well-run resort **Villa Cayo Levisa (** (07) 666075 is limited to 20 moderately priced beach *cabañas*, which are comfortable and have satellite television, radio and telephones. There is a lively restaurant and bar

Western Cuba is renowned for the quality of its tobacco.

and a small boutique. Horizontes recently took over and plans to expand this into a more luxurious resort. Facilities include basic diving and snorkeling equipment, and arrangements can be made for fishing trips and excursions to Viñales. Advance reservations are advised.

The inexpensive **Villa Rosario ℭ** (08) 93828, Granja Rosario in Puerto Esperanza, is housed in a nineteenth-century mansion that once belonged to a wealthy landowner and later housed the area's Communist Party headquarters). This quirky hotel and restaurant is a good base from which to explore this little-visited but very scenic region of small seaside villages and to make trips to surrounding keys. There are only four rooms. The restaurant features good home cooking using local ingredients.

WESTERN PINAR DEL RÍO

Not many visitors take the time to travel further westwards into Pinar del Río. However, this off-the-beaten-track region offers opportunities to appreciate some of Cuba's least developed natural scenery, and contains two important ecological reserves. Distances are short and if you are staying in Viñales, you can easily use your hotel as a base.

From the city of Pinar del Río, the standard route westwards is the main highway, which runs through this region's famous tobacco-growing area of Vuelta Abajo, where the leaves for Cuba's most prestigious cigars are grown, and notably the rustic towns of **San Luís** and **San Juan y Martinez**. The latter, which lies 23 km (14 miles) west of the city of Pinar del Río, is worth a stop to admire its pastel-colored houses.

Depending on the time of year you visit, you will see various stages of tobacco production. During the rainy winter and the early spring growing season, the tobacco plants are shielded from the ravaging effects of the sun by tarpaulins suspended from poles — which, en masse, appear like a sea of undulating fabric. You'll see countless drying sheds thatched with palm fronds where the precious tobacco leaves are dried in the traditional way to preserve their flavor.

Passengers prepare for departure.

Western Cuba

Further on, past the town of Sandino in a region of lagoons, fishermen continue to exist as they have for centuries, paddling their small boats out and using woven nets. **Laguna de Pesquero** is the most popular.

From here until the end of the highway, the road cuts through thick forests and swamps, a breeding ground for the region's large crabs, which often swarm out onto the roads.

A secondary road heads from the fishing outpost of **La Fé** toward **La Bajada**, the entry point for the Bahía de Corrientes, which is at the southernmost point of the peninsula,

where you have to pass through a military checkpoint.

La Bajada is home base of the **María La Gorda International Dive Center (** (082) 78131 or 78077, a diving resort which arranges diving expeditions to pristine reefs and sunken wrecks offshore.

In this area, María La Gorda (Mary the Fat) has entered local legend. Apparently she was a large Venezuelan woman in the eighteenth century who had the misfortune to be kidnapped by pirates and later left stranded here after a shipwreck. Taking stock of the situation, she soon became a sought-after attraction for passing sailors, and lived on in comfort to an old age.

On the other side of La Bajada is the **Guanahacabibes Peninsula**, one of the last refuges for the doomed Indian tribe, the Siboney (also known as the Guanahuatebey) during the Spanish colonization of the island. It is one of Cuba's largest forest reserves, and although rather unprepossessingly sparse in parts, is home to a great many endemic plant, bird, insect and animal species, a number of which are in danger of extinction. In theory, you can visit the reserve with a permit from the Cuban tourism authorities. However it is better to contact the Hotel María La Gorda, which can arrange for you to rent a jeep with a driver who can also serve as a guide. Or you can go with your own car and ask the park ranger at the entrance to accompany you. Entrance costs US$10, and you will have to arrange a fee with your guide. It is forbidden to camp here, and you should leave the reserve before nightfall.

The road that passes through the reserve follows a line of deserted sandy beaches along the Bahía de Corrientes before ending at the lighthouse of Cabo de San Antonio, from which all you can see is the endless expanse of the Gulf of Mexico.

WHERE TO STAY

Villa María La Gorda ((08) 43121 or (082) 78131 satellite **(** 683680510 FAX 683680510, Playa María La Gorda, is a fairly simple, inexpensive and practical establishment, designed with divers in mind. It is pleasant enough in its own right if you want a few days of swimming and seclusion. The 20 *cabañas* are comfortable (don't expect any frills), and the restaurant serves good meals featuring fresh seafood. The diving instructors and the staff here are very friendly and helpful.

FROM HAVANA TO VARADERO

It is an easy and well-signposted two-and-a-half-hour drive eastwards from Havana to Varadero along the two-lane highway Vía Blanca, which begins when you emerge from the Havana Bay tunnel and passes through the provincial capital of Matanzas.

Beyond the Pan-American Village, and further on, beyond the beaches of Playas del Este, as you drive along the coastal highway, your spirits may sink a little (hoping this is not an indication of what may be to come) as you pass plain beaches strung with clusters of plebeian bungalows and dreary cement-block hotels catering to Cuban workers, the Havana Club rum factory, and then a depressing industrial tract punctuated with dirty oil pumps, shelved with iron rock and carpeted with spiky *sisal* plantations.

The first moment of truly impressive scenery comes when you reach the **Yumurí Valley**, which lies at the entrance to the province of Matanzas, 80 km (50 miles) from Havana. Here, from the lookout point at **El Mirador**, you can break the journey with a drink (the juice of a freshly cut coconut or a *cafecito*) and survey the fabulous view across the valley, formed as a natural canyon by the Yumurí River and its tributaries. The surrounding landscape is sheathed in green forest, high above which you can see wheeling Cuban vultures, and beyond which coconut palms rim the coast. The valley, which is eight kilometers (five miles) wide and ringed by hills except to the west, is spanned by the **Bacanayagua Bridge**, the highest bridge in Cuba, completed in 1959.

MATANZAS

Only 20 km (slightly over 12 miles) from the Yumurí Valley is the historic colonial city of Matanzas, one of Cuba's main agricultural centers and industrial ports. It is also known as the vibrant home of many Afro-Cuban musical styles, including the danzonete, a variation on the danzon, which is traditionally played by charanga bands.

Background
By the mid-1800s, Matanzas was one of Cuba's most important trading cities. With its well-situated harbor and its surrounding countryside worked by thousands of slaves, it became the largest sugar exporter in the world, and the magnet for some of Cuba's most prominent intellectuals, scientists, musicians and artists. With its growing population of Creole elite, as well as the merchants and moneylenders who followed, Matanzas was a progressive city that saw the founding of Cuba's first printing press in 1813, its first newspaper in 1828, as well as its first philharmonic orchestra and its first public library. Today, you can see many fine nineteenth-century civic buildings and residences dating from this period.

Located around the large curving Bahía de Matanzas, surrounded by gently undulating hills and valleys and crisscrossed by the San Juan, Yumurí and Canimar rivers that flow to the sea, the city has a long history of settlement. Originally a Taíno Indian village called Yucayo, the Spanish founded the city in 1693, first trading in cattle, then tobacco and later, sugar.

It is not known for sure how Matanzas got its name, which means "place of slaughter." Some speculate that it could refer to the slaughter of cattle, but perhaps, more convincingly, it may refer to an unconfirmed account of 32 shipwrecked Spaniards who were killed here by the Taíno, and in an interesting twist, one of the survivors became the wife of the local Indian chieftain. Certainly, violence seemed to crop up in Matanzas: between 1825 and 1843, when slaves were revolting and attacking plantation owners, the Spanish colonial masters retaliated by brutally torturing and killing more than a thousand slaves in this region. In addition, the Spanish were particularly forceful in their attempts to proselytize, and consequently, the slaves here developed Christian disguises for their own gods, who they continued to worship. Thus, Matanzas became a key center for the development of Santería and other offshoots of Afro-Cuban beliefs, such as Palo Monte and Abakuá.

What to See and Do
You could easily spend an hour or two walking around Matanzas looking at its interesting buildings in the city center. Start with the imposing **Teatro Sauto**. Built in 1863 and designed by an Italian architect, it was the most impressive theater outside of Havana, and became the model for many theaters around the country. While the elegant five-story structure has a classical design, the ground floor incorporates the Cuban *portal*, into which carriages could drive. It is worth going inside to see the exceptional, and beautifully preserved interiors, where every detail was fashionable for its time, including the cast-iron seats and the elaborate painted neoclassical stage set, which could be raised and lowered mechanically. Many European touring companies — ranging from classical ballet to Italian opera — and stars, including Anna Pavlova and Sarah Bernhardt, performed here.

Near Playa Girón, a mid-stream jeep cleaning.

Nearby stands the **Matanzas Fire Station**, completed in 1900, which is among the country's first Republican-era civic buildings and occupies a prominent place on the city's original plaza. Also worth seeing is the **Museo Farmacéutico** (Pharmaceutical Museum) and the **Palacio del Junco**, both on the Calle Milanés, next to the Plaza de Armas, also known as the Parque Libertad. Founded in 1882, and housed in its original building, the museum is a fascinating place to visit, with all of the original copper and bronze instruments used for processing medicinal plants and distilling water, alcoholates and essential oils. The collection includes of thousands of labels, jars, tools and formulas, as well as an extensive library of books in four languages. The museum is open Monday to Saturday, 10 AM to 6 PM and Sunday 9 AM to 1 PM.

The Palacio, built for a wealthy sugar planter in 1842, houses the **Museo Provincial** which recounts the city's history and is open Tuesday to Sunday, 2 PM to 9 PM.

Other nineteenth-century buildings of interest are the **Hotel El Louvre**, a film-set period piece; the 1826 **Aduana** (Customs Building), and now the Palacio de Justicia (Courthouse); and the **Casa de la Trova y el Escritor** (House of the Troubadour and the Writer) which, if you are lucky, may be staging one of their memorable music ensembles the day you visit.

On the main square, look out for the early twentieth-century **Casino Español**, a former social club and casino notable for its ornate façade. It is now the municipal library, and you can take a walk inside to admire its marble staircase and the grandiose proportions of its rooms.

You can also visit the **Catedral de San Carlos**, the oldest church in Matanzas, which dates to 1730, but was remodeled with neoclassical elements, including the pilasters, a century later. Both the **Iglesia de San Pedro** and the **Capilla de Monserrat** chapel are influenced by Italian Renaissance architecture. The chapel's statues were added for a movie set and have remained there.

As you leave Matanzas on the road to Varadero, you will see a signpost on your right directing you to the **Cueva de Bellamar**, eight kilometers (five miles) away. Discov-

ered in 1861, this 3,000-m-long (over 9,800-ft) cave has an abundance of stalagmites and stalactites, with impressive galleries that drop to a depth of 48 m (157 ft), and a network of underground lakes and rivers. The cave is open daily from 9 AM to 5 PM.

Where to Stay and Eat

Matanzas is not really recommended as a place to stay to the extent that the Cuban government would rather that visiting foreigners stay in the purpose-built resorts further along in Varadero. To this end, although there are three vintage hotels — **Hotel El Louvre**, **Hotel Velasco** and **Hotel Yara** — they are peso-only, and non-Cubans are not encouraged. It's easy to imagine how all of them, especially the Hotel El Louvre, would look quite wonderful if they were restored to their former elegance.

Likewise, there is not much scope for a good meal in Matanzas. If you are desperately in search of a meal or refreshments, try **Mesón La Viña**, on the southwest corner of the main square. **Café Atenas**, opposite the Teatro Sauto, is another stand-by.

As you drive out of Matanzas towards Varadero, at the exit of the town is the **Ruinas de Matasiete**, an open-air establishment which serves drinks and snacks overlooking the bay.

CÁRDENAS

The sleepy, crumbling colonial town of Cárdenas lies just five kilometers (three miles) east of Matanzas. Here, horse-drawn carts bearing bales of hay and straw-hatted farmers atop bicycles outnumber cars. Despite its run-down ambience and the obvious hardship faced by many of its residents (which may open the eyes of many visitors to the harsh realities faced by many Cubans), there is a charming gentility to this rustic town. It is known as the "City of Flags" because the Cuban flag was first raised here in 1850, in a failed insurrection.

You should include in your visit a stop at the **Museo Oscar María de Rojas**, on Calle Cárdenas. Among its curiosities are an elegant nineteenth-century hearse, two preserved fleas trussed up in dancing costumes and a fountain-pen pistol which belonged to a Nazi spy who was captured in Havana in 1942. It is open Tuesday to Saturday, 1 PM to 6 PM and Sunday, 9 AM to 1 PM.

HOW TO GET THERE

Matanzas is 42 km (26 miles) west of Havana and 98 km (61 miles) east of Varadero. If you are driving, it is worthwhile exploring both Matanzas and Cárdenas en route from Havana, or as you return to Havana. If you are planning to continue on from Varadero to Playa Girón, you will pass through Cárdenas.

If you want to take the train from Havana to Matanzas, you will pull into the new Estación de Ferrocarriles at the city's southern edge. Most of the national trains travel through here from Havana en route to the island's main cities and towns, including Santiago de Cuba.

If you have set your heart on taking the Hershey Railway, which plies between Matanzas and Casablanca, you need to take the train at another station at Calles 55 and 67 in Versalles, close to the town center. Ticket sales begin an hour before departure.

VARADERO

Many visitors who arrive in Cuba on package tours are pitched directly into Varadero, Cuba's premier purpose-built beach resort, two and a half hour's drive east of Havana. Very often they never get to see any other part of the country, let alone the capital. While this may not be surprising, it helps explain why the culture of Varadero can be described as almost surreal. It's a playground for foreigners that is about as dislocated from the rest of the country as it is possible to be.

BACKGROUND

The Varadero that you see today — with its impressive row of luxury hotels best described as landscaped concrete-wonders lined up along an isthmus facing the Straits of Florida and nearly touching the Tropic of Cancer — was developed in the early 1990s as the centerpiece of the Revolution's bid to shore up its failing economy by re-starting the Cuban tourist industry after a long sabbatical.

Long before, the Spanish had set up a garrison here to keep watch for pirates and smugglers. As a resort, its popularity began during the late nineteenth century when the well-to-do from nearby Cárdenas began to build summer homes here. Then, in 1920, the pharmaceuticals magnate Eleuthère Irénée du Pont built a grand mansion here and bought up 512 hectares (1,265 acres) of beachside property, thus encouraging many fellow millionaires to holiday here. Later, during World War II, it became fashionable when prosperous Americans looked for

somewhere safer and closer to take a holiday than Europe. The Cuban elite also had their residences here, including the dictator Batista. After the Revolution, Varadero was just as popular with Cubans as well as sunseekers from the Soviet Bloc countries.

Varadero is said to have the most beautiful beaches in Cuba. Certainly the peninsula's 18 km (11 miles) of beaches are blessed with the necessary trio of soft white sands, palm trees and clear blue seas (with hardly a rock or a weed) to satisfy most basic requirements for a beach holiday. The hotels, a series of some surprisingly tasteful Canadian, German, French, Italian and even Jamaican

Oscar takes a reflective puff in his Varadero home.

investments in joint-ventures with the Cuban government, are designed for people who are content to stay within the confines of their hotel, or to shuttle between tourist-orientated cafés, bars, restaurants, shopping complexes and now, Cuba's largest, brand-new three-kilometer-long (nearly two-mile) 18-hole golf course. Meanwhile, planners intend to double the number of hotels here within a decade. Some joke that Varadero is presiding over its very own oil boom, the kind associated with suntans.

Varadero also has a reputation as something of a fleshpot: don't be fooled by the hotel schedules posted up in the lobby which suggest activities for almost every moment of the day, like a Baden-Powell-style British holiday camp. One observer commented that Varadero was only place he had ever seen prostitutes soliciting in the surf. If you go with your family, this aspect of the resort culture is pretty easy to overlook; indeed many couples and families have come to Varadero "for a change," but do expect to accommodate some of its problems.

GENERAL INFORMATION

Most hotels have information and tour excursion desks, and the leading hotels often house offices of the primary Cuban tour agencies. The main **Havanatur** ℂ (05) 667027 or 667589 office is at the corner of Avenida 1 and Calle 31.

The government's Centro de Información Turístico (Tourist Information Center) at Avenida 1 and Calle 23 has been replaced by a **Rumbos** ℂ (05) 612384 outlet that also deals in tourist information and excursions.

Asistur ℂ (05) 667277 or 662164, at Avenida 1 and Calle 31, can provide advice and assistance should emergencies strike. For example, they can help arrange medical treatment and insurance, legal advice and special-case cash advances, should you require it. Open Monday to Friday, 9 AM to noon and 1:30 PM to 4:30 PM; Saturday, 9 AM to noon.

Varadero's **International Clinic** ℂ (05) 667710 is located at Avenida 1 and Calle 61, opposite the Hotel Cuatro Palmas.

You can cash your traveler's checks at the **Banco Financiero International** ℂ (05) 667002, Calle 32 and Avenida Playa.

Varadero offers more Internet access than any other Cuban destination (including Havana). The **post office** at the corner of Avenida 1 and Calle 36 offers net service for US$5 per hour, although the lines are often "down" and hours are rather limited. Hotels are another option. Non-guests can log on for five hours at the business center in the lobby of the **Sol Elite Palmeras** ℂ (05) 667009 by purchasing a US$15 phone card.

GETTING AROUND

Getting orientated is not difficult. Varadero is located on the Hicacos Peninsula, and is a long, narrow isthmus of rocks and sand surrounded on both sides by sea, pocked (on the non-swimming side) by mangrove swamps and sand bars. The distance from the peninsula's entrance at the drawbridge over Paso Malo lagoon to its easternmost tip at the Punta de Hicacos is almost 20 km (about 12 miles) and its average width is no more than 700 m (about a half a mile). At its most bulbous point at the Punta de Hicacos, it is only 211 km (131 miles) from Key West, with a clear reception from Florida radio stations that is somewhat surreal.

The main roads lengthwise are the Avenida Kawama, Avenida 1 (which is the peninsula's main commercial strip), Avenida de las Américas and the Autopista Sur, which runs all the way to the eastern end of the peninsula. *Calles* (streets) run perpendicular to these main avenues and are numbered from 1 to 69, while the *calles* in the residential Villa Cuba section run from A to L.

A popular way to get around the relatively small confines of Varadero town is by rented motorcycle or bicycle (although renting bicycles on this lengthy beach can be a nightmare), allowing you to cruise along to different parts of the peninsula, stop at whatever beach looks inviting and investigate the town's cafés, restaurants and shops. Your hotel travel desk can assist you in renting a two-wheeled vehicle. Horse-drawn *calesas* are another option.

Most hotels also have car rental agencies, although be forewarned that you should do this well in advance to ensure availability. All of the major Cuban rental agencies have offices in Varadero including **Havanautos**

((05) 613733 or 614409, **Rex** ((05) 667600, **Via** ((05) 619001 or 611457 and **Transtur** ((05) 611444 or 667332.

WHAT TO SEE AND DO

Not surprisingly, most people prefer to simply lie on the beach, get sand in their paperbacks, gaze at — and swim in — the sea, and perhaps on an ambitious day, play a few rounds of tennis. Most of the hotels have bars designed around their swimming pools, so that swim-suited sun-worshippers

ing the **Museo de Varadero** ((05) 663189, housed in a candy pink and blue painted Key West-style house, set back in a garden by the beach, where all the local lore is documented. It is open Tuesday to Saturday, 9 AM to 6 PM, Sunday 9 AM to noon.

Don't miss the splendid Spanish Revival-style Du Pont family vacation home built in 1926, which now sits within the new 18-hole **Varadero Golf Club** ((05) 668482 or 662113 FAX (05) 668180 or 668481 WEB SITE www.varaderogolfclub.com. The Rumbos-operated complex was devised to

can indulge in rum-based *cuba libres* and get sozzled as they get sizzled. Varadero specializes in sun, sea and sand vacations, with watersports, diving and sailing expeditions by day, and plenty of discotheque and cabaret diversions at night.

This being said, the town of Varadero has a few places of interest tucked away, and you can always visit Matanzas or nearby Cárdenas if you are curious to see some "real" Cuban towns.

The historic part of Varadero — where the remains of the nineteenth-century Spanish garrison can be seen, now painted pink and green — lies between Calles 42 and 54 and Avenidas 1 and 2. Some of the wooden houses are quite charming. It is worth visit-

be a "golfing hotel" with comfortable rooms and the exclusive Xanadú restaurant. Some rooms have been left as they were originally, and there is a wonderful Moorish sea-facing terrace with details hand-carved in mahogany and romantic lamps at the corners. The golf course was designed by the Canadian firm Golf Design Services, headed by Les Furber, who worked with the great Robert Trent Jones.

Parque Josone is a tourist complex, full of restaurants, shops and cafés. Of all Varadero's shops — which include well-stocked supermarkets and casual-wear boutiques, **Casa del Habano** ((05) 667843,

Vegas (tobacco-drying sheds) dot the fertile west.

on Avenida 1 between Calles 63 and 64, is notable as a Mecca for cigar-smokers with its stock of Cuba's best brands.

If you want to drive to the end of the peninsula, follow the two-lane Carretera del Sur all the way past the hotel developments, past the **Marina Chapelín** ((05) 668440 FAX (05) 668441, and soon all you will see will be swampy marshes on your right and low-lying shrub to your left. The marina offers a number of interesting adventure excursions including a two-hour **"jungle tour"** on speedy jet skis into the nearby mangroves. Several popular catamaran cruises are also based at Marina Chapelín. **Cubanacán Seafari** ((05) 667550 or 667800 is a day-long voyage to Cayo Blanco that includes snorkeling, lunch and open bar. **Jolly Roger** ((05) 667565 or 667757 tenders a similar cruise on an almost identical boat.

Directly across the street from the marina is Varadero's brand new **Delfinario** ((05) 668031, which stages three dolphin shows per day. Open 9 AM to 9 PM. The small marine park also offers an opportunity to swim with dolphins.

Another new maritime attraction is based at Puertosol's Marina Dársena at the other end of the peninsula: the **Varasub One** ((05) 667027 or 667589, a boat with an underwater seating area and huge picture windows that allow passengers to get "up close and personal" with Varadero's offshore coral reef. It's almost like you're in a real submarine and is especially popular with children. Rates are US$25 for adults and US$20 for kids. Book your voyage at the main Havanatur office at the corner of Avenida 1 and Calle 31.

WHERE TO STAY

The most important factor in choosing a room in Varadero is location. The nicest, soft-sanded beaches are found between Calle 55 and Punta Hicacos, which means that it is worth checking before you book that your hotel is actually located in this more desirable part of the peninsula. The least attractive beaches are located near Vía Blanca and Avenida Kawama areas. It is at least useful to know in advance why you may have been given such a good rate on hotels and villas that are located on the way

into Varadero, such as Superclub Puntarena and Villa Punta Blanca.

Expensive

The **Meliá Varadero** ((05) 667013 FAX (05) 667012, Autopista Sur km7, Playa Las Américas, is still the undisputed queen of Varadero's deluxe resorts. You may feel quite content to simply commute between your room, the beach, the swimming pool and the buffet table without really feeling the need to leave. You can stay in a bungalow or a sea-facing terraced suite (which comes equipped with a mini-bar, satellite television and VCR). Among its restaurants, the Fuerteventfura is reputedly one of the best and most expensive in Cuba. The only drawback is that while the hotel beach is very pleasant, it is truthfully not the best on the stretch.

Located alongside, the **Meliá Las Américas** ((05) 667600 FAX (05) 667625, Autopista Sur km7, Playa Las Américas, is another luxury hotel in the same mold, run by the same Spanish-Cuban joint-venture as the above, with a similar standard of amenities and services. It also boasts several "golf suites" with direct access to the adjacent Varadero Golf Club.

Along the same stretch of sand is a third Meliá luxury property, the crescent-shaped **Sol Elite Palmeras** ((05) 667009 FAX (05) 667008, Autopista Sur km8. It's an attractive place to stay, with gorgeous landscaping, brightly colored stucco bungalows, good facilities, excellent service and direct access to the beach. Note: All three Meliá's offer a choice of all-inclusive or à la carte rates.

Despite a steel-beam façade that resembles an airport terminal, the **LTI Tuxpan Resort** ((05) 667560 FAX (05) 667561, Avenida de las Américas, Autopista Sur km4, offers comfortable accommodations with standard facilities, including a range of restaurants, boutiques, shops and convention rooms. This all-inclusive, German-managed hotel features a wide stretch of fine wide sand and an artificial island with coconut palms in the middle of its swimming pool. Most of the 233 rooms have ocean views. With a separate children's pool and kiddy club, the Tuxpan is especially popular with families.

Farther east is the quite popular **Hotel Beaches Varadero** ((05) 668470 FAX (05) 668335, on Autopista Sur at km14, a Jamaican-Cuban joint-venture operated by the same people responsible for Beaches Negril and Sandals in Montego Bay. It is not as classy as the Meliás but far superior in terms of decor and service to the peninsula's other all-inclusives. You can expect all sorts of organized fun and sports activities.

At the other end of the Varadero, **Villas Punta Blanca** ((05) 667090 or 668050 FAX (05) 667004, Avenida Kawama, is another beachfront all-inclusive, run with panache by Gran Caribe. You can choose among a

Anyone with a strong sense of history (or irony) should spend at least one night at the **Mansión Xanadú** ((05) 668482 or 667750 FAX (05) 668481, Avenida de las Américas, Autopista Sur km8.5, on the grounds of the Varadero Golf Club. This sprawling seaside villa was built in the late 1920s as a vacation home for chemical and munitions tycoon Eleuthère Irénée du Pont. The eclectic design features Asian, American and Spanish colonial elements. Six rooms in the old "guest cottage" are available for overnight stays, each with sea-view balcony and private

selection of spacious villas and houses spread along the beach at the quiet western end of the peninsula. There are several restaurants, including an Italian eatery in a beach house that once belonged to gangster Al Capone.

The only thing west of Punta Blanca is the hulking **Superclub Puntarena** ((05) 667120 FAX (05) 667074, Avenida Kawama, which consists of two ugly, stalwart-looking seven-story buildings known locally as the "Twins." Since the Jamaican Superclub chain assumed management several years ago, the dining and recreation facilities have shown a marked improvement. But that still can't compensate for the inconvenient location, the surly service or the unattractive beach.

bath. You can order room service from the same menu as Xanadú's gourmet restaurant. In addition to a small beach, registered guests have unlimited (free) access to the golf links, which is perhaps reason alone to stay here.

Moderate

Varadero's first luxury hotel, the faded pink, concrete, 1950s classic **Hotel Internacional** ((05) 667038 or 667039 FAX (05) 667246, Avenida de las Américas, is no longer in the luxury category. It's located on one of the loveliest beaches in Varadero, which makes

Billboard reminders of the aborted Bay of Pigs invasion.

it much easier to tolerate the hotel's idiosyncrasies and only average service and facilities, although this has improved with a recent renovation. The beach alone, as well as the slightly louche atmosphere at the beach bar, makes the Internacional a great place to stay. If you only plan to come to Varadero for the day, you can rent one of their beach cabins as a place to change, rest and shower for a nominal fee.

The **Hotel Arenas Doradas** ((05) 668150 or 668156 FAX (05) 668159, Carretera Punta Hicacos, Playa de Los Taínos, a well-run joint-venture between Cuba's Gran Caribe group and Spain's Hoteles C chain, is located towards the end of the peninsula, away from Varadero's main hotel strip. Attempts have been made to integrate the hotel with its natural surroundings, and there are plenty of thatched umbrellas on the pretty, soft-sanded beach. The rooms flaunt bright Caribbean color schemes and there's a pleasant pool area with a thatched-roof, swim-up bar.

The salmon-pink **Coralia Cuatro Palmas Resort** ((05) 667040 FAX (05) 667208, Avenida 1 between Calles 61 and 62, is set in lush vegetation that once harbored the beach house of Cuban dictator Fulgencio Batista. Its rounded *portales*-style arcades, balustrades and pillars lend it a pleasant Cuban atmosphere. Importantly, it is located on a lovely stretch of beach, is also close to the commercial district and has good watersports facilities. Since France's Mercure chain took over management several years ago, the resort has improved by leaps and bounds.

Villa Cuba Resort ((05) 668280 FAX (05) 668282, Avenida de las Américas, is located near the Du Pont mansion. These pleasant one-, two- or three-bedroom apartments — some more luxurious than others — are an excellent choice for families — but can be private and secluded as well. The beach is very lovely.

The Spanish-style (think Costa del Sol) **Villa Kawama** ((05) 667155 or 667156 FAX (05) 667334, Avenida Kawama and Calle O, is not entirely without charm, with two-story bungalows close to a palm-dotted, if uninspiring stretch of beach, which, not surprisingly, is quite private. On the other hand,

this is perhaps the cheapest all-inclusive you can find in over-priced Varadero.

Inexpensive

The homegrown Horizontes hotel chain has no fewer than a dozen properties in Varadero, all of them in the budget category. Most aren't worth mentioning, but a few stand out.

The fan-shaped **Horizontes Herradura** ((05) 613703 FAX (05) 667496, Avenida de la Playa, between Calles 35 and 36, overlooks Varadero's main beach, one of the few cheap hotels with its own stretch of sand. Rooms boast air conditioning and safe-deposit boxes, but you share the living room, kitchen area and balcony with one or two other units. You could find yourself sharing with smokers or all-night party animals. Hot water is problematic. But there's that gorgeous beach and warm turquoise water right outside the door.

Hotel Horizontes Pullman ((05) 667161 FAX (05) 667495, Avenida 1 between Calles 49 and 50, is the most charming of Varadero's inexpensive hotels, renovated in a quirky mansion, and located close to both downtown Varadero and the beach.

WHERE TO EAT

In addition to an abundance of restaurants, pizza bars and cafés that have sprung up along Varadero's beachfront stretch, you can consider the following recommendations.

Expensive

Fuerteventura ((05) 667013, Hotel Meliá Varadero, has to be Varadero's most exceptional restaurant, with excellent cuisine from Spain ranging from Basque specialties to creatively prepared paella and lobster.

Mansión Xanadú ((05) 668482 or 667750, Avenida de las Américas, Autopista Sur km8.5, the former Du Pont mansion, was Varadero's most elegant expatriate mansion in its day, and much of the atmosphere lingers on. Sections of the mansion have been preserved, with family photographs and book-lined rooms. The menu tenders a number of dishes not normally found in these parts: seared goose liver pâté, octopus and paprika salad, grilled albacore tuna, quail stuffed with foie gras, and honey roasted duck magret in port sauce. Even if you don't eat here, quaff a drink in the top-floor bar with its lavish Moorish woodwork and sweeping sea views.

Moderate

One of Varadero's more unusual restaurants is **La Casa de Al** ((05) 668050, Avenida Kawama just beyond the entrance to Villas Punta Blanca, a coral-stone beach house originally built in the 1890s and then purchased by American gangster Al Capone in the early 1930s. History aside, the beachfront eatery also has some rather unusual menu items: Bloody Spaghetti, Soup Mafiosa, Al Pacino and Godfather salads, and a range of "Cosa Nostra" main courses. Service is excellent and the shoreline setting is very romantic.

Set within this peaceful marina with sea views, **El Galeón** ((05) 663712, Marina Gaviota, Carretera del Sur, is a pleasant place to have lunch, with excellent seafood dishes.

Mesón del Quijote ((05) 667796, Avenida de las Américas, serves Spanish food of unexceptional but reliable quality, and the surroundings are pleasant, overlooking a nineteenth-century Spanish lookout tower.

Casa del Queso Cubano ((05) 667747, Calle 62 and Avenida 1, is not for the calorie-conscious, the specialties of this restaurant being cheese, meat and chocolate fondues. Whatever else, this is certainly a singular dish. **La Barbacoa** ((05) 667795, Avenida 1 and Calle 64, serves barbecued meats and seafood amid a baronial-colonial atmosphere.

Inexpensive

The best place in Varadero for typical Cuban and Creole dishes is **El Bodegón Criollo** ((05) 667784, Avenida Playa and Calle 40, with inexpensive prices and an entertaining musical trio. Among the house specialties are offbeat Cuban dishes such as *ropa vieja* (spicy minced meat), *tasajo a la criolla* (jerked beef), *palomille grille* (roasted dove), *costilla de lorno ahumada* (smoked loin chop), and a mixed seafood grill of lobster, shrimp and a fish called *mariscadas*. Like its much older namesake in Old Havana, El Bodegón's walls are covered in customer autographs and signatures, so remember to bring a pencil, pen or marker.

New along the waterfront is **Restaurante la Vega**, Avenida de la Playa, between Calles 31 and 32. Perched on wooden stilts above the sand, it offers a wide range of dishes like grilled fish and shrimp, *arroz con pollo* and vegetarian paella. If you're really hungry try the *fidelia vuelta abajo*, a mixed grill that includes shrimp, lobster, pork and squid.

For good seafood and international dishes amid rustic beach surroundings and palm trees, try **Mi Casita** ((05) 613787, Camino del Mar between Calle 11 and 12. **Lai-Lai** ((05) 667793, Avenida 1 and Calle 18, is regarded as Varadero's best Chinese restaurant, set in a rambling old colonial mansion beside the beach.

It is fun to visit the so-called Honey House, or **Casa de la Miel**, Avenida 1 between Calles 26 and 27, where you can sample intriguing dishes, sweets, juices and herb teas sweetened with honey and royal jelly. There are also cocktails with a honey and rum sting.

Avenida 1 in "downtown" Varadero sports a number of budget eateries. **El Caney**, at the corner of Calle 40, offers a nice garden setting with thatched-roof pavilions and a menu that seems to have everything from grilled lobster to hamburgers and ice cream. **La Viccaria** ((05) 614721, at the corner of Calle 38, offers a similar spread, including lobster, for a mere US$10.

NIGHTLIFE

Cabaret Cueva del Pirata ((05) 667751, Carretera Las Morlas, Autopista Sur km11, is located in a limestone cave, a dramatic, if somewhat claustrophobic setting, lit up with flashing strobes and dry ice. After the nightly cabaret show, which begins at 10:30 PM, dancing is *de rigueur*.

The poshest place on the peninsula to listen to live tunes is **Habana Café** ((05) 668070, Avenida de las Américas at Calle K, next to the Sol Club Las Sirenas resort. Modeled after the Hard Rock Café chain, many of the capital's best acts take the stage here.

Nightly Latin music and dancing, as well as live bands, have made **Discoteca La Bamba** ((05) 667560, LTI Tuxpan Resort, Avenida de las Américas, one of Varadero's most popular venues. The action runs from 10 PM to 4 AM nightly.

If you're in the mood for nothing more than a *mojito* and good old-fashioned street music, find yourself a table at **La Fondue**, Avenida 1, opposite the Hotel Cuatro Palmas, and listen to the music that pours forth from the outdoor stage on Friday and Saturday nights.

From the cocktail hour onwards, the **Piano Bar** ((05) 667013 at the Meliá Varadero, Autopista Sur km7, is a civilized place to enjoy musicians perform traditional Cuban songs and Afro-Cuban jazz. Another great place for a quiet drink and some music is the top-floor bar at the **Mansión Xanadú** ((05) 668482, reached by means of a 1930s vintage Otis elevator.

How to Get There

The **Aeropuerto Internacional Juan Gualberto Gómez** ((05) 613016 is located 16 km (10 miles) west of Varadero. See GETTING THERE, page 306, in TRAVELERS' TIPS, for information about international and domestic airline flights to Varadero, as well as its main ports of entry.

From Havana, there are various options for reaching Varadero by road. Aside from renting a car, you can opt to make the journey on a minibus. Your hotel travel desk or front desk can make the arrangements; the cost is about US$30 each way. Taxis between Havana and Varadero are roughly US$100 each way.

Another option is the modern, air-conditioned coaches of **ViAzul** ((05) 614886, Autopista Sur at Calle 36 in Varadero, or ((07) 811413 in Havana. ViAzul also offers regular bus service between Varadero and Trinidad.

If you decide to drive yourself, Varadero lies 142 km (87 miles) due east of Havana via a modern, four-lane highway called the Vía Blanca, which often offers spectacular views of the coast.

You can also travel between Havana and Varadero by sea on a 300-passenger ferry called the **Crucero Jet Kat Express II** ((05) 668727 in Varadero or ((07) 336566 in Havana. Departures from Varadero are Tuesday, Thursday and Saturday at 8:30 AM from Marina Chapelín. Ferries from Havana de-

part at the same hour on Monday, Wednesday and Friday.

THE ZAPATA PENINSULA

Within several hour's drive from Varadero is an exceptional region on the southern coast of western Cuba. The area encompasses Playa Girón — a region more memorably known as the Bay of Pigs, the site of an abortive invasion of Cuba by exiles and mercenaries in 1961 — and the immense Zapata Peninsula, the island's finest nature preserve and its largest area of pristine wetlands, which has been turned into a national park that also offers isolated beaches, crystal-clear waters, beautiful limestone *cenotes* (sunken lagoons) as well as exceptional fly-fishing opportunities.

You can explore this area — which lies on the sparsely populated southern coast of Matanzas Province — within a few days, perhaps setting out from either Havana or Varadero. From the southern coast of Matanzas, you can continue onwards to explore central Cuba.

The easiest way to reach this region is to take the main exit for Playa Girón from the Autopista Nacional, near the intriguingly named town of Australia. If you are driving from Varadero, via Cárdenas, you will be on secondary roads that pass through scenery that becomes increasingly lush, dominated by its *llanos*, its flatlands, fecund with a patchwork quilt of sugarcane and orange plantations, rimmed by a distant horizon of royal palms.

Along the roads, scenes of small town life flash by: women with curlers in their hair tending horses, old trucks wheezing by crammed with plantation workers, schoolchildren going to learn the ways of the field in the Russian-design agricultural camps.

What to See and Do

Just off the main highway for Playa Girón (which goes through Playa Larga first), is the roadside **Fiesta Campesina**, a tourist village where air-conditioned tourist buses usually make a scheduled stop. A miniature zoo has been constructed here, displaying lizards, baby crocodiles, prehistoric pike or *majuaní*, the rodent-like *jutias* and even guinea pigs. The house specialty is delicious Creole coffee, served in a small clay cup with a stick of sugarcane, and the other typical drink of the region, the *fiesta campesina*, made with sugarcane liqueur and rum. If only for rest, this is a convenient stop.

The town of Australia is notable for its hulking giant of a **sugar mill**, which Castro used as his personal headquarters as he and his Revolutionary Armed Forces staged their defense of the during the Bay of Pigs invasion. That victory is commemorated by a row of solemn concrete tablets that rise from the side of the road, sporadically at first, and then peppering the roadside, en route to Playa Larga. They honor 161 of Castro's soldiers who died in action. They stand where the soldiers fell during the three-day battle in April 1961.

Near the entrance to Playa Larga, to the left a vast marshland marks the western fringe of the **Laguna del Tesoro** (Treasure Lake), Cuba's largest natural lagoon, which spans 92 sq km (over 35 sq miles) and is tightly ringed with bulrushes, mangrove swamps and thick palmetto-shrub forest. Were it not for the mosquitoes, this scene would be the picture of implacable serenity. But beware: this area is also home to one of Cuba's few potentially deadly creatures, the Cuban crocodile.

As the Spanish went about colonizing Cuba, this was one of the few regions that they largely left alone. Christopher Columbus mentioned in his missives that these rivers and swamplands were inhabited by large quantities of "enormous monsters." However, within a few centuries, indiscriminate hunting turned the beasts into an almost extinct species, and only those that managed to hide away in intricate areas of the swamp system survived. Since a protection campaign was begun in 1961, thousands of the reptiles have been bred at the adjacent **La Boca Crocodile Farm**.

At La Boca, you can walk around a large circular enclosure where about 50 of the crocodile equivalent of teenagers and mature adults lurk in small swamps, hideout under rocks, gaze up longingly at visitors leaning over the wooden platforms, and make sudden lunges at any movement.

Feeding time — which takes place twice weekly — is a gruesome experience. Although these crocodiles can apparently live up to 150 years, they rarely do, and often finish up being attacked and eaten by other crocodiles. Smaller enclosures contain younger, smaller crocodiles who do not appear so threatening. One of the musicians of the inevitable trio that performs at the entrance of La Boca puts a tiny crocodile through its cabaret paces. You can get your photograph taken with one if you like. Admission to the croc farm is US$5.

To see even more crocodiles, there is a crocodile nursery across the road. Although it is not open to the public, if you are traveling independently and are prepared to give a donation ask the keeper if he can arrange a guided visit. At the nursery, some 45,000 or so crocodiles are nurtured from egg through all stages of their "childhood." They are held in steel pens divided up by age and size, and released at the age of 17. The workers who look after them know all sorts of crocodile stories, and some extend a munched arm or scarred stomach to show their own personal experience. Crocodiles, they say, can run up to 60 km/h (37 mph) for short spurts, and they don't recommend spear fishing in the shallow waters around here. No one is exactly sure how many crocodiles are "out there" now; apparently many escaped from the nursery when Hurricane Lili devastated the area in 1996.

La Boca is also the embarkation point for **Guamá**, a resort village that is quite unique in Cuba, situated on a series of islands connected by wooden walkways deep in the Laguna del Tesoro. The boat ride (US$10 round trip) takes you through the lagoon for several kilometers, then approaches the resort, which is supposedly sited on what was once a Taíno Indian village. According to legend, when the Taíno realized that the Spanish had finally discovered their home, they hid all their gold and valuable possessions in the lagoon, hence its name.

It was Celia Sánchez, Fidel Castro's revolutionary companion, who was inspired to create the Guamá resort, and *El Jefe* himself has often visited (having acquired a first-hand, in-depth knowledge of the surrounding topography during his rout of

CIA-backed Cuban exile mercenaries), tending towards adventurous fishing expeditions. On an island near the resort, you can explore a reconstructed Taíno village with its life-size sculpted figures depicting Taíno Indians by Cuban sculptor Rita Longa; sample *saoco* (rum and coconut water); and wander through the complex of thatched *cabañas* connected by pathways and bridges. It is unquestionably a beautiful place to visit, and you can linger at the restaurant for an hour or so and take the next boat back, but bring strong mosquito repellent regardless.

Fishing enthusiasts will be interested to know that the lagoon is rich in trout, haddock, carp, and the local Cuban *biajaca* as well as the alligator gar or *manjuarí*.

The only blot on the experience of visiting Guamá is the environmentally unfriendly diesel exhaust emitted by the boats, fuel shortages being as dire here as everywhere else in Cuba.

WHERE TO STAY AND EAT

Get back to nature at **Villa Guamá ℂ** (059) 5687 or 5551 FAX (07) 4131, on the shores of the Laguna del Tesoro. This ecoresort offers a series of circular thatched *cabañas* made from native woods, perched on stilts above the lagoon and surrounding swampy marshes, linked together by wooden walkways. The moderately priced *cabañas* may look rustic, but they are comfortable and air conditioned, with a bathroom and telephone and television. The resort has a restaurant and a discotheque (be warned that the nightly music may defeat your desire for tranquility), as well as fresh-water fishing supplies, binoculars for bird watching, and row boats to explore the lagoon. The Villa Guamá also arranges three-hour-long guided fishing trips on Laguna del Tesoro. The food is not very good, aside from freshly snared grilled fish you may catch. The resort can only reached by boat, a journey of eight kilometers (five miles) from the landing at the La Boca tourist complex on the Australia-Playa Larga Highway. Round trip boat fare is US$10 per person, even if you're staying overnight.

Overlooking the lagoon at **La Boca** is a ranch-style restaurant of the same name,

which serves excellent Creole dishes as well as roast crocodile tail, said to be an aphrodisiac. Similar fair is served at **Restaurante Colibri** in the same complex.

Several tourist restaurants are situated between Australia and the Autopista including the popular **Fiesta Campesina**, which always seems to have a herd of buses parked outside.

PLAYA LARGA AND ZAPATA NATIONAL PARK

From La Boca, the road continues through the marshlands to the beach resort of Playa Larga, 14 km (about nine miles) away. Lying at the head of the Bahía de Cochinos (Bay of Pigs), this was the secondary landing site during the Bay of Pigs invasion. Playa Larga is not the loveliest beach in the region. However, it is the entry point to the Zapata Peninsula's Parque Nacional de la Ciénaga de Zapata, the vast swamp that is Cuba's most important bird reserve. The modest-looking International Bird Watching Center is based here, close to Buena Ventura, the reserve's entrance, and operates bird-watching tours.

The reserve's designated fishing areas are also becoming something of a Mecca for fly-fishing enthusiasts, primarily for its tarpon and bonefish.

No unauthorized access to the sanctuary is allowed, and all visitors — including bird-watching and fishing groups — must be accompanied by government tourist guides assigned here. Consequently, many visitors, including ornithologists, stay at the modest Hotel Playa Larga, set on a fairly nondescript beach. From here, you can make individual or guided forays into the reserve, which has a well-established network of day and night observation sites and walkways.

GENERAL INFORMATION

Try to book a guide to lead you through the Zapata reserve in advance when you make your accommodation reservation. The Hotel Playa Larga runs excursions that start at US$20 per person. You can discuss with the staff about the type of excursion you wish to go on and negotiate your guide's time and fees. Guides can also be hired through the Fiesta Campesina complex: ask to speak to the manager.

You can contact the government agency **Cubatur** ((07) 334155 FAX (07) 333529, Calle F 157 at the corner of Avenida 9 and Calle Calzada, Vedado, Havana, for their information pamphlet on bird watching, as well as their bird-watching excursions in the Zapata Peninsula. In the United States, the specialist tour company, **Wings of the World** TOLL-FREE IN US (800) 465-8687, 1200 William Street, Suite 706, Buffalo, New York 14240, offers eight-day bird-watching tours to this re-

birds such as warblers, herons, terns, swallows and several birds of prey. Of Cuba's 23 endemic bird species, 18 inhabit these swamps. If you are lucky, you may see the *zunzuncito*, the *trogon* or *tocororo*, the Gundlach hawk, the blue-headed quail dove, the reclusive gnome owl, the island's rare species of woodpecker, and many Cuban parrots.

Most birding excursions make their first stop at **Santo Tomás**, about 30 km (19 miles) west of Playa Larga, where flamingos and spoonbills gather during the migratory season.

gion (as well as to Parque Nacional La Güira in Pinar del Río) on special request for a minimum of two people. While they recommend doing it in the rainy season, they will stage it at any time of year. The cost is US$2,295.

The best time to visit the reserve is between April and October, when vast numbers of birds arrive for the migratory season.

WHAT TO SEE AND DO

Within easy reach of Playa Larga, the national park's lush scenery is a paradise for some 190 species of birds, the majority of them migratory. Those seen most commonly are rosy flamingos, black-necked stilts, white ibises, parrots, wild-fowl and migratory

One of the most beautiful journeys in the reserve is to visit **Las Salinas** (which lies near the coast about two hour's drive southwest from Playa Larga), a huge expanse of marshes, flatlands and islets where many communities of birds make their home. To reach it, you have to take a dirt road which winds and twists its way through what feels like (and is) true wilderness: sometimes the road gets flooded, and crocodiles are known to live in the surrounding marshes. It is compulsory (as well as both a comfort and educational) to have a guide along with you here. There are plans afoot to make this reserve more accessible for ecotourists.

Crocodiles are raised at a nursery across the road from La Boca Crocodile Farm.

Within the Zapata Peninsula a 70 km-long (43-mile) limestone crevice snakes through this landscape, riddled with *cenotes* (sunken lagoons) and underwater cave systems. Washed by both sea and fresh water, these mysterious caverns teem with all sorts of life, including crocodiles, manatees and aquatic reptiles. Having just seen those crocodiles at La Boca, you might want to take your guide's advice about which *cenotes* are swimming and spelunking friendly.

Fly-fishing enthusiasts will be interested in the two designated areas for fishing — Laguna de Salinas and the 200-m-wide (650-ft) Río Hatiguanico, which snakes through mangrove swamps to the sea, branching out into many cross-streams. See SPORTING SPREE, page 31 in YOUR CHOICE, for details about arranging fishing trips here.

WHERE TO STAY

Hotel Horizontes Playa Larga ((059) 7225 or 7294, Playa Larga, is a good, inexpensive base for exploring Zapata National Park and that Bay of Pigs battle mural in the lobby is pretty cool. But the beach is not among Cuba's best and the resort has a fairly Spartan atmosphere — not a place to linger beyond meals and after a day's outing. However, local staff are very friendly and make an effort to ensure you are looked after.

EN ROUTE TO PLAYA GIRÓN

From Playa Larga, the historic town of Playa Girón lies 33 km (about 20 miles) away on the peninsula's eastern coast. Along the road, the scenery is spectacular, with clear blue lapping up against mangrove forests and small rocky beaches, and dotted by secluded coves, some of which have tempting *cenotes*.

If you weren't too impressed with Playa Larga, you might want to stop at **Caleta del Rosario**, about three kilometers (nearly two miles) from Playa Larga, an excellent little bay with good swimming. You may want to drive five kilometers (three miles) on to have lunch at **La Casa del Pescador**, a tranquil spot serving simple seafood and Cuban dishes. Its balcony overlooks one of the most impressive *cenotes* along the coast: **El Cenote**, in which you can snorkel or

dive amid schools of brightly colored tropical fish, which sparkle like gems in the dazzlingly ice-blue water. Adjacent, the small diving center attached to El Cenote rents equipment and gives advice about what to see. According to local lore, an unexploded projectile, dating from the Bay of Pigs invasion, is wedged within the depths of the *cenote*.

Further along (15 km or nine miles from Playa Larga), the **Cueva de los Pesces** is another impressive *cenote* and a perfect place to return for an afternoon of scuba diving. It drops to a depth of 70 m (230 ft), and its flooded caverns are filled with fish.

PLAYA GIRÓN

As you drive on to Playa Girón, which lies at the mouth of the Bahía de Cochinos, giant billboards announce that you are entering a politically charged zone. "Playa Girón: The First Rout of Imperialism in Latin America!" says one. During the rainy months of May and June, this is where you will see masses of insect-sized crabs swarming across the pavement, their shells black and their legs vermilion. They make driving an act of mass crab homicide, and dangerous, with sudden slippery skids.

BACKGROUND

In the early seventeenth century, these coasts were the domain of a notorious French pirate, Gilbert Girón. He was ultimately decapitated by a Spanish captain, who then displayed the head in a jar of brine in order to claim a reward from the Spanish Crown.

Playa Girón is best known as the main site of the April 17, 1961, invasion by some 1,500 Cuban exiles, backed and trained by the CIA, who code-named themselves Brigade 2506. Within a day, Castro's pilots were bombing the invading army's boats and planes, and had the bay surrounded by a volunteer army of 20,000 soldiers and peasants, led by Castro himself. By dusk on April 19, 1,200 of the 1,500 exiles had been taken prisoner and were eventually exchanged for more than US$50 million worth of medicines and supplies from the United States.

General Information

Facilities are few. The small town of Playa Girón has a pharmacy and a dollar-shop opposite the museum. A few modest fast-food *paladares* have sprung up.

Rental cars, as well as bicycles and mopeds are available at the **Transauto** office opposite the Villa Horizontes.

What to See and Do

The **Museo Girón** is a housed in a well-kept bungalow, with its lawns rightly mowed and everything almost self-consciously spic-and-span. Outside, stands a British-made *Sea Fury* fighter that was flown by the Cuban air force, along with the remains of the Brigade 2506 aircraft.

Inside, the museum displays dioramas charting the hour-by-hour progress of the invasion and the counter-attack, with detailed maps and photographs of the invading mercenaries as well as the martyrs of the Bay of Pigs, whose 30-year-old blood-stained garments, weapons, letters and other possessions can be seen here. It also documents the Revolution's efforts to improve the living conditions of residents of this region, many of whom are descended from poverty-stricken charcoal-makers. The museum is open Tuesday to Sunday, 9 AM to 5 PM.

Facing the pretty Playa Girón beach is the **Villa Horizontes Playa Girón** resort, which has simple *cabañas* with basic facilities, but the azure coast makes staying here a more attractive prospect than Playa Larga. There are two beaches, both stony as opposed to sandy — Playa Girón itself, which is not very big, but has safe calm waters, and another known locally as Enamorados (Lover's Beach), which is more secluded and unspoiled, both popular with Cuban vacationers.

The potential for scuba diving in the waters off Playa Girón is beginning to attract much attention. You are likely to see manatees as well as many species of tropical fish, and the submarine *cenotes* that are such a feature of this region provide opportunities for the adventurous for underwater spelunking. Contact the **International Scuba Diving Center** at the Villa Playa Girón.

Where to Stay

Villa Horizontes Playa Girón ((059) 4118 or 4110 FAX (059) 4117, Playa Girón, offers inexpensive accommodations. Here, almost 300 rooms and small concrete bungalows are spread out facing the beach, each equipped with a refrigerator and a television. There is a choice of restaurants, tennis courts, a swimming pool, and tourist facilities such as a shop, doctor's office, car and motorcycle rental. Its International Scuba Diving Center may well be the reason you stay.

How to Get There

If you are interested in visiting this region, but don't want to rent a car, join an organized tour from either Havana or Varadero. There are reasonably priced overnight packages to Laguna del Tesoro, the Zapata Peninsula and Playa Girón. Contact **Tour & Travel** ((07) 247541 or 241549 in Havana.

CALETA BUENA

Having come this far, you should not miss spending a day or half-day at one of loveliest swimming spots in the area, Caleta Buena, which lies eight kilometers (five miles) east of Playa Girón at the end of a long coral road along the coast. This idyllic, sheltered sea lagoon is perfect for swimming and lazing, with natural pools and transparent waters alive with multi-colored fish that are ideal for snorkeling — and further out — for scuba diving, with an ocean floor carpeted with corals, gorgonians and sponges. A small restaurant run by friendly locals serves snacks, cold drinks or lunch, and you can use their facilities as a changing room. Deck chairs and thatch umbrellas have been discreetly spaced to ensure privacy. On a beautiful day, this place is simply perfect, and long may it stay that way.

The Cuban Heartland

CIENFUEGOS

Spread around a dramatically wide harbor, Cienfuegos, which means "a hundred fires," was earmarked for rapid industrial development under the Revolution and is now Cuba's most important port, with the country's largest cement and plastic factories, sugar terminal and oil refinery plant. Still, the surrounding sea and the seaside life of its citizens, strolling and cycling and the Malecón, make Cienfuegos one of the prettiest provincial towns in Cuba.

Known as "La Perla del Sur" ("the Pearl of the South"), Cienfuegos has the advantage of not being full of tourists, *jiniteros*, or scrums of urchins. Its unsightly edifices are more than offset by its magnificent setting, boulevards and mansions. Located 250 km (155 miles) from Havana, Cienfuegos is a good place to stop for a night or two if you are traveling further into central Cuba.

BACKGROUND

The history of Cienfuegos is inseparable from its sweeping natural harbor, Bahía de Cienfuegos. Remains of a large settlement of aboriginal Siboney Indians have been found here. The Spanish recognized its potential from the beginning. Christopher Columbus sailed through the bay on his second expedition to Cuba in 1494, and a decade later, the conquistador Sebastián de Ocampo made a careful survey of the bay during his exploration of the island. Pirates and smugglers were lured here from the Isle of Pines (now known as Isla de Juventud) and Jamaica by the prospect of plundering ships moored off the bay. In order to protect the early colonial settlement from attack, the Spanish constructed the Castillo de Jagua in the mid-eighteenth century, a small fortress which still dominates the harbor's entrance.

As a city, Cienfuegos has the unusual distinction of having attracted an intrepid mixture of early immigrants, including many of French and Spanish descent from Baltimore, New Orleans, Jamaica and other Caribbean cities. Merchants, shippers and moneylenders soon followed the expansion of the sugar industry in the region, and the city

quickly gained the reputation of having the country's highest concentration of wealthy families. It was founded in 1819 by Louis de Clouet, a Creole trader from New Orleans, who named the city Fernandina de Jagua in honor of King Fernando VII, but also out of respect for the native name for this site. As the city grew, settled by a colony of French planters from Louisiana, it was soon renamed Cienfuegos after Cuba's then-governor, José Cienfuegos.

GENERAL INFORMATION

The best the city has to offer in the way of tourist information services is the **Buro de Turismo** ((0432) 451234 or 451174 in the Cubanacán office on Avenida 54 near Parque Martí in central Cienfuegos. There's a second branch on Calle 37 at Avenida 12 in Punta Gorda. Another source of information is the local **Ministry of Tourism Cienfuegos** ((0432) 451631 or 451627, on Calle 37 (near the Servi-Cupet gas station).

If you need medical treatment, legal advice or emergency cash advances, contact the local branch of **Asistur** ((0432) 666402 or 666190. **Banco Financiero Internacional** is located on the southeast corner of Parque Martí. It is open Monday to Friday, 8 AM to 3 PM. International calls can be placed from the **Etecsa** kiosk on Calle 37 opposite the Hotel Jagua. Right down the block is the local **Clínica International,** which has a doctor and nurse on 24-hour call.

GETTING AROUND

To contact **Turistaxi**, call ((0432) 96256 or 96212. Or, like the majority of Cienfuegans, board a horse-drawn cart (*mulo*).

Marina Puertosol ((0432) 451241 in Punta Gorda offers various sight-seeing cruises of the bay, including one that stops at the Castillo de Jagua.

Cubanacán ((0432) 451234, on Avenida 54 near Parque Martí in downtown Cienfuegos and at the corner of Calle 37 and Calle 12 in Punta Gorda, offers a city sightseeing tour, as well as excursions to Trinidad, nature walks from El Nicho in the Sierra del Escambray, visits to the Jardín Botánico, boat trips to the Castillo de Jagua and other destinations.

WHAT TO SEE AND DO

If you are staying at the Hotel Jagua, then you are already in the heart of **Punta Gorda**, a small peninsula on a sliver of land lapped by the sea at the other end of the city. This peaceful settlement, dotted with palm trees and tiny piers, is characterized by wood-frame gingerbread houses, many of which were prefabricated in the Gulf Coast of the United States and assembled here at the turn of the century.

Immediately opposite the hotel, the **Palacio de Valle** is perhaps the most extraordinary sight in Cienfuegos. This exuberant, ostentatious, neo-Moorish confection was commissioned by Aciclio Valle in 1890. He enlisted the help of Moroccan craftsmen to create this curious marvel of elaborate fretted interiors, stained-glass windows and balustraded rooms. It was completed in 1917. The Valle family fled Cuba after the 1959 revolution, and since 1990, its ground floor has been converted into the city's top restaurant. You can wander through its many rooms and up its winding iron staircase to the rooftop bar, which has magical views across the bay at sunset. Admission is US$1 including a rum punch in the rooftop bar.

Since Punta Gorda is some two kilometers (slightly over a mile) from the city center, you will need to continue your tour by a taxi or car, passing along the seafront Malecón. As you leave the sea, the Malecón becomes the **Paseo del Prado**, the city's central boulevard, which is lined with colonnaded colonial houses and monuments and crossed by streets in a regular fashion. This is the best place to begin your stroll, admiring close-up the colored façades, porticos and balustrades of these houses, painted in a rainbow of hues. Many of the ground-level houses have been transformed into peso- and dollar-shops, ice-cream and fast-food parlors and *paladares*. Numerous horse-drawn carts — referred to as *mulos* by locals — act as service taxis along the bustling Paseo del Prado, which is the center of commercial activity in Cienfuegos.

Turn right on Avenida 56, known as El Boulevard, a pedestrian section lined with dollar-shops that has become a main meeting point for young Cienfuegans. Continue to walk four blocks and you will reach **Parque José Martí**, the city's beautiful historic center, with its ensemble of nineteenth- and early twentieth-century buildings that are collectively considered a national monument. At one end, the park's entrance is guarded by two white marble lions on high pedestals; while a triumphal arch, a statue of José Martí and various monuments complete the sense of civic pomp.

At one corner stands the yellow-tinged **Catedral de la Purísima Concepción**, built

in 1819, notable for its particularly fine stained-glass windows depicting the 12 apostles. Nearby is the **Teatro Tomás Terry**, an elaborate theater named after the sugar- and slave-rich Venezuelan philanthropist who built it for the city in 1890. Make sure you see the elegant *fin de siècle* interior, with its three-tiered auditorium, mosaic murals and painted ceiling. The legendary Enrico Caruso once performed here, among many other famous entertainers. Although it is now seriously dilapidated, national dance and folklore productions are still staged here.

PREVIOUS PAGES: Trinidad's Plaza Mayor LEFT, a colonial-era gem. RIGHT: Vividly- hued houses in Cienfuegos. ABOVE: The 1890 Teatro Tomás Terry, where Enrico Caruso once performed.

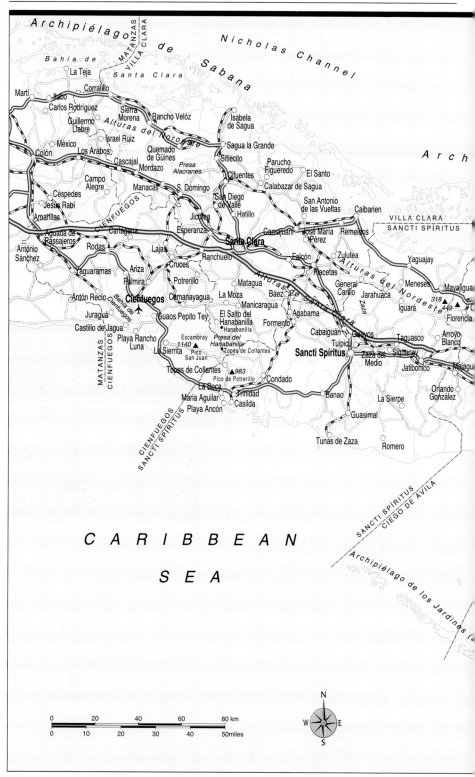

THE HEARTLAND

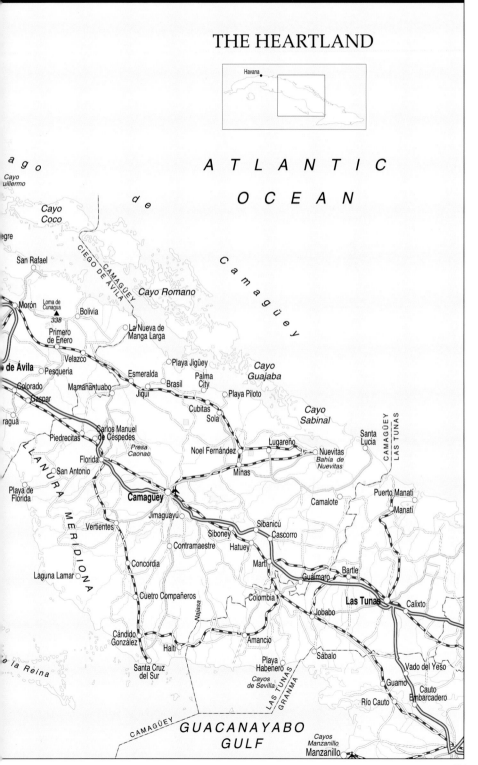

Continuing counterclockwise around the square, there are various notable buildings, including the **Biblioteca Provincial** (Provincial Library) housed in an early colonial building. Across the park is the **Palacio de Ferrer**, a strikingly ornamental building. Once a residential mansion, it is now the **Casa de la Cultura**, and is worth exploring for its grand winding staircase and elegant rooms lined with gilt mirrors. Likewise, the nearby **Museo Provincial**, displays antique furniture and memorabilia to recreate the bygone ambience of homes owned by the city's wealthy nineteenth-century bourgeoisie. The **Colegio de San Lorenzo**, also in the square, was inaugurated in 1927.

El Palatino, a tavern right on the square, offers a brief respite and a colonial atmosphere. Its renovated 1842 building has high vaulted roof, tiled floors; its stools are made from rum casks.

Parque Martí also boasts some of the city's best shopping. **Galería Maroya** on the south side represents dozens of local artists including funky folk paintings and interesting wood sculptures. Antiques and clothing are also on sale. At the southeast corner is **Imagen Cuba** which stocks a broad range of arts and crafts, as well as books, T-shirts and rum.

EXCURSIONS FROM CIENFUEGOS

Outside Cienfuegos, there are several worthwhile places to visit, making a morning or afternoon's excursion. Lying 18 km (11 miles) east of the city, the **Jardín Botánico Soledad** is one of the true highlights of visiting Cienfuegos. Indeed, this garden is the most beautiful — and the oldest — of its kind in Cuba. It is laid out across nine kilometers (five and a half miles), and was originally founded by the American sugar millionaire Edwin F. Atkins. Later it was taken over as a research center by Harvard University. Chosen for its ideal climatic conditions, one of the initial tasks of its founders was to create new, more profitable varieties of sugarcane. It soon expanded to include some 2,000 tropical and subtropical plants from all over the world, including 400 types of cactus, 248 timber-producing trees, 241 medicinal plants, 200 types of cactus, 89 different rubber plants, 69 varieties of orchids and 23 types of bamboo. From

Cuba itself, it contains 23 species of the *mariposa*, Cuba's national flower, as well as a complete collection of Cuban palm trees, including the "pot belly" and the "cork screw" palms, which are considered to be a living fossil. The entrance fee of US$2 includes a guided tour, and there is a refreshment bar near the parking area. It is open from 8 AM to 4 PM daily.

The Jardín Botánico Soledad is located along an unmarked road and can be tricky to find. A taxi there which will cost up to US$40 for a round trip. If driving from the Hotel Jagua, follow Calle 37 to Avenida 18. Turn

right and continue four blocks to Calle 45, then make a left until you reach the municipal stadium. Look out for a sign marked Clínica Estomatológica, which is your cue to turn right onto Avenida Cinco de Septiembre. This is the main road to the Rancho Luna beach. On the outskirts of Cienfuegos this is lined with micro-brigade estates and communal gardens. Take the turnoff onto the Circuito Sur (Southern Ring Road) and look out for the entrance to the garden before the Pepito Tey sugar mill between the villages of San Antón and Guaos.

En route is the charming **Tomás Acea Cemetery**, easily spotted along the Avenida Cinco de Septiembre a short distance outside the city. It has a monumental marble portico designed as a replica of the Greek Parthenon, supported by 64 columns. Set among gravel pathways and trees are elaborate funerary statues and mausoleums which reflect the fashionable tastes imported by the city's French colonial inhabitants.

Another suggested excursion from Cienfuegos is a visit to the Spanish-built **Castillo de Jagua**, located at the entrance to the city's harbor. Completed in 1745, it was intended as a defense against roving pirates, however it never came under serious attack. Now restored, its main attraction is the roving view from its parapets, which takes in small seaside villages and the wide sweep of the sea and the bay. There is a bar and restaurant within the castle and the surrounding settlement has some very charming colonial mansions near the water's edge. However, it is hard not to be dismayed at the ugly sight of the nearby Chernobyl-era Juraguá nuclear plant and the equally ugly Ciudad Nuclear, built as residential quarters for the plant's workers. Cuba's only nuclear power station was begun in 1983 with the help of the Soviet Union, then abandoned before completion in 1992. It is now in development limbo waiting for fresh foreign investment.

A rather Gothic legend is attached to the Castillo de Jagua, dating from the time of its first commander, Juan Castilla Cabeza de Vaca. According to the story, the guards became alarmed when, every night, a blackbird would swoop around the fort and then, upon alighting, would turn into a lady dressed in blue robes and wearing a vengeful expression. All the men were too terrified to stand guard at night, but one night, a soldier dared. The next morning, he was found prostrate on the floor, clutching his sword and surrounded by pieces of blue cloth. Apparently, he was left a gibbering wreck and spent the rest of his life in an asylum, and the mystery was never solved. Some said that the unearthly visitor was the commander's beautiful wife, whose remains are buried under the castle's chapel floor.

You can reach the Castillo de Jagua by road, after about an hour's drive from Cienfuegos. Or, perhaps more fun, you can take a peso-only ferry, which leaves from the jetty at Muelle Real, Avenida 46 and Calle 25 at intervals throughout the day. The trip takes

40 minutes and stops off at several small seaside fishing villages and the ugly Pascabello Hotel en route, which incidentally, should be avoided. The most enjoyable place for lunch or dinner in the area is the **Casa de Pescador** in the seaside village of Perché.

Also within an hour's drive from Cienfuegos along a road lined with mango plantations is **Playa Rancho Luna**, a sheltered, crescent-shaped and sof t-sanded beach with calm shallows. There are several hotels and marked scuba diving areas in the vicinity, but the best place to stay is the **Hotel Hori-**

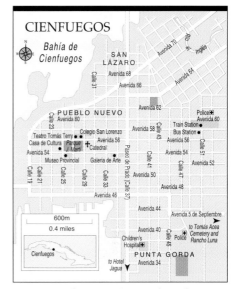

zontes Rancho Luna. As you drive there you may notice the collective farm, Communidad "Martires de Barbados," which is named in honor of the 80 Cuban athletes who died when anti-Castro terrorists bombed a Cubana de Aviación airline mid-air over Barbados in 1976.

WHERE TO STAY

There is only one hotel reserved for foreigners in Cienfuegos itself; otherwise there are several alternatives by the beach, within an hour's drive of the city.

Moderate

Most recently renovated in 2001, **Hotel Jagua** ((0432) 451003 FAX (0432) 451642, at

Cienfuegos offers fine examples of art nouveau, such as the Palacio de Ferrer.

the southern end of Calle 37, Punta Gorda, is the best hotel in or around Cienfuegos. It was converted from a Batista-era gambling haven into something that now approaches international standards. Peacefully located in the leafy peninsula of Punta Gorda, the Jagua has panoramic views from its upper rooms across the bay and the city from the terraces of its 145 rooms, and the hotel also overlooks and operates the Palacio de Valle next door. It has a saltwater pool and a nightclub, which stages a cabaret most evenings. The hotel has a Turistaxi stand as well as horse-drawn carts.

Inexpensive

Horizontes Rancho Luna Hotel ((0432) 48120 or 451012 FAX (0432) 48131, Carretera Rancho Luna, is located 16 km (10 miles) east of the city, on its own small but pleasant beach, with simple accommodation provided by a terraced red-tiled concrete row of rooms set in landscaped gardens. There is a restaurant, cafeteria, bar and shop, as well as a car rental office.

Located close to Playa Rancho Luna, the small **Cubanacán Faro Luna** ((0432) 451389, Carretera Rancho Luna, has 24 sea-facing rooms each with a small terrace. It has a salt-water swimming pool and scuba diving facilities.

WHERE TO EAT

Moderate

Right next to the Hotel Jagua, the flamboyant palace **Palacio de Valle** ((0432) 451003 has been converted into the city's best and most expensive restaurant, serving a wide variety of dishes. The main dining room used to be the Valle family's drawing room, and has a resident pianist, a grande dame, Carmen Iznaga, a niece of Nicolás Guillén. The rooftop terrace bar is perfect for cocktails. It closes at 10 PM.

The **Casa de Pescador** ((0432) 8160, Punta La Milpa, Carretera de Pasacaballo to La Milpa, Perché, is tucked into the entrance to the bay, with a view of the Castillo de Jagua, making it a charming place for lunch. The fresh seafood — such as lobster, shrimp and

Shady arcades and a *paladar* in Cienfuegos.

fish — served here, is the best you will find in Cienfuegos. Open for lunch until midnight.

La Finca Isabela ((0432) 7606, Carretera de Rancho Luna, a former colonial estate set among mango plantations several kilometers from the city, has been restored as a *campesino*-style restaurant for tourists, with roast pig, Creole dishes and evening performances.

Inexpensive

Located in an old green seaside mansion opposite the Hotel Jagua, La Cueva del Camarón ((0432) 8238 specializes in seafood;

the celebrated theater, offers ice cream and cold drinks throughout the afternoon and early evening hours. Its leafy patio is a perfect place to rest your weary feet.

HOW TO GET THERE

Cienfuegos lies 250 km (155 miles) southeast of Havana. The city's **Aeropuerto Internacional Jaime Gónsalez** is five kilometers (three miles) northeast of Cienfuegos. Aerotaxi, Aerogaviota and Aerocaribbean make scheduled flights to Cienfuegos, but Cubana

the bar terrace is popular with local Cienfuegans and is open late.

Just down the waterfront is La Paella, with an outdoor dining area perched on stilts above the harbor. The menu features the renowned Spanish rice dish as well as other seafood delights.

Palacio de Valle recently opened a snack bar called El Bodegon, which rustles up inexpensive burgers, sandwiches and salads. Friday and Saturday nights there's live music and karaoke from 9 PM to 2 AM.

In downtown Cienfuegos, El Palatino serves up light snacks and cold beer in a breezy sidewalk café setting overlooking Parque Martí. On the opposite side of the plaza, Sodería Terry, on the ground floor of

de Aviación does not. For more information on international charter and domestic flights, see GETTING THERE, page 306 in TRAVELERS' TIPS.

There are daily trains from Havana, which is a seven-hour journey on the Havana-Santiago train, and the **Terminal de Ferrocarriles** is located at Avenida 58 and Calle 4, almost adjacent to the bus station.

FURTHER AFIELD

Although most of Cienfuegos Province is relatively flat, it encompasses the lush, green Sierra del Escambray to the east, one of Cuba's three largest mountain ranges. If you are driving, you can either make a day trip into the Sierra del Escambray's **Ebse Hanabanilla** (Lake Hanabanilla) area from Cienfuegos, or you could make this excursion the first stop en route to Trinidad. Other excursions into the Sierra del Escambray are best made from Trinidad, and are covered in that section.

To reach Ebse Hanabanilla, leave Cienfuegos on Avenida 64, which is the main highway to Trinidad, and take the turnoff toward Cumanayagua, which you will see after several kilometers on your left. The lake is roughly equidistant — about 48 km (30 miles) from both Cienfuegos and the provincial capital Santa Clara. It's an interesting drive, passing first through undulating tobacco plantations and a military air base, then climbing into a mountainous region dotted with small agrarian hamlets, where at every turn, astride their horses, men have the weather-beaten faces of true *gauchos*, their mouths clenched on *puros*.

Lake Hanabanilla, which spans 36 sq km (about 14 sq miles), is formed by a large dam across the Río Hanabanilla. Surrounded by gentle forests, with beautiful, winding passages, the lake is a popular fishing spot for bass. The Hotel Hanabanilla, located right on the lakeside, is a good base for fishing expeditions. Depending on the time of year, the hotel is either reached by road or by launch, as sometimes the road may be flooded over. (You can expect to pay up to US$4 per person for the launch trip.)

There are also some wonderful walks, hidden limestone caves, waterfalls and natural swimming pools to be found in the surrounding mountains, notably at **El Nicho**, near the small village of Camilo-Che and set amid coffee plantations. Up from the village, there is a row of rough bungalows that were once used by Cuban army troops undergoing specialized guerilla training by visiting North Vietnamese commandos. A guide from the village can lead you through the lush forest to the magical **Cueva El Calvo**, which is filled with calcified limestone shapes, and on to a clear (and cold!) natural waterfall pool.

Along the way, look out for what the locals call the *chichicates* or "smoking trees," which send up plumes of pollen, as though blowing out smoke.

WHERE TO STAY AND EAT

Hotel Hanabanilla ((042) 491125, Salto del Hanabanilla, Muncipo Manicaragua, Villa Clara, is an inexpensive Soviet-style resort run by Isla Azul, which specializes mostly in Cuban holidays. It is very popular for romantic getaways and "honeymoons." The rooms are very simple and the food can be good. From here, you can easily explore the lake with boat and fishing trips, and there are some beautiful lakeside walks.

Río Negro is a pleasant, lakeside ranch-style restaurant which makes an excellent base for fishing expeditions, and its fabulous setting makes it one of the highlights of a visit here. It can be easily reached by launch from the Hotel Hanabanilla. Perhaps oddly, considering that the lake is renowned for its bass, the house specialty is *pollo saltón a la piña* (chicken with pineapple), but the chef may be amenable to serving bass if he has some in stock.

TRINIDAD

A colonial-era gem, much of Trinidad feels as though it has remained unchanged for centuries, as though one is stepping back to a fragile, untouched world. It is unquestionably charming and tranquil, with a warren of narrow, often steep streets lined with brightly colored, thick-walled townhouses adorned by porticoed windows and red tile roofs. Amid streets hazily lit by wrought-iron lamps, restored mansions have been polished up as museums, while horse-drawn carriages clip-clop lazily over the cobblestones. Often as you walk through the back streets people will invite you for a local coffee and a tour of their house. Some of these old houses packed with antiques, and most have an interesting story attached to them.

Preserved to an astonishing degree, Trinidad has a decidedly baroque air, unsullied by much of the usual tourist tat that often accompanies such full-scale restoration. Much less hectic than other major Cuban towns, Trinidad is also very manageable. From *palacio* balconies or nearby hill-

Trinidad's Cuban-style colonial church.

sides, expansive views sweep across green marshlands to the glittering Caribbean Sea and the surrounding, flower-splashed mountains of the Escambray.

BACKGROUND

Trinidad is Cuba's third oldest settlement. It was founded in 1514 by Diego de Velázquez, who was initially lured by reports that local Taíno Indians had struck gold in nearby rivers.

After quickly subjugating the large Taíno population in the region, the Spanish set

about establishing their fortunes, first by gold mining, then cattle ranching, tobacco farming and slave trading. The town's apogee — when it became known as a kind of El Dorado — occurred during the seventeenth and eighteenth centuries, when sugar plantations mushroomed in nearby Valle de los Ingenios (Valley of the Sugar Mills) and Trinidad became one of Cuba's richest trading ports, exporting one-third of the island's sugar to Europe, South America, the United States and Spain.

The *criollo* (Creole) bourgeoisie, as well as the new influx of French planters from Haiti, flourished on the steady flow of sugar and contraband, as thousands of black African slaves toiled. The colonial *Trinitarios* established elaborate homes, the wealthiest vying to out-do each other's monogrammed Meissen and Limoges collections, and intent on copying the latest fashions from Paris. They were also proud of such cultural institutions as their newspaper, language school (teaching English, French and Italian) and an academy for music, dance and theatre.

However, by the end of the nineteenth century, three factors contributed to Trinidad's ruin: the collapse of the slave trade, the establishment of Cuba's new republic and the growth of vast sugar estates elsewhere on the island. Opportunistic incursions by roving pirates created even more dismay. Trinidad was soon all but deserted, and for almost a hundred years, existing buildings were left to slide into dilapidation; nothing new was added to the town's historic architecture. Due to its economic collapse, Trinidad was left alone, and ultimately untouched in architectural terms. Restoration work did not begin here until after the Revolution, when the new Cuban government declared it a national monument. Later, along with Havana, Trinidad and the Valle de los Ingenios were designated World Heritage Sites by UNESCO.

You can easily spend two or three days in and around Trinidad, including a visit to the Valle de los Ingenios and to the nearby beach resort of Playa Ancón. Don't leave Trinidad without sampling its unique cocktail, a delicious concoction called *la canchánchara*; it is made of honey, lemon juice and distilled sugarcane brandy, or *aguardiente*.

GENERAL INFORMATION

The local **Infotur** outlet and **Rumbos (** (0419) 2264 or 4414, are both situated in the old Cremería building at the corner of Calle Gustavos Izquierdo (de La Gloria) and Calle Simón Bolívar. Either one can arrange hotel reservations, city tours, excursions to the surrounding countryside and tickets for the Valle de los Ingenios *tren turístico*.

Trinidad's only Internet café — indeed one of the few in all of Cuba — is **Las Begonias**, on Calle Gustavos Izquierdo across the street from Rumbos. Rates are US$1 for 10 minutes or US$5 per hour, but there's usually a long wait for the two computers. Service is available

Monday to Friday 9 AM to 1 PM and 3 PM to 10 PM; Saturday and Sunday 9 AM to 1 PM.

Your hotel is your best option for changing foreign currency, making telephone calls or finding a taxi. If you need to rent a car, ask at the Hotel Las Cuevas in town or the Hotel Ancón out at the beach. Otherwise try **Havanautos** ((0419) 6301.

Should you need any medical attention, try the **Clínica Internacional** ((0419) 3391 or 6240, Calle Lino Pérez (San Procopio) 103 at the corner of Calle Anastasio Cárdenas.

You'll notice that many of Trinidad's streets are known by both their pre-Revolution and post-Revolution names. The most frequently used names are listed here, with alternatives in parentheses.

WHAT TO SEE AND DO

Trinidad is a place that can be easily explored on foot — its steep, winding and narrow cobblestone streets defy any other method of getting around. Many are slanted towards the middle to drain away rainwater. Many of the large, uneven paving stones originated as ships' ballast, transported to the town from New England. This being said, the first thing to recommend is a comfortable pair of shoes.

The obvious place to begin is the **Plaza Mayor** (Parque Martí) in the heart of the town. All around, impressive colonial buildings reflect the growth in fortunes of the town's sugar-rich grandees, many part of the original settlement founded by the Spanish. In the eighteenth century, the original square was embellished with the addition of square palm gardens, decorative iron fences, statues, classical urns and bronze sculptured greyhounds.

The only two-story building on the square is the canary-yellow **Palacio de Brunet**, on Calle Fernando Hernández Echerrí (del Cristo). This classically beautiful, carefully restored colonial residence set around a plant-filled inner courtyard houses the **Museo Romántico**, perhaps the most interesting and charming of Trinidad's many museums, and also a popular venue for marriage ceremonies. It meticulously recreates the coquettish atmosphere of its erstwhile inhabitants: Count Brunet and his household, which included 12 children and some

20 slaves, lived here during the nineteenth century. Admission is US$2.

The building itself dates back to 1740, although the upper floor — a great rarity in Trinidad — was built much later. Unusually large for a provincial town, it evokes the *palacios* of Havana. Many of the *palacio's* 13 rooms are decorated with grandiose fresco paintings and trompe l'oeil, and furnished with a collection of exceptional period antiques as well as utensils in its perfectly recreated period kitchen. Look for the cedar wood ceilings, the mother-of-pearl-studded bed, mahogany staircase, marble floors, scalloped windows and the stunning views from the balcony across the main square.

To your left as you leave the museum, is the cream-colored, vaguely Gothic-looking **Iglesia de la Santísima Trinidad**. As it stands, this church was built in the late nineteenth century, although an earlier version had occupied this site since 1787. Built in an archetypal Cuban style, with three naves each fronted by a door, it is worth visiting for its venerated *Cristo de la Vera Cruz*, carved in Spain in 1731, which has an unusual history. The figure of Christ was carried on a boat from Spain to Mexico that stopped in Trinidad's port: three times the boat left to complete its journey only to be swept back by heavy storms. Ever since, the Christ figure has remained here, believed by locals to have sanctifying powers.

As you continue around the Playa Mayor in a clockwise direction, you will come to the **Museo de Arquitectura Trinitaria**. Not only does this museum showcase a remarkable collection of colonial architectural construction techniques and styles, it is also a distinctive building in its own right, made up of two former homes (one built in 1738, the other in 1785) that were joined together in 1819, sharing a beautiful patio. It was the townhouse of the Sánchez-Iznaga family, who owned and operated large plantations in the region. The timber roof is worth seeing alone. It is closed on Fridays.

Continuing clockwise, still on Playa Mayor, to the left is the **Casa de Alderman Ortiz**, now an art gallery which exhibits works by contemporary Trinidadian artists.

One of Cuba's varied means of transportation.

Opposite, on Calle Simón Bolívar (Desangaño) stands a restored eighteenth-century mansion housing the **Museo de Arqueología Guamuhaya**, which displays archeological finds and Indian artifacts, notably utensils, tools, decorations and ceramics constructed by early Indian settlers. A somewhat macabre addition displays exhumed skeletons taken from an African slave cemetery on the Iznaga sugar plantation in the Valle de los Ingenios. According to local historians, the house that originally occupied this site was lived in by the conquistador Hernán Cortés before he left to conquer Mexico. Closed on Sunday.

Heading away from the Playa Mayor, walk down the main cobbled thoroughfare of Calle Simón Bolívar, formerly the most fashionable address for Trinidad's colonial elite. To your right is the **Palacio Cantero**, now the **Museo Histórico Municipal**, with a collection that traces the town's history. It was owned by Justo German Cantero, paterfamilias of one of Trinidad's wealthiest families and owner of six sugar mills, but also a doctor, poet and aesthete. This impressive *palacio* includes a large central courtyard with shaded patios and spiral stairs leading up to a rare watchtower. The careful specialty and neoclassical decoration of the formal salons — with delicate, gilt-etched and exuberant patterns set against pale walls, Bohemian chandeliers and gleaming mahogany furniture — evoke the sensation that this residence has remained untouched for generations. Off the central patio, the kitchen is distinguished by an enormous oven and chimney system built of plastered *mamposteria*. The climb up the watchtower is rewarded by stunning views, not only across the plaza and the town, but across to the Iglesia de la Popa, a ruined eighteenth-century church.

From here, walk along Calle Francisco Toro towards Calle Piro Guinart (also known as La Boca) and turn right to reach **Plaza Real de Jigüe**. A native tree — the *jigüe* — and a plaque commemorates the site where Diego de Velázquez and his band of fellow expeditionaries held their first Christmas Mass in 1513, a year before Trinidad was founded. An attractive tile-studded colonial house shaded by the *jigüe* tree is now an elegant restaurant, **El Jigüe**.

Around the corner, after turning left on Calle Ruben Martínez Villena (Real de Jigüe) is **La Canchánchara**, a charming rustic-style building with an interior patio garden that serves the house drink of the same name.

Returning to the Plaza Real del Jigüe, walk down Calle Piro Guinart (Boca). To the left, at no. 302, are the remains of Trinidad's old town hall and jail. Further down at the next corner is the **Archivo Histórico Municipal**, interesting especially for its documents tracing the story of early immigrants from Manila, Macao, Buenos Aires, Philadelphia, Boston, New Orleans, Amsterdam and Belgium.

On the adjacent square, between Calles Fernando Hernández Echerrí and Piro Guinart, stands a former eighteenth-century **Franciscan convent** notable for its four-story bell-tower, which is in fact all that remains of the original structure and from which there are marvelous views across Trinidad. This former home for novices now houses the **Museo de Lucha Contra Bandidos** (The Museum of the Struggle Against the Bandits). It graphically illustrates the verve with which the Castro government condemned and crushed the band of counter-revolutionary rebels who held out in the nearby Sierra del Escambray mountains. The fascinating exhibit includes photographs, clothes, weapons, maps, pieces of a U-2 reconnaissance plane and even a hammock used by Che Guevara.

From here turn left, back along Calle Fernando Hernández Echerrí and continue along until you reach Calle Ciro Redondo (Calle San José). To your left, you will find **La Luna**, a delightful tavern that has been a fixture of Trinidadian society since the nineteenth century.

Turn right on Calle Jesús Menéndez (Alameda) to reach Plaza de Segarte. Here you will find Trinidad's delightful **Casa de la Trova**, located in an eighteenth-century house, where there are almost daily performances by local musicians. At the end of the patio there is a music shop and a small bar where you can enjoy a drink while you listen to the music.

OPPOSITE: Colonial Trinidad has been well restored and maintained. RIGHT: Detail of the eighteenth-century Museo de Arquitectura Trinitaria.

Beyond its historic center, Trinidad's other sights are more spread out. If you are staying at the Hotel Las Cuevas, you can't miss catching sight of the **Plaza Santa Ana**, which lies at the hotel's entrance gate. Here, next to the ruined **Iglesia de Santa Ana**, the former prison, painted a strident yellow, has been turned into the city's largest cultural center: Trinidad's Folk Ensemble regularly performs Afro-Cuban music and dances for visitors within the cobbled courtyard, which is also ringed by an art gallery, a handicrafts bazaar and a shop run by the Cuban Cultural Heritage Fund. There is also a lookout bar and a restaurant.

Elsewhere, away from Trinidad's tourist sights, the **Parque Central** (about 10 blocks south of Plaza Mayor) is a good place to take the town's pulse. This is where you will find Trinidad's peso-shops and markets, government ration dispensaries and the **Iglesia San Francisco de Paula**.

Several kilometers outside Trinidad, is the **Villa María Dolores**, set along the banks of the Río Guaurabo, which organizes horse treks through the surrounding countryside. It also has simple accommodations and a popular restaurant which often hosts a *fiesta campesina*, or farmer's night featuring spit-roasted pig, Creole dishes, hearty rum cocktails and *guateque* (folk) performances.

WHERE TO STAY

In Trinidad itself, the best place to stay is the inexpensive **Hotel Horizontes Las Cuevas** ((0419) 6133 or 6135 FAX (0419) 6161, Finca Santa Ana. Located on a hill overlooking the city and the distant Caribbean Sea, this hotel has stunning sunset vistas, so ask for a room with a balcony view. Its villa-style bungalows are spread across the hillside around a central bar and swimming pool area. The rooms are among the best the Horizontes chain has on offer in Cuba, especially the newer villas which are comfortable and spacious, with pleasant balconies. The main advantage of staying in Las Cuevas is its proximity to Central Trinidad, a fairly short walk down a steep hill away. The hotel takes its name from the numerous caves nearby, one of which houses a popular discotheque.

Given the number of young backpacker tourists who blow into Trinidad, the town boasts a number of budget *casa particulares*. One of the best is the family run **Hospedaje Mirelys** ((0419) 4336, Calle Antonio Maceo (Gutiérrez) 313, which offers simple but clean and comfortable rooms (with and without air conditioning) off a central courtyard where you can lounge in geriatric rocking chairs. The old colonial house is filled with black-and-white photos and antiques. Similar digs can be found at the **Hostal López Santandar** ((0419) 3541, 313 Calle Camilo Cienfuegos, which also has parking available for rental cars.

On the outskirts of Trinidad is the **Villa María Dolores** ((0419) 6481 or 6394, Carretera Circuito Sur. Inexpensive, rustic, retreat-style accommodation is offered in attractive, thatched-roof bungalows clustered beneath huge shade trees. The newer units, more comfortable and spacious, were added in 2001. The villa also organizes horse-treks.

WHERE TO EAT

Moderate

Trinidad Colonial ((0419) 3873, Calle Antonio Maceo (Gutiérrez) 402, is housed in an attractive restored colonial mansion and is considered Trinidad's finest. The specialties are Creole-style fish and seafood dishes and always accompanied by *fufú de platano* (fried bananas). You can dine inside or in the breezy courtyard.

El Jigüe ((0419) 4136, Calle Ruben Martínez Villena, is situated in another historic courtyard, this time in a prettily tiled colonial house on the square where Trinidad's first Christmas mass was celebrated in 1513.

Inexpensive

Located in an eighteenth-century building, the partly open-air, vine-covered tavern **La Canchánchara** ((0419) 4345, Calle Ruben Martínez Villena between Calles Piro Guinart and Calle Ciro Redondo, is a charming place to visit at any time of day. There is usually a high-spirited performance of traditional music going on and deftly made cancháncharas, a drink made with *aguardiente* (local brandy), honey, lime juice and ice. Apparently this drink was invented by the *mambisas*, the revolutionary guerillas who fought for independence against the Spanish in the nineteenth century. According to the manager, it is guaranteed to cure colds, especially if served hot according to the original version of the recipe. Accompanying Creole-style snacks are also served.

Shaded by bougainvillea, **Mesón de Regidor** ((0419) 3756, Calle Simón Bolívar between Calles Ruben Martínez Villena and Gustavo Izquierdo, is a pleasant courtyard restaurant and bar situated in a sprawling 1801 colonial building that has served as a

Cuban fair with dishes such as *camarones a la diabla* (shrimp in hot sauce), *medallones de langosta a la criolla* (Creole-style lobster slices) and *parrillada real* (a mixed grill of fish, shrimp and chicken).

A former prison-turned-cultural center is the venue for the **Restaurante Santa Ana** overlooking the square of the same name. Seafood, steak and chicken dishes are served in a rustic setting. Be forewarned that it often fills with large tour groups at lunchtime. Out at Playa Ancón, the **Grill Caribe** quite naturally specializes in seafood, served on simple

butcher shop, plant nursery, art gallery and museum before its conversion into an eatery. Mesón serves delicious Creole food, including grilled shrimp and lobster enchiladas. You will often be entertained by Trinison, a talented band of three brothers on the guitar, bongos, flute and *baracas*.

If you are in the mood for a somewhat orchestrated good time, **Fiesta Campesina** ((0419) 6481 or 6394, Villa María Dolores, Carretera Circuito Sur, can be fun, and the food is always abundant. Specialty of the house is cerdo asado criollo (roast pork).

Vía Reale, Calle Ruben Martínez Villena near Calles Piro Guinart and Ciro Redondo, situated in yet another attractive colonial mansion, offers an alternative to the usual

tables beneath a thatched roof beside the sea. You'll find it a short walk (or drive) north of the Hotel Costa Sur.

NIGHTLIFE

Aside from the **Casa de la Trova**, where you can hear excellent live music by seasoned traditionalists as well as well-known Cuban bands, there are two other places to put on your list. **Bar Daiquirí**, Calle San Proscopio between Calles Gracia and Jesús María, is a friendly and relaxed place to have a drink under the night sky, and perhaps meet some locals, since this is a popular gathering place.

Nineteenth-century French porcelain in the Museo Romántico, former palace of Spanish Count Brunet.

Disco Ayala, near the Hotel Las Cuevas, is Cuba's most bizarre dance and music venue, tucked within a huge natural limestone cavern, with underground walkways that lead to a strobe-lit clearing which functions as the dance floor, with a bar area to one side. It is very popular with young locals, who come here to dance into the night, and perhaps, meet foreigners. As you leave the cave, you'll notice a Santería shrine.

HOW TO GET THERE

Located 82 km (51 miles) from Cienfuegos and 462 km (287 miles) from Havana, Trinidad is best reached by road — there is no train service. If you don't have your own wheels, the only viable option is regular **ViAzul (** (0419) 2404 or 3737, bus service to/from Havana and Varadero. Trinidad's bus station is situated on Calle Piro Guirnart at the corner of Antonio Maceo and Gustavo Izquierdo.

For such a popular destination, the air service is fairly skeletal: two Cubana de Aviación flights a week from and to Havana.

TRINIDAD'S BEACHES

Located some 12 km (seven and a half miles) from Trinidad near Casilda Bay, both **Playa Ancón** and **Playa Costa Sur** and have white sandy beaches fringed by palms with hotels of the same name. This can be a good base for exploring Trinidad and enjoying the beach as well. Sheltered by a sandy peninsula, the bay's Caribbean waters are warm and clear quite shallow close to the shore, although coral reefs are fairly close by. By wading out about a hundred meters (a hundred yards) you can snorkel around coral and rocks to see many different types of tropical fish, and you may see a lobster or two.

Next to the beach is the **Marina Cayo Blanco (** (0419) 6205, run by Puertosol, where you can rent equipment for scuba diving and snorkeling. It also offers scuba diving, fishing and daily boat expeditions to nearby coral reefs and tiny islets, including Cayo Blanco and more distant excursions to the Archipiélago de los Jardines de la Reina. Prices for such excursions range from US$35 per day to US$400 for the latter option.

Another beach option is **La Boca,** which lies five kilometers (three miles) west of Trinidad. During the weekends, La Boca is a relaxing place popular with locals .

WHERE TO STAY AND EAT

By far the best accommodation in the area (town or beach) is the brand new **Brisas Trinidad del Mar (** (0419) 6500 or 6507 FAX (0419) 6565 on Playa Ancón. An expensive, all-inclusive property developed by Cubanacán, the resort features Mediterranean vil-

las with red-tiled roofs, wooden balconies and wrought-iron window fixtures spread village-style along the beach and around a pleasant pool area.

Moderately priced **Hotel Ancón (** (0419) 6120 or 6125 FAX (0419) 6151, Playa Ancón, Carretera María Aguilar, is a large and somewhat austere hotel, but the beach it stands on is very pleasant and helps take the edge off the hotel's shortcomings. Rooms are comfortable, and of course, you should request a sea view. Facilities include a restaurant, bar, cabaret, swimming pool, watersports, currency exchange, shop and car and bicycle rental office.

Inexpensive **Hotel Horizontes Costa Sur (** (0419) 6172 or 6174 FAX (0419) 6173, Playa

María Aquilar, Casilda, is located on another of the bay's soft-sanded beaches, and prettily landscaped with *flamboyán* trees. This hotel is otherwise fairly uninspiring and basic. It is preferable to stay in one of the 20 beach bungalows next to the main hotel complex, some of which have nice beach views. Buffet meals are nothing to get excited about, and the swimming pool can be less than tranquil. There is a tennis court.

VALLE DE LOS INGENIOS

You cannot miss visiting the nearby Valle de los Ingenios (Valley of the Sugar Mills), which lies 12 km (seven and a half miles) from Trinidad. You can easily explore its sights within a day, perhaps partly by steam train if you are so inclined. Along with Trinidad, the valley is an UNESCO World Heritage Site, and aside from its architectural value, it is an extraordinarily lush rural spectacle, with a patchwork of greens as the eye follows the horizon to the Sierra del Escambray mountains in the distance.

BACKGROUND

Trinidad's wealth is easily explained by just one statistic: by 1827, some 56 sugar mills in this valley were producing over 7,000 tons of sugar a year. Today, the valley encompasses some 65 sites of historic interest, including the remains of many steam-powered *ingenios*, 15 plantation mansions in various states of restoration, a village that was once home (or shall we say more correctly, prison) to generations of African slaves, sugar warehouses and a bell tower at the Manacas-Iznaga plantation. Eventually these sites will form what is being planned as a giant open-air Museum of Slavery, still under development. While you can miss seeing many of these sites, make sure you manage to see those described below.

WHAT TO SEE AND DO

Within the heart of the valley, the eighteenth-century **Hacienda Manacas-Iznaga** is one of the best preserved and most impressive *palacetes* or country mansions in the area. It belonged to the wealthy Iznaga family, who owned several townhouses in Trinidad, and it was from here that they ran their large sugar plantation and mills. Now, the hacienda contains a modest museum that details the history of the region's sugar industry. Apparently, when the Valle de los Ingenios Museum of Slavery is completed, this will contain much more information about the history of slavery within Cuba, and in the Caribbean in general. A section of the hacienda has been turned into a delightful restaurant (presumably where family members used to have their meals). According to

the manager, the back steps here contain small niches in which slaves were chained as punishment.

By now, you will have noticed and perhaps already explored the nearby **Torre de Manacas-Iznaga**. This baroque, seven-story look-out tower — almost 44 m (144 ft) high — has spectacular views across the valley, and was used to keep an eye on the slaves working on the surrounding plantations. Admission is US$1.

Also within the valley, you should see the **Casa Guachinango**, further along on the Carretera Sancti Spíritus. This modest eighteenth-century plantation house has been

Portraits of Trinidad old-timers.

turned into a restaurant, with tables along its broad verandah. Inside are a beautiful and unusual array of fading frescoes under restoration, depicting mythological beasts and figures, that were painted in the eighteenth-century by an Italian artisan.

You could spend a day exploring the valley from here by horseback, accompanied by a local guide.

The Valle de los Ingenios, with its many working sugar plantations, is a worthwhile place to witness the *zafra*, or **sugar harvest**. You can ask Rumbos in Trinidad for more information about visiting plantations, or simply drive through the valley, taking any road alongside the fields where you see sugarcane being cut. The *zafra* begins around December 15 and goes on through around June 15.

WHERE TO EAT

Restaurant Hacienda Manacas-Iznaga ((00419) 7241, Carretera Sancti Spíritus, is a charming, moderately priced restaurant that serves excellent regional dishes and good coffee, perfect for contemplating the outstanding views across the valley. You can dine indoors or outside on the verandah.

HOW TO GET THERE

It is possible to make a day trip to the valley from Trinidad by the Valle de los Ingenios **Tren Turístico**, a vintage steam-train, which makes stops at various historic sites, including Hacienda Manacas-Iznaga and Casa Guachinango. Check with the Rumbos office in Trinidad for details. If you're Cuban, the rail journey costs but a single peso; tourists must pay US$13 for the trip alone, or US$23 for a package that includes lunch. Officially, the train runs on Wednesdays, Friday and Sunday, but departures often vary depending on the ebb and flow of large tourist groups.

TOPES DE COLLANTES

The nearby Sierra del Escambray mountains provide a change of scene from Trinidad's historic charms and its beaches, although parts of this region have been sectioned off

as a military zone, definitely off-bounds to tourists. For this reason, you are advised to have a Cuban guide or driver with you.

The logical place to head for is the mountain's main hill station, Topes de Collantes, at an elevation of 771 m (about 2,530 ft), which is located within a large national reserve. Here, there are two hotels from which to set out on nature trails amid coffee plantations, hidden caves, waterfalls and dense vegetation. This very fertile area has its own microclimate, which encourages swathes of giant ferns, endemic palms and native orchids.

Although Topes de Collantes lies only 19 km (12 miles) away, the road requires slow going as you wind up steep inclines and countless hair-pin turns. The higher the road goes, the greater the profusion of sweet-scented eucalyptus trees and Caribbean pines. This is really the only way to reach the Topes de Collantes at present, since the other road, which leads from Manicaragua on the other side of the Sierra del Escambray, is too risky a proposition for most rental cars, or even jeeps, especially during bad weather.

BACKGROUND

Topes de Collantes was developed during the 1950s Batista-era as a sanatorium for sufferers of tuberculosis and other respiratory ailments. It is rather hard to ignore this fact if you check into the Kurhotel Escambray, a decidedly institutional health resort run by Gaviota, in which foreign tourists mingle bemusedly with Cubans undergoing treatments on health sabbatical. More inspiring is the Hotel Helechos, which caters to regular tourists.

The entire Escambray mountain range spans an area that is 90 km (56 miles) long and 40 km (25 miles) wide. The range's highest peak is Pico San Juan (1,156 m or 3,793 ft), with a lower peak, Pico de Potrerillo (931 m or 3,054 ft) frequently the goal of hikers in the region.

WHAT TO SEE AND DO

Aside from Pico de Potrerillo, one of the most popular trails is to the **Caburní Falls**, which is a fairly arduous hike three kilometers (nearly two miles) down the ravine to the bottom of the 75-m-high (246-ft) falls, which are deservedly beautiful when you get there. This is a strenuous climb and not recommended unless you are in good physical condition.

A much less difficult excursion is to drive six kilometers (about four miles) to the **Finca Codina**, a turn-of-the-century ranch that belonged to a Spanish coffee grower. From here, an easy and extremely beautiful trail wanders past mountain caves and luxuriant forest, alive with butterflies, *zunzuns* (bee hummingbirds) and an incredible variety of plants and flowers, including many medicinal plants, orchids and the fragrant *mariposa*, Cuba's national flower. Back at the Finca, you can try their delicious cocktail, made of ginger root, honey and rum.

With the area's changes in temperature and the sudden downfalls of rain, rain gear, a change of warm clothes and mosquito repellent are essential, even though none of the above might seem important while you are basking in Trinidad's strong sunlight.

It is well worth asking the hotel staff to arrange a local guide to accompany you on the nature trails in the area, someone who can point out and explain the fascinating medicinal properties of the region's plants, explain local history and make sure you don't get completely lost in the dense forest.

WHERE TO STAY

Los Helechos ((042) 40180 or 40227 FAX (042) 47317, Topes de Collantes, Escambray, Sancti Spíritus, is a far better proposition than the clinical style Kurhotel, located close by. It has 38 quiet, comfortable and inexpensive rooms with mountain views, as well as a pleasant restaurant, a swimming pool, sauna, shop, and car rental facilities.

The **Kurhotel Escambray** ((042) 40219 or 40321 FAX (042) 40288, Topes de Collantes, Sancti Spíritus, another inexpensive accommodation aoption, is an admirable national institution where many Cubans come for rest and treatments for various ailments, and as such it functions as a sanatorium, with patients using the swimming pool, Jacuzzis and steam baths as therapeutic treatment. It has a distinctly institutional quality and is much dingier and depressing than it sounds.

Running into color-coded track-suited patients in the corridors and lifts, you may start to feel like a patient yourself. There are more than 200 rooms, most of which have a mountain view, with television and radio, and there are two restaurants, one for patients and one for tourists.

HOW TO GET THERE

In theory, you could take the daily bus from Trinidad, however, this is not necessarily a viable option unless you wish to stand upright on the open back of a truck. It is always full with villagers trying to get home. Driving is your best option, or you can negotiate a fee with a *taxi particular* from Trinidad.

To reach Topes de Collantes, take the Carretera de Cienfuegos out of Trinidad, and after crossing the Río Guaurabo, just before the town of Piti Fajardos, take the turnoff to the right, and then continue on the main road which you will notice, starts to climb steadily. Regardless of how you get there, for this trip, you need to be in a vehicle with functioning brakes.

VILLA CLARA

Most visitors speed by the province of Villa Clara, bypassing its sights as they travel through on Cuba's main highway, the two-lane Carretera Central. The province lies in the center of the island, directly north of Trinidad, and is one of Cuba's most traditional agricultural beltways, with vast plantations of sugarcane and rice interspersed with fields of maize, beans, *yucca* (cassava root), citrus fruits and cattle farms.

After Pinar del Río, Villa Clara is Cuba's biggest producer of high-quality tobacco, and you will see countless tobacco fields, as well as the shaggy thatched *vegas* where the leaves are dried. Throughout this region, giant sugarcane rises above the road like green waves, and work-weary *guachos* astride their horses drive herds of bullock. During the tobacco harvest (between December and March), many farmers are happy to welcome visitors; it is interesting to see them working in the fields, and they'll give you a visit of the drying houses if you ask.

SANTA CLARA

The provincial capital, Santa Clara, was founded in the 1570s, after its Spanish settlers had to flee their original site, the town of Remedios which, being on the coast, was constantly threatened with pirate raids. Like the rest of central Cuba, Santa Clara's independence fighters suffered greatly during the wars of independence. In recent history, Santa Clara is best known as the city whose capture by Che Guevara on December 28, 1958, played a decisive factor in bringing Fidel Castro to power. It is also where the remains of Che's body were laid to rest in 1997, after almost 30 years of lying in a hidden mass grave in Vallegrande, in the Bolivian mountains.

With its ochre-tiled and thick stucco colonial houses and the occasional *palacio*, Santa Clara in many ways has the feel of a small Spanish town, and it definitely merits a visit, at least for an hour or so. In the distance, the foothills of the Sierra del Escambray are easily visible. Santa Clara is also a university town, and young students make up a large portion of its residents.

WHAT TO SEE AND DO

Be sure not to miss one of Cuba's most idiosyncratic museums, the **Tren Blindado** ("Armored Train") which stands on the fringe of the city center (next to the main highway to Remedios) at the very site where it was attacked and derailed by Che in late 1958. The train, which was crammed with Batista's soldiers and weaponry, is now a museum. You can peer inside the old wagons and muse over historical photos and wartime paraphernalia such as a Molotov cocktail fashioned from a Canada Dry ginger ale bottle. Admission is free.

In Santa Clara's massive **Plaza de la Revolución**, a monument honors Che Guevara with a large statue of the iconic revolutionary posed for action with a machine gun above his words, "Hasta La Victoria Siempre" and a stone tablet bearing a complete letter that Che wrote to his comrade Fidel. There is also a small **Museo de la Revolución** here.

Parque Vidal is Santa Clara's main civic square, a leafy cobbled square with a central gazebo, and it is lined with some interesting buildings. Housed in a colonial mansion, the **Museo de Artes Decoratives** has a charming collection of eighteenth- and nineteenth-century furnishings from the city's wealthiest households. The **Teatro de la Caridad** is one of Cuba's outstanding theaters, built in 1884 and funded by a local philanthropist, Marta Abreu du Estevez. Painted allegorical figures the interior dome, under which such greats as Enrico Caruso sang when he made a tour of Cuba.

Also facing the square is the **Palacio Municipal** (Town Hall) and the dilapidated **Hotel Santa Clara Libre**, its exterior is pockmarked with bullet holes from the battle that proved so crucial to Cuba's history.

WHERE TO STAY

"A Step in Nature's Direction" is the slogan of Cubanacán's inexpensive **La Granjita Village** ((0422) 22762, Carretera de Maleza km2, on the outskirts of Santa Clara. This must refer to the rustic-style theme of the thatched bungalows, landscaped by palms. With pleasant surroundings and good food, this is a great place for an overnight stop. The swimming pool is nice.

A similar resort mood prevails at the sprawling **Hotel Los Caneyes** ((O422) 218140, at Avenida de los Eucaliptos and Circunvalación de Santa Clara. This inexpensive and sedate Horizontes property is styled as though Johnny Weismuller, the actor famous for his role as Tarzan, might walk in at any moment, with faux Indian-style thatched *cabañas* surrounded by lots of lush foliage. A large billboard-size Indian welcomes you at the entrance with a "How." The hotel's Los Taínos restaurant is Santa Clara's best and the plush pool area is a great place to while away a hot afternoon.

There's not a awful lot of overnight choice in the city center, but one of the best bets is a pleasant little budget *casa particular* called the **Villa el Renancer** ((0422) 205470, Calle J.B. Zayas 111, between Calles Eduardo Machado and Tristá. Set in a colonial-style

The palm is a ubiquitous feature in Cuba, where hundreds of varieties can be found.

house, this family-run hostel tenders hot water, air conditioning and a nice central garden only a few blocks off the square.

WHERE TO EAT

By any stretch of the imagination, Santa Clara is not a culinary oasis and only thing approaching international quality is the moderately priced **Los Taínos** ((0422) 218140 at the Hotel Los Caneyes on the city's western outskirts. The menu seems typically Cuban — the usual pork, chicken and fish dishes — but dishes are prepared with a flair that puts other local eateries to shame. The service is also outstanding, as is the resident musical quartet.

Scattered around Parque Vidal in the city center are several budget restaurants mostly frequented by Cubans. Among the better choices are **Pizzeria Pullman** with its outdoor terrace on the Calle Independencia pedestrian street, and **Tuscana**, a pseudo-Italian eatery on Calle Máximo Gómez just off the square.

If all you crave is a cold beer or a shot of rum, pop into the lively bar on the ground floor of the **Teatro de la Caridad**, a popular late afternoon and early evening watering hole for locals.

HOW TO GET THERE

Aside from stopping in Santa Clara while driving or on an organized tour, it is most practical to travel here by train, rather than by bus. There are daily trains from Havana, Matanzas, Cienfuegos, Sancti Spíritus and Santiago de Cuba. The **Estación de Ferrocarriles** is located to the north of the town, off Calle Luis Estévez.

REMEDIOS

Located near Villa Clara's northern coast, Remedios, which lies 43 km (27 miles) east of Santa Clara, is one of Cuba's best-preserved late-colonial towns. In many ways, it is just as interesting architecturally as Trinidad, for although it lacks such grand *palacios*, it possesses an almost eerily time-warped ambience. Most of its surviving colonial buildings date from the eighteenth

and nineteenth centuries and are fairly modest and provincial. A church tower is the highest vantage point over low-lying red-tile roofs and sleepy, narrow alleyways. Few tourists come here, and there are virtually no cars (except vintage American cars in various stages of decay), just horse-drawn carts and bicycles.

Remedios was not one of the seven *villas* or settlements established by Diego de Velázquez, but it is still one of the oldest colonial towns in Cuba, founded in 1524.

WHAT TO SEE AND DO

At the town's center is the **Plaza Martí**, around which the main civic administrative buildings are arranged. On the eastern side of the square is the extraordinary **Iglesia de San Juan Bautista**, which was originally built in 1578 but was significantly remodeled in the seventeenth century. Inside, there is a magnificent Churrigueresque altarpiece which was carved of cedar and encrusted with gold leaf. The walls are covered with iconographic carvings and religious paintings, including a rarely depicted image of the pregnant Virgin Mary.

When you walk outside the church, you might want to stop at one of two nearby local cafés — **El Louvre** and **La Fé** — both of which have interiors that look as they have not changed for at least a century.

On the north side of the square, the **Museo de Música Alejandro García Cartula** is a shrine to the town's most famous musician, Alejandro García Cartula. It is housed in the elegant nineteenth-century mansion that was the musician's birthplace. Cartula, who was both a musician and a judge, scandalized *le tout* Remedios when he lived openly with his black mistress and was inspired to incorporate Afro-Cuban musical traditions in his compositions. He was murdered in mysterious circumstances. Admission is US$1.

Opposite is the **Hotel Mascotte**, the town's only hotel. In 1899, this was where General Máximo Gómez met with an aide of American President McKinley to negotiate the retirement of the *mambisas*, the independence fighters who had fought in the Spanish-American War.

Leaving the square, a short walk along Calle Máximo brings you to the **Museo de las Parrandas Remedianas** (Museum of the Frolics of Remedios), dedicated to Las Parrandas, the unique festival of the region, which used to be held each year. The festivities date back to the early nineteenth century and were apparently concocted by the local parish to try and drum up more attendance for the midnight Mass on Christmas Eve. Along with the carnival in Santiago de Cuba, Las Parrandas has been one of Cuba's most important historical fiestas.

For months before Las Parrandas took place — on the last Saturday of the year — two sections of the town each secretly prepared a huge float, called *trabajos de plaza*, which were premiered to great fanfare of the night of the fiesta, paraded through the town accompanied by musicians playing the polka, firework displays, and townspeople dressed-up in outrageous costumes carrying banners. Traditionally, each camp tried to sabotage or outdo the other's efforts in order to come up with the most spectacular display; causing as much hilarity in the town as the celebration itself.

Since the beginning of the Special Period, Las Parrandas, sadly, has been cancelled. You can get a good idea of the festival from the museum's displays of float models, photographs, costumes and lanterns. It is open Tuesday to Saturday, 1 PM to 6 PM, Sunday 9 AM to 1 PM and is closed on Monday. Admission is US$1.

Walking tours of historic Remedios are offered daily (at 9:30 AM and 2:30 PM) starting from the lobby of the Hotel Mascotte.

WHERE TO STAY AND EAT

The town's only abode is the lovingly restored **Hotel Mascotte ℂ** (0422) 395144 or 395467, Calle Máximo Gómez 114, a belle époque gem that overlooks the main square. The inexpensive rooms are a bit on the small size, but they're clean and comfortable. The hotel restaurant offers the best food in Remedios as well as a nightly "Cuban Fantasy Salsa Show" (US$5).

The only place in Remedios to get a proper sit-down meal is **Los Arcadas Restaurant** on the ground floor of the Hotel Mascotte, where the menu runs a typical Cuban gamut of pork, chicken, rice and beans. Breakfast is also served. For something less formal, try either of the café-bars on the plaza. **La Fe** serves traditional drinks such as mango juice and an intriguing concoction made with anise, as well as sandwiches, pizza and cheese snacks; **El Louvre** serves a few light snacks along with the traditional shots of rum and Hatuey beer.

HOW TO GET THERE

Remedios is 43 km (27 miles) due east of Santa Clara along a busy country road chocked full of tractors, trucks and horse carts. Buses — or rather re-constituted trucks — ply between the towns several times a day.

SANCTI SPÍRITUS

If you are planning to continue along the Carretera Central into central Cuba through the largely agricultural province of Sancti Spíritus, you may wish to stop briefly in the provincial capital, which takes the same name.

BACKGROUND

Founded in 1514 by Diego de Velázquez, and once an affluent sugar capital, Sancti Spíritus has faded into sleepy gentility, and now ugly industrial factories and sugar mills are encroaching on its fringes. Head for **Plaza Sánchez**, a large square surrounded by nineteenth-century neoclassical buildings, some of which were very ostentatious in their day. There is the ubiquitous bust of José Martí, and old men doze on park benches under the trees. If you look closely at many of the historic buildings, you can see traces of classically inspired motifs; many house exteriors were painted in a trompe l'oeil masonry pattern and have elaborate cornices.

Also seek out the **Iglesia Parroquial Mayor del Espíritu Santo**, which dates from 1512, and is considered to be Cuba's oldest extant church, although much of its construction dates from later centuries. The narrow streets surrounding the church contain many well-preserved colonial mansions.

From the church, Avenida Jesús Menéndez continues southwest two blocks to the Yayabo River, from which you should take the first right, on Calle Placido, to reach the **Palacio Valle Iznaga**, which once belonged to the sugar-wealthy family from Trinidad, whose townhouse and plantation estate you may already have seen if you have already visited that town. Today it is the **Museo de Arte Colonial**, which houses the usual display of colonial furniture, but is beautiful to behold. Nearby, the **Río Yayabo bridge**, built in 1522, is the only remaining arched stone bridge from the early colonial period to be seen in Cuba.

It is pleasant to take a stroll through the main core of Sancti Spíritus to appreciate how the influence of early twentieth-century French and Italian styles, as well as art deco, can be seen alongside traditional colonial architecture, even in Cuba's provincial towns. In particular, look out for the grand, three-story, nineteenth-century **Hotel Perla de Cuba**, which is being renovated.

WHERE TO STAY

Like so many of the less-touristy Cuban cities, the best digs are on the outskirts of the central city. Without a doubt the best place to bed down is the inexpensive **Hotel Zaza** ((0419) 28512 or 28334 FAX (0419) 28401, Finca San José, Lago Zaza, Sancti Spíritus. Located 10 km (six miles) southeast of town on Lago Zaza, a man-made lake and popular trout-fishing spot, this hotel makes a good rest stop if you're making the long drive from Havana to Santiago.

There's a similar relaxed ambience for similare prices at **Villa Rancho Hatuey** ((0419) 6172, Carretera Central, five kilometers (three miles) north of town, which offers both a swimming pool and a decent restaurant.

Until the ongoing renovation of the historic **Hotel Perla** is completed (and who knows what year that might be), accommodation in the city center will remain limited.

Don't judge a book by its cover when it comes to the inexpensive **Hotel Plaza** ((041) 27102, Calle Independencia on Plaza Sánchez. The shabby façade hides a nicely restored interior including a pleasant patio area with colorful plants set around Roman sculptures.

Rooms on the plaza side can be noisy, so ask for something away from the street.

Tucked into an old colonial building at the northeast corner of the plaza is **Los Richard's** ((041) 26805, a *casa particular* that offers small rooms with air conditioning, balconies and hot water.

WHERE TO EAT

There's not a lot of scope for finding a good meal outside the hotels recommended above. The best place to head for is **Restaurante 1514** ((041) 23514, Calle Céspedes Norte 52, which has a very basic menu amid fairly Spartan surroundings. At press time it was undergoing extensive renovation and due to open again sometime in 2002.

A great place to escape the afternoon heat is the recently renovated ground floor bar and adjacent patio in the **Hotel Plaza**.

HOW TO GET THERE

If you are driving directly from Trinidad, Sancti Spíritus lies 55 km (34 miles) away, and so makes a convenient rest stop, although tourists rarely stay long. However when the Autopista Nacional currently under construction is completed, it will not pass through the city as the Carretera Central does.

CIEGO DE ÁVILA

As you drive onwards through central Cuba, you enter the province of Ciego de Ávila, another mainly agricultural region, with an unbroken succession of cane plantations, pineapple farms, banana groves and citrus orchards. Here, the air is rich with Cuba's inescapable smell of jasmine.

Its capital, Ciego de Ávila, which lies 76 km (47 miles) east of Sancti Spíritus and 108 km (67 miles) west of Camagüey, has a quiet and suburban feel, and is usually only visited by tourists because it is located on the main east–west highway and makes a good rest stop.

However, it can make a rather convenient base if you plan to explore the **Archipiélago**

Traces of Spanish colonial founders in Sancti Spíritus.

de los Jardines de la Reina — a collection of unspoiled keys surrounded by clear waters with beautiful coral reefs, abundant fish and close to shore, many migratory birds — found off the province's southern coast, since many fishing and diving excursions to the keys originate from Ciego de Ávila.

Another goal of many visitors who pass through Ciego de Ávila Province is to head across to the northern coast to the exotically named Cayo Coco and its neighbor, Cayo Guillermo, which has become a popular, if remote, beach resort, and also happens to be

ground floor of the Hotel Sevilla, which serves the usual range of Creole dishes you find in the provinces. Down the street, **El Colonial** restaurant at Calle Independencia 110 offers similar food in a bygone setting. For refreshments, fast food and light snacks, try either **El Rápido** or **El Cabildo** on Parque Martí.

One of the better *paladares* is the **Mesón El Fortín (** (033) 28118, at the corner of Calle Máximo Gómez and Calle One west of the Parque Martí. Set in an historic Spanish arms house called the Fortín de la Trocha, it is open for dinner only. It's a good idea to ask around

one of Cuba's most important bird sanctuaries (see below).

for recommendations for any paladares that may have opened recently.

WHERE TO STAY AND EAT

Right off Parque Martí in the middle of town is the inexpensive and pleasant **Hotel Sevilla (** (033) 25603, Calle Independencia 57. Recently refurbished, the rooms are clean and comfortable but nothing fancy. The lobby, replete with caged birds and strange wooden sculptures, is a popular meeting place for the local elite. The hotel also boasts a restaurant, nightclub and tour desk.

Ciego de Ávila is not a great place for eating out. A welcome exception to that rule is **Restaurante Giralda (** (033) 25603, on the

HOW TO GET THERE

Ciego de Ávila's **Aeropuerto Internacional de Máximo Gómez (** (068) 3325316 is located at Ceballos, 25 km (nearly 16 miles) north of town. Many charter flights from Canada arrive here, with visitors bound for Cayo Coco. In addition, Cubana de Aviación flies here from Havana.

You can get there by train from various points in the island, including Havana, Matanzas, Holguín and Santiago de Cuba. The **Estación de Ferrocarriles** is located six blocks southwest of the town center.

TO THE CAYS

En route, you will pass through a town by the unlikely name of **Morón**, the epitome of rural life in Cuba, and notable for its large metal rooster programmed to crow at dawn and dusk. Despite its backwater atmosphere, the town shelters one of the finest small hotels in all of Cuba — **La Casona de Morón** ((0335) 45463 or 55107, Cristóbal Colón 41, managed by the Horizontes group. The seven rooms are scattered around the upper floor of an old colonial mansion behind the train station, allegedly the home of Morón's first stationmaster. Despite their age, rooms are outfitted with air conditioning, private baths and satellite television. Meals are served downstairs in an equally ancient dining room.

Nearby, a road winds the scenic and bass-filled **Laguna de la Leche** which earned its name from its milky waters, created by lime deposits at the lake's bottom. It is a beautiful sight when flamingos flock here in large numbers. Further on, the smaller **Lago La Redonda** is also popular — Horizontes Hotels has a lodge here, well-equipped and situated for fishing excursions.

Several kilometers after leaving Morón, you see the rather surprising apparition of an entire farming community constructed as though it were a hamlet in the Netherlands, complete with peaked roofs, chimneys and windmills. It is named the **Communidad Celia Sánchez**, and was created by Fidel's longtime confidante and private secretary after she returned from a trip to Holland and declared herself besotted with Dutch architecture. The plump cattle you see grazing here are the result of an artificial insemination program, crossing European breeds with existing livestock.

CAYERIA DEL NORTE

From the mainland and onwards to the keys beyond lies a 34-km-long (21-mile) stone-fill causeway across the Bahía de Perros (Bay of Dogs) known as the Cayeria del Norte (also known as the "Pedraplen") that was completed in 1989, partially built on water, and one of the most complex engineering feats of the Cuban roadway system. Environmentalists worry that the landfill bridge has cut off the sea's current, and the waters are becoming stagnant, causing the mangrove swamps to rot, and that bird life will suffer.

The drive along this causeway is one of the most memorable parts of a visit to Cayo Coco and the neighboring Cayo Guillermo, which are the most developed islands within the Archipiélago de Sabana.

At times it feels as through you are literally driving over the sea itself, and in the right season, you will see flocks of flamin-

gos, pelicans, diving birds and flying fish on either side. The Pedraplen toll is US$2 per vehicle.

CAYO COCO

Cayo Coco is named, not for the coconut palms seen here as you might expect, but for the bird the locals call "coco": the long-legged white ibis. It also has Cuba's largest flamingo colony, estimated to be at least several thousand strong. This mangrove-dense region is an important migratory retreat for many thousands of birds and is also home to 158 year-round endemic species including sea swallows, herons, egrets and the Cuban cuckoo.

More than half of the 22-km-long (14-mile) cay is covered in mangrove and bracken forest where wild horses, wild boar and wild livestock roam free, but for how long is the question. Initially, only ornithologists, scientists and biologists came out to this region to

OPPOSITE: The Sancti Spíritus library was a casino in the 1920s. ABOVE: On the road to Ciego de Ávila.

study the fragile inter-dependency of this mangrove and marine ecosystem.

The Cuban government seems to be going ahead with its plan to develop the area's beaches as its next Varadero, and is poised to complete an airport. (The nearest airport is currently at Ciego de Ávila.)

Certainly, the Sabana archipelago — with its hundreds of keys and sandbars spread over hundreds of kilometers, most unexplored, connected by a vast underwater system of reefs — is widely regarded on the island as one of Cuba's last great unspoiled

the much smaller Cayo Guillermo. Like the Cayeria del Norte, this dyke has also caused a disruption in the ecology of these islands.

ACROSS TO CAYO GUILLERMO

If you have read Ernest Hemingway's *Islands in the Stream*, you will recognize the author's description of this sketchy patchwork of sandy coves, dark green mangroves, and soupy lagoons filled with rosy-colored flamingos. This is where he led his protagonist, Thomas Hudson, in search of Nazi sol-

frontiers for snorkeling and diving. Other parts of the archipelago, such as **Cayo Romano** and much further east, **Cayo Sabinal**, will likely be developed in future.

Today, Cayo Coco has two large tourist resort complexes, which between them share about a thousand hotel rooms, and apparently, the government plans to build as many as 20 more hotels on its northern Atlantic-facing coast in the near future.

When you approach the end of the causeway and arrive at Cayo Coco, the road branching northwest will lead you past the main resorts.

Beyond the airport, another causeway leads 17 km (over 10 miles) across tiny stepping stones of mangrove-covered islets to

diers. The story is based on his real-life adventures patrolling for German U-boats off this coast in his boat *Pilar*, accompanied by his captain, Gregorio Fuentes.

Cayo Guillermo's **Playa El Paso** is a very peaceful and relaxing place to stay, admire the bird life and scuba dive amid the offshore reefs which teem with rich and varied marine life.

WHAT TO SEE AND DO

There is plenty of nature to enjoy, and you can decide what sort of pace appeals to you, and whether you like the sound of hotel-organized excursions or prefer to do your own exploring. You can either swim on the beach in front of the hotels or venture to other beaches within the keys.

Hotel information desks generally have maps for the local bird-watching sites, nature trails and swimming lagoons in the keys, as well as the tourist-orientated facilities set up by Rumbos, notably on Cayo Coco where a series of attractions such as beachside restaurants, a horseback-riding ranch and trails have been landscaped throughout the cay.

You can rent bicycles, mopeds and, if necessary, cars, at all the major hotels. These resorts also offer a range of special events and excursions, such as cruises retracing Hemingway's fishing trips, sunset cruises and moped tours across the keys.

Marina Puertosol ((033) 301738, on Cayo Guillermo, and **Blue Diving** ((033) 308179 or 308180, on Cayo Coco, can arrange scuba diving or snorkeling trips to nearby waters. Sport-fishing excursions (for bonefish, mackerel, pike and marlin) can be organized trough Puertosol or **Base Nautica Aguas Traquilas** ((033) 301221, at the marina near the eastern tip of Cayo Coco.

WHERE TO STAY

Expensive
Standing head and shoulders above the competition is the sparkling **Meliá Cayo Coco** ((033) 301180 FAX (033) 301195 at the eastern end of the main beach strip. Spacious rooms are situated along the beach or in romantic two-story houseboats on the lagoon. There are handicap-access rooms, as well as special programs for honeymooners and families with children. In addition to five restaurants and four bars, the all-inclusive resort features a fitness center with massage, sauna and workout equipment. Recreation includes scuba diving, sailing, windsurfing, horseback riding, tennis, aerobics and beach volleyball. What more could you ask for?

By comparison, the **Sol Club Cayo Coco** ((033) 301280 FAX (033) 301285 looks a bit tarnished. But make no mistake: this is still a first-class hotel, slightly older than the Meliá but managed by the same Spanish hotel group. Aimed at a younger, faster crowd, this spiffy all-inclusive is probably the closest thing in these parts to a Florida or Cancún "Spring Break" hotel.

Another new entrant in the Cayo Coco hotel sweepstakes is a huge Canadian-Cuban joint-venture called **El Senador** ((033) 301470 FAX (033) 301490, launched in the summer of 2001. From the beautiful modern lobby full of ferns, palms and stained glass, to the earthy tones (red, ocher and brown) used in the guest rooms, everything about this new all-inclusive abode is classy. There are a number of accommodation options including villas and suites.

Continuing down the beach in a westerly direction, the all-inclusive **Tryp Cayo Coco** ((033) 301300 or 301311 FAX (033) 301386 or 301376 is an entire village fashioned against what used to be empty mangrove swamps. Apartment-style condominiums (some complete with Jacuzzis) are linked by walkways which lead to an array of swimming pools, restaurants, bars, cafeterias and shopping centers, designed to create the idea that you are in some sort of unnatural beach village. The beach *is* lovely, with soft sands and plenty of space to roam. You can rent equipment for a full range of watersports, including jet skiing and water skiing, and explore surrounding beaches by boat. Make sure you request a room with a balcony facing the sea.

Villa Vigía ((033) 301760 FAX (033) 301748, Cayo Guillermo, is a good luxury choice if you want to be away from the huge tourist villages that dominate Cayo Coco.

Moderate
Villa Cojímar ((033) 301712 or 301714 FAX (033) 335540, Cayo Guillermo, is a fairly luxurious, all-inclusive resort with a secluded atmosphere, good facilities for watersports and scuba diving, and a white sand beach that is very pleasant to loll on. It is an Italian-Cuban joint-venture, meaning that the food is much better than usual. The Cojímar stands out as one of the few moderate options along an otherwise pricey coast.

WHERE TO EAT

Aside from the hotels there are several places worth considering, most offering inexpensive meals. Rumbos has various beachside and roadside eateries, notably **Parador La**

Colorful plazas and antique cars abound in Cuba.

Silla, located in one of the small islands before you reach Cayo Coco, which has a lookout for flamingos.

Cueva del Jabalí (Wild Boar's Cave), six kilometers (four miles) west of the Hotel Tryp, is a popular nightspot with a cabaret show from 9 PM to 1 AM (nightly except Monday). Its restaurant and bar have been constructed within a cave. Although atmospheric, it can be a little damp and mosquito-prone. It's open for dinner only.

Before you reach the cave, at the point where the coast road turns away from the

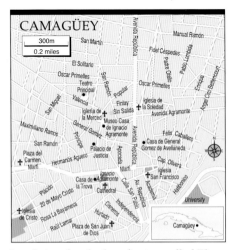

beach, is a thatched roof eatery called **Playa Prohibida** that serves typical Creole seafood and some pretty mean cocktails from a perch right beside the beach. The bugs can get a little aggressive, even during the middle of the day, so bring some repellent.

In the Servi-Cupet gas station complex on the big roundabout in the middle of the island is an **El Rápido** fast-food outlet that serves cold beer, light snacks and Copellia ice cream.

How to Get There

In keeping with the rapid expansion of tourist facilities, an airport is scheduled to open on Cayo Coco, and will receive both domestic Cubana de Aviación and international charter flights, primarily from Canada.

By road, the only way to get there is by rental car, unless you are arriving as part of a tour, or by an airport shuttle bus from a charter flight from Ciego de Ávila airport.

JARDINES DE LA REINA

Some 80 km (50 miles) off the south coast stretches the Archipiélago de los Jardines de la Reina, an extensive chain of secluded low-lying coral islets rimmed by beautiful, if small, white sand beaches and reefs. This is a pristine habitat for a spectacular array of marine life and birds. The Jardines de la Reina sprawl across the offshore boundaries of Ciego de Ávila and Camagüey provinces.

The only way to reach the keys is as part of an organized excursion from **Marina Júcaro ℂ** (033) 98104, 24 km (15 miles) south of Ciego de Ávila, or aboard your own private yacht. These diving packages can be organized by **Puertosol ℂ** (07) 245923 or 245782 FAX (07) 245928, Avenida 1 and Calle 30 no. 3001, Miramar, Havana (see SPORTING SPREE, page 31 in YOUR CHOICE).

CAMAGÜEY

Cuba's largest province, Camagüey has a tough cowboy reputation, famous throughout the island for its horse-adept *vaqueros* and its immense flatlands of sugarcane plantations and grazing cattle.

The provincial capital of the same name, Camagüey, was originally called Santa María del Puerto del Principe. It was among the seven townships founded by Diego de Velázquez. The original settlement was founded in 1514 near the present port of Nuevitas on the north coast, but after constant attacks from pirates, it was moved inland to its present site in 1528. Camagüey's settlers soon thrived from newfound prosperity in marketing contraband livestock to nearby French, Dutch and English Caribbean islands. Soon, the notorious English pirate Henry Morgan got wind of the treasures that were piling up, and he and his men ransacked the city mercilessly in 1668; another pirate attack followed a decade later.

Fear of pirates is evident in Camagüey's resulting early-colonial architecture. The town's inner core is surrounded by a labyrinthine network of winding streets, abutting in squares of all shapes and sizes, blind alleys and forked streets — and all with only one exit. Should the city ever find itself under siege, the plan went, the assailants would find the tables turned on them once they were trapped in this so-called "City of Squares."

The city is also known for its trademark bulbous clay pots, called *tinajones*, used to store precious rainwater for times of drought. A family's prosperity was measured by the number of *tinajones* they possessed, and the pots have since become a symbol of the city. An old legend has it that if a young woman from Camagüey gives a

very modest looking, neither brightly painted nor embellished with any form of decoration. However, the most attractive feature of these houses lies unseen behind discreet doors: the courtyard patio, which in Camagüey is the center of the home. Planted with shady trees, these courtyards are traditionally surrounded by roomy galleries, or in the case of less wealthy homes, supported by unembellished wooden eaves. Large pots of medicinal plants, flowers and herbs are also a traditional touch, as are the *tinajones*.

visiting stranger water from a *tinajón*, he will find himself so smitten with her that he will be unable to tear himself away from the city.

For anyone driving eastwards through central Cuba, Camagüey is an inevitable place to make an overnight stop. Despite the fact that it is very spread out — this is Cuba's third largest city — once you get to the colonial center, which has recently been named as a national monument, you can easily spend several enjoyable hours wandering around its maze-like and intensely traditional streets.

Wandering about the town, you will notice that most of the colonial buildings that line Camagüey's narrow streets are

GENERAL INFORMATION

There are few facilities for visitors in Camagüey. However, you'll find a **Banco de Crédito y Comercio** and a **post office** on Plaza de los Trabajadores. There is no Clínica Internacional, although the city has several hospitals and there's a 24-hour pharmacy, the **Farmacia Alvarez Fuentes** at the corner of Calles Oscar Primelles and Avellaneda.

Havanautos ((0322) 72239 has a car rental office at the Hotel Camagüey. There are two **Servi Cupet-Cimex** gas stations, located on the Carretera Central to the south of the city, close to the district of La Caridad.

Horse-drawn carriage transports tourists at Playa Santa Lucía.

WHAT TO SEE AND DO

Start by heading for downtown Camagüey, where you can leave your car behind to navigate your way through the city's narrow one-way streets on foot. Like many rustic capitals in Cuba, you may see more horse-drawn carriages and bicycles in these streets than cars.

You can begin at **Plaza de los Trabajadores** (Worker's Square), which in the nineteenth century was used to stage bullfights. You can't miss the enormous placard of Che Guevara. Just off the square, off Avenida Agramonte, lies the **Museo Casa de Ignacio Agramonte**, the birthplace and home of one of Cuba's most revered military revolutionaries and Camagüey's hero, General Ignacio Agramonte (1841–73). He was renowned for many feats of bravery, and took part in an estimated 45 battles while commanding troops during the Wars of Independence. His favored military strategy — much admired by Castro — involved using a small detachment to distract the enemy, then to simulate a retreat, only to lure the enemy troops into the thick of his army, much like the design of Camagüey itself. Although only the piano was an original possession of the Agramonte family, the house has been furnished to create the impression that the general has just stepped out. The museum is open Monday and Wednesdays through Saturday from 1 PM to 6 PM and Sunday from 8 AM to noon; it is closed on Tuesday.

Directly opposite is the **Iglesia de la Merced**, built in 1748 and restored after a 1906 fire. Although the exterior has a stern, almost fortress-like quality, the interior is ornate. An altarpiece made of carved wood, silver and marble is startlingly impressive. To the left, a side chapel contains an image of the Infant Jesus of Prague, much revered by locals. Elaborate confession boxes face the courtyard of the adjacent convent.

From here, walk westwards along Calle Valencia for two blocks and look for the marble façade of the **Teatro Principal**, built in 1850 and the home of the Camagüey Ballet, which, after Havana, is the second most prominent ballet in Cuba. As you return to

the square, look for Calle Salvador Cisneros. This will lead you into the labyrinthine maze that can be found at the city's heart; the streets here are lined with impressive colonial-era houses.

Further along Calle Salvador Cisneros to reach the **Palacio de Justicia** (Court House), a notable mid-eighteenth-century construction housed in a former seminary. Nearby, the **Centro de Promoción Cultural** often stages exhibitions by Cuban artists as well as jazz concerts, and is usually a lively place to visit. From here turn right on Calle Hermanos Aguero, where on the corner, is the birthplace of the Cuban poet Nicolás Guillén, which is open to the public as a small library. Keep walking until you reach the **Plaza de Bedoya**, unusual for its row of bright pastel-

painted colonial houses — a sudden splash of welcome color. At the end is the run-down **Iglesia del Carmen**.

From here, take your bearings and head for Avenida Martí, immediately parallel, which will lead you onto the **Parque Agramonte**, between Calles Independencia and Cisneros. Here, a 1916 statue of General Agramonte brandishing his sword and flanked by a sculptured relief of his cavalry soldiers presides over the square. The four palm trees at each corner of the square are also monuments in a sense: they commemorate four Cuban independence fighters executed by the Spanish in 1851, and were planted by locals as a secret homage to their slain compatriots unbeknownst to the colonial authorities. To the south side of the square is Camagüey's cathedral, the **Nuestra Señora de la Candelaria**. On the square, on Calle Salvador Cisneros, you will also find the city's **Casa de la Trova**.

A short walk three blocks south on Calle Cisneros, and then left on Calle Hurtado brings you to one of Camagüey's gems: **Plaza de San Juan de Dios**. Built in the eighteenth century, it is easy to see why this cobble-stoned square is a national monument. Since it has been restored, its red-tiled houses painted in their original colors, it looks straight out of a film set. It is flanked by the **Iglesia de San Juan de Dios**, built in 1728 and the first hospital to be established in the town. Inside the cobbled square, you can

Happy rodeo spectators.

visit a ceramics workshop, and perhaps, buy a *tinajón*. Within the square, two colonial-style restaurants, **Parador de los Tres Reyes** and **Mesón La Campaña de Toledo** are the city's most inviting places to dine.

From here, you may want to climb aboard a horse-drawn *calesa* to get back to your starting place on this tour.

If you have time for one last sight on your visit to Camagüey, see the lovely baroque **Iglesia de la Soledad**, built in 1775 with impressive fresco paintings in its interior. It lies at the corner of Avenida Agramonte and Avenida República, south of the railway track.

As you leave Camagüey, you can't fail to notice the ornate **Palacio de Matrimonio**, the yellow-and-white mansion that once belonged to a wealthy Cuban family (long-gone to Miami, one supposes) and is now used to officiate civil weddings.

The **Parque Casino Campestre** is where the city's school-children go to play; as well as having a small amusement park for younger children, donkey-rides are especially popular in the park. At the park's entrance, a statue commemorates the two Spanish pilots, Barberan and Collar, who completed their flight from Seville in Southern Spain to Camagüey in 1933, a unique achievement, and the first direct flight between Cuba and Europe.

WHERE TO STAY

Inexpensive **Hotel Maraguán** ((0322) 72170 or 71854, Camino de Guanamaquila, Circunvalación Este, is a modest and pleasant Cubanacán hotel, built as a series of stone cottages on the outskirts of the city, and probably best suited as a rest stop for those traveling by car as it is some distance from the center. The buffet meals are very good. Facilities include a small swimming pool and a bar.

Another low-cost alternative is the 1970s-style **Hotel Camagüey** ((0322) 287267 or 287270 FAX (0322) 287180, Carretera Central Este, Jayamá. The ugly concrete-block facility has seen many a tour bus come and go. The rooms are lackluster and showers are often without hot water. It is redeemed by the friendliness of its staff, the attempts to brighten up the place with artistic ceramic

sculptures by a local artist, and the talented musical trio who entertain here. Right next door, Camagüey's cabaret nightclub puts on a nightly show.

Located close to Camagüey's rail station, **Hotel Plaza** ((0322) 82413 or 82415, Avenida Von Horne, is an idiosyncratic, turn-of-the-century hotel that has a lot of old-fashioned charm and is a good choice if you want to be located within the city center and don't mind going without some comforts. You can request a room with air conditioning and a private bathroom. Rates are inexpensive.

WHERE TO EAT

La Campana de Toledo ((0322) 87223, Plaza de San Juan de Dios, is a moderately priced eatery housed in an attractive colonial house, with tables set outside on the cobbled courtyard over-hung with vines. This is the most enjoyable and atmospheric place to dine in Camagüey. The menu is one of the more intriguing in central Cuba with dishes like boliche mechado (beef steak stuffed with bacon), *camarones rebasados* (breaded shrimp) and *picadillo a la Habanesa* (finely minced meat in a spicy tomato sauce). Open 10 AM to 10 PM.

The charming tavern **Parador de los Tres Reyes** ((0322) 86339, Plaza de San Juan de

Dios, is a pleasant place to unwind and has a very local atmosphere. It is the best place to sample the local beer, Tínima, along with chorizo sausage. Open 10 AM to 5 PM.

HOW TO GET THERE

Camagüey Ignacio Agramonte Airport ((0322) 61862 or 61020, lies 14 km (about nine miles) northeast of the city. There are direct charter flights from the United Kingdom and Canada. There are regular scheduled flights with Cubana de Aviación from Havana and Santiago de Cuba.

By train, Camagüey is a main stop on the daily Havana–Santiago railway service. The **Estación de Ferrocarriles** is located at Calles Avellaneda and Finlay, opposite the Hotel Plaza.

PLAYA SANTA LUCÍA

On Camagüey's north coast, the beach resort of Playa Santa Lucía is a perfect place to spend a day or two recuperating if you are driving across Cuba. Over the past few years, it has become popular destination for the pale hordes of tourists who arrive on sun-seeking packages during the winter months, most arriving by direct charter flights from Britain, Canada, Holland, Germany, Finland and Argentina at either Camagüey or Holguín, the nearest international airports. It has to be said that most visitors simply come for a beach holiday and barely get out to see much of the rest of Cuba from here.

From Camagüey, the 112-km (70-mile) journey takes a couple of hours and follows a road that heads northeast and winds through Wild West-style pasturelands and pan-flat fields rimmed with bulrushes, where cattle ranches are overseen by brawny-looking cowboys or *vaqueros*, who frequently trot along the road with horses or cows in tow, cigar at the mouth, with a tip of the hat to passers-by. You should bypass the ugly industrial port of Nuevitas and head straight on to Santa Lucía, which now has five resort hotels which among them have all the usual resort facilities, including an international diving center and horseback excursions.

GENERAL INFORMATION

Playa Santa Lucía bears two distinct personalities: the eastern end of the strand is given over to Cuban-owned beach houses and local tourism; the western end is reserved for international hotels and foreign tourists.

Dividing the two zones is a huge traffic circle with a spanking brand new **Servi-Cupet** gas station, mini-mart and **El Rápido** fast-food outlet. Just west of the roundabout is an **Etecsa** telephone call center.

Facilities in the eastern zone include a police station and an international clinic.

WHAT TO SEE AND DO

Although the little settlement of Santa Lucía looks like nothing more than a shabby shantytown, Playa Santa Lucía is an exceptionally pleasant beach, with soft white sands stretching for more than 20 km (12 miles), fringed by palm trees and shrubs. In many ways, Playa Santa Lucía offers a much more relaxing beach experience than, for example, Varadero or Cayo Coco. It is still not as devel-

Bright colonial houses OPPOSITE in Camagüey, an area with a tough cowboy reputation ABOVE.

oped and has a much more Cuban atmosphere. Just three kilometers (nearly two miles) west of Playa Santa Lucía, you should not miss a visit to the characterful little village of **La Boca**, with its own beach and seaside restaurants run by friendly locals.

Playa Santa Lucía's main bay is protected by a coral reef close to the shore, and its enticing, clear blue and warm waters make it an excellent site for snorkeling and scuba diving with more than 15 dive sites. The surrounding reefs are home to more than 50 different coral species, including vivid bright orange sponges and black coral, as well as many species of fish, gorgonians, crustaceans and mollusks. Divers report that nurse sharks and barracudas can often be seen, but they are not described as posing a serious threat. Schools of dolphins are also frequently seen, as are flying flamingoes, which settle in seasonal flocks alongside the lagoon behind Playa Santa Lucía.

As a staging area, Santa Lucía is increasingly being promoted as an access base to Cuba's northern Sabana archipelago. You can also dive wrecks within the Bahía de Nuevitas, including the steamship *Motera*, which sank in 1898, and lies just meters below the ocean surface, now embalmed with colorful coral, and home to turtles, fish and the odd shark.

Snorkeling and scuba diving excursions — as well as specialized and beginners courses — are offered at local hotels and two independent operators: **Shark's Friend Diving Center** ((032) 365183, between the Cuatro Vientos and Caracol resorts, and **Marina Tararaco** ((032) 36222, next to the Hotel Escuela Santa Lucía. The hotels also offer chartered sport-fishing trips for *macabí* and *sábalo*.

Nearby, there are several beautiful beaches are to explore. **Playa Los Cocos**, at the mouth of the Nuevitas Bay, is a good swimming beach, with a broad strip of white sand protected from the ocean winds. It also has several simple, yet atmospheric, seaside restaurants.

Through your hotel in Playa Santa Lucía, you can also arrange a visit to **King Ranch**, a working ranch, where you can watch local *vaqueros* herding cattle, stage a rodeo show, and eat at a *campesino*-style restaurant. You can also rent horses and go riding. The ranch, which was owned by the Texan owners prior to the Revolution, lies just west of the entrance to Santa Lucía.

Separated from the mainland by a narrow inlet with shallow waters that can be reached from Playa Lucía by excursion ferry, **Cayo Sabinal** has a 33-km (over 20-mile) stretch of lovely beaches — including aptly named **Playa Bonita** — and inlets which attract flocks of migratory flamingos. Casual beachside restaurants, camping grounds and diving huts have been set up to make an excursion to Cayo Sabinal more tourist-friendly. In fact, the Cuban government plans to do more than that: a recent study on the tourism potential of Cayo Sabinal estimated that the area has a tourism capacity for 12,000 hotel rooms. Developers have been placing their bids.

WHERE TO STAY

Moderate

Located directly on one of the nicest stretches of the beach is the all-inclusive **Club Amigo Caracol** ((032) 365158 FAX (032) 365307, Playa Santa Lucía. Recently refurbished, the compound spreads along the shore village fashion, two-story units with red-tile roofs and rust-colored walls. Rooms are quite luxurious, with the usual amenities for this range of accommodation, including a small living room area, a mini bar and a beach view. Good facilities for children include an activities program. There is a large swimming pool, a cabaret with dance area, a watersports and diving center, car rental, horseback tours, shops and hair-dresser.

Right next door is the **Gran Club Santa Lucía** ((032) 365146 FAX (032) 365147, Playa Santa Lucía, another all-inclusive beach resort, also caters mainly to package tourists, but is more orientated toward younger clients, rather than young children. It has the same facilities as its neighbor, but also has a discotheque and a beachside restaurant and bar. Every morning, a catamaran departs to cruise out to a nearby coral reef, allowing scuba divers and snorkelers to explore, and then to have an Italian pasta and lobster lunch on board.

Hotel Cuatro Vientos ((032) 36160 or 36140 FAX (032) 36142, Playa Santa Lucía, is another possibility along the same beachfront strip. Recently renovated the hotel should be open again by the time you read this, with much nicer rooms and better facilities.

Inexpensive

At the far western end of the beach strip, **Hotel Escuela Santa Lucía** ((032) 36222 or 36410 is on the shoreline site of the old villa Tararaco resort. Make no mistake: there's nothing fancy about this place. But the price is

The best eats in town are at **Las Brisas**, in an old whitewashed building opposite the police station. The menu includes local seafood delights like cream of shrimp soup, grilled lobster, a mixed grill of lobster, shrimp and fish, and a mighty filling dish called *bistec las brisas* (breaded beef, pork and cheese).

At the western end of the beach, Hotel Escuela Santa Lucía offers two eateries: **Restaurante La Barca** offers a typical Cuban menu of chicken, pork and fish dishes, while the **Parrillada el Ancla** specializes in barbecued meat and fish dishes.

right, the service friendly and the ambience very relaxed. Thirty-one rooms sprawl motel-style along a palm-shaded beach, all of them air conditioned with private bath and satellite television. Recreation includes swimming pool, beach volleyball, sailing, windsurfing, billiards and scuba diving (at the adjacent Marina Tararaco). The school also boasts some of the best eateries and bars in Santa Lucía.

WHERE TO EAT

There are several good inexpensive restaurants at the eastern end of the beach strip including the thatched-roof **La Concha**, which is next to the old gas station on the main road out of town.

HOW TO GET THERE

Almost all visitors to Playa Lucía arrive on package tours, and therefore are ferried here on resort shuttle buses from Camagüey, 112 km (70 miles) away. There is one daily bus service between Camagüey and Santa Lucía.

Volleyball on the beach of Playa Santa Lucía.

Eastern
Cuba

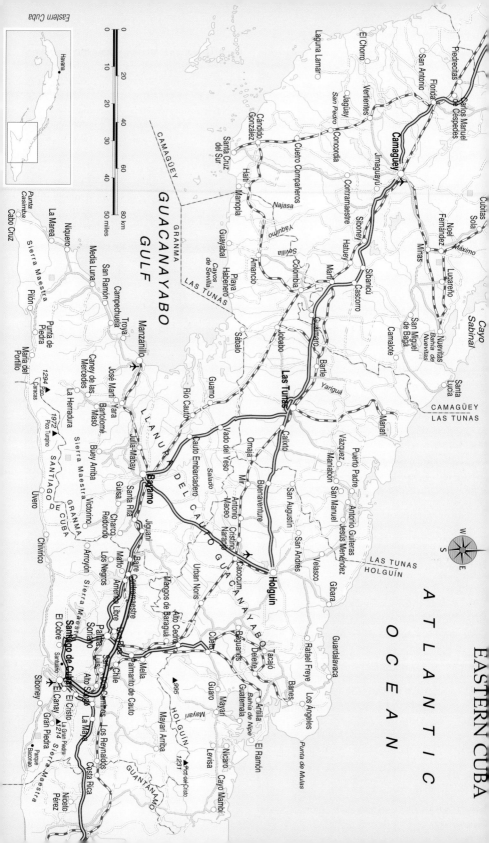

HOLGUÍN

Not an attraction in itself, the provincial capital of Holguín is an inevitable stop on the main highway from Las Tunas on the way to Bayamo. It is also a transit point for the many tourists who fly into its international airport to reach the nearby beach resort of Guardalavaca. Few foreign visitors linger long here, yet as the country's fourth-largest city, Holguín is a good place to stop to explore for an hour or two, simply to appreciate the street life and the reality of existence for many Cubans, away from places tourists would usually visit. It's not recommended as a place to stay overnight, unless you are recuperating from an international flight and arrived at Holguín's airport.

During the late colonial period, many Spanish and Creole ranch owners settled here, and the city has its own brand of reserve and conservatism. Cubans regard Holguín as having a rich cultural and intellectual life. Since the revolution, the province of Holguín has benefited from the creation of research institutes, universities and the modernization of its sugar industry.

GENERAL INFORMATION

Generally speaking, you are best advised to go directly to the Hotel Pernik's information desk if you need directing for any practical needs. The Hotel Pernik has a doctor's office, and it also has a **Transautos** office for car rental. The **Havanautos** office is located in Motel El Bosque. The **Servi Cupet-Cimex** station is located three kilometers (nearly two miles) outside town, on the Carretera Central en route to Las Tunas.

WHAT TO SEE AND DO

The best place to start is **Plaza Calixto García**, a desultory colonial park encircled by colonnaded houses, named for Holguín's most celebrated denizen, General Calixto García, a formidable rebel commander during the Second War of Independence. In dusty patches of sunlight, sitting in chairs and drinking *cafecito*, you'll see the proprietors of the local museum, art gallery, **Casa**

de la Trova and various small shops debating the latest gossip. Tradition has it that for generations, amorous assignations and marriages were inspired around this small green square, during a weekly ritual in which the whole town would stroll here at dusk, men promenading in one direction, women in the other.

Facing the park, on Calle Frexes, the **Museo Provincial de Historia** was built in 1868, first used as a grand house and venue for elaborate parties and later as the seat of the municipal government. It has been called

La Periquera ("the Parrot Cage") ever since the First War of Independence, when rebel forces, known as *mambisas*, besieged the Spanish infantry here, whose flamboyant uniforms could be glimpsed behind the building's barred windows. "Come out of your cage, you parrots," the *mambisas* are said to have jeered. The museum is worth visiting for its archeological and historical exhibits as well as its section on Santería, the Afro-Cuban religion, which displays a mock shrine. Open Monday to Saturday, noon to 7 PM, closed on Sunday.

PREVIOUS PAGES: Resting *vaqueros* or cowboys LEFT and RIGHT a *guajiro*, or traditional Cuban farmer. ABOVE: A child dwarfed by the sugarcane in Holguín Province.

On nearby Calle Maceo, just south of the park, is the **Carlos de la Torre Museo de Historia Natural** (Natural History Museum) ((024) 423935 WEB SITE www.ilam.org/cu/cuba_main.html, which has Cuba's most outstanding collection of brilliantly colored *polymita* snail shells, which are endemic to the coasts of Eastern Cuba. There is also a display of stuffed birds and mammals, along with sponges, conches and shells. It is open Tuesday to Saturday from 8 AM to 6 PM, Sunday from 8 AM to noon, and is closed on Monday.

On the northern outskirts of Holguín, a fairly strenuous climb up 450 steps leads to the lookout at **Loma de la Cruz** (Hill of the Cross), with a cross that was placed here in 1790, and a bird's-eye views across the city below. Every May 3, the Day of the Cross is celebrated by a pilgrimage here.

Another scenic view is from the **Altura de Mayabe** (Mayabe Heights), eight kilometers (five miles) southeast from the city. A tourist complex, the **Mirador de Mayabe** ((024) 422160, which features restaurants, bars, shops and a small motel, marks the lookout

As you walk along Calle Maceo to the Parque de San Isidoro, you will see the **Iglesia de San Isidoro**, built in 1720 and dedicated to the city's patron saint. Inside, the altar was transported here on foot by slaves from Bayamo, after the church there was burned to the ground. Outside, in the square stands a statue of Karl Marx.

On the city's eastern fringe, near the university, is the massive **Plaza de la Revolución**, in which stands a bronze statue and an imposing mausoleum containing the remains of General Calixto García. The general's birthplace, which is now a museum devoted to his life and times, is located nearby at the intersection of Calle Frexes and Calle Miró.

point with views across at the beautiful Mayabe Valley, with its clusters of palm trees, sugarcane plantations and *bohíos* (the traditional wooden houses of the Cuban countryside). The star attraction here is **La Taberno Pancho**, home for many years to a donkey called Pancho, famed for his beer-drinking exploits; he is now on display, stuffed.

WHERE TO STAY AND EAT

One of Cuba's finest examples of hideous Soviet "concrete chic" design is the hulking **Hotel Pernik** ((024) 481011 or 481667 FAX (024) 481371, Avenida Jorge Dimitrov near the Plaza de la Revolución. The property is named after the birthplace of the Bulgarian national hero, Geogry Dimitrov, whose country was partly responsible for its construction. This inexpensive hotel exudes classic Soviet-era style, with a huge mausoleum-like lobby, poorly maintained facilities, incredibly sluggish service and cafeteria dining hall. Despite this, it offers the city's best option for a comfortable stay. Be wary of using the elevators, which are known to break down regularly.

Just down the road and only slightly less obnoxious is the similarly priced **Motel El Bosque (** (024) 481012, Avenida Jorge Dimitrov, a sprawling, low-rise complex that sports a swimming pool and popular nightclub, El Pétalo. However, the noise and lack of value for money may make you wish you had chosen the Hotel Pernik instead.

Set amid lush tropical vegetation, Cubanacán's **El Cocal Village (** (024) 461924 or 461902, Carretera Central km7, is the best option for an overnight stay outside the city, with simple, two-story bungalow buildings arranged around a swimming pool. It is conveniently located near the airport. Rates are inexpensive.

WHERE TO EAT

Holguín dining was a pretty dreary affair until the launch of **Hacienda Compay Gallo (** (024) 30132, Carretera Guardalavaca km3, in early 2001. Located in a rural area northeast of the city, Gallo offers excellent food and friendly service at inexpensive prices. Among the more offbeat dishes are *codorniz a la vinagreta* (quail egg salad), *chilindrón de carnero* (lamb stew), and *fricase de conejo* (rabbit), as well as grilled seafood and chicken cordon bleu.

Otherwise, the most enjoyable place to eat is the **Mirador de Mayabe (** (024) 422160. This restaurant serves a limited but reliable repertoire of simple Cuban dishes under a thatched roof.

HOW TO GET THERE

Holguín's **Aeropuerto Internacional Frank País (** (024) 462512 or 462534, lies 13 km (eight miles) south of the city. Regular direct charter flights arrive here from Europe and Canada (see GETTING THERE, page 306 in

TRAVELERS' TIPS). Cubana de Aviación has daily scheduled flights from Havana.

Holguín is a main stop on the railway network, and is connected daily by train services from Havana and Santiago de Cuba. The Estación de Ferrocarriles is located to the south of the city center, on Calle V Pilar.

EN ROUTE TO GUARDALAVACA

For many arriving in Holguín, the real goal of their journey is Guardalavaca, 50 km (31 miles) away on the northeast coast.

GIBARA

If you are driving, it is well worth including a detour to the small port and fishing town of Gibara, 32 km (20 miles) directly north of the provincial capital. Both routes meander through cultivated fields and small towns, and especially in the case of the latter, some dirt track roads lined with cacti fences.

Gibara remains almost completely unvisited, and is an unspoiled haven of crumbling colonial shipwrecks of houses, narrow cobbled lanes, sleepy fishermen's bars and barnacle-encrusted fishing boats. A certain has-been grandeur seems part of its salty air. Gibara's claim to fame is that it was the crucible of many sea-borne fortunes when it served as a key port along Cuba's eastern coast during the nineteenth century. It is also the birthplace of the prolific, exiled novelist and essayist Guillermo Cabrera Infante.

OPPOSITE: Green pastures line the roads in Holguín Province. ABOVE: Horse-drawn carts transport tourists in Guardalavaca.

While you are in Gibara, wander along the waterfront which is bounded by the small **San Fernando Fort**, built in 1817, and find the main square, **Plaza de la Iglesia**, named for the nearby Church of San Fulgencio. Also visit the **Museo de Arte Colonial**, on Calle Independencia, the town's main street. The museum has all the classic decorative features of a nineteenth-century colonial home as well as art deco embellishments, including distinctive fan-shaped stained-glass windows. It is open Tuesday to Saturday from 8 AM to noon and 1 PM to 5 PM; Sunday, 8 AM to noon.

outcrop that does indeed resemble a saddle that dominates the horizon.

The turnoff to visit the landing place monument starts from Rafael Freyre, a town known for its antediluvian sugar mill fed by the bushels of sugarcane ferried from surrounding fields by steam locomotives. Although it's barely a 20-minute drive away, be sure your vehicle is suitable for a rough ride along the unsealed road, which dips in and out of small streams in places.

Located at the narrow tip of Cayo Bariay, on a forested beach scattered with coral

For lunch, try **El Faro** restaurant on the waterfront, which offers a variety of seafood dishes, including lobster, and charges reasonable prices.

PARQUE MONUMENTO NACIONAL BARIAY

Whether or not you make the detour to see Gibara, you can include another stop as you drive en route to Guardalavaca: the place where Christopher Columbus first sighted and then set foot on Cuban soil, after he sailed into **Cayo Bariay** on October 28, 1492. Although historians have argued about where exactly the explorer landed, his diary entries unmistakably describe the Silla de Gibara (Saddle of Gibara), a giant mountain

rock, the monument — built in 1992 to coincide with the 500th anniversary of Columbus's discovery of America — is strikingly eccentric, with its row of truncated neoclassical-style columns and ochre-colored sculptures resembling indigenous Indian gods and amulets.

The park has been embellished in recent years with the addition of a modest restaurant and an information kiosk. Archaeologists have also discovered the remains of an ancient indigenous settlement thought to be the village that Columbus described in his diary. A replica of the village has been erected nearby. Historians have also speculated that Columbus may have visited an Indian village across the bay at nearby Punta de los Gatos.

More interesting than visiting the monument itself, is seeing the Cuban families, *guajiros* (rural workers) and small children of this area going about their lives, sitting on rocking chairs in front of their wooden *bohíos*, listening to transistor radios, or mending fishing nets, loading vegetables on makeshift trucks, with an entourage of farm dogs, pigs, horses and chickens. Any hint of a genuine wave or smile from strangers, and they reciprocate with friendliness.

Near Cayo Bariay, **Playa Don Lino**, where a modest hotel complex sits on a small, white sand beach, has long been a favored destination for government officials. It's not recommended as a place to stay.

However, several beach resorts along this coast located on the **Bahía de Naranjo**, within the **Parque Natural Bahía de Naranjo** — as well as on the outlying island of **Cayo Saetía** — offer an enticing alternative to staying on the main beach of Guardalavaca.

Back on the main road, you will soon reach Guardalavaca.

GUARDALAVACA

Following close on the heels of Varadero, Guardalavaca is a popular and ever-growing beach resort. As beaches go, these are pretty enough, with soft blond sands fringed with plentiful palm trees to loll under. Although you may hear that this is one of the loveliest beaches in Cuba, it is in fact merely very pleasant, its azure waters still clear despite creeping seaweed, and its warm, swimmable shallows are suitable for keeping an eye on small children.

In fact, the most beautiful beaches along this coast — much more deserving of such a claim — are found close by, especially Playa Esmeralda in the Bahía de Naranjo, which has superb landscapes lined with coconut palms and the best hotels.

It has to be said that the scale of hotel development in Guardalavaca seems somewhat out of proportion with the size of the beach, given the fact that there are few other attractions in the vicinity. Still, for many of the foreign tourists who visit Guardalavaca on package tours from Canada and Germany, it is luxury enough being away from cold winters at home. Not surprisingly, with all this focus on tourism development, the resorts here are designed to be as self-contained as possible. Few tourists venture beyond the beach once they arrive from the Holguín airport, and consequently see little, if anything, of the rest of the country — just the way Fidel likes it.

Rather than making it a destination in itself, Guardalavaca is a good place to recuperate if you are on a driving expedition around the country.

GENERAL INFORMATION

In Guardalavaca, hotels cater to most practical needs. For medical assistance contact the resort town's 24-hour **Clínica Internacional** ((024) 30291. Other sorts of trouble can be sorted out through the local branch of **Asistur** ((024) 30148.

There is a branch of **Banco Financiero Internacional** in the resort's **Centro Comercial**. Nearby is a modest supermarket that seems to stock more rum than anything else. However, a new shopping center is under construction directly opposite the Hotel Guardalavaca.

Long distance calls can be made from the **Etecsa** kiosk next to Pizza Nova on the town's main roundabout.

All of the all-inclusive resorts have tour desks where local excursions can be arranged. Among the main operators in the area is **Gaviota Tours** ((024) 30903 or 30909.

There are car and moped rental offices at the Las Brisas Resort, Hotel Guardalavaca and Hotel Atlántico, as well as the Sol Meliá hotels at Playa Esmeralda. Fill up at the **Servi-Cupet** gas station on the Holguín Highway about one kilometer (half a mile) west of town, before the turnoff to Playa Esmeralda.

WHAT TO SEE AND DO

Guardalavaca's main beach is a fairly relaxed scene, with vendors selling coconuts, cold drinks and snacks. Further afield, you can also explore the beaches and coves around **Playa Esmeralda** in Bahía de Naranjo several kilometers southwest. The best way to

Resident of the Bahía de Naranjo, Holguín.

explore these beaches and coves is by rented car, moped or bicycle.

Aside from swimming, there are plenty of opportunities for diving and snorkeling around offshore reefs and outlying coral keys, especially around the Bahía de Naranjo. The waters within this marine reserve are renowned for their spectacular diving opportunities, as well as the many large and colorful sponges and deepwater gorgonians. Swordfish and barracuda are commonly seen off a sharp cliff drop well known to diving guides here.

Most hotels can arrange diving trips or will direct you to Guardalavaca's **Marlin Watersport Base**, which offers certification courses.

French tour operator **Lookea** runs a water-sport kiosk on the main beach, right below Pizza Nova. Ostensibly the equipment is for their clients, but they will rent to anyone with cash. Sea kayaks are US$5 per hour, windsurfers US$10 per hour and Hobbie cats US$10 per half hour. You can also contact the **Marina Naranjo**, four kilometers (two and a half miles) southwest of the Sol Meliá hotels at Playa Esmeralda, which organizes diving and fishing charters.

Yet another way to explore the waters off Guardalavaca is a **catamaran cruise** out of Vita International Marina. The excursion includes snorkeling and seafood lunch. Book through Gaviota Tours ((024) 30903 or 30909.

WHERE TO STAY

It is a challenge to find inexpensive accommodation in any of Cuba's tourist destinations, and Guardalavaca is no exception. It is worth checking in advance for any low season discounts. In the Bahía de Naranjo, Playa Esmeralda has become a beach resort in its own right, and is located close enough to Guardalavaca to be included in this section.

Expensive

Far and away the best place to stay in the Guardalavaca area is the superb **Meliá Río de Oro** ((024) 30090 FAX (024) 30095 at Playa Esmeralda. This all-inclusive, Spanish-run luxury hotel offers just about anything you could want in a Cuban beach resort including a fine white sand strand, excellent restau-

rants, nightly cabaret, shopping, tour desks, rental car and watersports as well as golf, tennis and horseback riding.

Across the lagoon are two older but only slightly less luxurious Meliá resorts. Serious divers will appreciate the well-equipped international scuba center at **Sol Club Río de Luna** ((024) 30030 to 30034 FAX (024) 30035, which offers PADI-licensed courses for beginners. This all-inclusive resort has a range of restaurants, bars and sports activities, plus two swimming pools, one for children. Many of its rooms face the beach and the suites have Jacuzzis. Bicycle, moped and car rental is available.

Slightly larger than its sister resorts, the all-inclusive **Sol Río de Mares** ((024) 30060 FAX (024) 30065 is pleasantly landscaped overlooking the bay, and also offers luxury suites with Jacuzzis, as well as two handicap-adapted suites, in addition to its standard rooms. It has an almost identical array of facilities and services — including golf, tennis, scuba and horseback riding — as the other Meliá resorts at Playa Esmeralda.

Only five *cabañas* — each with air conditioning, satellite television and a refrigerator — and one suite comprise the hideaway **Cayo Saetía Hacienda** ((024) 42350 or 52193, Cayo Saetía, Mayarí, situated on an idyllic bay and reachable only by boat or helicopter. Meals are served on your balcony or at the resort's small restaurant. Perfect for a peaceful retreat and exploring the island's wilderness by jeep or horse.

Moderate

With rooms overlooking the sea, the all-inclusive **Las Brisas Club Resort and Villas** ((024) 30218 FAX (024) 30418 offers a higher level of comfort, better buffet meals and better value for money than elsewhere along Playa Guardalavaca's main beach. It also has one of the nicer stretches of sand. Otherwise it has all the standard features that any veteran of these types of resorts will expect, including orchestrated entertainment programs, diving excursions, watersports, tennis court and volleyball games in the free-form swimming pools. They also have a massage center. Parents may appreciate the resort's children's activity programs, and there is a good variety of bars and restaurants. The hotel's travel desk can arrange excursions, bicycle and car rental.

The all-inclusive **Atlántico Hotel and Bungalows** ((024) 30180 or 30195 FAX (024) 30200, Playa Guardalavaca, is large and modern with comfortable facilities. This Cubanacán hotel's main advantage is its large swimming pool with a pool bar and restaurant which serves reasonable Italian dishes and seafood. Ask for a room with a sea-facing view. It is located quite close to the town's commercial complex and can arrange car, bicycle and moped rental. Activ-

WHERE TO EAT

El Ancla sits on an outcrop at the western end of the beach overlooking the sea and is undoubtedly the most pleasant of Guardalavaca's restaurants, especially as the sun sets. It has inexpensive prices, a varied seafood menu, including lobster dishes and is a good place to linger for cocktails. You can reach it by walking west along the beach from the Atlántico Hotel or driving down a dirt road that runs north off the Holguín

ities include horseback riding, water skiing, windsurfing, diving and fishing.

More than its neighbors, **Club Amigo Guardalavaca** ((024) 30121 FAX (024) 30221, Playa Guardalavaca, feels especially tailored for large groups, with its cafeteria-style dining hall rather unromantic, to say the least. The other major drawback is the fact that it's located somewhat back from the beach. However, the rooms are comfortable, with private bath and air conditioning, grouped in rows of bungalows around the swimming pool. And with a Kiddy Club and other pre-teen activities, the resort is especially aimed at families with children. Like other local abodes, the Guardalavaca is all-inclusive.

Highway about one kilometer (half a mile) west of town.

Overlooking the big roundabout in the middle of town is the inexpensive **Pizza Nova** ((024) 30137, with delicious pizza and pasta dishes, plus a fairly good wine selection. Sit outside on the breezy patio or in the air-conditioned gazebo with its odd blend of wood paneling and Chinese lamps.

Two other restaurants on the main beach, **El Patio** and **El Cayuelo**, are within easy strolling distance of all the Guardalavaca hotels, and offer simple, local cuisine.

Playa Esmeralda has several places where you can eat outside of the big all-inclusive

An example of a Spanish-Cuban joint-venture resort hotel at Playa Esmeralda.

resorts including the charming little **Conuco Mongo Viña**, which offers typical Creole dishes such as roast pig and fried chicken in a simple thatched-roof setting beside the bay for inexpensive prices.

NIGHTLIFE

Disco music is pumped out with strobes on the sands at the beach nightclub of **La Rocha**, which is a magnet for local Cubans. **La Piazza** is a more up-market, yet predictable nightspot, at Los Brisas Resort.

Playa Esmeralda is gradually evolving its own after-dark scene including **Bar Oasis** and the adjacent **Arco Iris Disco** in a grass shack off the main access road to the big hotels.

HOW TO GET THERE

The only way to get to Guardalavaca is by road, an excellent highway that stretches 70 km (43 miles) between Holguín and the beach resort. You can take your chances on the bus service from Holguín. In theory, this bus service connects with the arrival of the daily train from Havana, departing from the station. A taxi from Holguín will cost about US$40 each way.

EXCURSIONS FROM GUARDA-LAVACA

The following suggestions are daytrips. Aside from the visit to Cayo Saetía, which needs to be booked in advance, these excursions are within convenient driving distance.

CAYO SAETÍA

It is easy to arrange a boat or helicopter day trip from Guardalavaca to the "island" of Cayo Saetía, which has some of the most beautiful beaches in this region of Cuba. Until recently, this cay, which lies at the end of a narrow causeway off the eastern-most side of the entrance to the Bahía de Nipe, was off-limits to visitors because it was a favorite retreat for top officials, including Fidel.

Exotic animals such as zebras, antelope and ostriches were imported to breed and to become targets within this hunting preserve, which in Cuban doublespeak is also referred to within the same breathe as a "wildlife reserve."

You can visit for the day and explore by jeep safari or horseback, and swim from the cay's perfect white sand beaches.

Gaviota Tours ((024) 30903 or 30909 arranges daily excursions to the island including a buffet lunch on the beach.

BAHÍA DE NARANJO

This large, protected bay is one of Cuba's loveliest areas of coastline, with a magnificent landscape of sweeping coconut palms circling a pristine bay. It also lies within the Parque Natural Bahía de Naranjo, one of the island's important marine reserves, most notable for its main beach, Playa Esmeralda (also known as Playa Estero Ciego). Even if you are not staying here, it is worth visiting, and is just four kilometers (two and a half miles) away from Guardalavaca. Its soft, scrunchy white sand makes it one of the best swimming beaches in the area.

Right in the middle of the bay is a small mangrove-fringed island called Cayo Jutia, which plays host to the **Parque Recreativo Cayo Naranjo** ((024) 30132 or 30434. This Gaviota-run marine recreation complex which includes boat tours, a pretty good seafood restaurant and dolphin aquarium. The site of the aquarium is superb, reached by boat from a dock five kilometers (three miles) southwest of Guardalavaca. Dolphin shows with watery acrobatics are staged daily at noon. Admission to the park is US$12. Private swims with dolphins can also be arranged (US$40 per person).

MUSEO CHORRO DE MAITA

Two of the country's best archaeological museums are located close by. Just five kilometers (three miles) south of Guardalavaca, a turnoff on the road to Banes leads to one of Cuba's most important archaeological sites, the Museo Chorro de Maita, a Taíno Indian burial ground thought to have been used between 1490 and 1540. Some 108 skeletons have been discovered here, making this the largest aboriginal burial site in the Antilles. Part of the site has been turned into a museum, with more than 50 skeletons visible in the exact position they were found. Glass cases display offerings that were left alongside the dead, mostly shell and bone objects and ornaments. Anthropologists have speculated that one of the female skeletons, numbered "57," belonged to a young woman of high rank, since a rare gold idol and copper ornaments were found draped on her remains. Equally interesting is the presence of a Caucasian skeleton, presumed to be a Spaniard, who

ested in going to the small, unassuming town of Banes, once the site of a large Taíno Indian settlement and worth visiting for its compelling archeological museum.

Banes is also something of a quirk of history, for in more recent times, it was founded in 1887 by North American planters and became the headquarters for the United Fruit Company, a United States conglomerate, with its "Barrio Americano" (modeled on a North American town complete with golf course and country club) for its expatriate executives.

appears to have lived with the Taíno community. Most of the Taíno dead were buried in the fetal position, yet some were found arranged horizontally, with arms crossed over the chest in the Christian manner, suggesting further evidence of contact with Europeans. The site is open Tuesday to Saturday from 9 AM to 5 PM, Sunday from 9 AM to 1 PM and is closed on Monday. Across the road, a replica village has been built with displays on the lifestyles and times of the Taíno Indians. Admission US$3.

BANES

Continue along the same road for another 30 km (just over 18 miles) if you are inter-

Located off the main square of Plaza Martí, on Calle General Marrero, the **Museo Archaeology Indocubano** offers a fascinating collection of ceramics, utensils, jewelry and other objects unearthed in this region, some dating back more than 5,000 years. One of the prized exhibits is a distinctively Mesoamerican gold figurine of a woman with a feather headdress holding a bowl. It is easy to miss the innocuous-looking *espátulas vómicas*, which were used by the Taíno Indians to induce vomiting before taking hallucinogenic potions. The museum is open Tuesday to Saturday, 9 AM to 5 PM, and Sunday, 8 AM to noon. Admission is US$1.

Cold drinks for sale on the beach.

FROM GUARDALAVACA TO MAYARÍ

If you are planning to venture further into the countryside, perhaps stay overnight in the mountains, then do make time to visit the beautiful hill station of **Mayarí**, which is a two-hour drive east from Guardalavaca and a good base for walking excursions. From Mayarí, it's impossible to continue without a four-wheel drive vehicle with which to head up into the **Sierra del Cristal mountains** along bumpy, unpaved roads. The tranquil views, scents and wilderness of these mountains are worth the effort.

As you ascend these mountain roads, you'll notice the distinctive color of the soil, which changes from light brown to a soft red to a dark, densely iron-rich rust red — referred to by locals as *mocarrero*. Plantations of pine trees and coffee are grown up here — the coffee that grows in this rich soil is famous in Cuba for its taste. Famous also are the varieties of orchids that grow here along mossed slopes and out of rock clefts.

Visit the Scientific Station at regional national park, **Jardín de Pinare**. The park has set out trails, one of which leads you through 12 different ecosystems, from cacti shrubland to clearings amassed with flowers, coffee plantations and small waterfalls. Look out especially for the *cupey* plant, whose thick, waxy leaves were used by revolutionaries as paper to send messages during the War of Independence against the Spanish.

Set against a breathtaking landscape, the mountaintop **Villas Pinares de Mayarí** ((024) 53308, Mensura, Pinares de Mayarí, is built in the rustic style of traditional Cuban houses, with rough-cut timber and natural stone walls. There are 25 rooms and nine larger cabins. A restaurant, bar and a swimming pool are part of the complex.

GRANMA PROVINCE

Named for the famous leaky yacht that carried Fidel and his 81 fellow revolutionaries safely ashore in this region on December 2, 1956, Granma (literally, "Grandma") is in many ways the quintessential Eastern province. Drama permeates both its history and its landscape. Over the past two centuries some of the most decisive moments in Cuban history have been played out here, against the cinematic backdrop of giant camel-toned Sierra Maestra mountains hinged against an unruly, boulder-strewn coastline and a sparkling, marine-blue Caribbean sea. Its people seem carved from the same rough-hewn mold and they pride themselves on their tough self-reliance in this blisteringly difficult environment. Rain is a rarity in this southwestern region, which is the country's hottest and driest.

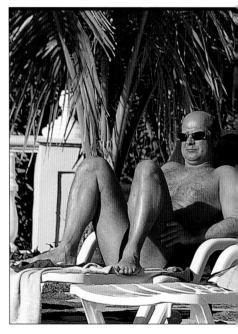

There's a reason many Cubans jokingly refer to this part of the country as the Wild West, for a discernable frontier spirit remains intact. If you make the effort to travel through this sparsely populated, poor and fiercely traditional region, you will see one of the few authentically unspoiled parts of the country.

To appreciate the best the province has to offer, you should spend a few hours in Bayamo, and then head along the southwest coast to stay at the beach resort of Marea del Portillo, perhaps making sorties to explore the magnificent Gran Parque Nacional Sierra Maestra, and enjoy the drive through sugarcane country and small coastal towns in this easy day's drive.

BAYAMO

Capital of Granma Province, Bayamo makes an interesting place to stop for an hour or two, before pressing on to explore the rest of the province. If you do want to stay overnight, it has reasonable facilities for visitors.

BACKGROUND

In 1513, San Salvador, as it was first named, was the second colonial township to be depot for French and Dutch contraband, with manufactured goods and fabrics from Europe being exchanged for meat, leather, sugar, coffee and indigo.

Although Bayamo is one of the earliest colonial towns, there is little evidence of that fact in the colonial architecture you will see here. During the first War of Independence in 1869, the townspeople of Bayamo deliberately started a fire to destroy their city, so that the Spanish troops who were massed to take it over would have nothing to seize except a smoldering ruin. In effect, Bayamo

founded by the expeditionary Diego de Velázquez on behalf of the Spanish crown. The original site beside the Yara River was moved inland soon afterwards to its present location, and was called San Salvador de Bayamo. As soon as the local church and the town council were installed, this was the town from which Velázquez set forth to capture and colonize the rest of Cuba.

Snuggled against broad flatlands on the banks of the Cauto River, the longest in Cuba, and protected from pirates due to its inland location, Bayamo was well placed to become a key trading center. It followed that when the Spanish Crown imposed heavy new restrictions on commercial traffic, Bayamo prospered as an active smuggling was the epicenter of the independence movement, and it was the provisional capital of the new republic before it was razed to the ground. One of the most famous figures in the town's history was Carlos de Manual Céspedes, so-called "Father of the Nation," whose call for independence and abolition of slavery from La Demajagua, his sugar mill near Manzanillo, set the revolt in motion.

GENERAL INFORMATION

Many of the facilities for visitors, such as the **Servi Cupet-Cimex** station, the **Hotel Sierra Maestra** and the **bus station**, are located on

Guardalavaca offers the complete Caribbean resort experience.

the Carretera Central, southeast of the town center. The **Banco de Crédito y Comercio** is at Calles Saco and General García.

WHAT TO SEE AND DO

One of the first things you will notice about Bayamo are all the horse-drawn carriages in use, many of them looking little changed since the nineteenth century. Bayamo is one of the Cuba's few cities, like Cárdenas and Remedios, which retain these carriages for everyday transportation, and you'll see everyone using them, from schoolchildren to police officers.

The place to begin your short walking tour is the **Parque Céspedes**, around which, as with all Cuban towns, life revolves. This square is a little different, however. Not only was it the first square in the country to be given this title, it commemorates the uprising against Spain that began in 1868 rather than Fidel's Revolution in 1959. At the square's center stand statues of Bayamo's two most famous figures: first, Carlos Manuel de Céspedes and, second, Perucho Figueredo, the author of Cuba's national anthem. It was on this square, in the former town hall, that Céspedes signed the decree abolishing slavery.

One of the few structures that survived the fire was **Casa Natal de Carlos Manuel Céspedes**, the hero's birthplace, also on the square. This two-storied mansion has been turned into a museum, and each of its 12 rooms contain displays of memorabilia relating to his life as well as the history of Bayamo and the struggle for independence. You can also see his printing press and copies of his *Cubano Libre* ("Free Cuban"), the first independent newspaper to circulate in Cuba after the capture of Bayamo. It is open Tuesday to Saturday from noon to 7 PM, Sunday from 9 AM to 1 PM, and closed on Monday. Admission is free.

After you emerge from Céspedes's house, to your right is the **Museo Provincial de Granma**, which has all sorts of relics and displays relating to the history, geography and natural sciences of the province. There are mangled remains from the fire of 1869 and the original copy of the national anthem. The simple colonial building in which it is housed was the home of Manual Muñoz, who composed the tune for the national anthem as well as Bayamo's much-loved song, *La Bayamesa*. In late 2001, the museum was temporarily closed and undergoing massive renovation.

If you continue along the same street, you come to the **Iglesia de San Salvador**, Bayamo's main church. Although it was first built in 1613, virtually nothing remains of the original except the baroque Dolores chapel, which dates from 1740 and survived the 1869 fire. Adjacent to the church is **Plaza del Himno** (Anthem Square). This is apparently where Perucho Figueredo was inspired to write the lyrics for the national anthem as he watched a triumphant Céspedes ride into Bayamo on October 20, 1868, having just claimed the city for the independence fighters. Tradition has it that the author was so overcome by the moment that he jotted the words down on the nearest thing that came to hand — on the back of his saddle. On one corner of the square, at no. 36, is the **Casa de la Nacionalidad**, a colonial building which houses a historical research center.

As you leave Bayamo's old quarter, try to at least drive by **Plaza de Patria**, the city's huge gathering place for political rallies and meetings, where a large sculpture honors the nation's revolutionary heroes.

WHERE TO STAY AND EAT

The recently refurbished **Hotel Royalton** ((023) 422290 or 422224, in a whitewashed colonial building on Parque Céspedes, is the best place to stay in the city center. The inexpensive rooms are rather simple, but nonetheless clean and comfy, and some offer sweeping plaza views.

On the outskirts of town is the pleasant **Bayamo Village** ((023) 423102 or 423124, Carretera via Manzanillo and Mabay road, is in the same price category. Although located at a distance from the city, this small spread-out complex is a more comfortable place to stay overnight than the Hotel Sierra Maestra. With a restaurant (specializing in roast pork and chicken), bar area and a swimming pool, this is not too bad.

Despite a recent coat of pink and yellow paint, the budget **Hotel Sierra Maestra**

((023) 427970, Carretera Central, is still a dismal hulk of a hotel that may have seen better days. It does have a restaurant, bar, swimming pool, shop, tourist office and nightclub, although none are very inspiring. If you find yourself stuck here, ask for a *"habitación especial"* — a larger room with balcony and garden view.

Although the menu is similar to a hundred other Cuban eateries, the **Restaurante Plaza** ((023) 422290, on the ground floor of the Hotel Royalton, is one of Bayamo's more enjoyable places to dine. Prices are inexpensive. Around the corner on Calle Palma is a modest café called **El Mayin**, which is open for both lunch and dinner. On the sidewalk outside is an all-day fruit juice and snack stand. **Bar El Pedrito**, at the northeast corner of Parque Céspedes, also serves light meals.

NIGHTLIFE

Head for the Parque Céspedes, where you can see what is playing at the **Casa de la Cultura**. If you're in the mood for nothing more than a drink both the **Bar El Pedrito** and the little tavern on the ground floor of the **Hotel Royalton** stock plenty of Cuban rum and cold beer.

HOW TO GET THERE

By air, Bayamo is linked by Cubana de Aviación with Havana three times weekly. Bayamo's **Carlos Manuel de Céspedes Airport** ((023) 43916 is located four kilometers (two and a half miles) north of town on the road to Holguín.

By rail, there are daily train services to Bayamo from Havana, Camagüey and Santiago de Cuba. The **Estación de Ferrocarriles** is at Calles Saco and Línea, one kilometer (slightly over half a mile) east of town.

FROM BAYAMO TO MAREA DEL PORTILLO

Two roads lead to Marea del Portillo, both of which branch from Yara. The recommended main route road passes through sugarcane plantations, historic small towns and beautiful coastal scenery, with some worthwhile stops and sights along the way. From Bayamo,

the first main town you'll encounter is **Yara**, 33 km (slightly over 20 miles) away. This was where Velázquez originally founded San Salvador. Yara is also famous in Cuban history books as the place where the Indian chief Hatuey began his uprising against the Spanish in 1512, and where, legend has it, he was burned at the stake rather than convert.

GRAN PARQUE NACIONAL SIERRA MAESTRA

Unless you have Indiana Jones-style nerves and a four-wheel drive jeep, it's not a good idea to take the more direct route which cuts across the Sierra Maestra mountains, despite the fact that it is marked on the map as a main sealed road. However, if you have come prepared, this is the route to take to explore the Gran Parque Nacional Sierra Maestra, the largest protected reserve in Cuba.

In 1956, returning from a one-year exile in Mexico, Fidel Castro, his brother Raúl, and the young asthmatic Argentinean doctor Che Guevara, along with 79 other men, were shipwrecked along the coast of this province, and battled their way up into these seemingly impenetrable peaks. Only about 15 men, (including Fidel, Raúl and Che) survived the journey. Traditionally one of the country's most isolated regions, the Sierra Maestra became a battlefield between 1956 to 1959, during which Castro's guerilla campaign gained control of the ever-expanding area they called "Free Territory." The park is scattered with rebel bases, including Castro's own headquarters, which has been preserved and can be visited.

From Yara, a steep road runs south to the park's entrance 32 km (about 20 miles) away. Your first stop should be at **Santo Domingo** (reached via Bartolomé Masó), which was a key rebel camp during Castro's guerilla campaign in the late 1950s. Located in the heart of the park, it is now a tourist complex, with cabins for an overnight stay. From here, you can contemplate the site's history, swim in a nearby river, or take walking or horseback trails through the mountains.

Or you can hike up **Pico Turquino**, which at 1,973 m (6,470 ft) is Cuba's highest peak. Located in the Parque Nacional Turquino, this trail is a full day's hike, and it can be very steep in parts. While you are still climbing the mountain's lower, shrub-covered pastures, you are likely to pass herds of goats, bells tinkling, and even see wild horses grazing at a distance. As you climb higher up the mountain flanks, the forest paths lead through ever-denser enclosures of mahogany and cedar trees, and if you are lucky, you may see a wide variety of butterflies, insects, birds and some wildlife. When you reach the summit, the rewards are tremendous views in all directions, across the surrounding mountains and over the Caribbean.

Where to Stay and Eat
Balcón de la Sierra Villas ((023) 595180, Bartolomé Masó, Santo Domingo, offers inexpensive accommodation and meals in a rustic mountain setting. This is the base camp for hiking to the Pico Turquino summit and La Plata command post. There are 20 cabins with bath and air conditioning. There is a simple restaurant and bar.

MANZANILLO

The port city of Manzanillo, 56 km (nearly 35 miles) from Bayamo, is the second-largest city in the province, but despite the certain dilapidated elegance of some its colonial buildings, it has little to delay the stranger. Its people, however, make this a very friendly and charming place. The city is also credited with being the birthplace of son, Cuba's famous traditional musical style, and the city's orchestra, La Orquesta Original de Manzanillo, is known throughout Cuba as one of son's best exponents.

Of places to visit, see the Moorish-influenced gazebo, known locally as **La Glorieta**, in Parque Céspedes, the main square. **Parque Masó**, with its promenade along the sea, is best place to see the sunset across the Gulf of Guacanayabo.

Do try to see the **Monumento a Celia Sánchez**, located seven blocks southwest of Parque Céspedes. Born in nearby Media Luna, this intriguing, courageous woman was one of the legendary figures of the Revolution. She was Fidel Castro's assistant in the Sierra Maestra and later in Havana, and was the closest companion *El Jefe* ever had until her death from cancer in 1980. Although her grave is in Havana's Colón cemetery, this memorial, whimsically shaped like a staircase and decorated with sculptured sunflowers and doves, touchingly shows how much she was loved in this province.

The inexpensive **Hotel Guacanayabo** ((023) 54012 or 53590, Avenida Camilo Cienfuegos, is located right on the seafront. This is the best place to stay in Manzanillo, and its rooms have a view of the bay. It has a selection of restaurants and cafeterias and a swimming pool.

SOUTH FROM MANZANILLO

About 10 km (just over six miles) from Manzanillo, on the road to Marea del Portillo, is the turnoff to **Parque Nacional de Demajagua**, where Cuba's first War of Independence was launched. It can be difficult to find: turn south along the road to Niquero after the Servi Cupet-Cimex station and after driving for about 15 minutes, you should see the park's entrance.

La Demajagua was the name of the hacienda and sugar mill owned by wealthy landowner Carlos Manuel de Céspedes. It was here, on October 10, 1868, that Céspedes first urged his fellow Cubans to fight for independence and the abolition of slavery. The ruins of La Demajagua form an open-air museum, which displays such objects as the bell with which Céspedes gathered his slaves to set them free and to launch his rebellion.

Back on the main road onwards from Manzanillo, the road hugs the coast until you reach the village of **Media Luna**, with its painted wooden houses and small museum devoted to Celia Sánchez. From here, if you are really interested, you can make a 20-km (12-mile) detour through Niquero to **Playa de los Coloradas**, the narrow, mangrove-covered beach famous as place where the *Granma* landed on December 2, 1956.

As Che Guevara recounted, "It wasn't a disembarkation, it was a shipwreck." Off-course, behind schedule and seasick, Castro and his band had to abandon the leaking six-berth cabin cruiser and wade for two hours through mosquito-infested mangrove swamps before they reached dry land. A monument marks the actual landing place of the famous yacht, and a long wooden pathway across mangrove swamps to a jetty apparently follows the route taken by the rebels as they waded ashore. Three days later, the men had their first encounter with Batista's troops at Alegría de Pío, south of Niquero.

After visiting Playa de los Coloradas, you will probably want to retrace your way back to the main coastal road. Otherwise, you could continue down to **Cabo Cruz**, where a 1877 lighthouse marks the very tip of the western peninsula of Granma Province. Dramatic, layered marine terraces are a feature

MAREA DEL PORTILLO

Continuing along the main coastal road from Media Luna, it's a 40-km (25-mile) drive across the hills of the Sierra Maestra to Marea del Portillo. The road leaves behind the wide expanses of sugarcane plantations which are lined with tired workers waiting at train crossroads. The landscape becomes more arid, with tussocky bleached grass, horse farms and small hamlets. Rain is rare in this region, which is one of driest and hottest

of this coastline, some rising from sea level to more than 200 m (650 ft) high. The surrounding densely forested region, which extends as far as the eye can see, is the **Parque Nacional Desembarco del Granma**, also known as El Guafe.

Before the arrival of the Spanish, this was a Siboney Indian settlement, and an intricate network of cave dwellings, burial grounds and archeological remains have been all uncovered here — most notably a cave containing an idol carved from a stalagmite. Signposted walkways are being gradually established with the aim of creating an ecological reserve here, but at present you need a guide to explore, otherwise it is very easy to get lost.

parts of the country. Along the route, you'll see giant billboards with illustrations and slogans which elaborately recounts the progress of the rebels as they made their way up into the mountains.

At first glance, this small, black-sand crescent of a beach, tucked alongside mangrove swamps and flatlands dotted with coastal palm trees, looks like an unpromising location for a resort. However, the particular charm of this place takes a little time — at least a few hours — to percolate. There is something special about Marea del Portillo, and it is easy to see why many of the foreign tourists — mostly Canadians — who come

Freshly harvested coffee beans: the *cafecito* is an important Cuban institution.

here return again and again. Unlike so many destinations in tourist-apartheid Cuba, this resort manages to be genuinely relaxing, and a palpable sense of goodwill, as well as many friendships, have been built up between the local community and the tourists.

It makes the perfect place to stop for a few days of relaxation if you are driving around this part of Cuba by rental car.

WHAT TO SEE AND DO

The black-sand beach is pleasant enough to look at from your balcony, and at sunset, the view across the bay is ravishing, burnishing the sea red. But it's not recommended as a place to swim. Indeed, this coast is known for its sharks. Instead, at set intervals during the day, a minibus and ferry connection takes guests to nearby **Cayo Blanco**, which the three hotels in the area use as their main beach. This perfect little island has soft white sand, natural sun umbrellas formed by sea-grape trees and is lapped by clear, blue sea with good visibility for snorkeling. A delicious barbecue lunch is served on the island each day, and you can choose to be as sociable or private as you like.

Ask the hotels about their guided, all-day excursions by jeep or horseback into the lush foothills of the nearby Sierra Maestra mountains, along tracks exploring small villages, low-lying forest and waterfall havens where you can picnic and swim. Many routes that used to be taken for horseback rides in this area are currently off-limits for military reasons.

There are plenty of rewarding opportunities for scuba diving in and around the offshore keys in the area, with some 25 established diving spots. These include visits to dramatic calcified limestone sea terraces, the wreckage of a Spanish galleon and to a site off Cabo Cruz where you are almost guaranteed to see manatees, grouped in small herds of six or seven.

The mangrove swamps that surround the main beach at Marea del Portillo support a thriving number of oyster beds, which are farmed by local, state-controlled cooperatives. You can watch fishermen working from their catamarans (noiseless, so as not to annoy the oysters) and take a catamaran ride yourself through the mangroves to visit an oyster bar,

open seasonally, where freshly shucked oysters are served with beer or wine.

WHERE TO STAY AND EAT

A recently-formed joint-venture between the Canadian company Journey's End and Cubanacán means that all three hotels in Marea del Portillo have been renovated and improved. Although they vary in price, all operate as all-inclusive resorts.

Moderate
Farallón del Caribe ((023) 597081 or 597032, Carretera Granma, Pilón, is attractively landscaped on a hill facing the bay on one side and the Sierra Maestra mountains on the other. This modern hotel is the most luxurious of the three recommended and has become a favorite with Canadian visitors for its relaxing atmosphere and excellent value. All of the pleasantly furnished rooms have sea views, balconies and satellite television. Facilities include a restaurant, bar, shop, swimming pool and games rooms.

    Punta Piedra Village ((023) 597009, Carretera de Pilón, located close to Cayo Blanco, set on the hillside overlooking the bay, is made up of 12 private cottages, including four suites, all with television. It is private, has a nice restaurant and is very pleasant if you prefer to be away from the crowds and don't mind not having all the facilities.

Inexpensive
Located on the beachfront, the recently renovated **Marea del Portillo Hotel** ((023) 597081, Carretera Granma km12.5, Pilón, has comfortable rooms with balconies from which you can step directly onto the sands. There is a restaurant, cafeteria, shop and palm-thatched outdoor bar around the swimming pool. The resort has a large pet iguana called Guana which is tame and eats mosquitoes. Admiring visitors often tempt it from its hiding places to eat pancakes.

HOW TO GET THERE

Most visitors reach Marea del Portillo by hotel bus, having arrived at Manzanillo's **Sierra Maestra Airport** ((023) 526800, 110 km (68 miles) away, on a charter flight from Canada. Cubana de Aviación flies to Manzanillo twice weekly from Havana.

DRIVING TO SANTIAGO DE CUBA

The 196-km (122-mile) drive from Marea del Portillo to Santiago de Cuba is one of the most spectacular in Cuba, and being less-traveled than other stretches in the country, has a certain maverick quality to it. It is made for those who enjoy solitary adventures: you will often find yourself completely alone on these roads, rarely seeing another car. A new tar-sealed road has recently been completed, and apparently the Castro government is planning to open this remote area up for tourism development. At present, facilities are few and the local inhabitants are often very shy, but always friendly. If you stop to talk with those you see on their long mountain treks by the roadside, always offer food and water as a friendly gesture, which will be greatly appreciated. Allow about four hours for the drive.

The road winds around the coast and is full of starkly beautiful vistas: sparkling sea views and black-shingle sand on one side, with increasingly vertiginous arid tussock-grass mountains and sporadic impoverished-looking hamlets on the other. Herds of goats and grazing horses are a common sight, and villagers sometimes emerge by the roadside seemingly in the middle of nowhere. Further on, the mountain sides become huge calcified limestone cliffs, with big boulders lapped by the sea.

Don't be unduly alarmed if you are stopped at an impromptu checkpoint made with a string and rags: locals with rifles slung over their chests are apt to check passing vehicles to make sure that farmers from the region are not heading to town with pigs that might spread an African pig disease that has been rife in this area. Although the men look like vigilantes they make these checks with the blessing of Cuban armed forces, and if they see tourists, will wave them on.

En route, you will pass through the town of **Uvero**, where Fidel Castro's revolutionary guerillas won a decisive battle on May 28, 1957. Further on is **Chivirico**, a tidy little town on the water's edge, its tree-lined streets usually busy with perky horse-drawn *calesas*.

Chivirico has two popular beach resorts, one of which has an international diving center.

Two of the nicest swimming beaches in the area are **Playa Sevilla** and **Playa Blanca**. Further on, the road will lead you to Santiago de Cuba.

WHERE TO STAY

Distances are given from Santiago de Cuba, from which these hotels are within an hour or so's easy driving distance.

Crawling up a mountainside of lush tropical forest, the all-inclusive **Super Club Sierra Mar** ((0226) 26319, Carretera Chivirico km60, is one of the best places to stay on Cuba's south coast. Managed with panache by the Jamaica-based Super Clubs chain, it flaunts a gorgeous beach and is unquestionably luxurious by Cuban standards, virtually a fully self-contained village in its own right, with elevators down to the beach and a walkway out to a thatched stilt-bar. Rooms and suites are very comfortable and soothingly pastel; rates are expensive. The higher up the mountain, the more dramatic the view from your balcony. Aside from the excellent international diving center here, facilities include a Nautilus equipment-stocked gym, a watersports center (with catamarans, windsurfing, diving and snorkeling equipment), day and nighttime tennis, a medical center, shops, car and bicycle rental. There is a large free-form swimming pool with a water-slide and swim-up bar. This is probably the best beach resort catering to young families: even children as young as two can be looked after at the Kids Kamp, which has a playground, Nintendo, a swimming program, nightly movie and cartoon program, watersports and other activities for older children.

Right up the coast is a sister property, also in the expensive category, called **Super Club Los Galeones** ((022) 26160, Poblado de Chivirico km72, near Guamá town. This quiet 34-room, all-inclusive resort perches on a hilltop near the ocean with wonderful views over the Caribbean Sea and the Sierra Maestra mountains. It is much more intimate than the Sierra Mar, and better for couples or serious divers. It has a small private beach and unlimited access to all facilities at Sierra Mar.

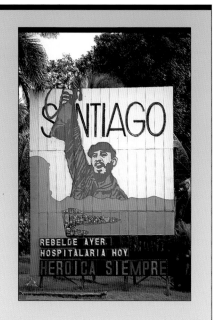

Santiago de Cuba and the Far East

SANTIAGO DE CUBA

It's easy to understand why Santiago is called the "most Caribbean" of Cuba's cities. Not only is it more tropical in temperature, but due to its geographical location, it has always had close links to neighboring islands (like Jamaica and Haiti). More predominantly *mulatto* than Havana, this influence also goes some way to explain the extraordinary tradition of musical innovation for which the city is celebrated. It has also helped make the city's legendary carnival (Fiesta del Caribe), which draws performers from all over the Caribbean, the most exuberant in Cuba.

BACKGROUND

At first glance, as you drive in from the airport, Santiago has the feel of a lush, heat-opiated backwater. In fact, it is Cuba's second largest city, with more than 400,000 inhabitants, and it was the island's original capital. With its rolling hills ranged around a wide, easily navigable harbor, Santiago was an obvious location for a strategic port within Spain's empire, despite proving somewhat earthquake-prone.

It was founded in 1515 by the island's first governor, the conquistador Diego de Velázquez. Another famous conquistador, Hernándo Córtez, used the settlement as his base for expansionist forays into Mexico and Central America. At that time, Santiago's fortunes had closer ties to what was then Hispaniola (now Haiti and the Dominican Republic), the North Caribbean and parts of South America than to the rest of Cuba, as inland communication and transportation were hampered by a natural barrier of formidable mountains. Santiago remained the capital until 1607, when that status was transferred to Havana.

Santiagüeros are also proud of their city's historical and cultural importance — "Hero City" and "Cradle of the Revolution" are the post-Revolution titles given to Santiago, and you'll see them proclaimed by ubiquitous roadside slogans. Support among the population was crucial during the nineteenth-century War of Independence, and it was also here that Fidel Castro and his rebels staged

a daring attack on Moncada Barracks, thus setting in train the sequence of events that were to make him *El Jefe*.

Santiago's colonial core is an intriguing mélange of early Spanish colonial administrative buildings and dandified mansions constructed by French plantation owners who settled here after fleeing the slave revolt in Haiti during the 1790s. Although Santiago cannot compete with Havana's architectural splendors and the cosmopolitan outlook — and is clearly suffering considerably from shortages and power cuts during the

Special Period — the city's intimate scale, not to mention the gutsy brinkmanship of its people and their passionate relationship with all aspects of music, make this one of Cuba's most special places.

GENERAL INFORMATION

Apart from the tourism desks in most of the hotels, you can consult **Asistur (** (0226) 686128, on the lower ground floor of the Hotel Casa Granda. Crowded into the same

PREVIOUS PAGES — LEFT: View from the road in Baracoa, Guantánamo Province. RIGHT: Billboard announces the entrance to Santiago de Cuba. OPPOSITE: Children tempted by roadside sweets. ABOVE: A young woman celebrates her coming of age on her fifteenth birthday.

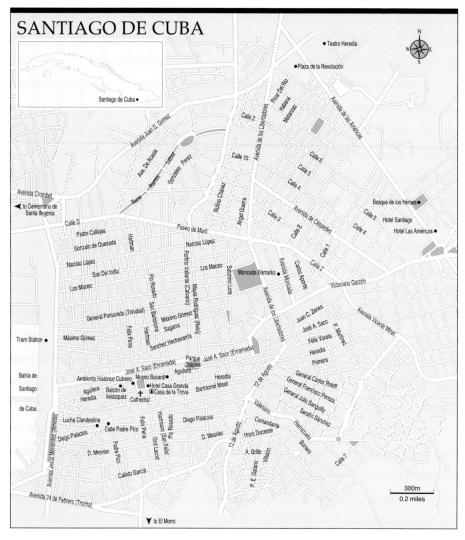

SANTIAGO DE CUBA

small space are a moped rental agency and a helpful **Havanatur** desk.

The **Dirección Provincial de Cultura** ((0226) 654571, Calle San Pedro 604, publishes a weekly newspaper on the Santiago arts scene called *Cartelera Cultural* that lists upcoming music, dance and cinema events. Pick one up at the front desk of the Hotel Casa Granda.

Another cultural institution, the **Casa del Caribe** ((0226) 42285 FAX (0226) 42387, which is at Calle 13 no. 154 at the corner of Calle 8, Vista Alegre, is a good place to ask about *casas particulars* or private home-stays.

Rumbos Travel and Tours ((0266) 22222 can be found opposite the Casa Granda Hotel

on Calle Heredia. This office can help with most queries and can arrange tours, both in and around the city, as well as to Parque Baconao and Guantánamo Province.

The central branch of the **Banco de Crédito y Comercio** is located at the corner of Calles Aguilera and Lacret, on Parque Céspedes. Otherwise, exchange facilities are available at all the main hotels, but hotels in Santiago tend to charge exorbitant commission to cash traveler's checks.

Should you need any medical attention, if it is not too serious, try the doctor's office at the Hotel Santiago de Cuba. Otherwise, go to the **Clínica Internacional** ((0226) 42589, Avenida Raúl Pujol in Vista Alegre, which has been set up specifically to cater to foreigners. It offers a 24-hour service and in addition to doctors, a dentist is also available.

Despite the city's enormous size, about the only place that a visitor can log onto the Internet at the present time is the ground-floor business center at the **Hotel Meliá Santiago** ((0226) 687070, Calle M and Avenida de las Américas. Service is available daily from 8 AM to 8 PM, at a rate of US$5 per hour. With only two PCs in service, there is usually a wait.

GETTING AROUND

Car rental is available through the **Cubanacán** desk at the Hotel Meliá Santiago ((0226) 54518; **Havanautos** at the Hotel Las Américas ((0226) 41388; and **Transautos** at The Villa San Juan.

The main tourist taxi stand is in front of the Meliá Santiago; there is another line outside the Hotel Casa Granda in Parque Céspedes. You will also notice *taxis particulares* or private taxis available for short rides around the city, and in some cases, you can negotiate a daily rate with the driver. They tend to congregate around the Plaza de Martí.

WHAT TO SEE AND DO

A Walking Tour

The obvious place to begin is **Parque Céspedes**, a tree-dotted square from which you can easily explore much of central Santiago by foot. You could begin with a *cafecito* on the expansive balcony of the colonial-era **Hotel Casa Granda** at the corner of the square in the shadow of the cathedral. From here, feeling bathed in the flowering scented space and chatter floating up from the park, you will surely see almost all of the city's personalities parade by eventually: wizened men gather to exchange gossip over their walking sticks; a double-bass soloist gives an impossibly brilliant, impromptu performance; shoals of children pass by in either mustard or red uniforms; flirtatious hustlers of both sexes wave and beckon with outrageous directness.

The Casa Granda itself is a city landmark. For decades leading up to the Revolution, it was a playing ground for the Cuban elite, a magnet for intrigue, assignations and international spies. Now, gleaming restoration by a major hotel group has almost expunged the louche atmosphere described by Graham Greene in 1957. Greene, who arrived in Santiago hoping to interview Castro in his Sierra Maestra hiding place, sprinkled his book *Our Man in Havana* with recollections of his Santiago stay, sending his character Wormold on an espionage mission disguised as business trip here.

On the balcony, unsteady *turistas* clad in "I love Cuba" T-shirts may be on their first

mojito of the day, recovering perhaps from a night at the Santiago Tropicana, while a deaf mute magician and his Lycra leopard skin-clad assistant move from table to table. The top floor offers yet another excuse for a *cuba libre* (in keeping with Santiago's fabled revolutionary zeal) and mesmerizing views across the red-tiled roofs out to the harbor. Next to the Casa Granda is the **Casa de la Cultura**, currently undergoing massive renovation. This is a good place to see local artists exhibit their work, and sometimes, to meet them. Look out for the work of Luis Rosaenz, a talented artist whose paintings fuse primitive colors and a distinct, Santería-

A Santiago de Cuba street scene.

influenced naive style. Upstairs, the **Casa de Matrimonio** is where civil marriages are officiated, some no-nonsense affairs, others with as much wedding pomp as can be managed.

Within the center of the square is a monument to Carlos Manuel Céspedes, the former Cuban plantation owner who, by freeing his slaves and fighting for independence against the Spanish, was dubbed "Father of the Nation." Around it are some of Santiago's most historic and interesting buildings. Imposingly large, the yellow and cream **Catedral** is dominated by a statue of the Angel of Annunciation, blowing her horn, apparently on the verge of flying away in a burst of Márquezian magic realism. The original church built on this site — the Santa Iglesia Basílica Metropolitana — dates back to 1523, yet many successive versions have since been built, it having been destroyed by earthquake and pillaged, with sections re-built as recently as 1810 and 1922. It is said that Diego de Velázquez was buried in the original cathedral, but his remains have never been found. Inside, an ecclesiastical museum documents the history of Catholicism in Cuba. The sacred and profane mingle at street level, where the cathedral encompasses various dollar-shops.

As you walk clockwise around the square, on Calle Félix Peña, you come to the **Museo de Ambiente Histórico Cubano** (Museum of Cuban History), also known as the Casa de Velázquez. This is Cuba's oldest residence, built between 1516 and 1530 as the home of Diego de Velázquez. It retains many original details and some furniture from that period — the entrance pavestones and heavy doors, the ornately decorated cedar ceiling (reminiscent in scent and design of a Kashmiri houseboat) and fresco designs that adorn the upper floors, Velázquez's living quarters. Moorish-style fretted wooden balconies add a distinctly Oriental effect. The ground floor was a frenzy of activity, functioning as the island's Office of Commerce, as well as a foundry where gold ingots were smelted and then shipped off to Spain.

Velázquez's quarters now house a collection of furniture and objects from the sixteenth through to the eighteenth centuries, including original wall hanging bearing his personal coat of arms, Spanish ceramics and paintings, and eighteenth-century silver and gold ornaments from Germany, Mexico and Cuba. The Spanish-style kitchen still contains some of the original utensils and ceramics. During the nineteenth century, the residence was used as a hotel, with a new wing added, along with the playful crescent-shaped stained-glass windows and fresco decorations popular with the French *haute bourgeoisie* who settled in Santiago de Cuba after fleeing Haiti. These rooms give a good impression of a wealthy planter's home of that period, with Bohemian chandeliers, Murano glassware, Napoleonic and Franco-Cuban *palisandro* furniture, and rattan rocking chairs — then a recent invention deemed perfect for the tropics. The museum owes its existence to one man: Dr. Francisco Prat, a Professor of Cuban Art at the Universidad de Oriente (University of the East). When, in 1965, the building had fallen into such disrepair that the city ordered its demolition, Dr. Prat fought for its restoration, and it is his donated personal collection that makes up most of the museum's exhibits. The staff who conduct guided tours are very friendly and informative; they also speak English. It is open Monday to Saturday from 8 AM to noon and from 2 PM to 6 PM, and Sunday from 9 AM to 1 PM; admission US$2.

Further up Calle Félix Peña, you'll see the local office of the **Partido Comunista de Cuba**, the **Casa de Galicia** cultural association and the **Academia Municipal de Ajedrez** where chess players gather throughout the day and into the evenings to play beneath the whirring fans, rum on hand. Nearby is the Cine Rialto movie-house and an open-air nightclub popular with *santiagüeros*, where avid flirtation and frenetic dancing occur most nights.

On the northern side of Parque Céspedes is the **Ayuntamiento**, or Town Hall, a large, white colonial building with blue wooden balconies. The original structure on this site was built by Hernán Cortés, however there have been several reconstructions. Used as the headquarters of the Spanish crown and later the American military government, it now houses the city government offices. It was from this central balcony that Fidel Castro made his first victorious speech as the nation's leader on January 1, 1959, to a crowd of cheering thousands.

From here, a web of cobblestone alleys and avenues branch out, any one of which will plunge you into Santiago's heady street life. Life spills out from the open doors and fretted balconies of wooden houses: a band rehearses from the recesses of a dusty schoolroom and with them, a clear alto voice soars with frisson-inducing melancholy; Lycra-wearing women with their hair in curlers shoot quizzical glances; a crowd jostles to fill bottles with rations of *aguardiente* (sugarcane brandy); unseen, a pig's squealing is suddenly silenced and

cians, actors and dancers to entertain, a spectacle not to be missed.

Further down Calle Heredia at no.208, near the intersection with San Félix, is Cuba's best loved **Casa de la Trova** ((0226) 623943 or 651708, an inevitable destination. Whether you are an aficionado of popular Cuban music or not (yet), spending a few hours listening to Santiago's famed veteran troubadours perform here is one of the most memorable experiences to be had to in Cuba, the tropical afternoons and evenings alive with almost continuous, intoxicating sound.

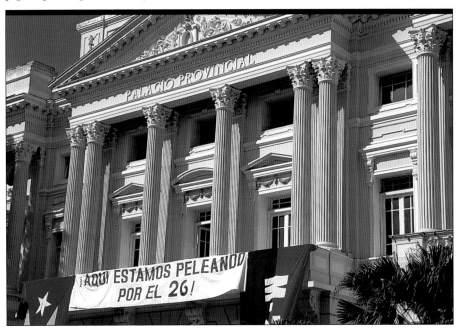

red frothy blood trickles into the gutter; the smell of cigar smoke mixes with the scent of the sea. In the still of a hot afternoon, a siesta-shuttered inertia takes hold.

One of the oldest streets is **San Basilico**, a cobblestone row still illuminated by antique gas lamps (used on occasion to hang suspected revolutionaries by Batista's hit men), while one of the prettiest is **Padre Pico**, with its historic steps. However, start with the liveliest street, **Calle Heredia**, east of the square, just off the Hotel Casa Granda, which is lined with colonial mansions, many with traditional ironwork balconies, some of which have been turned into art galleries, shops and offices. On weekends, this street is closed to traffic to allow musicians, magi-

The traditional ballad form (*trova*), a blend of African percussion and Spanish guitar rhythms with passionate lyrics, originated in Santiago.

An eclectic and unpredictable range of performers take the stage here, ranging from talented amateur musicians to established professionals. The "stage" is a simple raised platform, with rows of fold-up chairs in the front, surrounded by walls covered with paintings of famous performers of time gone by, including the Trio Matamoros. Sometimes, it has a party atmosphere, with the audience breaking into an impromptu cha-cha-cha. Weekends are the best time to come, but music

Santiago de Cuba's neoclassical Palacio Provincial.

plays throughout the week. Within the complex, a shop sells compact discs and cassettes of groups that have performed here, as well as musical instruments and souvenirs.

Further along, **Casa Heredia** is the museum-birthplace of the Santiago's most famous poet, José María Heredia (1803–39), after whom the street is named. Heredia was one of the first Cubans to speak out against the Spanish in favor of independence. Here you can find a small library of the poet's works as well as other Santiago writers. One of the more interesting shops along Calle Heredia is the **BFC Liberia**, a small shop, run by the affable Eddy Tamayo, selling second-hand books, songs by Pablo Milanes, atlases of Cuba, histories of the Revolution and selections of compact discs. You might also want to pop into the **Galería de Arte UNEAC** (Union of the Writers and Artists) down the block, where art shows, literary discussions and lectures take place.

Across the Calle Pío Rosado, on the next block, at Heredia 303, is the **Museo del Carnaval**, housed in a former prison. The phenomenon of Carnival in Cuba began at the end of the seventeenth century during the Spanish colonial period, and has undergone many mutations of form and content since. Nowhere else in Cuba has it been celebrated with as much gusto as in Santiago, where it officially began. Originally called Fiesta de las Mamarrachos (roughly translates as a "festival of the masked grotesques"), it took place on the feast days of Epiphany and Corpus Christi before it came to be held in July. The museum houses a diverting display of masquerader costumes (ranging from glittery bikinis for *mulatta* beauties to androgynous Pierrot attire), ornamental capes, giant papier-mâché heads, musical instruments, banners and drums used by competing bands over the past century. It is open Tuesday to Sunday, 9 AM to 6 PM, and closed on Monday.

Next door, lawyers may be intrigued to peer in at the **Casa del Jurista** which functions rather like a bar association. Here, lectures and meetings are held, and the legal community meet to gossip over subsidized rum.

From here, retrace your footsteps to the Calle Pío Rosado. At the intersection with Calle Aguilera is the **Museo Bacardí**. This unmistakably imposing structure is the oldest museum in the country, built for the purpose in 1899 by the rum clan's patriarch, Emilio Bacardí Moreau (1844–1922). When not presiding over the family fortune (or wearing his other hat as Santiago's mayor), Bacardí was a tireless collector and made the creation of this museum one of his passions. At entrance level, a section documents Cuba's early colonial history, with much memorabilia — some of it fascinatingly personal — belonging to a phalanx of leaders in Cuba's War of Independence against the

Upstairs, one of Cuba's most important collections of European and Cuban colonial paintings from the sixteenth to the nineteenth centuries is displayed (many of which have aroused much interest and been authenticated by the Prado Museum), including distinctive works by the well-known portrait artist of the Cuban colonial period, Federico Martinez Matos. A small wing displays contemporary Cuban art and sculpture, notably by Lucia Victoria Bacardí and Alberto Lesay, whose striking sculpture of Che Guevara dominates the

Spanish. Here, for example, is José Martí's tuxedo, and the bloodstained campaign hammock and scarf in which Antonio Maceo, one of Cuba's most feted national heroes, was fatally shot.

Elsewhere, even prosaic displays of nineteenth-century doctor's kits (complete with alarmingly large syringes) and clothes and shoes made from plant fiber are interesting. Tinseled crowns date from one of the few celebrations allowed to African slaves by their plantation owners — the annual "Day of Three Kings" — during which a slave king was crowned for the night. Look out for the handmade torpedo crafted in 1895 by Cuban rebels intent on blowing up Spanish ships moored in Santiago Bay.

room. From the adjourning courtyard runs **Callejón Bofill**, a cobblestone row of preserved colonial houses typical of the Santiago's colonial era, with authentic colors, intricate ironwork, wooden doors, stained-glass windows and street lamps.

A separate entrance in the building leads to the archaeological hall, which includes a collection of mummies from Egypt and South America. Bacardí (who seemed to have a taste for the macabre) is said to have personally removed the elaborate headdress of the Egyptian mummy — thought to be a 25-year-old princess who lived more than 2,000 years ago — which now lies un-

OPPOSITE: The Museo Bacardí traces Cuba's colonial history. ABOVE: School in Santiago de Cuba.

wrapped alongside her mummified crocodile, ibis and cat. Other exhibits include a pair of Peruvian mummies, a man and a woman whose skin and bodies were petrified together as if hewn from a tree, and the 400-year-old shrunken head of a 23-year-old woman from the Amazonian Tsantsa de Jibaro tribe. After this, the Cuban archaeological exhibits dating from the aboriginal Taíno Indian period seem somewhat tame: bones, shells, carved idols, ceremonial seats made for Indian chiefs, and deformed skulls that show how inhabitants of the

rants, as well as an ice-cream parlor, set in restored colonial houses — all exceptionally well-managed by the tourist company Rumbos, which won an award for the plaza's restoration. The church on the square has been converted into a concert hall and this is the best place to hear classical music performed in Santiago, usually at the weekend.

As you stroll back along Calle Aguilera to Calle Pío Rosado, look for Calle Saco, better known as **Enramada**, Santiago's main commercial thoroughfare. Dilapidated signs from long-gone cabarets, restaurants and

time successfully used wooden slats to mold the foreheads of infants to create a desired gorilla-like slope-effect. Open Tuesday to Saturday, 9 AM to 6 PM, and Sunday, 9 AM to 1 PM, the museum is closed on Monday. Admission is US$2.

As you walk up Calle Aguilera, you'll come to a pretty square known locally as **Plaza Dolores**, located between Calles Calvario and Reloj. At the intersection with Calle Calvario is **La Isabelica**, which serves only coffee, which patrons tend to take spiked with Cuban rum or *marasquino*, a sweet liqueur. As usual, the popularity of this characterful institution with tourists means that dollar prices are inflated. Otherwise, the plaza contains an array of restau-

hotel still flap in the tropical breeze, while lackluster shop windows and a grimy cinema showing kung-fu movies attract long lines. The main commercial activity seems to be the demand for *cafecitos* or *rallado* (shavings of ice dribbled with syrup). Men play dominoes in the neighborhood café, alternately long-faced, then grinning as they tell *chistes*, jokes, to pass the time. The **Hotel Venus**, one of the most popular pre-Revolution bars in Santiago and reputedly where the daiquiri had its commercial debut, is off the side street as you approach the Casa Granda. Like its mascot, an eye-less, armless Aphrodite placed glumly in the front window, it is a moldering wreck and is currently closed.

Walk two blocks down to reach Calle Heredia once more, but this time, continue in the opposite direction. In the second block on the right, between Calles Corona and Padre Pico, is the **Casa de Orfeon Santiago**, a paint-peeling colonial mansion with a courtyard and interiors that are worth a look. Occasional evening musical performances take place here — this was once the home of Cuba's most prestigious choral society.

To the left, a little further along is **Calle Padre Pico**, the famous street of stone steps that climbs to the top of a steep hill where the views across the city and bay are spectacular. The swaying hips of the women who climb these steps was supposedly the inspiration for a local ballad. As you ascend, houses are stacked, higgledy-piggledy, many of them helter-skelter incarnations of earlier abodes dating back to the sixteenth-century, some sweet-looking, balconies aflow with rambling plants. This district, known as **El Tivolí**, was originally the home of French settlers.

At the top of the steps, to the right, is the **Museo de la Lucha Clandestina** (Museum of the Underground Struggle), on Calle General Jesús Rabí. On November 30, 1956, a group of Castro's revolutionaries led by Frank País fire-bombed this building, which was then the Santiago police headquarters and often used for interrogations. The attack was meant to divert attention away from the planned landing of the *Granma*, en route from Mexico with Castro, Che and other comrades on board, however, it was mistimed. Many of those who took part were gunned down, some of them on the Padre Pico steps.

Inside this former colonial mansion, you'll see an exhaustive exhibition devoted to the underground struggle against the Batista regime. It is open Monday to Saturday, 8 AM to 6 PM, and closed on Sunday.

When you return to the stairs, instead of going down, take the next street, leading to the old tramway-lined Calle Corona. Look out for an archway at the corner of Calle Bartolomé Masó: it leads to a small open cobbled square lined with flowering plants called the **Balcón de Velázquez**. During the early Spanish colonial era, this lookout was used to keep watch over the arrivals and depar-

tures of galleons. Its beautiful setting is now used by the typically musical-minded *santiagüeros* as the city's Peña del Tango (Tango Club). From here, you are only a block away from Parque Céspedes.

En Route to El Morro

Although the first suggested city tour is designed especially to be done on foot, the other excursions suggested here require a car, as you will need to cover quite a lot of distance.

Begin at the **Hotel Meliá Santiago**, even if you aren't staying here. For many Cubans, this Canadian-designed, Spanish-managed hotel represents the apex of privilege, and party members are awarded short stays here as incentives. Across the avenue, is the much less salubrious **Hotel Las Américas**.

As you drive along Avenida de las Américas — the city's main boulevard — you'll see a number of **Universidad de Oriente** faculties, and pass the **Bosque de los Héroes**, a monument commemorating Che Guevara and his band of Bolivian guerillas. Further along are a series of structures, rather sternly utopian, all commissioned by Fidel Castro in preparation for the Fourth Communist Party Congress in 1993. Here you'll see the monumental **Teatro Heredia**, used for such events as Fidel's annual July 26 speech, and the **Estadio de Béisbol Guillermón Moncada**, which can hold some 350,000 people and where regular baseball games, frequently starring Santiago's own "Orientales," are played. The avenue all leads to the **Plaza de la Revolución**, where an immense futurist bronze monument to Antonio Maceo (whose nickname during his heyday was "Titan of Bronze") depicts the hero astride his rearing horse amid a circle of 23 red machetes that point victoriously towards the heavens. The monument symbolizes March 23, 1878, the day Maceo resolved to continue his spirited campaign against the Spanish. At the base of the monument is a very strange, small museum which contains holographic representations of icons symbolizing each stage in Cuba's path to Revolution.

Turn left just before the monument and continue along the same street to reach the

A slogan heralds the *zafra,* or sugar harvest.

corner of Portuondo and Moncada, off Avenida de los Libertadores. You may need to ask directions to the **Moncada Barracks**, since it is not well signposted. Surrounded by mustard-yellow stucco walls, this bullet-splattered garrison represents one of the most crucial events in the remarkable story of Castro's rise to power. (The bullet holes are reconstructions based on historical photographs, since Batista's men filled them in after the attack.)

On July 26, 1953, a 26-year-old, then little-known lawyer named Fidel Castro and 125 militants made an assault on Moncada, one of the island's most important military installations during the Batista era. Although daring, the attack was an unmitigated disaster in which most of the assailants were either machine-gunned down or later brutally tortured to death. However, Castro himself survived to stand trial and to make his first famous speech, which became the basis for his new revolutionary manifesto, the Movimiento 26 de Julio, known in revolutionary shorthand as M-26.

Now the **Museo Histórico 26 de Julio** holds a collection that is an exercise in revolutionary patriotism, with sections devoted to the nineteenth-century War of Independence, the guerilla struggle led by Castro throughout the 1950s, and the glories and achievements of the Cuban Republic. The assault on Moncada is scrupulously documented, and the blood-stained uniforms of those who died taking part in the siege are particularly graphic. Some of the military equipment used by the Castro-led M-26 movement in the Sierra Maestra mountains can be seen here, including handmade weapons and grenades, Castro's khaki uniforms and sharp-shooter rifle and Che Guevara's mud-stained boots. Outside, a large part of the barracks has been turned into a school complex, known as "School City July 26." The museum is open Monday to Saturday, 8 AM to 6 PM, and Sunday 8 AM to noon.

Retrace your route and head for Avenida Jesús Menéndez, which curls around Santiago's desultory dockfront, past warehouses, custom offices and the Parque de la Alameda with its slumbering, horse-drawn *calesa* drivers. Close by, **La Trocha**, a district cluttered with dilapidated wooden houses, is considered to be the site of the original Santiago carnival, as it was here, during the colonial period, that slaves were permitted to celebrate once a year. Continuing on, as you pass the train station.

Just north of the train station is **Barra del Ron Caney**, Cuba's oldest rum distillery, opened in 1862 by an astute Spanish immigrant called Don Facundo Bacardí. The Bacardís were among the wave of wealthy business clans who hastily left Cuba after the revolution, and having left Cuba, continued to rebuild their rum empire in various other countries, including the Bahamas, Puerto Rico, Canada, Mexico and Spain. Until the mid-1960s, the Cuban government, having nationalized the industry, continued to market

rum under the Bacardí label, but when the state tried to export the rum, the Bacardí family filed a trademark infringement claim in the World Court and won. Now the rum that is produced here is labeled "Havana Club," and it is regarded by many rum purists as a better product than the original Bacardí. Some 60 percent of the rum produced here is exported to Canada and Spain, and the rest consumed in Cuba. Factory tours have been suspended, but the shop here is a good place to buy 15-year-old Havana Club rum, difficult to find elsewhere.

As you continue north, past a giant replica of a rum bottle, there are two places of interest in the area. The **Yarayó Fort**, a small, unprepossessing, yellow and tile building, was the first of 116 fortifications built by the Spaniards. From here, turn left, and follow the Avenida Combret to the **Cementerio de Santa Ifegenia**. A necropolis of marble angels, crosses and extravagantly wrought tombs, this is one of Cuba's oldest and most interesting cemeteries, once strictly segregated by social rank and race. It is also the burial place of Cuba's revered heroes of the independence movement. Among those buried here are José Martí, Carlos Manuel de Céspedes and Tomás Estrada Palma (the first president of an independent Cuba). A tomb shaped like a small mock castle contains the remains of those who died in the war of independence, while the victims of the Moncada Barracks attack are also buried here.

ABOVE: View of the El Morro parapet.

From here, retrace the route to La Trocha, and turn right on Avenida Eduardo Chivás, which becomes the road to **Castillo del Morro**, eight kilometers (five miles) away. As you scan the horizon from the stalwart, honey-slate Spanish fortress, it is obvious why this spectacular location, with its commanding views across the seas at the entrance to Santiago Bay, was chosen. Started in 1638, during the governorship of Pedro La Roca, its construction was masterminded by Giovanni Baptista Antonelli, the same Italian architect known for Havana's famous fortress.

Once inside the main drawbridge, an elaborate labyrinth of time-scoured stone passageways, stairwells and alcoves reveal the headquarters from which generations of commanders strove to protect Santiago from a string of savage attacks. (In 1662, however, the fortress was briefly besieged and partially destroyed by Dutch pirate Christopher Myngs, after which additional fortifications were added.) Wonderfully atmospheric, its small blue-washed chapel contains its original wooden cross carved in the sixteenth century; while tiny cramped dungeons once housed African slaves in transit and other hapless prisoners. During the War of Independence, the Spanish authorities imprisoned many Cuban rebels here, among them Emilio Bacardí Moreau. Restored in 1978, and then again in 1997, the fortress is open Monday to Friday, 9 AM to 5 PM, and during weekends, 8 AM to 4 PM. Admission is US$4, plus US$1 for cameras.

After visiting the fortress, the nearby **La Taberna del Morro**, an open-air patio sheltered by vines, which overlooks the sea from the bluff, is a good place to relax. It's located just before you reach **El Faro**, the lighthouse.

WHERE TO STAY

Make sure you have booked in advance during July, when the carnival festivities can attract a considerable influx of tourists.

Expensive

Much local pride has focused on the monolithic **Hotel Meliá Santiago de Cuba ((0226) 687070, FAX (0226) 687170, Calle M and Avenida de las Américas in Vista Alegre. The funky pop-art colors and offbeat steel design are a welcome relief from the Soviet-style concrete hotels you find in so much of the island. Unlike the Casa Granda, do not expect colonial charm. But do expect fast, efficient service and a broader range of amenities than any other hotel in eastern Cuba. Facilities include health club, three swimming pools, sauna, shopping complex, conference rooms, child care, car rental and travel agencies, doctor's office, pharmacy, business center with e-mail service and even an international phone kiosk next to the front desk. There are several restaurants and an array of bars. The rooftop terrace bar on the fifteenth floor offers stunning views and the chance to hear some of Santiago's most talented musicians.

**Hotel Casa Granda ((0226) 86600 FAX (0226) 86035, Calle Heredia 201 next to Calle Lacret, overlooks the Plaza Céspedes in the heart of the old town. The Casa Granda is to Santiago what the Hotel Nacional is to Havana — a place where both locals and visitors gather to socialize and people-watch for hours at a time. Completely renovated after years of lingering between picturesque decay and near squalor and now managed by the French Sofitel group, it has 58 rooms (described by the management as decorated in "neoclassical and Renaissance style"), including one for handicapped guests. Even if you are not staying here, the Casa Granda sports the old town's best restaurant and bar, including excellent coffee. Aside from its other facilities — boutique, rental car agency and travel office — it has the best postcard stall this side of Havana.

Moderate

The 68-room **Hotel Las Américas (** (0226) 42011 or 87225 FAX (0226) 87075, Avenida de las Américas and Calle General Cebreco, pales somewhat beside the Hotel Santiago,

hotel consists of a series of villas, each consisting of three to five rooms, which can be taken separately or all together. It has a pleasant, private atmosphere. Amenities include satellite television, mini-bar, swimming pool and a baby-sitting service.

Inexpensive

Crowning a hilltop near the airport in a leafy, residential neighborhood, the **Versalles Hotel (** (0266) 91016 or 86603 FAX (0266) 86145, Alturas de Versalles km1, is a good choice for a peaceful stay. Its landscaped row of

just across the road. Despite its need for a major renovation, this Horizontes property offers comfortable rooms and friendly (if not quite efficient) service.

A much better bet is a nearby Horizontes hotel called the **Villa San Juan (** (0226) 87200 or 87116 FAX (0226) 87117, Carretera Siboney km1.5. Located on the slopes of historic San Juan Hill, the modern rooms are arranged motel-style around a swimming pool in a peaceful park-like setting. Facilities include a restaurant, a bar, car rental, travel agencies, dollar shops and nightly Cuban cabaret.

Nearby is the charming **Santiago de Cuba Village** (formerly the Villa Gaviota) **(** (0266) 41368 FAX (0266) 61385, Avenida Manduley 502, Vista Alegre. This small resort

rooms and bungalows are air conditioned and have small balconies. There is a swimming pool and a small shop.

Perched on a cliff-top above the Caribbean close to the Castillo del Morro, the 1960s-era **Hotel Balcón del Caribe (** (0226) 91011 FAX (0226) 22049, Carretera del Morro km7.5, has an incredible setting. There are drawbacks, however: sluggish service and uninspiring rooms. It is difficult to climb down to the sea, and the swimming pool is not much consolation. Everything could do with a fresh coast of paint and the parking lot needs a good sweep. With an overhaul, this hotel

OPPOSITE AND ABOVE: Two views of Castillo del Morro, which holds a commanding position at the entrance of Santiago Bay.

could be much nicer. But like they say: you get what you pay for and this place is definitely low rent.

WHERE TO EAT

Expensive

Restaurante ZunZun ((0226) 41528, Avenida Manduley 159, Vista Alegre, is named for a tiny Cuban hummingbird. Formerly called the Tocororo, this elegant eatery has a pleasant setting in an old colonial house close to the Meliá Santiago. The comprehensive menu

includes dishes normally hard to find outside Havana and the chic beach resorts: Spanish *tapas*, Caribbean seafood soup, medallions of shrimp and lobster, *calamares relleno* and lobster enchiladas. Add an excellent house guitarist and you've got all the makings of the perfect place for a romantic date.

Moderate

Located in a nineteenth-century mansion that was once the Santiago home of the Bacardí family, **1900 Restaurant (** (0266) 23507, Calle San Basilico 354, between Calles Pío Rosado and Hartmann, is a haven of faded rococo that attracts a steady clientele of Cubans with dollars to burn. Honestly, it's hard to see why. The service is rude and slow

as molasses, there's a silly dress code that seems to apply to everyone but the local Communist Party elite, and an obnoxious doorman who won't let you in if he doesn't like your looks. If none of this fazes you, the 1900 does serve good Creole dishes (including veal, rabbit and turkey) amidst giant chandeliers and antique furniture. There is a charming leafy roof terrace upstairs for cocktails. Open 7 PM until midnight.

Next to the Castillo del Morro, **La Taberna del Morro (** (0226) 87151 is a must on a sunny day, when the views from this cliff-top restaurant are perfect. Try to avoid the crush of tourist coach traffic though, arrive early or much later, or stay for sunset cocktails. Try a *morro helado*, the cocktail of the house. It blends rum, crushed ice and lemon with whisked egg white, the whole flavored with a dash of cinnamon and Angostura bitters. Creole/Cuban food is the specialty. Generally a simple *prix fixe* meal costs US$10.

Inexpensive

Despite its modest façade, **Pizza Nova** at the Meliá Santiago (** (0226) 687070, Calle M and Avenida de las Américas in Vista Alegre, cooks up some of the best Italian food in Cuba including delicious pizza and pasta dishes that actually taste the way they're supposed to. Among the savory dishes on offer are lobster pizza, penne arrabiata and fettuccini alfredo. Across the Meliá patio is another excellent little open-air eatery called the **Cafetería el Colmadito**, which serves burgers, hotdogs, fries and other snacks throughout the day.

The Plaza Dolores in old town Santiago has been transformed into a pedestrian complex of restaurants, ranging from moderate to inexpensive, each with their own specialty; there is also a 24-hour cafeteria. You can choose from the following: **Taberna de Dolores (** (0266) 23913 is charmingly arranged in an old colonial house, with tables in the courtyard. The Dolores specializes in roasts and is open from 7 PM until midnight. **Don Antonio (** (0226) 22205 serves international dishes in a hacienda setting with hospitable service and a saloon-style bar and quirky juke-box. It is open noon to 11 PM. **La Perla del Dragon (** (0226) 52307 serves unexpectedly good Chinese dishes (chopsticks on request), with a Chinese chef in residence; open noon to 11 PM. The decor and design of the waiters' costumes at **La Teressina (** (0226) 52307 are apparently inspired by the fact that "La Traviata" was sung in Santiago by the Cuban opera singer Teressina Paradi at the end of the nineteenth century, and an elegant effect is strived for.

Restaurant Matamoros ((0226) 22675 has historic status in Santiago: the Trio Matamoros once played here, and the Afro-Cuban band that now plays their songs are good too. You can choose to eat in a cafeteria-style section, or in a more elegant, candle-lit setting. The food is simple but well-priced including a delicious dish called *biftec boulevard* — steak, ham and cheese rolled into little balls and then roasted. The house drink is an offbeat combo of beer, tomato juice and Tabasco sauce called the "Gourd Blood."

NIGHTLIFE

Just about anywhere you go at night in Santiago will reveal why this city has such a reputation for its talented musicians and infectious dancing.

Music

Your first stop should be the old town's celebrated **Casa de la Trova (** (0226) 623943 or 651708, Calle Heredia 208, where the best of Cuban music unfolds each night on a simple wooden stage at the front of the funky old *sala principal* or outdoors in the breezy patio. The 8 PM show (US$1 cover) seems to attract more locals than tourists, people dancing in the aisles and between the seats. The 10 PM show (US$2 cover) is more a foreign affair, with waiter service and sedate seating arranged around tables.

Traditional Cuban music is also played every evening (from 9:30 PM onwards) in the relaxed, open-air terrace setting of **Patio Los Dos Abuelos**, Calle Francisco Perez Carbo 5, Plaza de Marte.

While not in the same league as the famous Casa de la Trova, **Café Cantante (** (0226) 43178, Teatro Heredia, Avenida de las Américas, is nonetheless worth a visit for its evening performances, where favorite Cuban songs through the ages are sung with great gusto and warmth.

Yet another venue for island tunes is the **Casa de la Música**, Calle Corona 564 near the intersection of Aguilera and Enramada. There's a different group each night, with shows starting at 10 PM. The cover charge is only US$5.

Cabaret

Located on Carretera del Morro, one and a half kilometers (almost one mile) out of town, **Tropicana (** (0226) 91287 is Santiago's version of the popular Havana cabaret, and although it lacks the professional flair and imagination of the original (nor are the performers quite as glamorous), it still puts up an energetic show with a large cast sashshaying about in flamboyant and titillating costumes, or performing magical tricks and acrobatics. The cabaret is staged in a large custom-built stadium (designed by the same architect responsible for the Hotel Santiago) with an attached piano bar and restaurant. Tickets are US$35.

HOW TO GET THERE

Santiago de Cuba's **Aeropuerto Internacional Antonio Maceo (** (0226) 91014 is located seven kilometers (four miles) south of the city. Although most visitors fly to Havana first, and then make a connecting flight, it is possible to fly directly here from many international destinations including nearby Jamaica (see GETTING THERE, page 306 in TRAVELERS' TIPS).

Cubana de Aviación has several daily direct flights from Havana, and a thrice-weekly flight from and to Baracoa. Contact **Cubana de Aviación (** (0226) 51577 or 51595, Calle Félix Peña, between Calles Heredia and Bartolomé Masó.

Aside from flying, Santiago can also be easily reached from many points of the island by train (see GETTING THERE, page 306 in TRAVELERS' TIPS). The **Terminal de Ferrocarriles** is located near the port, west of the city. Another option is the daily **ViAzul (** (0226) 28484, bus service between Havana and Santiago. The station is situated at the corner of Avenida de los Libertadores and Calle Yarayó, near the Plaza de la Revolución.

Hotel Santiago de Cuba, a somewhat dated monolith.

EXPLORING SANTIAGO'S ENVIRONS

CAYO GRANMA

If you fly into Santiago de Cuba, or look across the bay from El Morro, you will catch sight of this tiny, pretty island just off the coast.

Formerly known as Cayo Smith, for the wealthy English slave trader who owned it, the island was later renamed for the famous leaky boat that carried Castro and his men to

Located on the hillside overlooking Cayo Granma, close to the ferry, this peaceful out-of-town location is good for the Chinese dishes with a Creole influence served at **Kiam Sand Restaurant** ((0226) 91889, Carretera de Punta Gorda. You can sit on the shady terrace or in air-conditioned Chinese-style interiors. It is open from noon to 11 PM.

How to Get There

To reach Cayo Granma, you have to catch a ferry from Punta Gorda, several kilometers from Santiago. There are two ferries — leaving

Cuba from Mexico in 1956. It is worth exploring, if only to experience the tranquility of this picturesque backwater, with its single circular path leading from the ferry pier past ramshackle wooden houses swallowed in foliage and flowers. There are no cars, hotels and few amenities on the island, but it has a charming restaurant — El Cayo, which has a verandah that is one of the most relaxing places to idle in Santiago.

Where to Eat

Charmingly located, **El Cayo** ((0226) 90109, on Cayo Granma, serves moderately priced seafood and Creole dishes. It's a nice place to stop for coffee or a cocktail, even if you don't have lunch here. It is open from noon to 9 PM.

from different piers — one for Cubans, and the other (run by **Cubanacán Nautica**) for tourists. It's worth a visit, especially if you coincide your trip with lunch.

LA BASÍLICA DEL COBRE

Tucked away in the small hillside town of El Cobre, 16 km (10 miles) from Santiago, the basilica of **La Virgen de la Caridad del Cobre** (Virgin of Charity of Cobre) is Cuba's most important religious pilgrimage site. The Virgin is the island's patron saint, officially named as such in 1916 but regarded as a miracle-worker for centuries. During his visit here in 1998, Pope John Paul II blessed the Virgin with a papal kiss. Thousands of pilgrims from all over Cuba come here every year to worship and pray on September 8, when her festival is held. Many regard this destination as a Cuban Lourdes.

Background

El Cobre itself seems thick with history. It was the first open *cobre* (copper) mine in the Americas, first opening in 1550 with slave labor. Much later in 1731, this was where the largest slave rebellion in Cuba took place.

The legend of La Caridad begins in 1608, when two Indians and a young slave named

sign from above, and built a new chapel for her on that spot, where she became the patroness of the slaves working below. From that moment on, she became famous for her miraculous powers. The Virgin is frequently invoked as Ochún, one of the most powerful of the Yoruba goddesses in the Santería religion — and few Cubans would be so rash as to omit her in their prayers, especially in times of trouble.

Built in 1927, the present church rises from the nearby foliage with its three yellow towers topped by red cupolas. A long stair-

Juan Moreno, all mine workers, were at sea off the Bahía de Nipe, on Cuba's northern coast, on a salt-collecting expedition. The wind swelled high, and they feared for their lives, when from their boat they saw something floating in the sea. When they rescued it, they saw that it was a small statue of the Virgin on a wooden plank engraved with inscription: "I am the Virgin of Charity." The swells then subsided, and they returned to safety. When they bought the statue back to El Cobre, it was decided to build a new chapel for her at some distance away from town. In the three years that followed, the statue disappeared from its altar, only to mysteriously re-appear at the top of El Cobre hill. The slaves decided this was a

case leads to the main entrance, lined with street lamps. The statue of La Caridad del Cobre holding an infant Jesus is displayed in a glass case above the altar — her saffron and copper robes are also the color of Ochún, goddess of love and sexuality, protector of pregnant women.

Over the years, visitors have left offerings to the Virgin in a side chapel that is deluged with flowers, little scraps of cheap jewelry and cloth, wooden crosses, hand-written letters, autographed baseball bats, crutches, leg-braces, police badges, military medals, and all manner of other souvenirs from those who sought blessing here.

OPPOSITE: Santiago musician Emilo Cavailhon.
ABOVE: Traveling to the city by carriage.

One of the most famous offerings, unfortunately, can not be seen. After Hemingway was awarded the Nobel Prize in 1954, he turned over his gold medallion to the people of Cuba, requesting that it be displayed at the El Cobre basilica. After it was stolen in 1988, only to surface several days later when the culprits were caught, it has been held by the Archbishop of Santiago. Also in safe-keeping, perhaps considered too politically contentious, is the Catholic amulet given to the El Cobre basilica by Fidel Castro's mother as she prayed for her son's protection.

Unless you arrive very early, you will undoubtedly be approached by gangs of determined, sometimes quite aggressive, touts trying to sell you lumps of pretty but not very enticing pyrites that have been churned up in the nearby mines. They are best avoided.

SANTIAGO DE CUBA PROVINCE

You don't have to travel a great distance to appreciate the charms of this small province. Within a day or two you can easily explore some spectacular mountain scenery, see one or two quirky museums, and still be able to spend the afternoon by the sea, contemplating the sunset with the inevitable daiquiri.

There are a range of fairly modest places to stay in this area, east of Santiago. However, the two nicest beach resorts within driving distance are in fact located to the west of the city. The Super Club Sierra Mar and the Super Club Los Galeones are listed under DRIVING TO SANTIAGO DE CUBA, page 255 in the previous chapter.

To Parque Baconao

Encompassing a vast 80,000 hectares (nearly 200,000 acres), Baconao is the largest park in Cuba, stretching 52 km (32 miles) from the outskirts of Santiago to Laguna Baconao, and from the dense mountains of the Sierra de la Gran Piedra to the sandy beaches of the Caribbean coast. A nature park in the communist mold, the reserve was partly the brainchild of Celia Sánchez, Castro's long-time companion and ally, and was originally developed as a recreation center for Cubans, but has since come to embrace international tourists as well.

Part of the park has been designated a Biosphere Reserve by UNESCO, and represents an attempt to reforest Cuba with many endemic species of flora and fauna — it is a beautiful wilderness, crisscrossed with walking paths. Elsewhere, the park comprises a long series of beaches, some with hotels and restaurants, a so-called Valle de la Prehistoria (Prehistoric Valley), and numerous museums and other attractions. It is well worth a day's visit from Santiago, which can easily include a mountain walk and an afternoon by the sea, or you can stay within the park for several days. However, it should be noted that some of the park's primary attractions — including the Los Indios nature area and beautiful Playa Daiquirí — have recently been taken over by the Cuban military and

closed to the general public. Whether or not this portends the de-emphasis of Baconao as a tourist area remains to be seen.

As you leave Santiago along the Avenida de las Américas, take Avenida Pujol. You will see, on your right, the **Loma de San Juan** (San Juan Hill), the site of the last battle in the War of Independence, an event ingrained on generations of United States schoolchildren. For all the hype, the hill itself is very small. There's a small Spanish fortress near the Hotel Villa San Juan, and a large *ceiba* tree. It was under these branches that, on June 16, 1898, Spanish troops surrendered to the United States Army, handing Cuba over in a ceremony at which not a single Cuban was present. At the top of San Juan Hill, a row of memorials commemorates the *mambisas*, the

soldiers who fought for Cuba's independence, and there are also some in honor of American soldiers who died here.

The main memorial mentions the blood "of the brave and true Cuban insurgents and that of the generous American soldiers who sealed a covenant of liberty and fraternity between the two nations." Nowhere, however, on San Juan Hill is there any mention of Teddy Roosevelt and his famous Rough Riders, who led the American invasion in 1898.

From here, the road heads for Parque Baconao. This route has history branded into it: it was taken first by the invading Americans in 1898, and then later in 1953, by Castro and his revolutionaries on their way to

El Cobre, whose basilica draws pilgrims.

the Moncada Barracks. As you drive along, you'll see 26 stone memorials lining the road — Fidel's superstitious number "26" — in commemoration of the rebels who died in the aftermath of that assault. Incidentally, the number does *not* correspond to the body count of those who died.

LA GRAN PIEDRA

About 10 kilometers (six miles) east of town, before reaching the beach town of Siboney, a well-signposted turn-off marks the route to La Gran Piedra, an enormous boulder that perches almost supernaturally on a peak in the northern Sierra Maestra mountains. As the road winds ever upward (this is one of the steepest inclines you are likely to encounter in Cuba), a breathtaking landscape unfolds with each curve. Myriad hues of green trees and vines are splashed with fiery orange *flamboyán* blossoms and fragrant *mariposa* flowers, butterflies and birds flit through coffee and guava plantations, and views towards the coast grow increasingly spectacular. The heat of the coast subsides, and the air becomes cooler, fresher and moist from the tiny waterfalls trickling out from the side of rocks. The road itself is sometimes prone to landslides, and its steepness requires cautious driving — watch out for hikers, locals and wandering animals. (This is not a trip to attempt on a day when there is a torrential downpour.)

Shrouded in pine forest, La Gran Piedra, literally the "great rock," looms some 1,234 m (4,113 ft) above sea-level. It's a 432-step climb to the top, with plenty of places to rest and look at the exotic vegetation and lizards. Look out for the spiky *pandanao* tree, with its large nugget-sized seeds striped in reggae tri-colors which smell just like a banana.

From the top of La Gran Piedra, it's said, you can see Haiti and Jamaica on a clear day — or at least their reflected lights in the sky at night — but others scoff at this as fancy. You can see as far as the naked eye can stretch in all directions, however, with dazzling views southwards to the coast, and undulating green valleys to the north.

There are many mountain pathways to take for long walks through the Sierra Maestra, during which you may catch glimpses of the rare, tiny bee hummingbird, known as *zunzuncito* (a frenetic flash of blue, green and red feathers), and the exquisite *Greta Cubana*, one of only two clear-winged butterfly species in the world.

Roughly a 30-minute walk back down the mountain from Gran Piedra is a sprawling botanical reserve called the **Jardín Ave de Paraíso** where birds of paradise, jasmine, gladiolas, begonias and other tropical blooms are produced for florist shops in Santiago. For a donation of US$1 per person, the manager will give you a personalized tour of the various gardens.

If you stay up here, remember to bring a pair of good walking shoes, a jacket for cool evenings and mosquito repellent.

LA ISABELICA

Having come as far as the Gran Piedra, don't miss driving just a little further along the mountain-side to reach La Isabelica, an early nineteenth-century French coffee planter's estate that is now a museum. The Spartan stone hacienda is a moving sight, its walls alive with a creeping flame-colored lichen echoed by the surrounding red blossoming *flamboyáns*.

It was built in 1810 by Monsieur Victor Constantin Cuzeau, who set about rebuilding his fortune in this vertiginous and isolated place after fleeing the slave revolution in Haiti, bringing his slaves with him by force. An early daguerreotype shows him to be a tall, stern and maniacally alert figure in a top hat and suit. Yet he was obviously not without passion: he named his plantation for Isabel María, his slave mistress, who lived with him as slaves toiled below in their chains. The museum (closed for renovation at press time) encompasses the hacienda, coffee drying beds and plantation grounds, with displays of heavy tools and shackles. It is open Tuesday to Saturday 9 AM to 5 PM, Sunday 9 AM to 1 PM. Admission is US$1.

FROM MOUNTAIN TO COAST

As you return to the coast, take the turn along the main highway to Parque Baconao

Guajiros, or traditional farmers, at work.

that leads to **La Granjita Siboney**, located just before the beachfront town of Siboney. This is the farmhouse Fidel Castro and his comrades — disguised as chicken farmers — rented in 1953 a few weeks before their July 26 attack on the Moncada Barracks. Some 135 men loyal to Castro gathered here on the eve of the attack, and most had only hours to prepare themselves with the details of what their mission would entail. Despite warnings from Castro about the risks involved, most set off on the doomed assault with their leaders words ringing in their ears: "We will be free men or martyrs." Later, the farmhouse was the scene of grisly torture and butchering as many of those who participated in the raid were brought here by the Batista forces. Inside the museum, blood-stained khaki uniforms and objects retrieved from the Moncada assault tell the story. It is open Tuesday to Sunday, 9 AM to 5 PM, and closed on Monday.

Continuing on, Siboney's beach is very popular with young *santiagüeros*, but there are nicer beaches further. A road to the left at the junction just south of Granjita Siboney heads east to Laguna Baconao. Several kilometers on, you reach **El Oasis**, an artist's community. On the town's north side, just off the highway, you will see a rather large thatched restaurant and bar called the **Finca Guajira Rodeo ☎** (0226) 39526 where you can watch rodeos on Saturdays and Sundays (2 PM) or rent horses for rides. Tickets to the two-hour rodeo are US$2 for adults, US$1 for children.

After some 10 km (six miles) along the main highway, you will reach Damajayabo Valley, otherwise known as the bizarre **Valle de la Prehistoria**. The dusty landscape is dotted with almost a hundred life-like (well, almost, from a distance) replicas of prehistoric dinosaurs, mammals and Stone Age *Homo sapiens*, all frozen in action poses. (None of them were endemic to Cuba.) Wandering around them and posing alongside for wonderfully kitsch photographs takes about half an hour, with an optional drink in the Fred Flintstone-style cave. Admission is US$1 per person. The valley is open Tuesday to Sunday, 8 AM to 5 PM.

Farther along the coast road is the delightful **Museo de Autos**, which is well worth a

stop, either on the way there, or on the way back. It's really more rewarding than visiting the fake dinosaurs. This collection of antique cars was once a private and personal collection. Among its stars are the smallest hand-made car in Cuba, the '56 Ford Thunderbird that belonged to Ángel Castro (Fidel's father), Batista's blue '48 Oldsmobile, Beny Moré's Cadillac, and 2,070 miniature cars displayed indoors, tracing the history of automobile design.

From here, a side road leads down to the **Playa Daiquirí**, one of the area's nicest beaches and the site of the 1898 landing by Roosevelt and his Rough Riders. However, the beach was recently expropriated by the Cuban military and is no longer open to the public. Meanwhile, the Hotel Daiquirí and the adjacent scuba school have also closed and are allegedly being converted into a drug rehabilitation center. In other words: the entire beach area is now off limits to anyone who doesn't have special permission from the Cuban government.

It's said that the daiquiri was invented here, named for a nearby ore mine, after American soldiers adopted the local habit of mixing rum with sugar and water. With their addition of crushed ice, the drink became famous the world over.

Beyond the turnoff to Playa Daiquirí, the highway veers inland to loop around the nature reserve called **Los Indios,** which is currently closed to the public. Recently the park lodge was converted into a sanitarium for mentally ill Cubans. The highway hits the coast against at rocky **Playa Larga** and continues east past the **Jardín de Cactus**, which contains more than 400 desert plants. **Playa Sigua** harbors a decrepit little amusement park that has seen its better days, as well as a wave-splashed restaurant called the **Casa de Pedro el Cojo**, one of the few spots along this stretch of coast where you can pick up something to drink or eat.

Once you get past Sigua, the action starts to pick up again. The seaside **Acuario Baconao** offers dolphin shows and colorful Caribbean fish, while the adjacent **Club Amigo** resorts add a splash of Mediterranean color to the arid coastal landscape.

Roadside flowers on the way to Gran Piedra.

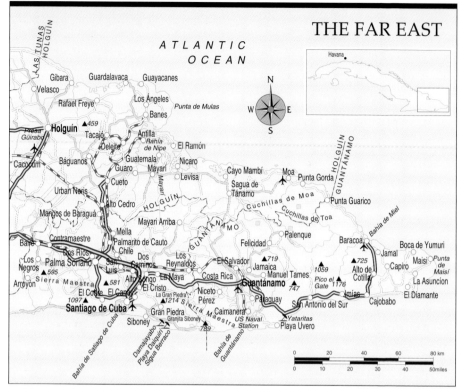

Nearing the end of the road you reach a tourist complex on the southern shore of **Laguna Baconao** where you can organize fishing, boating and horseback riding. The complex has a small zoo where lagoon dwellers like the Cuban crocodile and jutia (tree rat) are on display, although not exactly in their natural habitat.

WHERE TO STAY

Moderate

Coralia Club Bucanero ((0226) 686363 FAX (0226) 686073, Carretera Baconao, Arrollo la Costa near El Oasis, is the best choice along the Baconao coast. Located at the base of a coral cliff facing the sea and the mountains, this all-inclusive French-managed resort has a nice pool area and a small private beach nearby that's perfect for swimming. All rooms have air conditioning, satellite television, phone and mini-bar. Facilities include a choice of restaurants, bar, nightclub, watersports activities and a shop. There are regular shuttles into Santiago (US$5) with pick up and drop off at the Hotel Casa Granda.

Farther east is the German-managed **Carisol-Los Corales Resort (** (0226) 356113 or 356115 FAX (0226) 356116, Carretera de Baconao km31, Playa Cazonal, a well-maintained and comfortable hotel that sprawls along the coast like a red-roofed Mediterranean village. The beach isn't much to write home about, but there's an excellent pool area and an open-air amphitheater where Cuban-style cabaret is staged each night. Carisol-Los Corales is a good choice for families with children, with daily recreational programs and a range of sports activities including tennis, billiards, sailing, snorkeling and sea kayaking.

Inexpensive

La Gran Piedra ((0226) 86147, Carretera La Gran Piedra, 14 km (nine miles) from Santiago, can't be missed as you drive along the main road to La Gran Piedra. A refuge from the heat of summer, this is a very private, beautifully located Horizontes resort. Each of the 22 stone *casitas* have wonderful views (each have their own terrace) and many boast stone fireplaces to warm you on chilly winter nights. There is a restaurant, bar and games room, and horseback riding and walking tours can be arranged.

The seaside **Hotel Costa Morena** ((0266) 356126 FAX (0226) 356155, Carretera de Baconao km38.5 in Playa de Sigua, was under renovation at press time and Horizontes could not supply a firm date for reopening. When the resort finally does open up again, the 115 rooms will feature air conditioning, satellite television and balconies with ocean views. Sports facilities will include swimming pool, beach volleyball, tennis court and croquet field.

WHERE TO EAT

Despite its increasing popularity, there isn't a lot of choice in dining along the Baconao coast. Once the current renovation is completed, the inexpensive **El Curujey** ((0266) 356126 restaurant at the Costa Morena resort will once again be the best place to eat between Santiago and the end of the road. The thatched-roof dining area, poised on a bluff above the waves, is also very romantic.

A popular spot with Cuban diners is the **Casa de Pedro el Cojo** ((0226) 398160, Playa de Sigua, which serves excellent Creole dishes, most notably roast pig. Meals are inexpensive. Similar Creole delights are available at **Finca Guajira** ((0226) 39526 in El Oasis, where you can eat beneath a thatched roof in a simple restaurant overlooking the rodeo corral.

If you make it all the way to the end of the road, pop into the hilltop restaurant at the **Gran Laguna Baconao** tourist complex, which serves a range of light snacks including very tasty french fries.

HOW TO GET THERE

The easiest way to explore is by rental car or taxi, and of course, you'll need to negotiate the rate in advance. Renting a car, or arranging a day away with a car and driver is easily done, either through a car rental agency or from the taxi stand at Plaza de Marte in Santiago.

Otherwise, the best option for exploring the Parque Baconao is to take an organized excursion run by one of the main tour agencies from Santiago de Cuba. Rumbos has offices opposite the Hotel Casa Granda and in the Hotel Las Américas.

GUANTÁNAMO PROVINCE

Once you enter Guantánamo Province, be assured that you have strayed firmly off Cuba's beaten track. The province has much more to offer than just the controversial United States military base, and the drive to Baracoa, Cuba's oldest colonial town, across La Farola highway is one of the island's most spectacular journeys.

The remote and unpopulous province of Guantánamo runs from just east of Laguna Baconao to the easternmost tip of island, which is the least visited part of the island. The capital, also called Guantánamo, which lies 90 km (56 miles) east of Santiago, is a fairly unattractive prospect, with its bleak housing estates and swirling dust bales. Everyone in Cuba and a great many people around the world may perhaps recognize this as the province that is celebrated in the song *Guantánamera*, which is also the name of the famous Cuban director Tomás Gutiérrez Alea's last film.

BACKGROUND

Guantánamo is equally well known for the United States naval military base here, which is one of Cuba's great political oddities. In 1902, when Cuba was declared Republic, the price for the end of military occupation by American troops was that the naval station at Guantánamo be leased "in perpetuity." The continuing presence of the naval base has been a constant source of aggravation for Fidel Castro's government. As you enter Guantánamo town, you see a huge billboard which pronounces: "No Son Negociables" — Not Negotiable.

The Guantánamo naval installation is the largest in the world, spanning 72 sq km (about 28 sq miles), and is separated from Cuban territory by a 27-km-long (nearly 17-mile) fence and many thousands of Cuban and American landmines. It houses around 2,000 military personnel and about 1,500 civilians within a community of suburban houses and split-level ranches tidily housed on street-lit roads, administrative offices, shopping malls, recreation areas, a hospital, a church, a port and two airfields. The base was the setting for the film, *A Few Good Men*, starring Tom Cruise, Jack Nicholson and Demi Moore.

Every year the United States sends the Cuban government a nominal rent check for about US$4,000, but since Castro came to power in 1959, these checks have never been cashed, for the Cuban government is incensed by the situation and adamant that the United States should go. It is strictly forbidden for any transit to occur between the United States naval base and the rest of Cuba, although a dwindling number of graying Cuban employees — now entering their twilight years — still retain jobs on the base they have held since before 1959, and they are the only personnel allowed to come and go. Meanwhile, only approved United States military personnel and their families are allowed in from the United States.

WHAT TO SEE AND DO

With prior permission or by joining an organized tour (ask at your hotel in Santiago) you can enter the Cuban military zone and drive to a lookout located on a hill overlooking the base, **Mirador de Malones**, a restaurant and bar operated by Gaviota. From the military checkpoint, a road winds upward through dry plains and thick forests of prickly cacti, many of which were planted by the Cuban army as a "cactus curtain" to prevent Cubans from trying to seek political asylum in the base. From the lookout, it is a surreal experience to look through the powerful binoculars (made in Fairhope, USA) and to survey all that the eye can see of the base, from American soldiers in their watchtowers to trucks unloading at the docks, all the while aware that everything on your side is also being avidly scrutinized.

During the summer of 1994, when unprecedented numbers of Cubans were trying to flee in order to seek automatic political asylum in the United States, many of them were intercepted by United States coastguard patrols and returned to the Guantánamo base which served as a detention camp while the United States government tried to figure out what to do with them. Haitians fleeing turmoil in their country were also detained here — 40,000 of them, one-fourth of whom were sent back to Haiti. The detention camp was closed down, and at present, Guantánamo continues its normal duties of training the entire United States Atlantic Fleet.

Located to the southeast of Guantánamo town, is the small, sleepy fishing village of **Caimanera**, which borders the naval base. This is a restricted zone, and generally, the remaining Cubans who work on the base commute from here. Many Cubans have tried to swim into the base from here, and you need to pass through a checkpoint to enter, however you will only be allowed to pass if you have a reservation at the small, 17-room **Hotel Caimanera** ((021) 99414 or 99416, Loma Norte, Caimanera, which is a good place to break your journey and far more scenic than anywhere in Guantánamo town. It has a nice swimming pool and the staff are very friendly. In the bizarre-atmosphere stakes, this is a great place to stay: you can watch the lights of the naval base twinkle away nearby across the stretch of sea.

HOW TO GET THERE

Guantánamo's **Mariana Grajales Airport** ((021) 34533 or 34789 is located 16 km (10 miles) southeast of the town center. Cubana de Aviación has daily flights there from Havana.

By rail, there are daily train services connecting Guantánamo to Santiago de Cuba, Holguín and Havana. The **Estación de Ferrocarriles** is on Calle Pedro A. Pérez, just north of Parque Martí.

FROM GUANTÁNAMO TO BARACOA

From Guantánamo, the road continues for a time across empty arid hills and then along the empty southern coast, which is bordered cacti-covered hills with deep ochre cliffs that are thrashed by unruly waves. Small towns here sustain themselves on fishing and farming salt and mangoes. Although this is a poor region, it becomes increasingly beautiful, splashed with bougainvillea and hibiscus plants. Along the route, a few sheltered sandy coves are tempting places to stop for a swim, especially **Playas Yateritas** and **Imías**, near the village of the same name.

Just after Imías, the road turns inland and heads north towards the mountains. Then begins the winding ascent of **La Farola** ("The Beacon"), a 30-km-long (nearly 18-mile) roadway, which was finished in 1968 and is one of Cuba's greatest engineering feats. It snakes and winds its way across this region's steep mountain passes, and in many places is supported by columns. As you climb, you

BARACOA

For so many years, Baracoa remained a very isolated part of Cuba, and in many ways, this sultry backwater seems pickled in a peculiar unreality all its own. Tropical vegetation licks at its edges, and its air is sweet with the smell of damp plants and salt sea. It is an intriguing place to visit, with its lonely colonial fortresses and enveloping provincial life. Further afield, you can visit rural villages, swim in deserted

enter dense untouched tropical forest and a rarefied, almost alpine coolness chills the air. Clouds permeate the lush scenery and views across the coffee and cacao plantations, small villages and tropical vegetation are breathtaking (and at some vertiginous moments, a little nervous-making). *Guajiros* on horseback are a common sight. From the highest point, you can see both the northern and southern coasts of Cuba.

From here, the road twists and winds its way downwards to Baracoa's lush coastal flatlands. Be sure to drive across La Farola only during daylight hours and during good weather, as the roads are treacherous enough even by day, with switchbacks, sharp curves and steep hills.

beaches and perhaps even kayak or raft through forested stretches of river.

BACKGROUND

Located at almost the easternmost tip of the island, it was the island's first settlement; founded in 1512 as the first of seven cities founded by Diego de Velázquez, and for a very brief period, it was Cuba's capital. Baracoa sits beside the rounded curve of Porto Santo inlet, the second place Columbus stopped on his first voyage to America, and planted (so it is believed) a wooden cross, said to be Cuba's oldest relic, which can now be seen in Baracoa's Nuestra Señora de la

A family on the road among Guantánamo cactus.

Asunción church. Columbus admired the surrounding landscape and commented on the unusual square shape of El Yunque — 575 m (1,886 ft) high, the remains of an ancient limestone mesa which dominates the horizon — and the beauty of the nearby Río de Miel, the so-called "River of Honey," as well as the Toa and Duaba Rivers.

Many in Cuba regard Baracoa as the cradle of the island's civilization: it was home to a large settlement of Taíno Indians, evidenced by the quantities of Taíno pottery, objects made from sea shells and ancient human skeletons found here. After the conquest of Cuba, many Taíno Indians took refuge here (together with slaves who managed to escape from plantations), and they are believed to have survived longest here. Many Baracoans have Taíno features, being short of stature, with smooth, light bronze skin. The region's forested mountains are rich in pre-Columbian archaeological sites, and Baracoa itself has one of the best museums in the country, and has one of Cuba's most active centers of archaeological research.

Baracoa's strategic foothold location required fortresses and towers to protect its early Spanish colonists from pirates at sea, and most were built during the mid-eighteenth century. One of the fortresses, the Seboruco, sits high on a hill, and has been turned into El Castillo, a comfortable hotel with unmatched views across the so-called Bahía de Miel in one direction, and across another sea of green forest to El Yunque in the other. There are also fortresses at both ends of Baracoa: the Matachín and La Punta. The former is now a museum and the latter provides a dramatic setting for a restaurant.

GENERAL INFORMATION

Baracoa has little infrastructure for tourists, beyond its two main hotels, El Castillo and Porto Santo, and you will probably have to rely on their services for essentials such as cashing traveler's checks and changing foreign currency as well as post and telephone calls. Baracoa airport has a **Havanautos** ((021) 355419 car rental office.

You can check with **Rumbos** ((021) 43335, Avenida los Mártires at Maceo, to find out about and book excursions within Baracoa and to surrounding nature reserves, working farms and beaches, as well as kayaking trips down the Río Toa, and visits to Finca Duaba. They can arrange accommodation at the Villa Maguaná.

If you are interested in spending more time in the region's wilds, you should contact **Cubamar** ((07) 338317, 662524, 305536 or 662523 FAX (07) 333111 WEB SITE www.cubamar@cubamar.mit.cma.net, Paseo 752 at the corner of Calle 15, Vedado, Havana; or **Alcona S.A.** ((07) 222526, 222529 or 845244 FAX (07) 241531, Calle 42 no. 514, at the corner of Avenida 7, Miramar, Havana. Both companies can help you arrange guided nature walks, whitewater rafting and kayaking trips in the Baracoa area.

Should you need medical attention, one can only hope that it is not serious — the nearest well-equipped hospital is at Guantánamo, 150 km (93 miles) west, a journey that should not be made after dark. Baracoa Hospital, despite its well-trained doctors, is a study in the impact of the United States embargo.

WHAT TO SEE AND DO

Baracoa is small enough to explore on foot, especially if you are staying at El Castillo, which lies at the heart of the town. Most of the town's houses are dilapidated, red-tiled and made of wood. They are not very old, yet there is a strongly colonial influence in Baracoa's layout of streets and squares, in its small parks and its long seafront Malecón.

Whatever direction you take, it seems you are plunged into some vignette of neighborhood life: laughing children running in their blue Pioneer uniforms, housewives throwing buckets of water in the gutter, factory buses picking up workers, old men and athletic young boys playing dominoes, side by side.

You could start with a visit to the **Museo de Baracoa**, housed in the Fuerte Matachín, at the entrance to the town. The museum showcases discoveries (and Taíno skeletons) from some 56 archaeological sites from the area. Another collection of much interest is the museum's display of the beautiful polymites, or snail shells, especially the *polymita Pictas*, which is unique and endemic

A wooden shack stands amidst luxurious vegetation near Baracoa, Guantánamo.

to this region. Baracoa's well-respected city historian, Alejandro Hartman, has his office in the museum and has an encyclopedic knowledge of the region.

You should definitely visit the church of **Nuestra Señora de la Asunción de Baracoa** (Our Lady of the Assumption), which stands on Baracoa's Parque Central. Inside is the famous **Cruz de la Parra**, the cross that Columbus is believed to have planted when he landed in nearby Porto Santo. Apparently he placed it at the mouth of cove, with rough stones heaped around it, where according to legend, it was found under a vine in 1510 by Diego de Velázquez's expedition. Made of dark wood, about a meter (a yard) high and adorned with silver-plated metal, carbon dating has confirmed the antiquity of the cross, which is believed to have been made of wood from the area's native seascape tree. Over the centuries, it has survived unscathed — despite the fact that Baracoa's original church, founded in 1512, was destroyed, first by pirate attacks and later by fire.

Within the Parque Central stands a statue of the Taíno Indian chief, Hatuey, who the Spanish burned alive at the stake because he refused to become a religious convert.

From here, a block east takes you to Calle Antonio Maceo, one of the town's main streets, which is a good place to wander, passing the **"Socialismo o Muerte" bakery** and perhaps stopping at the **Casa del Chocolate** on Calle Calixto García, which sells cups of hot chocolate and locally made chocolate bars. You may see a few shops selling handicrafts for *turistas*, made of natural fibers native to the area, coconut husks, shells, and seascape wood carvings.

WHERE TO STAY

Moderate
With its commanding position and marvelous views across Baracoa and the harbor from its swimming pool deck, **Hotel Castillo** ((021) 42103 or 42125, Calle Calixto García, Loma del Paraíso, is an easy choice if you want to be in walking distance of the town. The hotel's stairs are protected by two old towers, while the rooftop bar has an excellent lookout. Rooms are simple but comfortable, and the restaurant food is good.

Hotel Porto Santo ((021) 43578, 42125 or 43590, Carretera al Aeropuerto, is located across the bay, close to the beach where Columbus moored his ship and left his cross. This hotel complex is Baracoa's most relaxing place to unwind, with its roomy bungalows, a large pool area with a swim-up bar and a nearby beach. It also has an outdoor restaurant and a cabaret.

Both the above hotels have recently been taken over by Gaviota, the tourist group run by Cuba's Ministry of Defense, and may be upgraded soon.

Inexpensive
The mustard-colored hotel right on the Malecón, **Hotel La Rusa** ((021) 43011, Calle Máximo Gómez, is named for the colorful Russian lady who established it, Magdalena Monasse. She was a fervent *Fidelista*, who settled here, perhaps preferring the climate. Fidel and Che stayed here in the past. Don't expect luxury.

WHERE TO EAT

La Punta ((021) 43335, La Fuerte La Punta, located within the historic fort, right at the harbor's entrance, is Baracoa's best restaurant, with delicious, inexpensive food served in a casual atmosphere, with tables outside if you prefer. Try the *pescado con leche de coco* (fish cooked in coconut milk), the *chatino* (fried green bananas) and the *arroz con coco* (coconut milk-cooked rice).

In deference to the local coconut industry, you should sample *vino de coco*, which is rather nice and tastes a bit like a sweet retsina, served with ice. It is also hard to resist the local *cucurucho*, a delicious soft, sweet coconut candy that is served wrapped in palm leaves.

Don't miss a visit to the **Casa del Chocolate** on Calle Antonio Maceo, where you can a drink of cup of locally produced chocolate.

NIGHTLIFE

At night, darkness settles across Baracoa almost eerily, the sunset honeying the sea

OPPOSITE TOP: Typical Baracoa wooden houses. BOTTOM: A Baracoa girl celebrates her fifteenth birthday.

and seemingly turning the surrounding forest into liquefied green.

From El Castillo's balcony bar, all the sounds of the town float up; you might hear the unmistakably unique tones of the *nengón* and the *kiribá* — instruments that are rarely heard these days in Cuba — and the frenetic chants which accompany the Afro-Cuban *Yambú Akalé* dancers. You can ask about attending one of these ceremonies, which are usually private.

Competing salsa music blares forth from the town's only discotheque, an open-air affair on the rooftop of a dreary building that is the social focus for miles around.

How to Get There

In an effort to promote tourism to this province, Cubana de Aviación has recently begun operating thrice-weekly flights to Baracoa from Havana via Santiago de Cuba or Guantánamo at a nearby modest landing strip — the **Gustavo Rizo Airport** ((021) 42580 or 42216 — which ends abruptly at the harbor's edge at Porto Santo. For information contact **Cubana de Aviación** ((021) 42171, Calle José Martí 181.

By road — whether you come by rental car, tour bus or hitching a ride on an old truck — Baracoa lies 150 km (93 miles) northeast of Guantánamo. You'll see Baracoa's sole Servi-Cupet at the entrance to the town as you drive in from Guantánamo.

EXCURSIONS FROM BARACOA

From Baracoa, there are two possible routes along the coast to explore: westwards towards the mining area of Moa and eastwards to the very tip of Cuba at Punta de Maisí.

West from Baracoa

To the west, the road first passes the inlet of Porto Santo, and then passes through a spectacular stretch of lush coconut plantations, Banyan-like *jagüey* trees, and inlets hiding unspoiled beaches.

Some, like **Playa Duaba**, near Porto Santo airport, have a decent swathe of beach; others are merely slivers of sand tucked between dense foliage. At Playa Duaba is a

commemorative tablet marking the spot where Antonio Maceo, the great independence fighter, put ashore with a band of like-minded companions and joined the War of Independence.

Within the district — a short distance inland — is the **Finca Duaba**, which stages *campesino*-style meals for tourists and is also a great place from which to swim in the Río Duaba. Visitors are welcome daily, but the *finca's* managers prefer to have advance bookings so that they know to prepare food that day. To guarantee yourself a good meal contact Rumbos ((021) 43335.

En route, it is interesting to see various stages in one of the region's main industries: coconut farming. The palms are harvested from seed banks set up by the Ministry of Agriculture, with as many as 19,000 coconut palms in each seed bank.

Further on, about 12 km (seven and a half miles) outside Baracoa, is the turnoff to **Playa Maguaná**, one of the best beaches in the area. Not many people drive onwards to **Moa**, further around the coast to the northwest. This arduous journey involves a fairly bumpy ride across a mostly dirt road, and is an alternative route to traveling back into central Cuba, if you are heading for Holguín or Guardalavaca perhaps. The initially scenic landscape of rustic villages and plantations becomes a harsh, sun-baked realm of burgundy-colored soil and metallic-like trickles of water. Here, three huge mines — including a brand-new mine that is a Cuban-Dutch joint-venture named after Che Guevara — are progressively mining Cuba's largest deposits of nickel. Not hugely recommended as an overland route.

On your way back to Baracoa from Playa Maguaná, take the turnoff to the **Cuchillas de Toa** ridge, which climbs for about two kilometers (just over one mile) to a lookout point offering dazzling views across the Alturas de Sagua-Baracoa, the Cuchillas de Toa and the Cuchillas de Moa, as well as El Yunque. All around, for some 220 sq km (85 sq miles), the surrounding virgin rainforest is a protected biosphere reserve, through which runs the Río Toa. Saved from the loggers, this reserve is one of the most beautiful, yet least visited in Cuba. It is the island's richest in endemic flora and fauna, with its many varying habitats and ecosystems. Those in the Cuban government who had the foresight to protect this area should be gratified that its success stories are many: the virtually extinct large ivory billed woodpecker seen almost nowhere else, lives here, as does the endangered royal woodpecker and Cuba's tiny endemic frog, which is no bigger than a fingernail. Just as tiny, multicolored polymite snails live here amid the forest floor's mosses and lichens.

As yet, there are few trails through the **Parque Nacional Alejandro de Humboldt**. Both Hotel El Castillo and Hotel Porto Santo arrange guided tours.

EAST OF BARACOA TO THE TIP OF CUBA

The most popular place to visit east of Baracoa is **Yumurí**, which lies 25 km (under 16 miles) away and is named after the river that snakes through it. It is a beautiful hourlong drive along a good road, which winds through the hills and then down to the coast, where you pass an array of idyllic little black sand beaches.

The village of Yumurí itself is very rustic and relaxed; the scenery here is breathtaking, with a towering backdrop of forested cliffs. The drive back is equally impressive for its vistas of El Yunque.

Should you wish to continue on (preferably in a four-wheel-drive vehicle) another 20 km (about 12 miles) on a bumpy dirt road brings you to **La Punta de Maisí**, the very easternmost tip of Cuba, 1,280 km (795 miles) from Havana, which has a small track leading to a lighthouse and a windswept, isolated village.

Baracoa offers views filled with gigantic ferns and exuberant vegetation.

The Islands

Although it is generally regarded as a single island, Cuba is in fact surrounded by over 4,000 (mostly tiny) islands and keys fringed with white sand and coral reefs. Most lie within four archipelagos that encircle the mainland: the Canarreos, to the island's southwest; the Jardines de la Reina to the southeast and the Sabana to the north, both reached off Ciego de Ávila and Camagüey provinces; and Los Colorados, off Pinar del Río Province. Most of those islands that can be visited fairly easily are already mentioned in this book within the relevant province or closest town from which they are most easily reached, such as Pinar del Río's Cayo Levisa; Ciego de Ávila's Cayo Coco and Cayo Guillermo.

However, two larger islands stand out as destinations in their own right, and for that reason they merit a chapter of their own: Isla de la Juventud and Cayo Largo. Both are located within the Archipiélago de los Canarreos (Archipelago of the Canaries), which is made up of some 350 islands in total, lying 100 km (62 miles) off the southwest coast of Cuba in the Gulf of Batabanó.

ISLA DE LA JUVENTUD

The second largest island in Cuba, the cauliflower-shaped Isla de la Juventud (Island of Youth) lies 138 km (just under 86 miles) southwest of Havana. It is 327 km (203 miles) long and spans 58 km (36 miles) at its widest point. Some 70,000 people live on what they term "La Isla," which is a special municipality, not a province.

It is an unlikely version of the so-called "paradisiacal island" — with its low-lying shrublands (the pine trees it was once named for have largely vanished) harboring wild boar, rodent-like *jutías* and indigenous crocodiles in its southern reaches. Yet many believe the island's offshore diving sites, especially those lying in the southeast, to be among the most outstanding and ecologically intact in the Caribbean.

BACKGROUND

Known formerly as Isla de los Pinos ("Island of Pines"), this island had a fearsome reputation during the seventeenth and eighteenth centuries as a hideout for pirates and roving

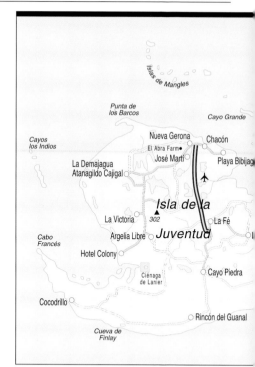

speculators from all latitudes, among them Sir Francis Drake and Henry Morgan. It was also a shady place of exile for runaway slaves. It seems from all accounts that when Robert Louis Stevenson wrote *Treasure Island*, he was writing about what is now the Isla de la Juventud, based on spectacular stories of buried treasure stolen from Spanish galleons, in addition to the usual rum-running, slave-trading and smuggling activities that went on here. The island's first inhabitants were the Siboney Indians, who left behind a series of elaborate cave paintings in a cave at Punta del Este, in the southeastern part of the island. However, when Christopher Columbus discovered the remote, pine-covered island in 1494, on his second voyage to America (baptizing it with the short-lived name, Evangelista) he noted that there were few indigenous tribespeople remaining.

In 1826, the Spanish decided to establish a penal colony here, where they could dispatch political prisoners along with dangerous criminals for a lengthy, perhaps indefinite stay. Cuba's famous independence leader, José Martí, was sent here while still in his late teens. In 1925, then-President Gerado Machado ordered the construction of his huge so-called

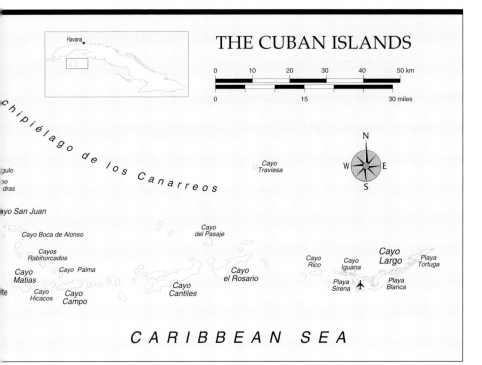

Havana

THE CUBAN ISLANDS

| 0 | 10 | 20 | 30 | 40 | 50 km |

| 0 | | 15 | | 30 miles |

Archipiélago de los Canarreos

gulo
oo
dras

yo San Juan

Cayo Boca de Alonso

Cayos
Rabihorcados

Cayo Matias

Cayo Palma

te   Cayo
Hicacos   Cayo
Campo

Cayo
Cantiles

Cayo
del Pasaje

Cayo
el Rosario

Cayo
Traviesa

N
W   E
S

Cayo
Rico

Cayo
Iguana

Cayo
Largo

Playa
Tortuga

Playa
Sirena

Playa
Blanca

CARIBBEAN SEA

Model Prison here. Later, its most famous prisoner was Fidel Castro, who was imprisoned here in a solitary cell for his attack on Moncada Barracks in Santiago de Cuba.

After the Revolution, Castro set about turning the island into a vast educational work camp for young people and thousands of "volunteer workers" were sent here to transform the newly named Isla de la Juventud into a major citrus-producing region.

In and around the main town of Nueva Gerona, over 60 secondary schools were built, typifying the extensive prefabricated complexes designed according to Cuba's centralized plan for education facilities throughout the country, and named for Cuban and Communist heroes, Soviet cosmonauts and revolutionary dates. During the 1970s, some 18,000 students studied here each year, many from Socialist-friendly African, Latin American and Asian countries that shared international programs with Cuba. Since Cuba has been in the grip of the Special Period, the number has declined to fewer than 10,000 students. Still, Nueva Gerona has a noticeably large population of young-faced students, many of them from Africa.

Today, much of the island is still wilderness. The chief attractions for foreign visitors are diving, fishing and exploring nature. This is also where Fidel Castro — a great outdoors enthusiast as well as an avid diver — has a country retreat, a modern ranch-style house in an isolated part of the island.

NUEVA GERONA

Isla de la Juventud's main town and administrative center is Nueva Gerona, located in the north of the island. Although it is not especially attractive, it has a piquant port atmosphere. It's liveliest around the downtown historical core of two-story, weather-beaten wooden houses with characterful verandahs, mostly centered along Calle 39 (Calle Martí). It is not recommended as a place to stay; noisy industrial quarries (mostly for marble) are located on the town's outskirts.

General Information
You will not find any facilities for visitors within the town of Nueva Gerona, beyond

PREVIOUS PAGES — LEFT: A stretch of Cuba's beautiful coastline. RIGHT: View of the tranquil Punta Francés beach.

the usual practical necessities. The **Banco de Crédito y Comercio** ((061) 24805 is at Calles 39 and 18. Try to attend to all your banking needs before you arrive, as the islands strong points do not necessarily include efficiency and cash availability. The car rental agency, **Havanautos** ((061) 24432 or 23256 is located at Calles 30 and 39, while an alternative agency, **Nacional**, is based out of the Villa Isla.

There is a **pharmacy** at the corner of Calles 39 and 24, and a **police station** at Calles 41 and 54.

political prisoners. The prison closed in 1966 and is now a museum, which is open from Tuesday to Sunday, 9 am to 5 pm.

Another museum now dedicated to a once-imprisoned leader, is the **Finca El Abra**, located a short distance from Nueva Gerona on the Carretera de Siguanea which runs along the coast southwest to the Hotel Colony. It was owned by a Catalonian farmer who convinced the local authorities that he could keep the youthful rebel under his charge, rather than sending him into a forced labor camp. José Martí arrived here in Octo-

The **Cubalse Supermarket** at Calle 35 between Calles 30 and 32 is the best place to stock up on provisions. It is closed on Sunday.

What to See and Do

A road east of town brings you to one of Cuba's oddities, the **Presidio Modelo**, or "Model Prison," completed in 1926 and now a national monument. This foreboding complex of four enormous circular structures with interior rings of cells was based on the design on a penitentiary in Joliet, Illinois in the United States, allowing prison authorities to see and control every aspect of the inmates' existence while remaining unseen themselves. It was designed to house some 6,000 inmates, among them Cuba's most dangerous criminals and

ber 1870, and spent two months here. You can see some of his personal belongings and the room where he stayed. It is open Tuesday to Sunday, 9 am to 5 pm.

Where to Stay and Eat

If for some reason you long to sleep near town rather than on the beach then your best option is the inexpensive **Isla de la Juventud Village** ((061) 23290 or 24486, Carretera Nueva Gerona-La Fé, a motel located two kilometers outside Nueva Gerona on the road to the fishing village of La Fé. This Gaviota-run establishment has 20 rooms and a swimming pool.

There are several good restaurants in Nueva Gerona. You'll also find a number of *paladares* along Calle 39. **El Río** ((061) 23217, Carretera Nueva Gerona-La Fé, between Calles 32 and 35, specializes in excellent Cuban fish and seafood dishes. **El Corderito** ((061) 22400, Calle 39 at the corner of Calle 22, next to El Cochinito, features lamb dishes as well as typical Creole food, while **El Cochinito** ((061) 22809, Calle 39 at the corner of Calle 24, has made roast pork and Creole dishes their specialty.

Nightlife

Due to the number of foreign students on the island, Nueva Gerona has a number of venues which play live music, and some which stage cabaret performances. All located on or just off Calle 39, **Cabaret El Patio** ((061) 22346, **Café de Cuba** and **Café Nuevo** all have live salsa bands during weekends.

You may wish to check listings for upcoming events at the **Casa de la Cultura** ((061) 23591, at Calles 37 and 24. The Isla's best band — **La Tumbita Crilla** — often perform their version of *sucu-sucu*, the local dance rhythm, at this venue.

THE WEST COAST

Elsewhere on the island, the **Hotel Colony** on the west coast is one of Cuba's most popular diving resorts and the base of the island's **International Diving Center**, which is fully equipped for serious diving and has one of Cuba's few decompression chambers, as well as a pool for practice dives.

From here, the hotel arranges diving excursions to various offshore locations, notably along the stretch between **Punta Francés** and **Punta de Pedernales**, on the southwestern tip of the island, which is the so-called **Costa de los Pirates**. Here, the offshore waters are lined with spectacular dive spots, including the Gulf Cliff, which teems with exotic coral formations, turtles and many species of fish. This offshore area is a marine reserve, and by law, can only be accessed if you are with an official Cuban guide.

Where to Stay

Hotel El Colony ((061) 98181 or 98282, Carretera de Siguanea, is undoubtedly the best place to stay on the Isla de la Juventud. This colorful Retro-style hotel dates from a 1950s effort to attract foreign tourists. With its blue post-art deco edges, it looks straight out of South Beach Miami. Rates are moderate. It sits on a superb beach to the southwest of the island, 41 km (just over 25 miles) from Nueva Gerona. It has 77 rooms overlooking the sea, a swimming pool, a nightclub, a good restaurant and facilities for other watersports besides the excellent facilities offered by its International Diving Center. Overbooking can be a problem. Many guests arrive on special diving packages, inclusive of all transport, accommodation and dives.

Wings of the World toll-free in us (800) 465-8687, 1200 William Street, Suite 706, Buffalo, New York 14240, organizes week-long scuba diving tours here from the United States.

From the Hotel Colony, a taxi to Nueva Gerona or to the island's airport costs about US$30 each way.

PUNTA DEL ESTE

You can also seek out the island's seven pre-Columbian caves, which contain ancient cave paintings thought to have been executed by the Siboney Indians. Most of them are located at Punta del Este at the southeast point of the island. The best known caves were discovered by a shipwreck survivor in 1910, and are notable for their mysterious black and red pictographs and symbols, with some 253 pictographs in total. Some speculate that the paintings may represent an ancient solar calendar. They are regarded

OPPOSITE: Statue dedicated to a record-winning milk cow, Isla de la Juventud. ABOVE: Isla de la Juventud snack-bar sign.

as the most important cave paintings in the Caribbean. You can reach the caves by road from **Punta Piedra**, but many of the tracks are unmarked and it is best to go there with the guide.

The caves are located 59 km (almost 37 miles) southeast of Nueva Gerona. You'll need a car or a taxi to reach them.

CRIADERO COCODRILO

Another attraction you may find interesting to seek out in Isla de la Juventud is the Cri-

Pinar del Río and Nueva Gerona. Nueva Gerona's **Rafael Cabrera Airport** ((061) 24259 or 22531, is located 15 km (just over nine miles) south of town.

By sea, there are various options — passenger hydrofoil, ferry or car barge — all reaching Nueva Gerona's ferry terminal from **Surgidero de Batabanó**, only 60 km (37 miles) south of Havana. The hydrofoil service runs between Nueva Gerona and Surgidero de Batabanó twice daily; the journey takes two hours. You can catch a connecting train to Surgidero de Batabanó from

adero Cocodrilo, a crocodile breeding farm, 30 km (almost 19 miles) south of Nueva Gerona on the coast. Here, more than 500 crocodiles live and breed amid a small settlement of wire pens. Ask at the Villa Isla and the Hotel Colony about tours.

HOW TO GET THERE

Make sure you bring your passport, which you will need to clear customs and immigration when arriving at Isla de la Juventud.

By air, Cubana de Aviación flies twice daily from Havana, and the smaller airlines, Aerocaribbean and Aerogaviota also make charter flights here from Havana and Varadero, while Aerotaxi flights operate between

Havana's Estación de Ferrocarriles, however, this service itself takes up to three hours and is frequently delayed. Call the Surgidero de Batabanó ferry terminal ((062) 85355 or 83845 for hydrofoil, ferry or barge reservations.

CAYO LARGO

The undisputed queen of Cuban beach resorts, Cayo Largo is as close to most people's concept of a tropical island paradise as it gets. With its perfect snow-white sands, dazzlingly clear turquoise waters and comfortable resort hotels, this is a far more beautiful place for the relentless pursuit of beach lounging and watersports than, for example,

Varadero. It is, however, as un-Cuban a place as you are likely to find in Cuba, and Cuban tourists are not allowed to come here, adding a surreal sense of tourist apartheid.

BACKGROUND

Situated at the eastern end of the Archipiélago de los Canarreos, 177 km (about 110 miles) southeast of Havana and 114 km (about 71 miles) east of the Isla de la Juventud.

Cayo Largo is only 27 km (about 17 miles) long and has been developed exclusively for

tourism. Until recently, the island was the uninhabited habitat for colonies of migratory birds, including flamingos, pelicans and storks, as well as sea turtles and iguanas. Apparently the Cuban government has pledged not to develop this ecological preserve too much or too fast. The maximum number of hotel rooms has been set at 3,000. Already, the development seems quite enough for such a pristine environment, so try to go soon before more construction mars the ambience.

GENERAL INFORMATION

The Complejo Isla del Sur tourist complex has an information desk and the island's

only medical center. Opposite the complex, you will find a telecommunications center, which includes a post office, international telephone and fax office.

WHAT TO SEE AND DO

Cayo Largo has some of the best beaches in the Caribbean — wonderful for diving, fishing, swimming and lazing about — and fewer than 10 hotels along its main seven-kilometer-long (just over four-mile) beach, **Playa Blanca**.

You can explore the island's many beaches, some of which can only be reached after a long walk along the shore. **Playa Sirena** at the western tip of the island, is the most popular swimming beaches, blessed with warm, sheltered waters, while **Playa Tortuga** at the eastern end of the island is home to a seasonal colony of sea turtles. Excursions can include a boat ride to nearby **Cayo Iguana**, a nature reserve with hordes of meter-long iguanas, or to the archipelago's other nature reserve, **Cayo Cantilles**, where there are monkeys along with other wildlife.

Facilities offered by the hotels include watersports; yacht and boat rental; bicycle,

OPPOSITE and ABOVE: Crocodile breeding farm on Isla de la Juventud.

moped and car rental — the road through the key runs from the marina past the airport and hotels along the beach and is only 10 km (six miles) long, so you may want to think twice about renting a car. Horseback riding, scuba diving and fishing (both saltwater fly and deep-sea fishing) can be arranged through your hotel or at the marina. Costs for these activities are not inexpensive, but quite reasonable by international standards. The hotels offer a range of restaurants and welcome outside guests. There are a couple of shops near the hotels on Playa Blanca selling basic provisions.

WHERE TO STAY AND EAT

Complejo Isla del Sur ℂ (05) 48111 FAX (05) 48160 is made up of a group of several different hotels (listed below) landscaped around the island's southern Playa Blanca and Playa Lindamar beaches, all operated by the Gran Caribe group. You can book an all-inclusive package if you wish, or book a room and pay for food, watersports and diving excursions separately.

The Complejo Isla del Sur has extensive facilities for diving and watersports, and you can rent bicycles to explore the beachfront roads. Buses run regularly from the complex to the marina stopping at each of the hotels and at the small airport.

Expensive

The only conventional-style hotel is the **Hotel Isla del Sur**, which has 59 rooms set in a two-story building built behind the beach, and was the first hotel to be built on the island. It has a swimming pool in its central courtyard, and has a complex of hotel bars, a buffet restaurant, an information desk and various shops. Guests staying at other hotels come here to book many organized activities, such as scuba diving, horseback riding and deep-sea fishing trips.

Hotel Pelicano ℂ (05) 48333 FAX (05) 48160, has 324 rooms, all with sea-facing terraces or balconies. Facilities include several restaurants, a discotheque, a swimming pool and a gym. Activities include watersports, volleyball and basketball. It has a car, moped and bicycle rental office.

Moderate

Within the Complejo Isla del Sur, you have a choice of four other hotels. All have en-suite shower rooms, air conditioning, satellite television and refrigerators. Also within the complex are a variety of restaurants and outdoor bars, some right on the beach.

The **Villa Coral** complex is made up of 60 simple but pleasant rooms landscaped along a coral pathway above the beach. The **Villa Iguana** has 52 brightly painted, two-story bungalows. The **Villa Capricho**, the most secluded of the properties, has 75 thatched *bohíos*, with sand verandahs facing the sea. They are perfect if you are looking for rustic accommodation, with hammocks and shady porches. Its **Blue Marlin Restaurant** is Cayo Largo's most attractive and popular

restaurant. The **Hotel Lindamar** has 63 air-conditioned, thatched, natural-wood *cabañas*, situated within a few yards of the beach.

How to Get There

There are daily Cubana de Aviación flights from Havana and Varadero, and weekly flights from Camagüey and Santiago de Cuba. Flights to the island are also operated by Aerocaribbean and Aerogaviota. A growing number of direct charter flights have begun operating from Canada, Mexico, the Grand Cayman Islands and Italy.

Because Cuba has designated Cayo Largo as a free port (with full customs facilities and duty-free), if you arrive in Cayo Largo on an international charter flight, you do not (at time of writing) need a visa, as long as you do not plan to travel to other parts of Cuba. You will be granted a 30-day visa upon arrival for a US$20 fee.

Outdoor boxing matches are held in a Nueva Gerona town park.

Travelers' Tips

THE TOURISM BOOM

Until 1959, Cuba was a hot destination for tourists, especially Americans. After the Revolution, tourism was condemned as the epitome of Batista-era decadence. Only since the early 1990s has Cuba welcomed the industry back like a long-lost lover, a shift towards revolutionary pragmatism forced by the collapse of the Soviet Union, which left the island badly in need of hard currency. Although the new Ministry of Tourism was only set up in

1994, tourism has become the top priority sector within the Cuban economy, destined to become the country's most important source of revenue. Meanwhile a hotel construction boom is sweeping the island.

Now, in the island where socialism meets salsa, communism with a dash of capitalism is becoming a heady brew. Upwards of two million international visitors a year have been arriving in Cuba, mostly from Canada, Latin America and Europe, particularly Spain, Italy, Germany, Holland and France. Even Americans are coming and for them, spending money here is a serious offence back in the United States, punishable by as much as a quarter of a million dollar fine under the Trading with the Enemy Act.

Spanish companies are the major source of capital for tourism projects, having pioneered joint-venture hotels on the island. It's estimated that Spanish companies have already poured more than US$300 million into Cuba. The Grupo Sol (the Sol Meliá chain), Europe's third-largest hotel chain, has been creating joint-ventures with the island's largest tourism organization, the government-owned Cubanacán. Among them, are the Meliá Cohiba in Havana, the Meliá Varadero, the Meliá Las Américas and the Sol Palmeras in Varadero, all five-star hotels.

Cubanacán also has joint-ventures with other foreign companies, including Spain's Barcelo Group, LTI International Hotels of Germany, the Amsterdam-based Golden Tulip group, Canada's Delta International and Commonwealth Hospitality chains, France's Accor and Club Med organizations, and Jamaica's swish Superclub resorts. By the end of 2001, Cuba could boast of 24 hotel joint-ventures with a total of 3,700 guest rooms in operation and another 11,900 on the drawing board — not too shabby for a nation that had virtually zero tourism arrivals a decade ago.

Several Cuban chains also run hotels, in some cases contracting out management to foreign partners. The top domestic operators are Gran Caribe (four and five star hotels), Horizontes (two and three stars) and a low-budget, domestic tourism chain called Islazul, which manages some of the island's most dreadful hotels. The Gaviota group is perhaps the most unusual of the Cuban tourist enterprises — a subsidiary of the Cuban Ministry of Defense, it often uses former armed-forces facilities, and offers specialist holidays involving, for example, hunting or fishing.

The state-owned company Habaguanex develops and runs hotels, restaurants and shops and offices in La Habana Vieja: a mini-capitalist empire which brings in millions, a percentage of which goes to reinvesting in its projects; the rest goes to the state.

It's helpful to understand the backdrop to the tourist industry in Cuba — it explains

PREVIOUS PAGES — LEFT: Tourist stops for a roadside shot in Baracoa. RIGHT: Local cookout in Santiago de Cuba Province. ABOVE: A resort hotel in Baracoa. OPPOSITE: A view from La Habana Vieja.

why you can expect somewhat elevated prices and why there is such a wide disparity between the dollar economy and the Cuban peso economy. An average meal served in a tourist restaurants can represent more than the average Cuban earns in a month.

It is also helpful to remember that the industry is new, and prices tend to change with disconcerting regularity. Cuba is only learning the tourism business, so you cannot always expect the same precision of information or thoroughness of service as you may find at more visited destinations. To

safe airline by the independent web site AirSafe.com based on eight crashes in 30 years. Since then, the airline has made a concerted effort to upgrade its fleet by purchasing or leasing newer aircraft including DC-10s and Airbus 320s. However, there are still Soviet-era aircraft (Ilyushin IL-62s) in operation on some routes. Cubana provides service from a number of overseas destinations including London, Paris, Rome, Frankfurt, Milan and Madrid in Europe; Montreal and Toronto in Canada; Mexico City, San José (Costa

enjoy your travels in Cuba, we recommend a dash of tolerance combined with a good dose of humor.

GETTING THERE

BY AIR

Almost all visitors arrive by air. Havana's **Aeropuerto Internacional José Martí ☎ (07)** 335177, 335660 or 454644 is generally where most flights arrive, however there are also international airports at Varadero, Cienfuegos, Camagüey, Holguín, Manzanillo, Santiago de Cuba and Cayo Largo.

Cubana de Aviación is the national airline. In 1999, it was rated the world's least

Rica), Panama City and Guatemala City in Central America; Bogotá, Buenos Aires, Caracas, Quito, Lima and Montevideo in South America; Kingston, Montego Bay, Santo Domingo, Martinique and Guadeloupe in the Caribbean.

However, Cubana is not your only option. A number of other airlines now offer regular service to Cuba from major destinations in Europe, North America, South America and the Caribbean including British Airways, Air France, Lufthansa, Iberia, Mexicana, Air Jamaica and Martinair (see list below). Be advised that many of the European and Canadian services are charter flights that go directly to an airport near a large beach resort rather than stop in Havana.

United States citizens traveling to Cuba have two flight options: direct charter flights from Miami, New York or Los Angeles (assuming you qualify under a general or specific license from the Treasury Department); or flights via a third country — Mexico (Cancún, Mexico City, Monterrey or Tijuana), Jamaica (Kingston or Montego Bay), Canada (Toronto or Montreal), Panama (Panama City) or the Bahamas (Nassau). Although you can call airlines such as Mexicana and Air Jamaica in the United States to inquire about flight availability and prices, you will need to book your flight by contacting the airline or a travel agency at their office outside the United States.

From Australia and New Zealand, the most direct route is to fly via Los Angeles, where you can connect with the overnight Air Jamaica service to Montego Bay and then onto Havana, or through Mexico. South Africans also have a long haul; the easiest way is through London, Paris or Madrid.

Airlines serving Cuba include:

Aero Caribe ((07) 333621 or 334423 in Havana or (098) 842000 in Cancún, Mexico; WEB SITE www.aerocaribe.com.

Aerolíneas Argentina ((07) 334949 EXTENSION 2320 in Havana TOLL-FREE IN ARGENTINA (800) 2228-6527.

Aeromexico TOLL-FREE IN MEXICO (800) 366-5400 or ((55) 5448-0990 in Mexico City; (664) 683-2700 or 831044 in Tijuana; or (81) 356-7455 or 340-8760 in Monterrey; WEB SITE www.aeromexico.com.

Air Europe ((07) 666743 or 666745 in Havana; TOLL-FREE IN ITALY (0800) or (02) 6711-8228 in Milan; WEB SITE www.aireurope.it.

Air France ((07) 662642, 662644 or 662634 in Havana; (0802) 802802 in France; WEB SITE www.airfrance.com.fr.

Air Jamaica ((07) 662447, 334098 or 662448 in Havana; TOLL-FREE IN NORTH AMERICA AND THE CARIBBEAN (800) 523-5585; or (1) 952-4300 in Montego Bay; or (1) 922-4660 in Kingston; WEB SITE www.airjamaica.com.

British Airways ((07) 334949 in Havana; (0845) 773-3377 in Great Britain; WEB SITE www.britishairways.com.

Copa ((07) 331503, 333657 or 331758 in Havana; or (0) 265-7814 or 265-7825 in Panama; WEB SITE www.copaair.com.

Iberia ((07) 335064 or 334743 in Havana; (902) 400500 in Spain; WEB SITE www.iberia.com.

Lacsa/Taca ((07) 333187 or 333114 in Havana; (296-9353, 232-3555 or 296-0909 in Costa Rica; WEB SITE www.taca.com.

LTU ((07) 333524 or (07) 333525 in Havana; or (0211) 941-8466 in Germany; WEB SITE www.ltu.com.

Lufthansa ((01803) 803803 in Germany; WEB SITE www.lufthansa.com.

Martinair ((07) 334364 in Havana; or (020) 601-1767 in Holland; WEB SITE www.martinair.com.

Mexicana ((07) 333531, 333527 or 334949 in Havana; (55) 5250-1792 in Mexico City; WEB SITE www.mexicana.com.mx.

The following airlines have their Havana reservations and ticketing offices in the Cuban airline building at the corner of Calle 23 (between Calles Infanta and P) in Vedado: Aero Caribe, Aerolíneas Argentinas, British Airways, Copa, Iberia; LTU, Martinair and Mexicana. Air France and Lacsa are in the Hotel Habana Libre; Air Jamaica in the Meliá Cohiba. Air Europe has its office in the Lonja del Comercio in Habana Vieja.

See TAKING A TOUR, page 70 in YOUR CHOICE, for a list of travel agencies that can help arrange your flights and obtain your Cuban tourist card.

OPPOSITE: Schoolchildren in a bus on Isla de la Juventude. ABOVE: Naïve painting by unknown artist.

It is important to check with your Cuba-bound airline that you can buy a Cuban tourist card once you arrive in the airport from which you will be traveling onwards to Cuba. In both Mexico City and Cancún airports for example, the Mexicana office can sell you the necessary Cuban tourist card for US$15 (see ARRIVING (AND LEAVING), below).

BY SEA

Due to the United States blockade, very few cruise ships ever call into Cuba's ports. The

of Youth, Grand Cayman, Cozumel and Mérida before returning to Havana.

Another possibility is a small cruise ship called the *Riviera One*, which sails between Cancún and Havana on seven-day/six-night cruises. For information and reservations contact the Canadian office ((416) 240-7700 TOLL-FREE IN US AND CANADA (800) 419-1635 FAX (416) 240-7701 WEB SITE www.forcuba .com, 2011 Lawrence Avenue West, Toronto, Ontario M9N 3V3.

If you plan to enter Cuba by private yacht or cruiser, you don't have to arrange a prior

Toronto-based Cuba Cruise Company was scheduled to start regular twice-weekly "educational" cruises between the Bahamas and Cuba in early 2001 but decided to shelve the project after a series of anonymous bomb threats and other intimidation, presumably from hardline Cuban-Americans opposed to further contacts with the Castro regime.

However, several other cruise ship companies have put Cuba on their itineraries. Athens-based **Festival Cruises** WEB SITE www.festivalcruises.com or www.festival.gr, launched a "Cuba Delights" cruise service in the winter of 2001-2002. The 1,200-passenger MV Mistral departs Havana weekly on a roundtrip voyage that includes the Isle

visa, but you will have to purchase a Cuban tourist card if you plan to stay longer than 72 hours. As you approach Cuban waters — 20 km (12 miles) away — it is essential that you make radio contact with the Cuban port authorities over channel 16 (VHF) or the National Coast Network over 2760 HF (SSB) before you cross the water boundary. Given the tense situation between Cuba and the United States, it is vital that if you don't make contact immediately, keep trying at regular intervals. You will then need to follow their instructions for clearance. When approaching, you need to give the name of your yacht, type and color of vessel, flag, port of registration, last port of call, estimated time of arrival and number of people on board. If possible, you should try to fax your target port of entry in advance.

Cuba's official points of entry are the Marina Hemingway in Havana, Marina Puertosol Dársena and Marina Gaviota in Varadero, María La Gorda International Scuba Diving Center in Pinar del Río, La Marina Marlin Cayo Coco in Ciego de Ávila, Base Nautica Gaviota Bahía de Naranjo in Holguín, Marina Marlin Punta Gorda in Santiago de Cuba, Marina Puertosol in Cienfuegos and Marina Puertosol Cayo Largo in Los Canarreos Archipelago.

ARRIVING (AND LEAVING)

Aside from a valid passport, you need a tourist card or *tarjeta de turista* to enter Cuba. Tourist cards are available from any Cubanacán-affiliated travel agents, Cuban tourist offices or consulates. You can also purchase them from the relevant airline office at the airport where you are making a connecting flight on that same carrier onwards to Cuba. In theory you can purchase a tourist card on arrival in Cuba, but in practice this may cause problems and it is recommended that you make this arrangement before you arrive. Cost varies: Air Jamaica charges US$15 for a Cuban tourist card issued at Montego Bay airport, whereas COPA charges US$30 for a card issued at Panama City airport.

The tourist card is valid for 30 days, and the date of departure is filled in by the official according to the return date marked on your ticket.

Although the tourist card is all most visitors require, you may need to apply for a special tourist visa if you intend to stay with a Cuban family (although this is the policy, it is unpredictably enforced), if you are intending to do business, to study or to do research, or if you are undertaking journalism activities.

For lost passports while in Cuba, contact your embassy or consulate. If you do not have diplomatic representation in Cuba, you will have to throw yourself on the mercy of your country's nearest (friendly) neighbor or political ally. For example, if your country is a Commonwealth country, excepting Australia and Canada, you should contact the British Embassy. However, Australia is represented by the Mexican Embassy. If you are an American who entered Cuba illegally and then has lost your passport or had it stolen, don't panic unnecessarily. You have no choice but to go to the United States Interests Section in Havana (see FOREIGN REPRESENTATION IN CUBA, below). The State Department warns that it may be difficult to assist distressed United States citizens, should emergencies arise. But they are known to be sympathetic to Americans who have lost their passport. However, you may face problems later — with United States Customs and Immigration or the Treasury Department — when you return to the United States.

ENTRY FOR AMERICANS

According to the Cuban government, about 200,000 United States citizens travel to Cuba each year. About a quarter of them (50,000) do so without permission from the United States government. Contrary to popular belief, Washington does not prohibit Americans from traveling to Cuba. It merely prohibits Americans spending money there under regulations set by the Treasury Department's Office of Foreign Assets Control (OFAC). Additionally, the Helms-Burton Act has raised the potential penalties on Americans who go to Cuba as tourists to US$250,000 in criminal fines and US$55,000 in civil fines.

Under the Clinton administration and previous White House occupants, these regulations were rarely enforced. However, the situation changed dramatically after George W. Bush took office in January of 2001. Bowing to pressure from rightwing Republicans and Florida's hardline Cuban immigrants, President Bush launched a crackdown on Americans traveling to Cuba. In 2000 (the last year of the Clinton administration), OFAC sent letters of inquiry to 188 United States citizens who had apparently violated the travel ban; during the first two months of the Bush administration crackdown, OFAC dispatched 443 letters. The letters ask the recipients to explain their reasons for traveling to Cuba without an official "license" from

The Havana Harbor.

the Treasury Department and to verify that they didn't spend any of their own money during the trip by showing proof that their visit was fully "hosted" (paid for) by a Cuban family or organization. Those found guilty of violating the travel ban are being assessed an average fine of about US$7,500, but fines are very often bargained down to between US$700 and $2,500.

If you receive an inquiry letter from OFAC, it's wise to seek legal representation. Two organizations specialize in Cuba-related matters: the **Center for Constitutional Rights** ((212) 614-6420 or 614-6430, in New York City; and the **Cuba Subcommittee of the National Lawyer's Guild** ((414) 273-1040, in Milwaukee, Wisconsin. The former performs legal advocacy work for Americans facing fines; the latter can put you in touch with lawyers who specialize in OFAC or Treasury Department cases.

According to the United States Travel Advisory Consular Information Sheet, attempts to enter or exit Cuba illegally (without the permission of Cuban authorities) are punishable by jail terms of up to five years. However, this particular law is primarily intended to keep anti-Castro, Cuban-Americans and their sympathizers from staging unauthorized, clandestine operations in Cuba.

Despite the ban, a number of Americans qualify for "general license" to spend money for Cuban travel, which means they don't have to seek prior permission from the United States government. These include:

Academics and students from institutions that hold a Cuba license from the Treasury Department; people with close relatives in Cuba; journalists (on assignment) who are regularly employed by a news-gathering organization like a television network, newspaper or magazine; United States government workers and Americans who are employed by international organizations like the United Nations who are traveling on official business; athletes (amateur and semi-professional) participating in an official event organized by an international sports body.

If you don't qualify under any of these categories, United States citizens can apply for a "special license" in the following categories: freelance journalism, research work, humanitarian assistance, individuals trying to identify commercial opportunities in Cuba, and people attending public performances, workshops, exhibitions or clinics. However, the OFAC cautions that special licenses are not automatic. For more information on Cuba travel licenses, contact the **Office of Foreign Asset Control** ((202) 622-2480 FAX (202) 622-1657 WEB SITE www.ustreas.gov/ofac, United States Department of the Treasury, 1500 Pennsylvania Avenue NW, Treasury Annex, Washington, DC 20220. Even if you have permission to travel to Cuba, OFAC mandates that United States citizens must spend no more than US$185 while in Cuba. Licensed travelers can return to the United States with US$100 worth of souvenirs and other purchases. However, there is no limit to the amount of "informational material" (books, magazines, etc.) or artwork that you can bring back. Save your receipts!

If you qualify for a general and specific license, Marazul Tours in New Jersey (see TAKING A TOUR, page 70 in YOUR CHOICE) can arrange flight and hotel reservations. You will have to apply for a Cuban visa or tourist card from the Cuban Special Interests Section in Washington, DC.

Assuming that you're not an academic or a journalist and you're granny doesn't live in Havana, the easiest way to visit Cuba legally to book one of the many special-interest tours organized each year by United States-based travel agents. These tours are usually based around a specific activity — ecology, sports, culture, performing arts, etc. — that falls within the special license category (see TAKING A TOUR, page 70 in YOUR CHOICE).

If you do decide to travel illegally to Cuba, please note that Cuban immigration normally stamps your tourist card rather than your actual passport. However, that doesn't mean that you're out of the woods. The Treasury Department is now using other means to identify United States citizens who defy the travel ban — including clandestine "surveillance" at overseas airports with Havana connections. If you have American-issued credit cards, you will find them nearly impossible to use in Cuba. See MONEY, below, for more details.

If you want to extend your permit to stay in Cuba, change your immigration status or marry a Cuban, you should contact the

Consultoria Juridica Internacional ((07) 242490 or 246294 FAX (07) 249469, Calle 16 no. 314, at the corner of Avenida 3, Miramar Playa, Havana.

CUSTOMS

Along with personal belongings, Cuban customs allow visitors to bring in one of each of the following: photographic equipment, binoculars, baby stroller, musical instrument, tape recorder, portable computer, tent, fishing equipment, bicycle, canoe, kayak or surf board (under five meters/16.4 ft long) and other sports equipment (not firearms), as well as gifts that do not exceed the value of 100 Cuban pesos and up to 10 kilograms

(22 lb) of medicine (excluding blood-based or veterinary medicines). If you are over 18, you can bring in three liters (quarts) of liquor, plus a choice of either 200 cigarettes, 50 cigars or 250 grams of uncut tobacco. Be prepared to declare all the items above (although it is likely you will not have to); and if so, they will have to be produced as you leave the country.

The import of any flora and fauna specimens, live animals, unprocessed food (including fresh fruits and vegetables) is restricted. Items that are forbidden to import into Cuba include narcotics, explosives, motorized vehicles, pre-recorded video cas-

Locals play dominoes on a Santiago de Cuba street.

settes and any pornographic or "morally offensive" material.

TAX

Departure tax is generally included in your ticket price, however, you may find that you have to pay US$20 when you depart.

EMBASSIES AND CONSULATES

CUBAN REPRESENTATION ABROAD

Australia Cuban Consulate-General ((02) 9311-4611 FAX (02) 9311-5512, 18 Manwaring Avenue, Marouba, NSW 2035.
Belgium Cuban Embassy ((02) 343-0020 FAX (02) 343-9195, Robert Jonesstraat 77, 1180 Brussels.
Canada Cuban Embassy ((613) 563-0141 FAX (613) 563-0068, 388 Main Street, Ottawa, Ontario K1S 1E3, Canada.
    Cuban Consulate-General ((416) 234-8181 FAX (416) 234-2754, 5353 Dundas Street West, Suite 401, Toronto, Ontario M9B 6H8, Canada.
    Cuban Consulate-General and Trade Commission ((514) 843-8897 FAX (514) 845-1063, 1415 Pine Avenue West, Montreal, Quebec H3B 1B2.
France Embassy ((01) 45675535 FAX (01) 45658092, 16 Rue de Presles, 75015 Paris.
Germany Embassy ((0228) 3090 FAX (0228) 309244, Kennedy Allee 22, 53175 Bonn.
Italy Cuban Embassy ((06) 575-5984 FAX (06) 574-5445, Via Licinia 7, 00153 Roma.
MEXICO Cuban Embassy ((55) 280-8039 FAX (55) 280-0839, Presidente Masarik 554, Colonia Polanco, 11560 México DF.
Netherlands Cuban Embassy ((070) 360-6061 FAX (070) 364-7586, Mauritskade 49, 2514 HG, Den Haag.
    Cuban Consulate (/FAX (010) 412-8970 Stationsplein 45, 3013 AK Rotterdam.
South Africa ((012) 346-2215 FAX (012) 346-2216, 45 Mackenzie Street, Brooklyn 0181, Pretoria.
Spain Cuban Embassy ((91) 359-2500 FAX (91) 359-6145, Paseo de La Habana 194, Pinilla 28036, Madrid.
United Kingdom Cuban Embassy ((020) 7240-2488 FAX (020) 7836-2602, 167 High Holburn, London WC1V 6PA.

United States Cuban Special Interests Section ((202) 797-8518 FAX (202) 986-7283, 2630 16th Street NW, Washington, DC 20009.

FOREIGN REPRESENTATION IN CUBA

Austrian Embassy ((07) 242825, Calle 4 no. 101 at Avenida 1, Miramar.
Belgian Embassy ((07) 242410, Avenida 5 no. 7408 at Calle 76, Miramar Playa.
British Embassy ((07) 241717 or 331286 FAX (007) 248104, Calle 34 no. 702 at Avenida 7, Miramar.
Canadian Embassy ((07) 242517, Calle 30 no. 518 at Avenida 7, Miramar.
French Embassy ((07) 242132 or 242308, Calle 14 no. 312, between Avenidas 3 and 5, Miramar.
Italian Embassy ((07) 333334 or 333376, Paseo no. 606, between Calle 25 and 27, Vedado.
Japanese Embassy ((07) 243355 or 243508, Centro de Negocios Miramar, Avenida 3 at the corner of Calle 80, Edificio 1, Fifth Floor, Miramar.
Mexican Embassy ((07) 242383 or 242666, Calle 12 no. 518 at Avenida 7, Miramar.
Netherlands Embassy ((07) 242512 or 242511, Calle 8 no. 307 between Avenidas 3 and 5, Miramar.
Spanish Embassy ((07) 338029 or 338025, Carcel 51 at the corner of Calle Zulueta, Habana Vieja.
Swedish Embassy ((07) 242831, Avenida 31 no. 1411, between Calles 14 and 18, Miramar.
Swiss Embassy ((07) 242611, Avenida 5 no. 2005, between Calles 20 and 22, Miramar.
United States Special Interests Section ((07) 334401 or 333551, Calzada between Calles L and M, Vedado.

TOURIST INFORMATION

ABROAD

Canada Cuba Tourism Board ((416) 362-0700 FAX (416) 362-6799, 55 Queen Street East, Suite 705, Toronto, Ontario M5C 1R6.
    Bureau de Tourisme de Cuba ((514) 857-8004 FAX (514) 875-8006, 440 Boulevard René Lévesque Ouest, Bureau 1402, Montreal, Quebec H2Z 1V7.

Sunset on Isla de la Juventud.

France Office de Tourisme de Cuba ☏ (01) 4538-9010 FAX (01) 4538-9930, 280 Boulevard Raspail, Paris 75014.

Germany Cuban Tourist Board ☏ (069) 288-322 FAX (069) 296-664, An der Hauptwachb 7, 60313 Frankfurt.

Italy Ufficio di Promozione ed Informazione Turistica di Cuba ☏ (02) 66981463 FAX (02) 6738-0725, Via General Fara 30, terzo piano, 20124 Milano.

Mexico Cuban Tourist Board ☏ (55) 255-5897 FAX (55) 255-5866, Insurgentes Sur 421, Complejo Aristos, Edificios B, Local 310, México 06100 DF.

Spain Officina de Promoción e Información Turística de Cuba ☏ (91) 411-3097 FAX (91) 564-5804, Paseo de la Habana 27, Madrid 28036.

United Kingdom Cuban Tourism Office ☏ (0171) 240-6655 FAX (020) 7836-9265, 167 High Holborn, London WCL.

IN CUBA

Infotur ☏ (07) 333333, 247036 or 240624 WEB SITE www.infotur.cu, the information wing of the Ministry of Tourism, has several walk-up tourist offices in Havana including Calle Obispo, between Calles Bernaza and Villegas in Habana Vieja; Calle 28 no. 303 in Miramar; Avenida 5 (at Calle 112) in Playa; and all three terminals at Aeropuerto Internacional José Martí. Infotur stocks brochures and maps, and can make hotel, car rental or tour reservations. The staff can be extremely helpful.

Asistur ☏ (07) 338920, 338527 or 338339 FAX (07) 338087 WEB SITE www.asistur.cubaweb.cu, Paseo de Martí (Prado) 212, La Habana Vieja, is a Cuban company specializing in assistance to international visitors. They can help if you require any of the following: emergency medical or dental treatment, repatriation, legal aid, currency exchange, travel insurance, help with tracing lost baggage and acquiring new travel documents.

Less urgently, they can also help you with tourist information and making reservations for tours, hotels, restaurants, nightclubs, excursions, transportation and performances.

You can also contact the main office of Cuba's largest tourist organization, **Cubanacán S.A.** ☏ (07) 280607 or 286063 FAX (07) 280107, WEB SITE www.cubanacan.cu, Calle 160 and Avenida 11, Playa, Miramar, Havana.

MONEY

As a tourist in Cuba, you will be expected to pay everything in United States dollars — few hotels, restaurants, shops, businesses and taxis accept anything else. It may seem rather ironic that the same United States dollars were illegal until 1993. In fact, Cuba has a triple-currency system: the official Cuban peso or *moneda nacional*, made up of 100 centavos and ostensibly linked to the United States dollar at the rate of one to one, but to all practical purposes, one United States dollar is worth about 26 pesos; the United States dollar; and the *peso convertible*, which is interchangeable in value with the dollar. You will probably receive this tourist currency in exchange for United States dollars during your stay in Cuba, but try to dispense with them before you leave — in theory they can be exchanged for United States dollars, but in fact, you may find it difficult to do so. In the unlikely event that you receive any Cuban pesos, you are not allowed to export them as souvenirs. In the summer of 2001, the Cuban government issued a decree that United States coins are no longer legal tender.

When bringing United States dollar cash, make sure you have plenty of small denominations. United States dollar traveler's checks and credit cards issued outside the United States (obviously American Express is not valid) such as Visa, MasterCard, Access, Banamex, Bancomer, Carnet and Diners Club as well as MasterCard, Visa and Diners Club traveler's checks are accepted in Cuba. Neither personal checks nor traveler's checks drawn on United States banks are accepted in Cuba. However, some cracks are beginning to appear in the economic blockade: Rex rental car in Havana and some other commercial enterprises are now able to accept payments in United States-issued Visa cards because the paperwork is processed through a Danish bank.

You can get cash advances on these major credit cards at the Hotel Nacional and Hotel Habana Libre as well as various banks in Havana. It is worth mentioning that Visa and MasterCard are the most widely accepted cards in Cuba. Your passport is generally required whenever you pay by credit card in Cuba. Generally, between two to five percent commission is charged.

Cuba's banking system has diversified in keeping with the gradual decentralization of the island's economy and a host of foreign banks have opened in Havana. Most European currencies are accepted for exchange at tourist centers and banks. You will probably find the Banco Financiero Internacional most useful. The Casas de Cambio S.A. (CADECA) in Havana and Varadero are frequently patronized by

rather than officially acknowledged, for most services. If you hire a driver, guide or translator, for example, they will be crushed if they perform well and you do not give them a decent tip at the end of your stay, although they will never ask you directly. Bear in mind, when you are trying to work out how much to tip in United States dollars that this does not represent a conversion into Cuban pesos; in effect, dollars have the same buying power for Cubans as they do for you. However, don't make the mistake of tipping in pesos: it will not be well received.

locals to change United States dollars and pesos back at the free-market rate. ATM machines are just beginning to make an appearance in Havana, especially in tourist-orientated La Habana Vieja.

If you should happen to require the services of a proper bank, the **Banco Financiero Internacional** ((07) 333003, 333520 or 333148, is located at Calle Línea 1, Vedado, Havana, and there is another branch at ((05) 337002, Avenida Playa and Calle 32, Varadero.

TIPPING

Service charges are not included in restaurant bills, and tipping at your discretion is greatly appreciated. Tipping is hoped for,

You may soon start to notice that tipping is unofficially courted everywhere, most notably by determined chambermaids, who construct elaborate swans and roses (and sometimes, even Santería *orishas*) from your bath towels to adorn your bed, and leave little flower-festooned notes in their attempts — quite touching — to communicate with you in whatever your language might be. You can leave a tip in an envelope on your bed when you leave.

You should tip (not over-tip) museum guides, hotel guards who watch your belongings or rental car, or anyone within the service industry who has been helpful. How-

The *peso convertible* is interchangeable with the dollar.

ever, don't offer money to Cuban government officials: anything smacking of bribery could be taken the wrong way and cause you considerable embarrassment.

On the other hand, the Cuban government is also concerned about tourists inadvertently encouraging young children to beg for pens, soap, sweets and money. Many Cuban parents and school teachers would prefer that tourists give donations of pens, crayons or other items for children to schools (see WHAT TO TAKE, below).

GETTING AROUND

You don't have to spend much time in Cuba to notice how the nation's transportation system is suffering under the Special Period. Makeshift vehicles of many ingenious kinds spluttering thick plumes of diesel are a common sight along the island's highways. Large trucks are converted into buses, while horse-drawn carts or *calesas* are frequently used in the provincial towns. Meanwhile, Cubans everywhere have a difficult and often frustrating time getting around: long lines form at city bus stops, at the exit of towns and at crossroads along highways. Yellow-clad officials known locally as *amarillos*, have the task of organizing those waiting for a ride. (Most government vehicles are legally required to pick up hitchhikers if they have the room.)

What this means is that if you intend to travel by public transportation in Cuba, be prepared to cope with all vicissitudes that come your way with the stamina and spirit of enterprise that Cubans themselves have spent years perfecting. This is precisely why many visitors who would otherwise travel independently decide to opt to join tours when they travel around Cuba. That doesn't necessarily mean you.

BY AIR

The national airline **Cubana de Aviación** ((07) 334446 to 334449 WEB SITE www.cubana.cu, with offices in the huge airline building at the bottom of Calle 23 (La Rampa) in Vedado, has an extensive domestic air network. There are daily flights from Havana between Santiago de Cuba and Varadero and regular flights to Baracoa, Bayamo,

Camagüey, Ciego de Ávila, Guantánamo, Holguín, Las Tunas, Manzanillo, Moa and Nueva Gerona (on the Isla de la Juventud) between two and three times a week. Flights within the country are not very expensive, however, they are 25 percent cheaper if you book them in conjunction with your international ticket abroad. Check with your travel agent about this. All payment must be made in United States dollars and tickets must be purchased at least a week in advance. Most domestic flights are on small veteran propeller aircraft — usually Russian Yaks and Antonovs, although Cubana recently acquired four Fokker F-27s. Cuba has two other airlines which fly some of these routes — **Aerocaribbean** ((07) 797524, in the airline building at the bottom of La Rampa; and **Aerogaviota** ((07) 230668, Calle 47 no. 2814 between Calles 28 and 34, Reparto Kolhy, Havana.

All three airlines depart from Havana's Aeropuerto Internacional José Martí. Any domestic flight requires you to check in 60 minutes in advance before flight time and the baggage limit is 20 kg (44 lb). It can be difficult to figure out which airport terminal to go to — there are no directions. Aerocaribbean's terminal is at the western end of the airport — not always easy to find. Always get directions about which terminal to go to from your local travel agent, or as a last resort — if you are getting there by taxi, make the driver wait while you check you have the right terminal.

RENTAL CARS

Traveling around Cuba in a rental car or jeep is probably the most satisfying way to see the country, although setting off on the road may not be for the timid. Cuba has the most extensive road system in the Caribbean, and has developed a fairly comprehensive network of dollar-friendly Servi-Cupet and Oro Negro gas stations, and Rumbos-operated roadside cafeterias, across the country. The Carretera Central (Central Highway) is not an expressway, but it does run from one end of the country to the other. The Vía Blanca is a four-lane expressway that runs from Havana to Varadero. The Autopista National is an eight-lane expressway that links Havana to Sancti Spíritus, Las Tunas, Bayamo and Pinar del Río.

There are many car rental companies in Cuba, and many different makes of rental cars and jeeps to choose from, some air conditioned and with a car radio and tape deck. You need to be at least 21 years old and have a valid driving license (either an international license or a license from your home country) and at least one year's driving experience. The rental fee must be paid in advance and a refundable US$200 to US$250 deposit is required, although a credit-card imprint may suffice. Two optional insurance plans are available, and you should probably pick one. Advanced reservations for car rental are recommended.

Horizontes offers the so-called Flexi Fly & Drive program designed to appeal to independent travelers. The rental car and accommodation packages range from six to thirteen days and are available from Havana, Varadero, Holguín and Santiago de Cuba, and they include vouchers that allow travelers to use all Horizontes hotels islandwide (only the first night's accommodation is pre-arranged; after that travelers can design their itinerary on a flexible day-to-day basis). A standard rental car is provided with unlimited mileage, as well as insurance. No drop-off charges apply for ending your journey somewhere other than your starting point. You will be given a complete list of Servi-Cupet stations and a suggested driving itinerary. For information and reservations contact **Horizontes** ((07) 334042 FAX (07) 334361 WEB SITE www.horizontes.cu, Calle 23 no. 156 between Calles N and O, Vedado, Havana; or **The Cuban Connection** ((941) 793-5204 TOLL-FREE IN US AND CANADA (800) 645-1179 WEB SITE www.cuba .tc, in the Turks and Caicos Islands. The program uses cars from three different rental car agencies: Korean-made Daewoo sedans from Havanautos, Korean-made Hyundai Accents and Japanese-made Mitsubishi Lancers from Transautos, and German-made Audis from Rex.

In general, expect the unexpected on Cuban roads. There are a few basic things to remember. In Cuba, traffic moves on the right. Make sure your horn works — you'll need it. Avoid driving at night at all costs: few roads or towns are lighted and potential dangers are cattle, potholes, tractors or bicycles without lights. Very often when you set out in the morning you will see the wrecks of cars that crashed during the night. Cuban drivers often don't indicate before stopping, turning or passing, so be alert. When you pass, blow your horn as you do so, especially if nearing a left-hand turn. Burst tires are unfortunately not an uncommon phenomenon in Cuba. (If it happens, accelerate ever so slightly into the direction of the skid — the last thing you should do is break suddenly, which can cause you to spin dangerously out of control.)

Your rental agency will give you a list of places to call for breakdown service. They either come and repair your car, or the agency will arrange for you to pick up another car and reimburse for the time lost or add extra days to your schedule.

Servi-Cupet and Oro Negro are the main gasoline distributors; many stations also sell diesel fuel. If you get a diesel car, the fuel costs are generally half the rate of gas, although of course, it is less environmentally friendly.

Make sure you have a good road map. The Cuban-produced *Automapa Nacional*, available at hotel shops or car rental agencies, which has up-to-date highway information and Cuban road rules. You'll find that road markings and signs are virtually nonexistent. Remember that dirt roads — often marked as secondary roads — sometimes become impassable during the rainy season. Try to see Tomás Gutiérrez Alea's film, *Guantánamera* for a sense of life on Cuban roads.

It is useful to discern the meaning of car plate colors: yellow plates mean private use or a foreigner's car; blue and red mean government-owned (can be asked to take people on board); green means military-owned; dark red belongs to a rental car agency; black belongs to foreign embassies; white license plates with red letters are owned by farmers cooperatives; and white license plates with blue letters indicate high ranking provincial or central government officials.

In the unfortunate event of an accident, **Roberto Gonzalez Sehweret** ((07) 326813 FAX (07) 333786, at the corner of Calles J and 23, Vedado, Havana, is a reputable attorney who specializes in car accidents involving foreigners.

The following are among Cuba's most established rental car agencies:

Cubacar (Cubanacán) ((07) 337233 or 242104 WEB SITE www.cubacar.cubanacan.cu.

Gaviota/VIA ((07) 240240, 666777 or 339781 WEB SITE www.gaviota.cubaweb.cu.

Gran Car ((07) 577338 or 417980, which offers lifts in vintage American cars.

HAVANAUTOS ((07) 332369, 239805 or 240646 WEB SITE www.havanautos.cu.

Micar ((07) 242444 or 552444.

Transautos ((07) 245532 or 245765.

Veracuba ((07) 330600 or 555657.

campers come well equipped, with mobile phone, air conditioning, gas stove, kitchen utensils, refrigerator, radio, hot water and bed linens. You also get a list of 20 motor campgrounds around Cuba. Rates vary between US$130 and US$148 per day depending on how long you rent; minimum rental is three days. Insurance is US$20 extra per day and you must leave a US$400 deposit before the trip starts. You can book a camper prior to arrival through British-owned **Go Cuba Plus** WEB SITE www .gocubaplus.com.

The country's most exclusive rental car and limousine company is **Rex (** (07) 339160 or 337788 FAX (07) 339159 WEB SITE www. rex-limousine.com, Avenida de Ranchos Boyeros and Calzada de Bejucal, Boyeros. Havana. Rex offers modern Audi convertibles and sedans and luxury Volvo limousines with professional bilingual drivers. Prices are high, but the company prides itself on its service. Unlike other rental companies, Rex requires renters to be over 25 years old.

New on the Cuba scene is **Campertour (** (07) 801542 or 806874 FAX (07) 805389, the only people on the island who rent motor caravan campers— Mercedes Benz turbo diesels that sleep one to four persons. The

BY TAXI

If you wish to travel around Cuba by car, but don't want to drive yourself, you may want to consider the option of a long-distance taxi. As with most things in Cuba, there are two versions: a *colectivo*, a service taxi (often a veteran American car or a battered Lada) whose driver negotiates a gaggle of peso-paying passengers along routes of varying length; and a privately hired version, involving the customer (you) hiring a driver and car, paying a daily fee as well as all fuel costs. Other add-on costs can include the driver's accommodation and food. Be sure to negotiate the price *before* the journey begins.

All of the companies listed below (apart from the Gran Car agency) operate modern, air-conditioned vehicles made in Europe or Japan. Cuba's top taxi companies include:

Fenix ((07) 635861 or 639720.
Gran Car ((07) 577338 or 417980, which offers lifts in vintage American cars.
Habanataxi ((07) 419600.
Panataxi ((07) 555555.
Transgaviota ((07) 339780 or 272727.
Transtur ((07) 335543.
Turistaxi ((07) 336666.

By Train

It is an interesting piece of trivia that Cuba is now the last Caribbean country with a functioning railway, now that the Jamaican rail system has been phased out. Trains somewhat erratically service all the regional capitals, and although not an easy ride all the way, are in general much more reliable and hassle-free than Cuban buses. Tickets are relatively easy to get and leaping on a train can be a colorful way to see the country.

Aside from these options, you can't fail to notice, or to lust for a ride in, Cuba's *taxis particulares*: old Chevrolets, Buicks, De Sottos and Kaisers that trundle along on balding tires in various states of repair. If you opt for one of these unlicensed taxis, you could find yourself in a debate with the Cuban police, but usually you are most at risk of breaking down with a flat tire or an empty tank. Still it can be worth the experience. Remember, for your own safety, it's better to tell the driver that you don't want his friend (or friends) to drive along with you. Always negotiate the rate beforehand. Some tourists come to a private arrangement when it comes to hiring a car and driver for longer trips, but this type of free-enterprise initiative is illegal in Cuba.

Cuba's railway system extends across the country from Havana, via Matanzas, Santa Clara, Ciego de Ávila, Camagüey and Las Tunas, from which provincial lines service Cienfuegos, Bayamo and Guantánamo. In addition, there is a very slow train that chugs between Havana and Pinar del Río; as well as the "direct" overnight train from Havana to Santiago de Cuba, which takes 15 hours to cover the 900-km (560-mile) distance. This can be a good alternative to flying or driving. A relatively short trip that allows you to experience train travel in Cuba is the so-called Hershey Railway from Casablanca, an electrified train that plies the old route past

OPPOSITE: Embarking on the road from Camagüey to Santa Lucía. ABOVE: Taxis for tourists in Havana.

sugar plantations once owned by the American Hershey chocolate company.

When riding the rails, prepare for billows of smoke from your fellow passengers in what are frequently sealed compartments.

To purchase tickets, you will have to go through the **Ferrotur** ((07) 223409 or 234036, agency in Havana, which allows tourists to buy tickets up to an hour before departure, although of course, prices are in United States dollars. Trains depart from the **Estación Central** ((07) 613509, at the corner of Calle Belgica and Arsenal in Habana Vieja.

With so many Cubans having to stand in line for what services actually exist, you may quite question whether it is really considerate to take away someone else's seat. If you do want to investigate getting about the country by bus, you will have to contact the state agency **Empresa Omnibus Nacionales** ((07) 816132 or 706155, Avenida Independencia 101, near the Plaza de la Revolución in Havana, which operates all inter-provincial services. You should try to book as much in advance as possible. Buses depart from the adjacent **Terminal Nacional** ((07) 703397 or 709401.

By Bus

Since 1991, Cuba's bus services have been badly hit by the Special Period. You'll see reconstituted buses made from converted trucks, often with two buses hitched together by all manner of spare parts (and in some cases, almost anything with wheels). Referred to as *guaguas* or *camelos* (camels), it would be hard to recommend these as a form of getting around. Cubans will roll their eyes at you and pronounce you *"loco"* if you express an interest in riding one. Since waiting for public transportation in Cuba is like waiting for Godot, most Cubans give up waiting at interminable lines and try to hitchhike (known as *hacer botella*, or making a bottle with the hand).

Overseas visitors can take advantage of a new tourist-only express bus service: **ViAzul** ((07) 811413, 815652 or 811108 FAX (07) 666092 WEB SITE www.viazul.cu, Avenida 26 at the corner of Calle Zoológico, Nuevo Vedado, Havana, which offers coach service from Havana to Varadero, Santiago, Trinidad, Baracoa and Viñales, as well as Varadero to Trinidad. Other ViAzul offices can be found in Varadero ((05) 614886, Autopista Sur at Calle 36; in Santiago ((0226) 28484, at the corner of Avenida de los Libertadores and Calle Yarayó, near the Plaza de la Revolución; and in Trinidad ((0419) 2404 or 3737, Calle Piro Guirnart at the corner of Antonio Maceo and Gustavo Izquierdo.

BY BOAT

Until recently, the only way to see Cuba by boat was to take a yacht cruises or charter (see SPORTING SPREE, page 31 in YOUR CHOICE). Now, new cruise terminals are being planned for Cuba, with the general mood in tourist officialdom being that some time in the future, the island will become a major cruise destination within the Caribbean.

One of the few options available at the present time is the MV *Mistral*, a modern

1,200-passenger steamer (home-ported in Greece) that offers eight-day "Cuba Delights" cruises. The voyage kicks off from Havana, with stops in the Isle of Youth, Grand Cayman, Cozumel and Merida before returning to the Cuban capital. For information contact **Festival Cruises** WEB SITE www.-festivalcruises.com.

You can also travel between Havana and Varadero by sea on the 300-passenger **Crucero Jet Kat Express II** ((05) 668727 in Varadero or (07) 336566 in Havana. This modern high-speed ferry departs Varadero's Marina Chapelín on Tuesday, Thursday and Saturday at 8:30 am; and Havana's Terminal Sierra Maestra on Monday, Wednesday and Friday at the same hour.

ACCOMMODATION

When you arrive in Cuba, a certain suspension of judgment seems to set in when it comes to appreciating (or not) the hotel you are staying in. After all, this is a country where things are not as they are elsewhere, a society with an economic siege mentality due to the United States embargo. When your chambermaid is a trained lawyer, your waiter earns more than a university professor, and when Cubans themselves are not officially allowed to stay in the nation's tourist hotels (although ladies of the evening seem to be a rather visible exception to that rule), it can interfere with your reasoning (see THE TOURISM BOOM, page 304).

You might experience the embargo for yourself: an elevator breakdown due to power-shedding or the lack of a spare part might mean you have to walk up to your hotel floor; perhaps the hotel doctor dispenses medicines donated by other tourists on their departure.

If you are staying at a large foreign-managed or joint-venture hotel complexes you can expect it to be of an international standard. They offer the best food on the island, although the food is often not especially Cuban. Although the prices of these hotels are usually higher, they are nonetheless recommended for the superior quality of their service.

The pricing category in this book has been divided as follows: **expensive** is above US$120, **moderate** is US$65 to US$120, and **inexpensive** below US$65. Sometimes, considerable reductions can be had (for fixed dates with advanced reservations), notably through Havanatur.

The star system used throughout the country is not an internationally recognized rating, but is awarded by the Cuban government. It does not, however, necessarily indicate a standardized level of taste or comfort.

For more information about other accommodation options, such as staying with Cuban families, see BACKPACKING, page 46 in YOUR CHOICE.

Train service in Cuba can be erratic, but the experience is inevitably colorful.

Below are the central offices of the major Cuban accommodations providers.

Habaguanex ((07) 338694 or 338694 FAX (07) 338697 WEB SITE www.ohch.cu/f_turi.htm, Calle Oficios 110, between Calles Lamparilla and Amargura, Havana.

Gran Caribe ((07) 330575 to 330582 FAX (07) 330565 or 330238 WEB SITE www.grancaribe.cubaweb.cu, Avenida 7 no. 4210, between Calles 42 and 44, Miramar, Havana.

Horizontes ((07) 334042 or 334090 FAX (07) 333722 or 334361 WEB SITE www.horizontes.cu, Calle 23 no. 156, between Calles N and O, Vedado, Havana.

Cubanacán ((07) 280607 or 286063 FAX (07) 280107 WEB SITE www.cubanacan.cu, Calle 160 and Avenida 11, Miramar Playa, Havana.

Cubamar ((07) 338317, 662524, 305536 or 662523 FAX (07) 333111 WEB SITE www.cubamar@cubamar.mit.cma.net, Paseo 752 at the corner of Calle 15, Vedado, Havana.

Gaviota ((07) 666777, 666773 or 666778, FAX (07) 332780 WEB SITE www.gaviota.cuba web.cu, Third Floor, Edificio la Marina, Avenida del Puerto in Miramar.

Islazul ((07) 320571 or 327718 FAX (07) 333458 or 324410 WEB SITE www.islazul.cubaweb.cu, at the corner of the Malecón and Calle G, Vedado, Havana.

Grupo Sol Meliá ((05) 667013 FAX (05) 667 162 WEB SITE www.solmeliacuba.com, Hotel Meliá Varadero, Carretera Sur, Varadero. The group also has numbers in the following countries: Belgium (0800 18866, France (0541-3165, Germany (0130-2301, Italy (1670-11692, Spain (901 144444, United Kingdom (0800 282720, United States ((800) 33-MELIA.

EATING OUT

The price categories given in this guide refer to the price of a meal per person, and are as follows: **expensive**, over US$30; **moderate**, US$15 to US$30; and **inexpensive**, under US$15.

BASICS

TIME

Cuban time is five hours earlier than Greenwich Mean Time, making it the same time as United States Eastern Standard Time (the same as New York), and six hours earlier than Central European Time. Daytime daylight savings applies from April to September, during which clocks are turned forward an hour, then turned back at the beginning of October.

ELECTRICITY

The common electrical voltage in Cuba is 110 volts, 60 cycles, exactly the same as in North America. However some joint-venture hotels have installed outlets that are 220 volts. Flat parallel plugs are the norm, so bring an adapter if your appliance differs. Confusingly some of the newer hotels have European-style outlets with two round plugs. For sensitive electrical equipment, keep in mind that current cuts and jumps are frequent.

WEIGHTS, MEASURES AND TEMPERATURE

Cuba uses the metric system, and measures temperature in centigrade.

BUSINESS HOURS

Shops are generally open from 8 AM to 8 PM, although never be surprised at mysterious "Cerrado" signs at any hour. That being said, most of the time and throughout the country, there is not often great deal to buy. Despite high summer temperatures, Cubans do not take a siesta. Banks and government offices are generally open from Monday to Friday from 8:30 am to 12:30 pm and then in the afternoon from 1:30 pm to 5:30 pm.

TRAVEL INSURANCE

Order medical insurance to cover any holiday accidents or illnesses. Cuba is generally a safe country, but it's wise to insure personal belongings. Ask your insurance company or travel agent for more information and make sure your travel insurance covers Cuba. If you're already in Cuba, travel insurance can be purchased from **Asistur** ((07) 338920, 338527 or 338339 FAX (07) 338087 WEB SITE www.asistur.cubaweb.cu, Paseo de Martí (Prado) 212, Habana Vieja, or the Asistur branches in Santiago de Cuba, Varadero, Cienfuegos, Playa Guardalavaca or Ciego de Avila.

COMMUNICATION AND MEDIA

You should be able to make international calls and send a fax from your hotel anywhere in Cuba. The top hotels have direct-dial satellite communications from you room; otherwise you need to go through the operator, which is generally fairly quick. You can call the United States, although you will always have to request this call through the operator. Naturally, surcharges are added to any telephone or fax service from your hotel.

Portable phones are available in Havana, Varadero and Santiago de Cuba — the concierge at the top hotels will be able to tell you who to contact.

Cuba has a national postal system that is fairly reliable, although don't be too sure that any gifts you may try to send back to Cuba later will actually reach your friends.

DHL has offices in Havana ((07) 241578 FAX (07) 240999 at Avenida 1, at the corner of Calle 26, Miramar; and in Varadero ((05) 667330, Calle 10 no. 319, Iberostar, Barlovento.

NEWSPAPERS AND TELEVISION

You can't go to Cuba and not read *Granma*, the nation's official Communist Party newspaper, named for the boat that carried Fidel Castro's band of revolutionaries back to Cuba from Mexico in 1956. (As the writer Martha Gellhorn noted with some amusement as she heard street vendors shouting out the name of the nation's newspaper, *Granma* means "Grandma.") *Granma International*, the weekly version, is published in English, Spanish, French and Portuguese. It usually carries long transcripts of Fidel Castro's speeches (often reminiscing about the old days in the Sierra Maestra with Che and Raúl). It reports variously on the latest progress in Cuban medical science, labor students in Pinar del Río, new economic accords with Norway or Canada, for example. It also carries articles such as "Who Are They Afraid Of," about the United States missile installations in Florida. You can buy *Granma Inter-*

national at the Centro de la Prensa (Press Center) on Avenida 23 in Vedado, Havana. You can also read Cuba's leading newspaper online at WEB SITE www.granma.cubaweb.cu (domestic edition; Spanish only) or WEB SITE www.granma.cu (international edition in English, Spanish, German, French and Portuguese versions).

There are several publications that visitors may find useful or interesting. The *Business Tips on Cuba*, *Prisma* and *Cuba Internacional* are all bilingual English-Spanish publications aimed at either tourists or busi-

ness travelers and sold at the main hotels or at the airport shop.

Other Cuban publications include *Trabajadores de Cuba* (the Worker's Party newspaper), the *Juventud Rebelde*, the *Tribuna de La Habana* and the *Habanero*. There are many other provincial and regional newspapers across the country.

Outside Cuba, one of the best publications for information about Cuba is the *CUBA Update*, published monthly by the Center for Cuban Studies in New York and available on a reasonably priced subscription (see the listing for the Center for Cuba Studies in TAKING A TOUR, page 70 in YOUR CHOICE). Another use-

Electrification for tourism near Rancho Hatuey, Sancti Spíritus.

ful publication to help you keep up to date is *The Cuba Report*. For subscriptions, contact ℂ (305) 372-1089, 501 Brichell Avenue, Suite 200, Miami, Florida 33131.

Cuban television has two national channels: CubaVision and Tele Rebelde, as well as provincial channels. Radio Rebelde, Radio Progreso, Radio Reloj and Radio Enciclopedia Popular (music-only) are the main radio stations. Cuba has one international radio channel, Radio Havana Club which operates 24 hours a day in several languages and Radio Taíno, which broadcasts in Spanish and English.

Satellite and cable television — including the CNN, ESPN, HBO and Discovery channels — is usually provided in Cuba's top hotels, while Canal del Sol is a tourist-orientated channel that broadcasts a mixture of advertising, sports and movies.

TELEPHONE

The country code for Cuba is 53. City codes are provided for numbers listed in this book. Drop the zero within the same area code.

ETIQUETTE

In general, Cubans are very conscious of good manners, and take great pains themselves to be hospitable, presentable and well-mannered to their foreign guests or business partners. Dressing in a dignified manner is *de rigueur* in formal or business situations, as is listening carefully and politely even if you are not conversant in Spanish. Humor and personal warmth are the qualities most likely to endear you to people on all levels of society in Cuba, and never underestimate Cuban pride.

If you want to take photographs of people, always ask beforehand (although this can change the nature of the photograph) by asking "*Puedo tomar una foto?*" (Can I take a photograph?).

Other important things to remember involve not inadvertently meddling with Cuban superstitions. When in Cuba, do as the Cubans do, and always pour a glass for the *orishas* when you open a bottle of rum. Never absent-mindedly set an empty rocking chair in motion when you are in a Cuban

person's home — this is viewed as calling death into the house. If you ever have cause to discuss another person's illness, never gesture to the same part of your own body as you describe the symptoms — Cubans believe this can result in you getting the same illness. Cubans will tell you not to look in a mirror during a thunderstorm and to smoke a cigar on Mondays to ensure good luck for the week. Finally, if you are a woman, never put your handbag on the floor, for Cubans believe that this invites bad luck with financial matters. Put it on a chair or table instead.

On the street, you may be taken aback by people making hissing sounds — this is not meant as a hostile gesture, merely a way of getting attention. Cubans also frequently hiss this way to attract attention in restaurants, but this may not be a habit that it is politic for you to adopt.

HEALTH

The risk of picking up any serious illness in Cuba is low; you are far more likely to come home with diarrhea — nicknamed *la turista* — than anything else. Vaccinations are not required to enter Cuba, however you would be wise to be inoculated against Hepatitis A. Other standard inoculations include typhoid, tetanus and polio. If you are going to spend an extended period of time in Cuba, you might consider getting a rabies inoculation.

The eastern region of Santiago de Cuba in particular reported a crop of cases of dengue fever ("breakbone fever"), a severe and painful flu spread by mosquitoes. For dengue fever (as for HIV and AIDS) there are no jabs, and there is no vaccine against food poisoning either. The government's response to the dengue fever threat has been regular insecticide sprays, sometimes by air and sometimes from moving trucks. Try not to breathe in the fumes, and make sure you bring and use a strong brand of mosquito repellant.

Hotels generally have a doctor on call, and the larger hotels have medical centers, but bring any medicines you require (plus a copy of your prescription which may have to be inspected at customs). Also bring your own contraceptives, vitamins and sunscreen. You may need to watch out for that intense

Cuban sun. If you are traveling with children, make sure they get enough (bottled) water and not too much sun, and bring with you any medication they may need.

Although Cuba has an enviable reputation within Latin America as well as other developing countries for its medical expertise and public health, at present Cuban hospitals and clinics frequently lack basic supplies. Antibiotics, bandages and painkillers can be very hard to come by due to the United States embargo. Tales of dirty syringes, sticky tape used in the absence of bandages

tralia. Cuba has engineered several unique treatments, such as PPG, which brings down high cholesterol (and reputedly has a stimulating effect on the male libido), and is also reported to be making progress on an AIDS vaccine.

In Havana, the **Clínica International Cira García** ((07) 242673 or 240330, Calle 20 at the corner of Avenida 41 in Miramar, is designed to cater exclusively to foreigners, while the capital's premier medical facility, **Hospital Nacional Hermanos Almeijeiras** ((07) 576077, Calle San Lázaro 701, off the

and surgery without anesthesia are sadly not at all uncommon.

On the other side of the coin, the Cuban government has set up a range of clinics offering treatment to foreigners as part of its so-called Health Tourism program, run by **Servimed** ((07) 242658 or 242023 FAX (07) 241630 WEB SITE www.cubanacan.cu/servimed, Turismo de Salud, Calle 18 no. 4304, between 43 and 47, Miramar Playa, Havana, which is a branch of Cubanacán. More than 5,000 people visit Cuba each year seeking specialized treatment, including heart and eye surgery, organ transplants, pediatric surgery, vitilago, psoriasis, alopecia and laser treatment; most come from Latin America, but some from as far away as Aus-

Malecón in Centro Habana, has two floors reserved for foreigners. Should you fall ill or need emergency treatment, you would be well advised to take advantage of these clinics, and not the hospitals reserved for Cubans.

Most hotels boil or filter their water, and thus it is potable, but you may wish to be on the safe side and drink only bottled water or boiled water. Otherwise, an unwelcome stomach upset, or possibly even Hepatitis A may result. Bottled water is plentiful at neighborhood supermarkets and street stalls, but always check when you buy it that the seal is unbroken. Drink a lot of water and

Reading a newspaper in Old Havana.

wear a hat and light loose clothing to prevent dehydration and heatstroke.

Finally, there is one ailment that can strike visitors, especially during the Cuban winter: the *catarro Cubano* ("Cuban cold"). The best way to deal with it is to take a lot of liquid, rest, hot weak tea (no milk), with plenty of honey and lemon, and perhaps the odd splash of rum. Aspirin should help to bring the fever down.

TOILETS

There's not much to say about toilets in Cuba except that they are of an "international standard" in most hotels. In La Habana Vieja, water shortages can be a slight problem from time to time. However, while on the road, be prepared for pretty appalling loos, which you can usually expect to find at Oro Negro or Servi-Cupet gas stations. Have a supply of packaged tissues and soap with you if you will be discommoded by the absence of these essentials.

SECURITY

Cuba is, generally speaking, quite a benign and safe country, especially compared to some other islands in the Caribbean. Still, the convergence of the rise of tourism and widespread economic desperation (born of the United States-imposed fetters on the Cuban economy, many say) has led to a rise in some petty crimes, such as pickpocketing, bag-snatching and theft of personal belongings from hotel rooms or even private houses. Be aware that, especially in La Habana Vieja, thieves often work as a pair, swooping past on bicycles for a swift getaway with your handbag. Crime is rarely violent however, and rarely directed at foreign tourists.

When you stray off the beaten path, in the semi-darkness of back streets in Old Havana for example, you should have your wits about you. Although Havana is truly a great city for the *flaneur*, if you have even a remotely cautious disposition, it is better not to be completely alone wandering the city in the middle of the night.

There is rarely a sense of menace — people usually either ignore you as you pass or

offer a crooked grin or even a welcoming wave. People may approach you from their doorways, offering various things, ranging from their house to rent, their car to "borrow" and even in some cases, themselves (or someone they know). While many friendships may be made on the street in Cuba, beware of outright hustlers — of either sex — and be careful about invitations to be taken to another part of the city by someone you have just met.

That takes us to the next segment of this advice column. Prostitution is an ever-present reality in Cuba. After dark, along Havana's Avenida 5, the Malecón and in La Habana Vieja, and increasingly in Santiago de Cuba as well as other provincial cities such as Camagüey. It can sometimes seem that there is a

veritable forest of women clad in tight Lycra or whatever finery they can muster and definitely on the prowl. Cuban taxi drivers often wryly joke that they only have one dangerous animal in their country — their *jineteras*, figuratively speaking, "female jockeys," or "women who go along for the ride."

Visitors should be aware that since April 1997, a series of small bombs were detonated in Havana hotels and nightspots popular with foreign tourists. The explosive devices were small but were potentially dangerous, and in one case caused the death of one individual. Be alert and wary of unattended packages or bags in public areas.

In Havana, the drug trade is a small, but burgeoning, fact of life. Penalties are high, and crackdowns are sporadic. You may notice that La Habana Vieja is now full of police in blue uniforms, who frequently stop people on bicycles or on the street to inspect their identity papers as part of the crackdown on petty crimes.

You should also be aware that as a foreign visitor, you are not allowed to photograph military or police installations, harbor, rail or airport facilities.

You can contact the **Tourist Police** at ((07) 600106 or 820116.

GAY AND LESBIAN TRAVELERS

A lesbian couple hold hands as they peruse paintings in the Museo Nacional de Bellas

Various means of transportation in Baracoa.

Artes in Havana. Gays openly socialize at a cabaret nightclub in Camagüey. A couple of men smooch on a Varadero beach. Cuba has come a long way from the days when homosexuality was considered unnatural and anti-socialist. Back in the 1960s, Castro declared that homosexuals do not "embody the conditions and requirements" of the Revolution. During the early days of his regime, Cuban gays were subjected to various forms of persecution including rural reeducation camps where it was hoped that a dose of sunshine and a whole lot of hard work would somehow transform them back into "real men." By the late 1980s, Castro had come full circle and mandated a complete halt to both the official and unofficial harassment of homosexuals. Given the fact that Cuba is still a macho Latin society, prejudice against gays and lesbians lingers — but perhaps no more so than North America or Europe.

For more information on the island's gay scene log onto **Gay Cuba** WEB SITE www.gay-cuba.com, or consult **Queers for Cuba (** (415) 995-4678 FAX (415) 530-9275, 3543 Eighteenth Street No. 33, San Francisco, California 94110. As an expression of solidarity with Cuban gays and lesbians, the latter group organizes annual fully hosted trips to Cuba.

DISABLED TRAVELERS

Cuba is still in the dark ages when it comes to assisting disabled or handicapped visitors. Very few hotels have special rooms for the disabled and few museums, shops, restaurants or other tourist-oriented venues are wheelchair accessible.

However, there are a few noteworthy exceptions. Santiago's elegant old **Hotel Casa Granda (** (0226) 86600 FAX (0226) 86035, Calle Heredia 201 next to Calle Lacret, recently refurbished under the discerning eye of the French Sofitel group, is one of the few Cuban hotels that offers special disabled rooms. And assuming you can get yourself up the front steps and into the building, the beautiful new Cuban wing of the **Museo Nacional de Bellas Artes (** (07) 613858 or 620140, Calle Trocadero between Zulueta and Monserrate in Habana Vieja, offers both ramps and elevators to access the various galleries.

WOMEN TRAVELING ALONE

Cuba is not an intimidating destination for women traveling alone. Indeed, especially if you are a business traveler or journalist, you will notice that male chivalry rather than Latin machismo generally comes to the fore. Foreign women on their own, much less frequently than their male counterparts, may find themselves approached by Cuban men, but this is very rarely threatening.

WHEN TO GO

With its tropical climate, Cuba is best visited during late-December, January, February and March. During these months, generally the sky is clear, the sun warm and the evenings delightful. This is, in fact, the Cuban winter, which begins in early December, with average temperatures around 21°C (75°F). (It pays to remind yourself that it is actually winter if a cold front hits creating unsettled or uncomfortably cold and wet weather.)

From April to December when it is *very* hot, with average temperatures from 30°C (86°F), you may take comfort in the remark that it is never as hot in Havana as in New York during summer. This may be a fallacy: it certainly *feels* hotter in Havana. In some parts of Cuba, the mercury climbs even higher, such as the island's hottest province, Oriente.

May to November is the wettest time of year (June being the wettest month); November is also hurricane season, with storms hitting the Cuban coasts from August to October as well. During summer, there are frequent thunderstorms with intense lightning, often preceded by formations of towering cumulus clouds, oppressive heat, then what the Cubans call the *aire de agua*, a fresh humid breath of air. When hurricanes hit, they can be ferocious and deadly, such as Hurricane Flora in 1963, which killed 4,000 people, and Hurricane Lili, which devastated swathes of Matanzas Province in 1996.

There are two seasons in Cuba for tourism: the high season between December 15 and April 14, and the low season from April 15 to December 14. Hotel rates can decrease by as much as 15 percent in the low season.

WHAT TO TAKE

It's always (or almost always) warm in Cuba. Bring light summer cotton or linen clothes and a light jacket for cooler evenings; also, air conditioning in hotels and restaurants can be freezing. Remember good walking shoes and sandals. Sunglasses are very necessary, as is a hat. Also take a warm sweater and woolen socks if you plan to visit mountain areas of Cuba, where temperatures become quite cool at night. Although casual dress is the norm throughout Cuba, looking sloppy is not considered chic and may offend your Cuban hosts. If you are working, then wear a semi-formal tropical version of your "work outfit." Only important business meetings require men to wear a tie and jacket. You can always take your cue from Cuban men who often wear the long-sleeved *guayabera* to official functions or the best restaurants. On the beach, of course, skimpy bathing suits are fine, but remember that topless bathing is confined to tourist areas.

When it comes to medication, very little is easily available in Cuba, and you should bring with you everything you think you might need, such as aspirin, or strong painkillers, first aid equipment, condoms (nicknamed "*el quitasensaciones*" or "killjoys" in Cuba), tampons and sanitary napkins, eye drops, and treatment for diarrhea, indiges-

An example of a recently authorized private enterprise: watch-battery installation.

tion, as well as vitamin supplements. Strong mosquito repellant is essential, as is sunscreen. Any left-over medicine will be gratefully received by the hotel doctor, or by Cuban friends.

If you stay in Cuba for several weeks, you may find that there are quite a few things you regret not bringing with you. They could include an electric kettle for making your own tea (tea-drinking is not an institution in Cuba); supplies of muesli and biscuits; adapter plugs for your appliances, which are very hard to get hold of once you are in Cuba; a plastic line and pegs to hang washing to dry; a cassette deck or walkman; and gifts for your new Cuban friends.

Gifts are personal things. However, if you experience warmth and hospitality extended to you by Cubans you meet, you may well wish you had something to give back to them. Gifts could include perfume, makeup, underwear, fashionable clothes for women; men often appreciate grooming essentials, such as aftershave, deodorant, razors, as well as T-shirts, baseball caps and cigarettes. Fashion magazines and novels are gratefully received. Soap, coffee, and basic toiletries are severely rationed in Cuba, so these can make small gifts too. Also, music cassettes of popular music abroad make excellent presents. If you plan to rent a car and driver for a stretch of time, he (drivers are almost always male) definitely appreciate car accessories and good car wax.

You can also pick up many gifts in the dollar-only stores.

LANGUAGE BASICS

From wafts of songs on street corners to snatches of overheard conversation, it does not take long to understand why the Cubans call their idiomatic version of Spanish "the loving tongue." You will quickly familiarize yourself with Cuban-Spanish if you already have a working knowledge of Spanish, although most Cubans will go out of their way to communicate with you and to make you feel welcome; many speak English. Cubans appreciate your attempts to learn and speak their language. Take a short course in Latin American Spanish or bring along a phrase book and try to speak at least a few basic phrases. At the very least, always remember to say *por favor* ("please") and *gracias* ("thank-you"). *Buenos días* ("good morning") and *buenas tardes* ("good afternoon") should always be used as a greeting, while you should preface your address to someone with either *señor*, *señora* or *señorita*.

In terms of pronunciation, Cuban Spanish has most in common with Puerto Rican or Dominican Republic Spanish, as well as Latin American Spanish. It does not have the Spaniard's "th" lisp. The letter "j" is pronounced "h" as in "hat" and "ll" is pronounced as "i" as in "machine."

Vowels are pronounced as follows: "a" as in "father"; "e" as in "bet"; "i" as in "machine"; "o" as in "note"; "u" as in the "oo" in "food." "Y" is considered a vowel when it stands alone or appears at the end of a word. When alone, it means "and" and is pronounced as the Spanish "i."

Consonants are pronounced as follow: "b" is pronounced as in English, and often replaces what in English would be "v," as in "Habana." "C" is pronounced like the "s" in "sea." If it is before "e" or "k," then "c" is pronounced like "k" in English. "Ch" is pronounced as in "church"; "d" resembles "h" as in "feather"; "g" is like a "h" in "hat" when placed before "h" and "i"; otherwise it is a hard "g" as in "go"; "h" is always silent; "ñ" as in "ny" of "canyon"; "q" is pronounced like the English "k"; "rr" is rolled; and "z" sounds like "s" as in "sass."

COMMON EXPRESSIONS

hello   *hola*
yes   *sí*
no   *no*
good morning   *buenos días*
good afternoon   *buenos tardes*
good evening   *buenos noches*
good-bye   *adiós*
see you later   *hasta luego*
thank you   *gracias*
please   *por favor*
My name is...   *Mi nombre es.../Me llamo...*
What is your name?   *¿Come se llama?*
How are you?   *¿Como esta usted?/¿Que tal?*
Fine, and you?   *¿Bien, y usted?*
Pleased to meet you   *Mucho gusto, encantado/encantada*

Friend or companion   *amigo/amiga* or *compañero/campañera*
I don't understand   *No   entiendo*
Do you speak English?   *¿Habla usted inglés?*
I don't speak Spanish   *No hablo español*
Pardon me   *Perdóneme*
Excuse me   *Con permiso*
Don't mention it   *de nada*
Where is...?   *¿Dónde está...?*
What is...?   *¿Que es...?*
I want...   *Quiero...*
How much is...?   *¿Cuanto cuesta...?*
Is there...?   *¿Hay...?*
Do you have any...?   *¿Tiene...?*
The check please   *La cuenta, por favor*
I am lost   *Estoy perdido*
I do not feel well   *No me siento bien*
Help!   *¡Socorro!*

DAYS

Monday   *lunes*
Tuesday   *martes*
Wednesday   *miercoles*
Thursday   *jueves*
Friday   *viernes*
Saturday   *sábado*
Sunday   *domingo*

TIME

What time is it?   *¿Que hora es?*
morning   *mañana*
today   *hoy*
yesterday   *ayer*
tomorrow   *mañana*
week   *semana*
month   *mes*
early   *temprano*
late   *tarde*
later   *después*

NUMBERS

one   *uno/una*
two   *dos*
three   *tres*
four   *quatro*
five   *cinco*
six   *seis*
seven   *siete*
eight   *ocho*
nine   *neuve*

ten   *diez*
eleven   *once*
twelve   *doce*
thirteen   *trece*
fourteen   *catorce*
fifteen   *quince*
sixteen   *dieciséis*
seventeen   *diecisiéte*
eighteen   *dieciocho*
nineteen   *diecinueve*
twenty   *veinte*
twenty-one   *veintiuno*
thirty   *treinta*
thirty-one   *treinta y uno*
forty   *cuarenta*
fifty   *cincuenta*
sixty   *sesanta*
seventy   *setenta*
eighty   *ochenta*
ninety   *noventa*
one hundred   *cien*
one hundred and one   *ciento uno*
five hundred   *quinientos*
one thousand   *mil*
one million   *millon*

DIRECTIONS

here   *aquí*
there   *allí/allá*
near   *cerca*
far   *lejo*
left   *izquiereda*
right   *derecha*
straight   *derecho*
at the corner   *a la esquina*
at the back of   *al fondo*
before   *antes*
behind   *atrás*
city block   *cuadra*
next   *proximo/proxima*
soon   *pronto*
entry   *entrada*
exit   *salida*
open   *abierto*
closed   *cerrado*
pull   *jale*
push   *empuje*

LOCATIONS

money exchange   *casa de cambio*
airport   *aeropuerto*

bus station   *terminal de omnibus*
bus   *guagua*
train station   *estacion de ferrocarriles*
ticket office   *taquilla*
post office   *correo*
gas station   *gasolinera*
hospital   *hospital*
bathroom   *baño, lavabo*

AT THE HOTEL

hotel   *hotel/villa*
room   *cuarto*
bed   *cama*
key   *llave*
front desk   *carpeta*
soap   *jabón*
towel   *toalla*
purified water   *aqua purificada*
hot   *caliente*
cold   *frio*
blanket   *manta*
bill   *cuenta*
credit card   *tarjeta de crédito*
What does it cost?   *¿Cuánto cuesta?*
per night?   *¿per noche?*

IN THE RESTAURANT

waiter   *camarero*
waitress   *camarera*
breakfast   *desayuno*
lunch   *comida*
dinner   *cena*
table   *mesa*
fork   *tenedor*
knife   *cuchillo*
spoon   *cuchilla*
wineglass   *copa*
glass   *vaso*
plate   *plato*
bowl   *tazón*
bread   *pan*
butter   *mantequilla*
sugar   *azúcar*
milk   *leche*
eggs   *huevos*
coffee   *café*
tea   *té*
ice   *hielo*
without ice   *sin hielo*
a little, please   *un poco, per favor*
beer   *cerveza*

soda water   *refresco*
mineral water   *aqua mineral*
bill   *cuenta*
change   *cambio*

SLANG

When it comes to Cuban slang, you are bound to pick up some along the way. Cubans will smirk if you ask for some papaya: in Cuban this word is slang for the female sex organ. Other slang words include *yuma* ("foreigner"), *bisbe da buisness* ("a dirty deal"), *dolores* ("dollars"), *puro* ("cigar"), *chisme* ("gossip") and *apagone* ("power cut").

RECOMMENDED WEB SITES

Cuba has discovered the Internet and embraced it with typical Latin passion. Nearly every week comes the launch of a new web site dedicated to some aspect of Cuban government, tourism, business or culture. The number is now somewhat overwhelming. Some of the more intriguing sites include:

Asistur www.asistur.cubaweb.cu provides information on the government organization that helps foreign visitors with emergency medical or dental treatment, legal aid, currency exchange, travel insurance, and lost passports.

Castro's Speeches www.cuba.cu/gobierno/discursos/index can also be found on line for those with a keen interest in Fidel ... and lots of time on their hands.

Cuba Online www.cubaonline.com.cu is a general interest site maintained by the Cuban government that includes articles about sports, music, books, cinema, art, humor, food, events and tourism. Spanish only.

Cuba Web www.cubaweb.cu/eng is a portal into hundreds of other Cuban web sites as well as a place where you can get Cuban news and information on all sorts of subjects including culture and art, science and technology, sports, business and events. Temperatures for various Cuban cities are updated hourly and there's also online shopping for Cuban products.

Go Cuba Plus www.gocubaplus.com is an independent (non-government) site dedicated to Cuban tourism that proffers information on myriad topics including domestic flights, ferries, rental cars, travel insurance and cell phone rental. Although based at Havana's Marina Hemingway, the site is maintained by British expats living in Cuba.

Government of Cuba www.cubagov.cu is a portal into all sorts of other sites maintained by the powers that be in Havana.

Granma www.granma.cubaweb.cu is the online version of *Granma*, the official daily newspaper of the Cuban Communist Party. Spanish only, while **Granma International** www.granma.cu is the digital online version

Oficina del Historiador de la Ciudad de La Habana www.ohch.cu gives detailed insight into the organization charged with the task of renovating and stimulating tourism in Old Havana.

One, Two, Three www.123y.islagrande .cult.cu is the official site of Isla Grande records, packed with information on the Cuban music scene including audio and video clips, artist interviews, information about events and general music industry news. It links to numerous other Cuban music sites.

of *Granma*'s overseas edition. Some of the articles are insightful, others nothing more than barely disguised party propaganda. You can choose to read in English, German, French or Portuguese.

Habanos S.A. www.infocex.cu/habanos gives you the lowdown on Cuba's largest cigar manufacturer.

INDER www.inder.co.cu is the island's official sports and recreation site, with information on upcoming international competitions in which Cubans are involved, as well as athlete interviews, feature stories and links to the country's various official sport organizations.

Infotur www.infotur.cu is the official site of the information wing of the Cuban Ministry of Tourism.

Science Cuba www.cubaciencia.cu posts information on events and publications related to all aspects of Cuban science, plus instant links to various other science and technology related sites.

UNEAC www.cubarte.cult.cu/uneac is the official sight of the Writers and Arts Union of Cuba.

University of Havana www.uh.cu provides general information on Cuba's largest center of higher learning and links to all sorts of university departments and programs.

VeraCuba www.dtcuba.com/eng is an official Department of Tourism site that posts everything from destination information and articles on health, sports and business, to

A café in Isla de la Juventud.

"hot deals" on hotels and rental cars to current weather conditions in Havana.

RECOMMENDED READING

Nobody should travel to Cuba without first picking up a copy of *Mi Moto Fidel* (National Geographic Adventure Press, 2000) by Christopher P. Baker. California-based Baker knows the island better than any contemporary English-language writer, as he proves time and time again in this account of his 11,265-km (7,000-mile) peregrination through urban and rural Cuba on a BMW motorbike he affectionately dubbed "Fidel."

Those with an interest in the machinations of civil war should take a look at *Revolution in Cuba* (Charles Scribner's Sons, 1975), a sympathetic exploration of the personalities, motivations and achievements of the Castro Revolution by Herbert L. Matthews of the *New York Times*, who interviewed Fidel Castro in the Sierra Maestra in 1957. Another good resource is *Cuba, or the Pursuit of Freedom* (Eyre & Spottiswoode, 1971) by Hugh Thomas. This 1,700-page epic is by one of the leading scholars of Latin America, and covers Cuban history between 1762 and 1962. Thomas is not a fan of Castro or his Revolution, yet this book is a superb historical reference.

A much more recent reference is *Conversations with Cuba* (University of Georgia Press, 2001) by C. Peter Ripley, who traveled to the island six times between 1991 and 1999 to speak with ordinary Cubans about their lives and the current state of the Revolution. Ripley's interviews capture both the frustration of decaying socialism and the immense pride that Cubans still have for their country.

Cuba is both the inspiration and setting for a lot of classic twentieth-century literature. Hemingway alone churned out three Cuban works: *The Old Man and the Sea* (Scribner's, 1952), *Islands in the Stream* (Scriber's, 1952), and *To Have and Have Not* (Macmillan Publishing, 1937). British author Graham Greene gives us another take on pre-Revolution Cuba in a wickedly satirical *Our Man In Havana* (William Heinemann, 1958).

Contemporary authors have also turned Cuba into rich reading ground. In *Havana Bay* (Random House, 1999), mystery writer Martin Cruz Smith resurrects the character (Renko) who earned him fame and fortune in his best-selling *Gorky Park* in this tale of post-Cold War intrigue and romance in Cuba. Elmore Leonard, the master of offbeat American noire fiction, turns his talented hand to a completely different theme, the fictional account of the Spanish-American War, in the pages of *Cuba Libre* (Delacorte Press, 1998). Celebrated travel writer Pico Iyer tries his hand at fiction in *Cuba and the Night* (Knopf, 1995), a haunting, voluptuous and atmospheric novel of passion and regret. Iyer's nonfiction account of a modern journey through Cuba in *Falling Off the Map: Some Lonely Places of the World* is also pertinent reading.

Cuba has also produced many of its own literary masters. The late Alejo Carpentier spent most of his life in Paris, but is regarded as one of Cuba's most famous contemporary writers. Among his trademark works are *Reasons of State* (Writers and Readers, 1977), *The Chase* (Farrar, Straus and Giroux, 1989), and *Explosion in a Cathedral* (Harper & Row, 1989).

Another great Cuban bard is Guillermo Cabrera Infante, who lives in exile overseas. *Mea Cuba* (Noonday Press, Farrar, Strauss and Giroux, 1994) is a humorous, political autobiography that explores the nature of the Cuban Revolution and the lives of those it has involved or affected, from political figures and writers to everyday people. His other works include *Infante's Inferno* (Harper

& Row, 1984), *Three Trapped Tigers* (Harper & Row, 1971), and *View of Dawn in the Tropics* (Farrar, Straus and Giroux, 1978).

Several recent coffee table books cover the island through the keen eye of master photographers. *Cuba* (National Geographic Books, 1999) by David Alan Harvey, is one of the most impressive books ever produced on the subject. Harvey capture's the island's spirit, faces and architecture in living color. *Havana* (Asteidl, 2001) showcases Robert Polidori's lush, evocative photos of modern Havana spread across 124 pages. With an incredibly discerning eye, he manages to capture both the vivacity and the decay of the Caribbean's largest city in what one reviewer calls a visual companion to the music of the Buena Vista Social Club. The book kicks off with a poignant essay by Eduardo Luis Rodriquez.

Anthologies of Cuban writing include *Chronicles Abroad — Havana* (Chronicle Books, 1996), edited by John Miller and Susannah Clark, and *The Reader's Companion to Cuba* (Harvest Original, Harcourt Brace and Company, 1997), edited by Alan Ryan.

Two girls reading in Trinidad.

QUICK REFERENCE A–Z GUIDE
TO PLACES AND TOPICS OF INTEREST